BEYOND THE FRINGE . . .
AND BEYOND

A Critical Biography
of
ALAN BENNETT, PETER COOK,
JONATHAN MILLER and DUDLEY MOORE

Ronald Bergan

VIRGIN

First published in Great Britain in 1989 by
Virgin Books
a division of W H Allen & Co Plc
Sekforde House
175–179 St John Street
London EC1V 4LL

Set in Melior by Greenaways, London
Printed and bound in Great Britain by
Mackays of Chatham Plc, Chatham, Kent

British Library Cataloguing in Publication Data

Bergan, Ronald
Beyond the Fringe – and beyond.
1. Comedies – Biographies – Collections
I. Title
791'.092'2

ISBN 1-85227-175-2

To Jonathan, Dudley, Alan and Peter

CONTENTS

ILLUSTRATIONS

ACKNOWLEDGEMENTS

I wish to thank profusely and alphabetically: Frith Banbury, John Bassett, Stuart Burge, Michael Frayn, Stephen Frears, John Gale, Patrick Garland, Alexander Goehr, Clive Hirschhorn, Roland Kenyon, Frank Kermode, Max Loppert, Catriona MacGregor, George Melly, Robert Ponsonby, Ned Sherrin, Karen Stone, Janet Suzman and John Wells for giving me their time. Also Jane Livingston at the ENO, Mary Fulton at the Old Vic, and Kent Opera for their assistance.

I'm also greatly indebted to the following indispensable publications: *The Private Eye Story* by Patrick Marnham (André Deutsch, 1982); *From Fringe to Flying Circus* by Roger Wilmut (Eyre Methuen, 1980); *Dudley* by Paul Donovan (W H Allen, 1988); *Dudley Moore: An Informal Biography* by Jeff Lenburg (Delilah Books, New York, 1982); *Footlights – 100 Years of Cambridge Comedy* by Robert Hewison (Eyre Methuen, 1983); *The Peter Hall Diaries* (Hamish Hamilton, 1983) and *Subsequent Performances* by Jonathan Miller (Faber and Faber, 1986).

A special thank you goes to Methuen for permission to quote so extensively from *The Complete Beyond The Fringe* (1987) as well as from *Dud and Pete – The Dagenham Dialogues* (1971), also to Faber and Faber, publisher of Alan Bennett's diaries and plays.

Above all, I would like to express my immense gratitude to Jonathan Miller and Dudley Moore for graciously submitting themselves to my questions.

Ronald Bergan, May 1989

PART ONE

Beyond The Fringe

'Future historians will thank me for providing them with a full account of the moment when English comedy took its first decisive step into the second half of the twentieth century.'

Kenneth Tynan on *Beyond
The Fringe* in *The Observer*,
14 May 1961

EDINBURGH

True or False? *Beyond The Fringe* was a Cambridge revue performed by four young amateur undergraduates on the Edinburgh Festival Fringe. Answer: False.

1) It was not a Cambridge revue, nor an Oxford one. In fact, it was not a university revue at all. It is true that Jonathan Miller and Peter Cook had made names for themselves previously in the Cambridge Footlights, and that Alan Bennett and Dudley Moore had performed in revue at Oxford, but the show did not come from Oxbridge.

2) The four performers were not undergraduates and although they were still very short in the tooth, Miller and Bennett were 26 years old, Moore was 25 and Cook 23. Miller had come down in 1956 with a medical degree, Bennett got a BA a year later, Moore was already the holder of a BA and BMus (1958), and Cook had just graduated in modern languages. The comedy, therefore, was strictly speaking 'graduate humour'.

3) Amateur-Shamateur! Despite the measly amount of money they got initially (£100 each for writing and performing), *Beyond the Fringe* was a professional show in both senses of the word. Peter Cook's name had already been in lights in Shaftesbury Avenue as writer of the revue *Pieces Of Eight* and he already had an agent; Dudley Moore had been a professional jazz musician for over a year, playing in the Vic Lewis and Johnny Dankworth Orchestras; Jonathan Miller had made many appearances on BBC television and radio; Alan Bennett had performed in cabaret.

4) The show was not part of the Edinburgh Festival Fringe. The title, which the performers accepted reluctantly, was meant, in its obfuscating way, to explain that it was *not* part of the Fringe but far better or *beyond* it. In the language of early 1980s British comedy, it was **Not** The Edinburgh Fringe. It was the 1960 Festival's *official* revue put on at its centre – the Royal Lyceum Theatre.

II

There is a publicity photograph for *Beyond The Fringe* taken by John Hedgecoe in 1960, depicting the four young performers looking through a glass door. Just perceptible in the background is the reflection of a fifth man looking in from the outside. As in the second half of Alan Bennett's 1988 play *Single Spies*, about Anthony Blunt, in which the Surveyor of the Queen's Pictures finds that after cleaning and X-raying Titian's 'Allegory of Prudence', there are not two men in the painting as originally thought, but five, the question arises: who is the fifth man?

If Hal Roach gets the credit for teaming Stan Laurel and Oliver Hardy, then the unsung and unknown John Bassett must accept the laurels for bringing these four very different young men together. Bassett, the same age as Miller and Bennett, was up at Oxford until 1958 when he got an Honours Degree in PPE. At university, Bassett played the trumpet in his own jazz band, with Dudley Moore on piano. Bassett was also an astute spotter of student talent and organised cabarets as well; on coming down, he applied for a job as Assistant Artistic Director of the Edinburgh Festival. But there would have been no *Beyond The Fringe*, had it not been for a pair of suede shoes . . .

Robert Ponsonby, the Artistic Director of the Festival since 1956, was totally undecided between John Bassett and another candidate. Stepping out of his office after the interviews, he went in to see his three secretaries.

'Well, girls, I really don't know who to choose. They're both excellent,' The secretaries chorused with one voice, 'You've got to choose Mr Bassett. The other man wears suede shoes, and we can't bear them.'

Ponsonby immediately rang Bassett to tell him that the job was his, without daring to mention that suede had swayed him, and invited his new assistant to meet him for lunch to celebrate. Ironically, Bassett changed into a pair of suede shoes for the occasion, bought for £8 a few years before as a celebration after leaving National Service. Had he worn them on the day of the interview, and the other candidate not . . .

Since the mid-1950s, the Edinburgh Festival had expanded to include unofficial events in church halls, pubs, cellars, attics and in the streets, open to any performers who could find the money and the space for a week or so in Edinburgh in August. The 'Fringe' gave the opportunity for experimental, amateur, school and college theatre groups to gain a wider audience – the Cambridge Footlights was and is a regular visitor – and the shows varied from the good, the bad, the ugly, the boring and the bizarre. Much the most interesting theatre was done on the Fringe, and because there was nothing the Festival proper could offer after around 10 p.m., the crowds flocked to the city's more obscure corners. Something therefore had to be done to attract the night owls.

'I always had a naughty corner in my mind,' says Robert Ponsonby, 'and it seemed to me that we were a bit pompous, and that late-night entertainment, which was of course flourishing on the Fringe, was something the Festival proper ought to be doing itself.'

The comic-chanteuse Anna Russell kicked off in 1958 with a week of her 'recitals' at 11 p.m. at the Freemasons' Hall, returning the following year to the Lyceum, where Flanders and Swann took over for the second week. In 1960, Ponsonby decided to go the whole hog and have three weeks of late-night shows. The first week was to be Louis Armstrong, the second *Les Frères Jacques* and the third Bea Lillie. When negotiations with 'Satchmo' collapsed, it seemed fate stepped in again for Bassett. As revue was the most popular type of entertainment on the Fringe, Ponsonby thought it might be a good idea for the Festival to have its own, but of a higher quality.

'I was tired of the Fringe continually stealing our thunder with brilliant revues from this or that university,' he explains, so together with Bassett he considered a possible meld of Footlights (Cambridge) and ETC (the Experimental Theatre Club at Oxford), which could be called, with no great originality, *The Oxbridge Revue*.

Bassett was familiar with Dudley Moore's wizardry on the ivories and his abilities as an actor and entertainer; he had seen Alan Bennett in cabaret at university, as well as in an Oxford revue called *Better Late* on the Edinburgh Fringe in 1959. He had been at Bedales school with Jonathan Miller's wife and sister-in-law and knew of the doctor's reputation as the 'Danny Kaye of Cambridge', a moniker that Miller, now at University College, London, was doing his utmost to repudiate. It was in the casualty department at the University of London, where Bassett visited him, that Dr Miller agreed to take a short break from University College Hospital to tread the boards.

'I still fiercely regret the distraction,' said Miller, many years later, 'I think that was a bad thing I did. Much better to have been a very funny comic undergraduate and forget about it – but I got on to this terrible treadmill.' A typical remark reflecting the schizophrenic attitude to his two callings that has punctuated his life. Like Laurence Olivier's Hamlet, Miller was 'a man who couldn't make up his mind'. It was Miller who suggested Peter Cook, the already legendary President of the Cambridge Footlights and author of most of the sketches of a West End revue starring Kenneth Williams, as a possible fourth member of the group. It was only a matter of convincing the others to do the show, and getting the four of them together.

Like Miller, Alan Bennett also had qualms about whether or not to participate. His reserve and insecurity, the feeling that he would have little to contribute, and the fact that he was in the midst of his Master's degree in medieval history at Oxford, made him look upon the whole idea as 'cockeyed'. In addition, which seems a trivial consideration, he would be the only one of the four from the North.

Peter Cook, who saw himself as 'the ghastly show business element', commented that: 'Jonathan had this doctor-comedian conflict and Alan had this academic-comedian conflict. I had no conflict whatsoever, nor had Dudley. It was rather boring. We kept trying to think of something such as "By day he is a Trappist monk, by night he is on the boards".'

In Bennett, who admits to having 'a streak of pure tinsel' in his character, the conflict has long been resolved, with the comic playwright and occasional actor sitting on top of the university don, only infrequently allowing him to surface. By now it is plain to the world that the theatrical mask has stuck so firmly to Miller's face that were he to remove it, like Max Beerbohm's *Happy Hypocrite*, he would have grown to resemble it. The scientist and the artist within him have had a stormy relationship but the marriage has lasted. There was a time when Dudley Moore had ambitions to be a choir master or a church organist, failing which he would be a full-time jazz musician and composer. The reason that the profane replaced the sacred was primarily due to the fact that beautiful women do not drape themselves over organs in churches in order to admire the player, an important consideration for the priapic, though repressed Dudley. He was – and still is – also a superbly inventive jazz musician with a flair for pastiche and a comic streak. Like Bennett, though, Moore was also extremely inhibited and felt trepidation in meeting, as he had been informed, three of the most brilliant young men of their generation; if he hadn't needed the job, he might have declined. But with Bassett urging and chivvying, the four disparate elements came reluctantly together.

III

On a spring day in 1960, the four of them arrived from different parts of London, descending on a little Italian restaurant near Warren Street station, where Thames TV and the MI6 building are now. The location was chosen partly because Miller could only get away from his hospital for an hour, and it was nearby. Bennett, who admits to having had a vague knowledge of London, recalls it as a 'distinctly unfashionable restaurant near Euston Station'.

'My knowledge of London was so hazy that whenever we went about I never quite knew where we were,' he remarked.

Their host, John Bassett, made the general introductions. According to Miller, they 'instantly disliked each other and decided that it might be a profitable enterprise'. Miller optimistically hoped that with the proceeds he might buy a house and then continue his medical research.

'At that time, the outlook for a junior doctor in England was appallingly dim; it's bad enough now, then it was absolutely dreadful,' Miller says. 'Then we worked eighteen hours a day for something like £5 a week. The prospects for promotion to registrarship were very bleak. The membership of the Royal College of Physicians exam failed something like ninety-five per cent. We lived in dreadful hospital residences, the chances of holding a permanent consultant post were slim. You saw tired, haggard registrars in their late thirties supporting families with wives they never saw. I thought, let's have some fun before all this closes in on me and get some money to enable me to have a comfortable house to go back to.'

At this initial meeting, they sniffed around each other suspiciously. The 5 foot 2½ inch Dudley Moore noticed first of all how 'extremely tall' the others were – all over six feet. (It is axiomatic that 6 foot 2 inches is the minimum height permitted for success as a comedian from Cambridge: e.g. John Cleese, Graham Chapman, Stephen Fry, Hugh Laurie. Being tall at Oxford is optional.) They all remarked subsequently to Bassett that none of them dared make the first joke. It was Peter Cook who broke the ice. Comic invention and creativity just flowed out of him. Dudley gradually lost some of his discomfiture, and did a Groucho Marx walk behind the waitresses going in and out of the swing doors. However, when the quartet began to discuss material, and Moore came up with an idea for a mime in which a violin behaved like a baby, Cook greeted it with derision. It was the start of a long and beautiful friendship.

The chronically shy Alan Bennett didn't say very much except 'Oh, dear me' from time to time. 'I had the slight feeling I was there under false pretences – a feeling that never really left me. Peter was very funny and, to my alarm, very fluent. He appeared to be able to ad lib excellent material in monologues of spiralling absurdity.' Moore claims that 'We were all very competitive when we met. We had had some success in our respective fields, but I couldn't compete on the literary, philosophical level at all. I had no knowledge there.'

While Dudley Moore was being silent or facetious, Alan Bennett taciturn and glum, and Peter Cook extremely witty, Jonathan Miller took the practical line, discussing the project realistically, while going off on rapid verbal tangents; even Cook found his loquacity rather inhibiting. Cambridge perhaps inevitably came out on top over its old rival on this occasion. It would have been quite feasible for Peter Cook to have addressed any eavesdropping clients at the restaurant in terms of the 'Real Class' sketch from *Beyond The Fringe*.

'I think at about this juncture it would be wise to point out to those who haven't noticed – and God knows it's apparent enough – that Jonathan Miller and myself come from good families and have had the benefits of a public-school education. Whereas the other two members of the cast have worked their way up from working-class backgrounds. Yet Jonathan and I are working together with them and treating them as equals, and I must say it's proving to be a most worthwhile, enjoyable and stimulating experience for both of us . . .'

IV

A few days later the foursome went to meet Robert Ponsonby at the Edinburgh Festival offices at 29 St James's Street. Ponsonby – Eton, Trinity and the Guards – is as tall, elegant, English and cultured as one would expect. 'They came and they played the fool, and I could see we were on to something, because they were sparking each other off just in conversation in a small room. I thought the show was going to be anarchic but very funny, or anarchic and not at all funny. In the end it was not anarchic, but very funny,' he recalls with a chuckle.

John Bassett suggested that the four of them pool the best of their already tried and tested solo material and write additional sketches bringing in one or more of the others, in order to make a one-hour show. They had about four months to write and rehearse in time for the Festival in August. Everyone agreed except Cook's agent, Donald Langdon, who advised Peter against getting involved with 'a little amateur revue up in Edinburgh'. When Cook refused this advice, Langdon, whom Bassett describes as a 'camel-hair-coated gent with the nap gone off the camel hair', then managed to negotiate a fee of £110 for his young client which, after his £11 commission, left Cook with a pound less than his colleagues.

The material that already existed for the show consisted of solos that had wowed Oxbridge students and there was no reason to believe that late-night festival-goers wouldn't lap it up as well. Bennett would do his silly sanctimonious clergyman, Miller the absurd tale of getting his trousers from the London Transport Lost Property department, Cook had his moronic man on the park bench, and Moore his Schubert and Fauré pastiches.

They then had initial creative meetings and started rehearsals, *sans* director. Some of them took place in Miller's room at the hospital.

'It was an odd scene,' Moore recalls. 'We rehearsed with him in between heart transplants.' Naturally, future director Miller took most control in shaping things although more than half the new sketches were written or conceived by Cook. However he and the others were used to being directed.

'There was no unified approach at all,' Bennett explained. 'We each had our own ideas of what we wanted to be funny about.' It was at these sessions that their different personalities emerged more clearly. Cook and Miller were able to improvise, sparking off each other most of the time, while Bennett worked more slowly.

'I realised I couldn't actually provide material at the meetings, that I'd have to think of things beforehand and come along with them,' he says.

The inhibited Dudley Moore hardly said anything at all.

'I felt totally constricted and overpowered. I was very out of place with the other three – totally out of place,' he recalls. 'I didn't contribute anything textually . . . Peter bends words and twists them and follows them through. Jonathan juggles with them. He throws them up in the air and you get a great firework display. I was quite shocked at their lack of inhibition. I kept saying things like, "But you can't do that." ' As Miller said, 'Dudley was very reluctant to do anything which might create offence.'

Cook, the devil-may-care diplomat's son, his ears still ringing with the sound of the laughter he had created in the West End, and the mercurial Miller, the 'godless Jew', son of an eminent psychiatrist, both oozed the confidence of their class. Facing them were butcher's son Bennett, bred in a back-to-back in Leeds, and Moore, the club-footed son of a railway electrician, brought up in an ugly housing estate in Dagenham – both a million miles away from the serene seascape at Torquay and leafy London suburbs, the childhood scenes of their Cambridge co-optimists. The two working-class men also retained, despite a spell at Oxford away from family influence, an inherited puritanism, the inevitable result of which was that both of them later became far more preoccupied and identified with the sexual side of life than the more liberated Cook and Miller. The church-going Alan Bennett, according to Cook, 'was completely different from them. I think he was genuinely shocked by the degree of filthy badinage. He was quite puritanical then; now he's the smuttiest of the lot of us.' For Dudley Moore, a virgin until he was 22, 'Sex was tied up with guilt, fear, shame, anxiety and roast lamb.'

After their first meetings, during which new ideas and cheap wine flowed, they confronted the task of getting the material down in written form. They would sit round a table, argue, discuss, improvise and record sketches and then transcribe them. Although the show was a communal effort, apart from the monologues, it is not difficult to attribute contributions to one or the other. A great many of the bogus Bardic pentameters in the Shakespeare parody were Jonathan Miller's; Peter Cook's singular voice rings out in 'The End of the World'; and Alan Bennett's tones can be heard in the capital punishment sketch. 'I think probably Alan had a little more anger in him than the rest of us,' Miller recalls. 'He brought a sense of austere intellectual severity and the belief that fatuity is abroad. Although we didn't get on very well, we both wanted to strengthen the satirical element. Peter provided an absolutely unique form of verbal surrealism, a sort of insane linguistic facility in the tradition of N F Simpson, Ionesco and Pinter.'

As they didn't yet have a director there was no impartial figure to arbitrate on what should go in or out and this resulted in a fair amount of heated disagreement. Cook originally didn't want 'The Aftermyth of War' included, and Miller and Bennett had to use all their powers of persuasion to get him to accept it. He then improvised the sections in which the man in the garden greets the news of every crisis, delivered to him by his wife during the war, with 'You put on the kettle, we'll have a nice cup of tea.' These conclude with his reaction to the news of rationing: 'Never mind, my dear. You put on the kettle – we'll have a nice cup of boiling hot water.'

'If something had to be taken out it was three of us ganging up on the fourth,' explains Bennett. 'We were very disparate personalities. Jonathan is very exuberant and I'm sort of inward-looking. Dudley was very reserved about anything other than music. Unlike the rest of us, he was not particularly verbal, whereas Peter is schizophrenic in his use of words. The things we did tended to be in line with the way we are.'

During the Festival they were all ensconced in a beautiful fourth-floor apartment, overlooking Edinburgh Castle, which contained a piano and space to rehearse. As they were a completely unknown quantity to the majority of Festival-goers, the bookings were poor, on top of which the dress rehearsal was a disaster. They broke down, they giggled, they hadn't got their lines or moves right. Ponsonby thought, 'This is awful. This is going to be a shambles, and I shall be blamed for putting it on.' He had a committee of 60 to whom he had to justify his actions, led by the formidable (his polite word for 'battleaxe') Lady Eva Rosebery.

'She did scare me but I wasn't cowed into compromising my artistic decisions,' he recalls. Having stuck his neck out over *Beyond The Fringe*, he risked having her chop his head off.

V

On Monday, 22 August 1960 at 10.45 p.m., following a rather undistinguished Old Vic production of *The Seagull*, the hour-long *Beyond The Fringe* opened at the Lyceum Theatre, playing to only 35 per cent capacity. Such was the triumph of the first night, however, that they played to 120 per cent capacity for the rest of the week, with two rows of standing room on every level, contravening safety regulations.

Apart from a few disgruntled guardians of sacred cows, audiences and critics received the show with enthusiasm. The anonymous scribe of *The Times* wrote under the headline 'Midnight Gaiety In

Edinburgh': 'The pleasingness of this revue is difficult to pin down in words. It keeps the midnight audiences in a continual ripple of easy laughter. The reason may be that each performer is coolly confident of his own power to amuse and also that the comedy is ruled by a nice sense of proportion.'

The show consisted of a dozen sketches, only half of which got to London. One that bit the dust in transfer was a parody of ITV's *Jim's Inn*, a puerile advertising playlet in which people in a pub, quite straight-faced, introduced products for praise into their conversation. In the takeoff, Moore ('Jim') is the barkeeper serving clients Miller ('Basil') and Cook ('Nigel').

Basil: Good gracious me – out of the corner of my eye I thought you were wearing a good cashmere.

Nigel: I'm glad you thought it was cashmere but it's not.

Basil: I'd put my money on it being cashmere.

Nigel: You'd lose your money, Bas. It's a Nablock Histamine Non-Iron Oven-Dry Visco-Static Dynaflo, all designed to make a nice sweater with peak purchasing power.

The sound of laughter, rather than any scent of revolution, emanated from the Lyceum into the Edinburgh air. There was general comment, however, on the show's 'Brechtian' conception, an adjective that meant a bare staging. Despite the visit, four years before, of the Berliner Ensemble, the British theatre-goer's perception in 1960 of the great German playwright's work was even more lamentably misinformed than it is today. *Beyond The Fringe* was simply, to paraphrase a line from a famous Dud and Pete sketch, 'deficient in the scenery division'. As the revue cost a mere £100, it was hardly likely to contain anything that could be called spectacular. Just four young men in grey worsted suits, plain shirts and dark ties (which they had to pay for themselves) and a piano. (Hugo Boyd, a young semi-pro bass player, did accompany Moore in one or two jazz numbers.) The virtue that emerged out of this necessity was the stripping away of the usual accoutrements of traditional revue. Although Cook flippantly remarks that, 'We'd have been delighted to have had a hundred chorus girls dancing about,' their absence turned out to be one of the show's strengths. (At one stage, there had been a suggestion of using the unknown 19-year-old Julie Christie in a running gag, in which she would wear as little as permissible, but it came to nothing. She came to something herself in 1962.)

Still, at the Festival, where cheap Fringe shows abounded (one could easily catch an entertainment which was twice as satiric and half as expensive, i.e. two men and a guitar), this official entry did not seem to go very far beyond the Fringe. It was only after the show was expanded to a full evening and presented in the glaring light of London's West End that its impact could be properly assessed.

2

LONDON

When news of the reception that had greeted *Beyond The Fringe* reached the ears of Donald Langdon, Peter Cook's agent, he promptly began to think of finding a producer to provide it with a commercial run, with himself representing all four performer-writers, and to that end contacted his friend Willie Donaldson, another ex-Cambridge man. Peter Cook had made his reputation in *The Last Laugh*, the notorious Cambridge Footlights Revue of 1959, and Donaldson had lost all his money soon after that by putting on a show adapted from it entitled *Here Is The News*. The 23-year-old Donaldson (later the anonymous writer of *The Henry Root Letters*) didn't think he had a hope in hell of getting the rights to an acclaimed show at a Festival where producers gathered each year like children at a birthday party to grab at any goodies that appeared, but despite the producer's gloom, Langdon flew up to Edinburgh to try to persuade 'the boys' to take him on as their representative and to give Donaldson the rights to present the show in London.

Langdon was not exactly greeted with open arms. Cook had not forgotten his negative approach to the project in the first place and knew that if he had been guided by Langdon he would not be sharing in an undoubted success. Miller, Bennett and Moore didn't take to him either, nor was Willie Donaldson's name one to inspire confidence, but success had obviously not yet gone to their heads and they agreed to sign with the agent, in the face of offers from fourteen other managements. John Bassett had asked to handle them but Langdon elbowed him out by threatening to take Cook out of the show (something he didn't actually have the right to do) if that happened. Bassett ended up with one per cent of the profits (about £30 a week) during the West End run.

'I thought rather naively that just as everything flowed over the boys, it would flow over me,' he recalls regretfully, but without bitterness. 'I thought there was bound to be a management that would say, "Who thought this up? Oh, we must get him to think up another show." But it didn't follow. From that springboard, I should have had a fantastic career.' After Lord Harewood took over the Festival in 1961, with the blessing of Lady Rosebery, Bassett in fact went on to work for the BBC as director on the early evening magazine programme *Tonight*, and later as Ned Sherrin's assistant on the weekly satirical show *That Was The Week That Was* (popularly known as *TW3*).

According to Donaldson, Langdon 'had been able to persuade them . . . that I was so stupid and inexperienced that I wouldn't interfere with what they wanted to do, whereas every other impresario who knew his business, and knew what he was doing, would interfere with it.' When the Festival was over, Donaldson and the cast met to discuss business at the White Elephant restaurant in London, the former hoping that the establishment's name was not the ill-omen it seemed. Here was a self-styled impresario ready to sign up a show he hadn't actually seen, and four performers willing to give the rights to a green producer without a penny to his name.

'I remember coming away with Jonathan from the session when the contract was discussed,' writes Bennett in a postscript to the *Complete Beyond The Fringe* book. 'He had hailed a taxi; it was the first London taxi I had ever been in and riding up Half Moon Street we discussed the terms. "They're very good," said Jonathan. "It's ten times what I'd be receiving as a junior doctor." It was fifteen times what I'd been receiving as a medieval historian but something told me even then that this was not really the point.'

A contract was duly drawn up and signed, and Donaldson was the owner of a small, stark revue featuring four relative unknowns called *Beyond The Fringe*, a title that created the opposite effect from that intended, that is to say, people never saw beyond the word 'fringe'. The 60-minute late-night show had had a success at Edinburgh, but was there life beyond the Festival?

II

In order to knock the entertainment into a more professional shape for London, the director-actress-choreographer Eleanor Fazan, affectionately known as 'Fizz', was brought in. She had already directed or co-ordinated three innocuous shows by ex-Footlighters: Julian More's

Grab Me A Gondola (More was one of the lyric writers on *Out Of The Blue* of 1954 in which Jonathan Miller appeared); Cambridge undergraduate Bamber Gascoigne's *Share My Lettuce*; and Peter Tranchell's *Zuleika*. Once more the foursome would gather to rehearse, this time at her Belgravia flat. Some items from Edinburgh were discarded and many more were added, including Cook's Macmillan imitation, and linguistic philosophy and civil defence sketches.

'Fizz' found it rather an uphill task: the cast would not regard themselves as a team but as four separate, competing entities. The overworked phrase, 'team spirit', in the theatre as in life, is not always a necessary ingredient for success and so it proved now. The fact that these very individual and intelligent yong men, thrown together by chance, felt that they had little in common and were often at odds with one another, may have created an underlying theatrical tension and counterpoint that would have been absent from a troupe of 'good companions'. They didn't seem to mind if there were arguments and rows. In fact, it was a way of establishing and protecting their own personalities. Only Dudley Moore was upset by the lack of harmony. 'He wanted everyone to be friends, everything to be jolly and fun,' Fazan recalls. 'He was slightly afraid if it wasn't.'

Willie Donaldson had a problem of a different order – how to find a theatre that would house the show. He approached Donald Albery (pronounced Al-berry), grandson of the dramatist James Albery and son of theatre manager Sir Bronson Albery, who owned the Criterion, Wyndham's, The New (renamed the Albery in 1973) and the Piccadilly. The total production cost was £8,000, half of which was put up by Albery. Donaldson, unable to raise his £4,000, received three-quarters of it from producers Peter Bridge and John Gale, who had already seen the four perform in cabaret.

'It turned out to be the best investment I have ever made,' says Gale, who was to produce the record-breaking *No Sex Please, We're British* in 1971. 'Unfortunately, I laid most of it off and just had £100, but from memory my £100 made something like £7,000 profit. Not a bad return!'

The future Sir Donald had bought the production unseen because he had heard good things about it, although what exactly he could not remember. When he came to see a run-through he was not only rather perturbed at some of the content, but pretty unimpressed by the style as well.

'Who's the one in the spectacles?' he asked Donaldson. 'We've got to get rid of him, he's no good.' Not calculated to help Bennett's already shaky confidence. Bennett, who remembers Albery saying, 'It would be all right except for the fair-haired one,' remarked in his careful, self-disparaging manner that 'I did understand what he meant.' It was only after Donaldson pointed out to the great man that no-one else could perform Bennett's own monologues, that he was an essential quarter of the whole enterprise and that the critics seemed to have liked him, that Bennett was not given the boot.

III

Like an army wishing to conquer the capital of a country, a play, musical or revue has to win battles in the provinces before it can gain the main prize. It was therefore arranged for the new extended *Beyond The Fringe* to play first at the Arts Theatre, Cambridge, followed by a visit to the Theatre Royal, Brighton. Albery had yet to decide which of his West End theatres it would come in to.

At Cambridge, home territory, so to speak, the revue was given an overwhelming welcome by the mainly undergraduate audience. The opening night started at 8 p.m. and was still going strong 4 hours and 35 items later. Peter Cook, especially, did almost every sketch he could think of. He and Miller performed a piece (lost in the transfer to London) entitled 'Under Canvas', in which Cook revealed that Constable was not a landscape painter at all but a great painter of nudes. 'I think most critics are agreed that Constable's handling of breasts is out of this world, but some maintain he falls down on his thighs . . . No other Victorian painter could touch Constable on his breasts.'

John Wood (who had directed Cook's last Footlights revue and was to become better known as the comic actor John Fortune), writing in the *Cambridge Review*, recognised that the cast 'also wrote all the material; so that they had the intuitive feel for it which inspires confidence and ultimate laughter'. It was a general rule until the 1960s, that comedians and revue artists, with notable exceptions, used stuff turned out for them by script writers and jokesmiths.

Next stop Brighton. The Theatre Royal has, over the years, traditionally served as a try-out venue for shows headed for the West End, rather as New Haven used to serve Broadway, but being less of a boneyard. In 1961, even before the building of Sussex University and the enlivening existence of a large gay community, Brighton was one of the more civilised of English seaside resorts – there was (and is) a range of good restaurants and a comparatively cosmopolitan atmosphere – but its Victorian theatre has always been a notoriously difficult place to play in. The audiences usually consist of retired people or holiday-makers desirous of seeing a bedroom farce starring some mediocre TV personality, plus a sprinkling of Brighton's more camp citizens who are keen to pronounce on productions before Fleet Street has had the chance to express its views. Alan Bennett remembers the refrain of 'We loved it, darlings, but don't take it in.' Sibilant sycophants might have expressed traditional dressing-room praise but there were generally few people left at the end of a performance, those old ladies who did remain resembling so many Madame Defarges. Seats would snap like guillotines throughout and the cast usually ended up outnumbering the audience.

The review in the *Brighton and Hove Herald* on 6 May 1961, written by one F T G, reflected this audience reaction.

'If you think that four bright young university men on the stage without feminine assistance, scenery, change of costume or an orchestra would find it hard to keep me amused for a whole evening with material they have written themselves – you would be right. The revue . . . presented by the four optimists nearly sent me to sleep . . . one person present seemed to share my opinion . . . after an unsuccessful attempt to start a slow handclap he stamped out noisily.' Yet despite finding 'the satire has as much sting as a blancmange', the anonymous critic thought it 'vaguely indecent for twenty-year-olds to be making fun of Battle of Britain pilots. No doubt I shall be told that their real target is the films about the battle. My answer is that most of those who endured the battle overhead thought the films were a worthy tribute to the "Few" who won it.'

Continuing to reveal his own prejudices, the reviewer asked 'Why be funny about Civil Defence?' He felt it was 'unworthy of university men to ridicule a youth with a non-U accent in a television religious programme and a comic scene in a death cell to me was atrocious'. The only sketch that amused the writer was the Shakespeare burlesque but 'even this was rather like schoolboys having fun at the expense of their school play'. The smaller *Brighton and Hove Gazette* was kinder in thinking that 'their special kind of irreverent debunking of sacred cows is the type that makes a sure appeal to a certain section of eggheads'. A little bit of detection on the part of the cast revealed that the critic of the *Brighton and Hove Herald* was, in fact, a homosexual boy-scout leader interested in philosophy and amateur dramatics, involved in Civil Defence and a local Tory bigwig. There was hardly a sketch in the entire revue that didn't touch on his life.

Despite the numerous disclaimers issued by the cast in years to come, insisting that *Beyond The Fringe* was 'in the tradition of English revue – light, silly, but very funny' (Miller) and 'not satiric in intent' (Bennett) – it obviously did knock a few cherished beliefs of the 'silent majority', if we are to take F T G (Fulminating Tory Gentleman?) as an example. Although Brighton was far from being in the sticks, the show's reception there demonstrated the vast distance that existed between the sophisticated audiences and critics of the Edinburgh Festival and London's West End, and 'the provinces' at the start of the 'sixties. At about the same time, *The Knack* was on its pre-London tour. Ann Jellicoe found that her own opinion of her play was modified by the different audiences with which she saw it. At Cambridge, the youthful audience convinced her that it was very funny; however, at Bath, among older and more conservative people, she thought the play rather obscene. Finally, in London, as part of a wised-up Royal Court audience, she found it innocent and childlike.

Making no adjustment to different audiences, the supposedly courageous producer Donald Albery, horrified at the reaction the show received in Brighton, decided that he had made an appalling misjudgement in taking 'the property' on in the first place and refused to allow it to be put on in one of his theatres, although he still retained a stake in it. For Miller, Bennett, Cook and Moore it was an abrupt awakening from a delightful dream. It looked as though *Beyond The Fringe* would go no further.

During the bleak week on the South Coast, a lawyer by the name of David Jacobs (neither the radio personality nor the creator of *Dallas*), representing the comic actor Bernard Cribbins, went down to see the show and thought it wouldn't have the legs to run more than a few weeks in London. Nevertheless, he considered it might do as a filler at the small Fortune Theatre where Cribbins had been appearing with some success since October in a revue called *And Another Thing*. The 440-seat Fortune, just opposite the imposing colonnade of the Theatre Royal, Drury Lane, was used to providing a cosy intimacy and seemed an ideal venue for *Beyond The Fringe*. One of its biggest hits had been the two-man entertainment, *At The Drop Of A Hat*, in which the bearded Michael Flanders in a wheelchair and the bespectacled Donald Swann at the piano put over comic songs and mildly satiric patter from 1957 to 1959.

A few weeks before the May opening at the Fortune, Peter Bridge and John Gale presented a revue called *On The Brighter Side* taken from a successful BBC series starring Stanley Baxter and Betty Marsden. 'We brought the show into the Phoenix Theatre,' remembers John Gale, 'but unfortunately for us *Beyond The Fringe* had been seen in Edinburgh by nearly all the London critics. The result of this was that *On The Brighter Side* was poorly reviewed by most of them and Bernard Levin finished his notice with the immortal words "Thank God for those four young men marching down from Edinburgh".'

The four-man show managed to keep the Fortune warm for 1,184 performances before transferring to the Mayfair in 1964. *And Another Thing II* never happened, because one whiff of *Beyond The Fringe* caused the death of traditional revue and civilisation as we knew it.

IV

Willie Donaldson, who had written of his life as a pimp and of his experiences of the Soho sex scene in *Both The Ladies And The Gentlemen* and *The Balloons In The Black Bag*, asked the four performers what treat he could provide for them before the West End opening. Having been regaled with some of his Runyonesque stories (some short, some tall), Peter, Dudley and Jonathan asked to see blue movies in a brothel. (Alan was not too keen on the prospect.) Although they were all in their mid-twenties, there was a naiveté in them that pre-dates the Permissive Society.

Donaldson arranged a visit to a 'house' in Bond Street. When the blowsy prostitute's maid, a retired 'tart' herself, opened the door, she was greeted by the unusual sight of Miller and his doctor wife Rachel, Cook and his wife-to-be Wendy, Moore and a girlfriend, Bennett and John Bassett. After a certain reluctance to let them in, she finally ushered them upstairs into a waiting room.

A great deal of nervous giggling went on amongst the group as they leafed through *La Vie Parisienne*, a magazine thought at the time to be terribly sexy, full of very arty drawings of ladies in black stockings and nothing else. Their laughter brought the maid in to tell them to keep quiet: they were disturbing the present punters' concentration.

The first performance over, they were ushered into a bedroom containing a large bed, the headboard covered in plastic to prevent grease marks, a French prostitute and a kidney-shaped dressing table on which were photographs of her children. She set up an old 8mm silent projector and began to comment on the ineptly shot flickering black-and-white images: 'Now zee gentlemen in zee audience will have an inferiority complex. Now zee gentlemen will be jealous,' she said as men appeared with gigantic phalluses.

The doctors Miller began to give medical details on what they were witnessing. 'If he does that again, he'll certainly do damage to the symphysis pubis,' or 'That is medically unsound.' Cook made appropriately witty remarks, Moore was necking and Bennett was unable to bring himself to look. The prostitute was slightly puzzled.

V

Beyond The Fringe opened at the Fortune on 10 May 1961. *The Times*, in those days the most influential daily, wrote a respectable short review which concluded that the 'work smacks a little of the Third Programme, but this need alarm nobody, for if the chosen ideas make hardly any contact with the clichés of Shaftesbury Avenue they are clowned in a way warranted to make a cat laugh'. Bernard Levin, who had fancied himself as a satirist in his 'Taper' column in the *Spectator* since 1957 and long before he came to see the Festival of Light, went characteristically overboard in the *Daily Express*.

'Gratitude that there should be four men living among us today who could come together to provide, as long as memory holds, an eighth colour to the rainbow,' he apostrophised. 'Satirical revue in this country has been, until now, basically cowardly. First, it has picked on easy targets. Second, however hard it hit its targets ... it left its audience alone, to leave the theatre as fat and complacent as it came in ... The satire then is real, barbed, deeply planted and aimed at things and people that need it. But this is still not all. For the final target ... is the audience. It is they who ... are thoroughly, healingly, beneficially, beautifully, and properly shaken up in the process. The four good, great men who have done this thing to and for and in the name of us all have written and performed the whole thing themselves.'

Though purple praise from Levin did the state of the box office some service, it was Kenneth Tynan's review in *The Observer* on the Sunday following the opening that turned the tide. It was Tynan who had single-handedly among critics changed the face of British drama in 1956 by writing 'I doubt if I could love anyone who did not wish to see *Look Back In Anger*. It is the best young play of its decade.' Always quick to seize on any stage work that could be used as a weapon with which to beat the British Establishment, Tynan took up the cause of *Beyond The Fringe*. Time and Tynan waited for no man. Heading his review 'English Satire Advances Into The Sixties', he was no less positive than Levin but far more perceptive. Although his piece contained the rather unfortunate turn of phrase that the show was 'the funniest revue that London has seen since the Allies dropped the bomb on Hiroshima', he concluded by putting the entertainment in perspective: 'It can justly be urged against the show that it is too parochial, too exclusively concerned with taunting the accents and values of John Betjeman's suburbia: *Beyond The Fringe* is anti-reactionary without being progressive. It goes less far than one could have hoped, but immeasurably farther than one had any right to expect.'

Just as, a few years before, writers like John Osborne, Kingsley Amis, Colin Wilson and John Braine had been labelled 'Angry Young Men' (later becoming Moaning Middle-Aged Men) and 'anger' was the word that had then buzzed round tables at dinner parties, now the word 'satire' was bandied about as if it had just been coined, echoing trendily throughout Hampstead and down the King's Road, Chelsea for the next few years. It was not long before Peter Cook's Establishment Club opened, *Private Eye* magazine cocked its first snook and *That Was The Week That Was* hit the airwaves. There followed endless discussions in the newspapers and on TV as to what exactly 'satire' was. Christopher Booker, one of the first editors of *Private Eye*, stated in *The Neophiliacs* in 1969 after his conversion to Christ, that 'to a large extent the underlying message of the satirists was simply that of "What's Wrong With Britain" journalists – only carried to a new, irresponsible, unreal and more destructive level'. Booker's retrospective disapproval aside, it was said that if one wanted real satire one wouldn't visit the Fortune Theatre but would go instead to the works of the eighteenth-century Augustans, such as Alexander Pope and Jonathan Swift, whose razor-sharp mockery, accompanied by an air of gravity, scourged the vices and follies of the age.

There was general agreement that, despite Levin's talk about the

Beyond The Fringe variety of satire being 'barbed and deeply planted', the skin of 'the establishment' was as thick as a rhino and that the established actually enjoyed the *frisson* of being mocked; after all, little was being done to change the structures that kept them in power. They sit there smiling at the darts that hit them before rising to trample upon the dart-throwers or to absorb them. In retrospect at least, and having moved on, the Fringe foursome refused to wear the lucrative 'satire' label being pinned on them. They have followed the time-honoured custom of artists in dissociating themselves from a move-ment they were part of. Jonathan 'Swift' Miller, always able to find an appropriate 'popular' analogy when need be, feels that the satiric banner was thrust into their hands 'rather like Charlie Chaplin in *Modern Times* finding himself at the head of a Communist parade... and we've been lumbered with it ever since'. However, the doctor's diagnosis as to why 'none of us approached the world with satirical indignation' cannot stand up to too much close inspection.

'We had no reason to – we were all very comfortably off and doing very nicely. Alan was all set to be an academic at Oxford, Dudley was doing very well as a jazz musician – and Peter and I came from professional middle-class families anyway and had nothing to com-plain of.' Even if this were true (neither Bennett nor Moore was especially well off or content at the time), the statement assumes that 'satirical indignation' derives only from the economically deprived.

Alan Bennett, it is true, has always eschewed satiric intentions in his work and talks rather of his comedy deriving from 'observation': 'I don't think we ever thought we could change things, but each of us, to some extent, concentrated on the things that irritated us. Some of these were small irritations, others had larger implications... The older I get and the more I do the less confident I am that one can achieve anything by comedy.' Dudley Moore thought the show merely 'great fun' while Peter Cook is prepared to admit reluctantly that 'certain parts of it were satirical': 'There were all sorts of things I would have liked to change in society but I didn't think they would be achieved by *Beyond The Fringe*. I thought it was important that the sketches had some real content and weight but primarily they were there to make people laugh.'

In his introduction to the published text, 1957 Footlighter Michael Frayn described satire as a 'poor, broken-winded idea'. Thus, the attitude today of many of the participants in the so-called 'satire boom' of the early 'sixties is rather as if they were being asked inquisitorially by the House of UnEnglish Activities 'Are you or have you ever been a satirist?' Labels, always dubbed 'journalists' phrases' – such as Mannerism, Impressionism, 'Kitchen Sink' drama, *La Nouvelle Vague* and Minimalism – are nonetheless useful and general guide lines to an ethos.

The mere mention, though all-encompassing, of a decade, say the thirties, immediately conjures up an atmosphere. Break it down further by saying thirties English poetry and a more specific picture comes to mind. Auden, Spender and MacNiece will mostly be mentioned, only because they were the most representative. The 'Satire Industry' in the early sixties means *Beyond The Fringe*, The Establishment Club – 'England's first satirical nightclub' – *Private Eye*, *TW3* (a TV programme that became not so much a programme, more a way of life for millions of viewers every Saturday night), followed by *Not So Much A Programme More A Way Of Life*, which was not so much a way of life, more a programme. Whether they were satiric in the sense of Swift, Pope, Hogarth, Gilray, Daumier, Voltaire, George Grosz *et al* is irrelevant. The perception at the time was that there had been a breakthrough in popular culture. It was the beginning of some kind of British *glasnost*. Jonathan Miller admits that 'after several years of this sort of activity ... a generalised scepticism in the face of political behaviour became characteristic of the British public'.

It is symptomatic of 'sixties Britain that, whereas the French make continual reference to *les événements de mai 1968*, the Germans to the Baader-Meinhof activities, and the Italians to the Red Brigade, the social watermarks of the English are *Beyond The Fringe* (considered to have started the ball of the Permissive Society rolling), *That Was The Week That Was*, the night Kenneth Tynan uttered 'fuck' on BBC TV and the day John Lennon said of the Beatles, 'We're more popular than Jesus now.'

VI

It is difficult to measure the impact that such an amiable, amusing and academic (in its scholarly sense) revue such as *Beyond The Fringe* had in the early 1960s, and to understand, in these days of *Spitting Image* and *The Comic Strip*, why it was seen as biting satire. One can assume that the belly of British society must have been pretty flabby to have been winded by such a mild punch, compared with today's

'Alternative Comedy' – another shorthand expression used to distinguish comics willing to look outside stereotypes and popular prejudices for their comedy, to take a political stance or, according to Dame Edna Everage, to describe comedians who are funny on alternate nights. 'There seems to be a popular picture of us lurching into a paddock full of sacred cows and laying about us with broadswords. But the so-called sacred cows had had foot and mouth disease for years,' explains Miller.

Of course, the powers that were had been slightly shaken by the Suez crisis, the Aldermaston marches, and by the plays and novels that *Look Back in Anger* engendered. But the long years of smug Tory rule and the reactionary Establishment's hold on the state institutions made any attack seem more daring than it actually was. That is why an extremely influential left-of-centre theatre critic like Kenneth Tynan saw so much hope coming from the direction of Messrs Bennett, Cook, Miller and Moore. Looking back on it nine years later, the rightof-centre columnist Bernard Levin, in his *The Pendulum Years*, felt that 'long before the end of its run it had suffered the inevitable fate reserved in England for rebels, namely affectionate absorption into the bosom of the Establishment that they are supposed to be out to destroy. Eventually the Queen went to see it, and was reported to have laughed heartily.'

Yet it was not so much the politics but the style that made the deepest impression. John Wells remembers going to the first night.

'I'd been working very hard to produce a revue for that year and it was still on the lines of the traditional cabaret. It was suggested we literally clean our teeth before the opening number. What was so surprising about *Beyond The Fringe* was it was exactly as if the curtain, the proscenium and the audience weren't there, and you were sitting in somebody's rooms in Oxford or Cambridge. It was a completely new and real tone of voice.'

Michael Frayn, in his introduction to the text, wrote of 'the sheer surprise of going to a revue and finding oneself addressed not by hired spokesmen, zombies with neatly squared-off, bulled-up theatrical faces, repeating someone else's jokes, but directly, by recognisable human beings, who talked about things that human beings talk about outside the theatre, and not special demonstration topics brought out of formaldehyde only for revues.'

Harold Hobson of *The Sunday Times*, the Morecambe to Kenneth Tynan's Wise in the double act of weekend theatre critics, thought the show, with no females, orchestra or band, and the bare staging, resembled 'the dock in a run-down provincial court'. Bare or simple, symbolic sets were not unknown in straight plays at the time – the entire cast of Benjamin Britten's 1951 opera *Billy Budd* was male, only a piano was used in *At The Drop Of A Hat*, and neither Flanders nor Swann was a woman – but for revue plainness constituted a breakthrough. More to the point, and continuing on the line of what the show *didn't* have, was its abandonment of comic and 'point' songs, of light and 'seriously though' musical numbers. Only Dudley Moore could carry a tune, and so it otherwise conformed to the dictionary definition of a revue (pre-dating *Beyond The Fringe*) as a 'theatrical production consisting typically of brief often satirical sketches and songs'.

The only musical interludes came from the nimble fingers of Moore at the piano, which were comments on music itself. The show opened with a hasty rendition of the National Anthem by Moore. The other three decide that the pianist cannot be English as he played 'the whole thing sitting down', and therefore must be Russian. Until the early seventies, all theatrical performances began with the playing of 'God Save the King/Queen', which prompted the audience, whether they found the ritual meaningful or not, to stand up. At least the traditional *trois coups* in France alerts the audience to pay attention rather than stand to it. Movie-goers only had to rise *after* the film performance and, as they were getting up anyway, it was not much of a bind and for a cinema manager it was a good way to clear the house quickly, since audiences were eager to escape detention.

The number, called 'Steppes In The Right Direction', continued with an effort to indoctrinate Moore (who says not a word) by explaining to him the benefits of living in England. 'Under the National Health Service for twelve shillings a week we are treated absolutely free.' ('Bit of satire in there straight away,' as Ben Elton, 'alternative' comedian of the 1980s, might say.) The only reaction they get from 'the Russian man' is the raspberry he blows every time they mention Macmillan. The sketch ends with the cast singing 'Macmillan' followed by a raspberry to the tune of 'The Volga Boatmen', not exactly the tone of sophisticated political satire.

The solo piano contributions from Moore were wickedly accurate and witty pastiches of 'classical' music. No need, as the Goons used to do, to urge audiences to 'nip out and get the pop corn' during the unwelcome musical interpolations by Max Geldray and Ray Ellington.

'Pastiche' is defined as a 'musical or other medley of borrowings done in general imitation of an artist's style'. Appreciation of it is commensurate with the knowledge of the subject being parodied or pastiched. On the whole, to imitate accurately is to know and love what you imitate. The intellectual dilemma of such an exercise derives from the fact that those listeners who know their Fauré and Schubert songs can laugh affectionately and with recognition at the brilliance of the take-offs, while others laugh as they would at the original. The pastiches thus created both erudite and philistine reactions at the same time.

The musical item that was billed as 'And The Same To You' was written by Moore in Edinburgh the night before the opening.

'I was desperate, so I took the most ridiculous tune I could think of. It went so well that I made it longer and longer.' This tune was a version of 'Colonel Bogey' in the style of Beethoven, with a never-ending coda. It was a *tour de force*, although its humour would have been familiar to those who had attended Hoffnung concerts. The audiences for the latter tended to be part of the wide, but closed, circle of music lovers who enjoyed letting their hair down in between listening to what used to be called 'long-haired' music, before the Beatles. Moore's contributions opened up classical music pastiche to the general theatre-going public, whose references were mostly musical comedy.

The Fauré was 'La nuit s'épanouit', 'in which the poet bemoans the evil spirits which are at the bottom of his garden'; and the Schubert was a setting of Heine's poem 'Die Flabbergast'. Moore, 'playing with himself' and singing the parts of both tenor and soprano in mock German, was far cleverer and less broad than Anna Russell, who used to do this sort of thing.

It was, however, his Benjamin Britten version of 'Little Miss Muffet', as sung in the strangled tenor tones of Peter Pears, that was the most original and seemed almost as 'shocking' as taking off the Prime Minister. Britten, who was considered, not without justification, to be the greatest English opera composer since Purcell and the saviour of British post-war music, had made a number of transcriptions of folk songs for Pears. Like the best of parodies, Moore's was close enough to be extremely funny, but not close enough to be mistaken for the real thing.

As Moore felt rather diffident about contributing anything to the content or structure of the revue, the Britten item only got in by the skin of its teeth, with him asking the others to listen to it about a fortnight before opening in London. 'He said he was just trying it out,' remembers Alan Bennett. 'He couldn't possibly do this, could he?' When Moore was invited to be a castaway on Roy Plomley's *Desert Island Discs* in 1969, he chose the Britten pastiche as one of his eight records. 'I must stress, however,' he told Plomley, 'that I do this out of absolute love and admiration for Britten and with no malice aforethought at all.' Britten and his life-long companion, Peter Pears, did see some malice in the title 'Little Miss Britten' that the item was given in the programme, and never went to see the show. They might also have been offended by the sketch in which three wrist-flapping actors mince into a studio to do a film advertisement for a cigarette called Bollard, a word slightly reminiscent of 'bollocks'. 'Bollard? That sounds exciting,' says a sashaying Miller. After chatting about their clothes and hairstyles, they don sou'westers and suddenly become terribly butch. 'Smoke Bollard – a *man's* cigarette.' Then the three of them shriek 'Whoops!' Blackout. It was the sort of routine that could easily have fitted into one of Hermione Gingold's wartime revues at the Ambassadors. It was also the reverse of a hoary vaudeville blackout sketch in which a tough gangster shoots a man dead. When asked why, he takes up a camp stance, and shrieks, 'He was sitting on my knitting!' Alan Bennett was relegated in the sketch to the role of neutral cameraman–director. 'I was never allowed to camp it up,' he complained. (He later indulged himself during his TV series, *On The Margin*, where he appeared each week as a queeny antique dealer.)

Before *Beyond The Fringe* was performed, the text, like every theatre script, had to be submitted to the Lord Chamberlain (until his unlamented departure in 1968) to see whether it contained anything that would 'deprave and corrupt those whose minds are open to such immoral influences and of a nature calculated to shock common feelings of decency in any well-regulated mind'. Although the Lord Chamberlain's office, in 1958, had recognised that homosexuality's 'complete exclusion from the stage can no longer be regarded as justifiable', it issued the licence on the understanding that the *stage direction* 'Enter two outrageous old queens' be changed to 'Enter two aesthetic young men' and that 'all homosexual gestures and business are omitted and "darling" omitted where it occurs, as being a feminine endearment'. Dudley Moore turned this to excellent advantage by substituting the original greeting of 'Hello, Girls' to the other two camp actors with 'Hello, Men' and got a bigger laugh.

Originally, the noble protector of the 'well-regulated' minds of the worthy citizens of Britain, specifically Edinburgh, wanted the 'Hello Sailor' sketch cut altogether. Robert Ponsonby, determined to save it, wrote to the Lord Chamberlain to explain, as he quaintly put it, that 'The moth we are pinning to the board is not homosexuality as such.' Gay Lib was still some years away; in fact, the homosexual act between consenting adults was made legal only in July 1967 and in Scotland not until 1980. There was a joke at the time about two men making love on a train going north and having to come before the border.

Effeminate actors playing hearty seamen (they could have done the same as members of the salty chorus in Britten's *Billy Budd* or *Peter Grimes*) is one side of a double-edged joke. The other is the strange perceived connection between cigarettes and the sea in contemporary commercials. Anthony Sampson asks, in his *Anatomy of Britain*, 'Is it the excitement of wetness, the suggestion of manliness, or the echoes of naval supremacy? Whatever it is, the lure of the sea is everywhere – as in Anchor, advertised by manly men in oilskins singing a ditty about how they hanker for an anchor; or Capstan, which requires an unfortunate young man to lug around a bollard with his girl-friend.'

Outrageous queens, or rather 'aesthetic young men', have always been a staple of comedy but the lampooning of a black politician entered new and more sensitive territory. Three years later John Bird was doing his imitation of President Jomo Kenyatta in *Not So Much A Programme More A Way Of Life*, which was bitterly criticised by the Kenyan High Commission; and in the 1970s satirists attempting to make Idi Amin the butt of their humour were neutralised by his own self-caricature. Lenny Henry (Britain's answer to Eddie Murphy) started his career with his 'Katanga' politician, which he dropped because it was, like the *Beyond The Fringe* sketch, dangerously close to Western prejudices. After all, Britain at the time still had a vicious open colour bar, unlike the vicious covert one operating today. In 1960, around seventeen countries became independent and the leaders of new African nations, whose independence had mostly been won in bloody struggles against colonialism, were giving blacks a voice in world affairs for the first time. But, as some of them were dictators and one kind of colonial rule was being replaced by another, as suggested in Jonathan Miller's productions of *The Tempest* of 1970 and 1988, they seemed fair game.

The black politician, played in a wavering African accent by Miller and called by the Japanese sounding name of Mr Nobitsu, complains that 'Everywhere the black man is misrepresented. For example, recently I went to London to see the play *Fings Ain't What They Used T'Be*, and in this play, there was a black man who was laying about all over the stage doing nothing, implying that all black men are layabouts.' When the interviewer (Cook) says, 'You might as well say the same play implies that all white people were pimps or prostitutes,' Nobitsu replies, 'Well, that is fair comment.'

Up to this point, the audience accepts the unblacked-up Miller as a black man, but theatrical licence is suddenly removed when Cook remarks, 'Mr Nobitsu, one thing rather puzzles me – your hair is extremely straight, and your complexion seems to be white in colour.' 'That is perfectly true. I have recently undergone an operation to straighten my hair and also to remove the pigmentation from my skin . . . I feel in this way I can represent the interests of my people best by speaking to the white man on his own ground. Besides, it is the only way in which I can get lodgings.'

The inclusion of politics (even with the smallest of p's) acted like sunlight entering the stuffy Miss Havisham room called the West End. When *Beyond The Fringe* took up residence at the Fortune in May 1961, some of its neighbours occupying the 30-odd theatres around the area where the musicals *My Fair Lady, Oliver!, Irma La Douce*, and *The Sound of Music*, farces such as *Watch It, Sailor!* and Brian Rix in *One For The Pot*, light comedies *Billy Liar, The Irregular Verb To Love* and *The Bride Comes Back*; there was also *The World of Susie Wong*, the everlasting *Mousetrap* and another thriller called *Guilty Party*. One would have to look hard for any politics or satire in Peter Cook's revue *One Over The Eight* and there was only the slightest whiff of politics in Terence Rattigan's *Ross*, in which Alec Guinness portrayed Lawrence of Arabia.

Although *Beyond The Fringe* did not set out to be a topical revue, it could not help but reflect events going on in Britain and the world, quite unlike any of the other shows mentioned above. In its opening month Britain bought Skybolt missiles from the USA and put more money into Civil Defence; President Kennedy increased his defence spending tenfold; Enoch Powell, the Minister of Health, announced an increase in Health Service charges for dentures and spectacles, and the cost of prescriptions was doubled. At the House of Commons there was a farcical scene when Anthony Wedgwood Benn was barred from entering by the Principal Doorkeeper because the House had refused him permission to renounce his peerage: he had gained it on the death of his father, Viscount Stansgate, and wished to remain an MP.

The 'Fringe' teams sketch on the idiocies of Civil Defence was presented primarily by Peter Cook and Alan Bennett; 'we shall receive four minutes' warning of any impending nuclear attack. Some people have said, "Oh, my goodness me – four minutes? That is not a very long time!" Well, I would remind those doubters that some people in this great country of ours can run a mile in four minutes.' And 'The first golden rule to remember in hydrogen warfare is be out of the area where the attack is about to occur – get right out of the area because that's the danger area where the bombs are dropping. Get right out of it – get right out of it – if you're out of it you're well out of it, if you're in it you're really in it. If you are caught in it when the missile explodes, for goodness sake don't move, stand absolutely stockstill – not under a tree, of course – that could be extremely dangerous.' As far as radiation is concerned: 'Jump into a brown paper bag. Draw it on rather like a shroud . . . the bomb drops, the dust settles, jump into your brown paper bag, and hop along to your local Civil Defence leader.' All this when John Cleese and Graham Chapman were not yet a gleam in Monty Python's eye.

Alan Bennett had a solo as a pompous reactionary gentleman giving a lecture in which he talks about international relations and attacks 'intellectual blighters' who 'just because there's some minor aspect of the internal policy of the legally elected government of South Africa that they don't agree with . . . think that by not eating pineapples they're going to improve the situation'. Although the piece, entitled 'Let's Face It', lasted only a few minutes, Bennett feels, 'There were great stretches of boredom in it. There were few laughs and I'd never dare do it today, but I was sustained because I did feel that it was sort of hard-core material.' Cook referred to the sketch as 'Boring Old Man time which will severely restrain the audience from laughter and lash them with guilt.' In a sense, without being the funniest item, it prepared the audience for the kind of attitude the four were taking on certain issues. Most of all, it warmed them up for another 'boring old man', the Prime Minister Harold Macmillan.

Nowadays, when imitations of leading politicians and even the Royal Family, are often extremely robust – Mrs Thatcher could be seen literally licking President Reagan's arse on TV's *Spitting Image*, the shock not being lessened by the fact that they are latex puppets – Peter Cook's take-off of Harold Macmillan seems extraordinarily gentle. (Near the end of his life, Macmillan made his appearance on *Spitting Image* as dried-up, mildewed and senile.) A few months before *Beyond The Fringe* opened, Macmillan, in his fifth year as Prime Minister, met the newly elected President Kennedy, 25 years his junior, at the naval base in Key West; attempted to prevent the Commonwealth prime ministers from expelling South Africa from its ranks; and started negotiations to join the Common Market. Macmillan, grandson of a crofter, came up through Eton School, Balliol College, Oxford, the Grenadier Guards, marriage into the aristocracy, the Ministry of Housing and Chancellorship of the Exchequer and finally Prime Minister. His motto was Gilbert and Sullivan's 'Quiet, Calm Deliberation Disentangles Every Knot'. The droopy moustache and eyes, the languid gestures and his Edwardian clothes masked a shrewd and often ruthless Tory politician. He was a staunch defender of the establishment, grouse shooting and the novels of Anthony Trollope, from whose pages he might have stepped. Didn't he once say that he liked nothing better than to go to bed with a Trollope?

According to Christopher Booker in his subjective chronicle of the times, *The Neophiliacs*, 'By 1959, Macmillan had become a "dream symbol" to friends and opposition alike. The essence of a dream symbol being that it carries no "value"; it is merely an image that for the time being is hypnotic, both for those who profess to dislike it and spend a disproportionate amount of their time explaining why; and for those who find it irresistible until such time as they become bored and seek another.' Cartoonists 'never had it so good', especially the left-wing Vicky, jester on Beaverbrook's right-wing *Evening Standard*, whose satirical creation of Supermac – Macmillan in a Superman outfit attempting to right wrongs, and occasionally wronging the right – had the opposite effect to the one intended. (Rather as the 'Iron Lady' tag affixed to the 'dream symbol' Thatcher was taken up by admiring authoritarians to be used as a compliment.) Vicky later changed tack by sketching Macmillan as Archie Rice, the faded music-hall comic of John Osborne's *The Entertainer*. There was little of Supermac or Macwonder about Peter Cook's TVPM who came out as a silly old buffer, 'one of the weary old men of Europe', in Cecil King's phrase, whose gestures were out of sync with his words.

'Good evening. I have recently been travelling round the world on

---

your behalf and at your expense, visiting some of the chaps with whom I hope to be shaping your future. I went first to Germany, and there I spoke with the German Foreign Minister, Herr . . . Herr and there, and we exchanged many frank words in our respective languages; so precious little came of that in the way of understanding . . . I then went on to America, and there I had talks with the young, vigorous President of that country, and danced with his very lovely lady wife. We talked of many things, including Great Britain's position in the world as some kind of honest broker. I agreed with him, when he said that no nation could be more honest; and he agreed with me, when I chaffed him, and said that no nation could be broker . . . '
Moving from world affairs, the PM then reads a letter from an old-age pensioner in Fife complaining about having to live on a fixed income of £2 7s a week. After tearing up the letter, he replies, 'Well, let me say right away, Mrs McFarlane – as one Scottish old-age pensioner to another – be of good cheer. There are many people in this country today who are far worse off than yourself. And it is the policy of the Conservative Party to see that the position is maintained.'

Peter Cook says, 'My impersonation of Macmillan was in fact extremely affectionate – I was a great Macmillan fan. He did have this somewhat ludicrous manner – but merely because it was the first time for some years that a living Prime Minister had been impersonated on the stage, a great deal of weight was attached to it.' Michael Frayn describes what he witnessed on the second night. 'The couple in front of me, as sound a pair of Young Tories as I have ever heard cachinnate, were right with us, neighing away like demented horses, until the middle of Peter Cook's lampoon on Macmillan, when the man turned to the girl and said in an appalled whisper, "I say! This is supposed to be the Prime Minister," after which they sat in silence for the rest of the evening. God knows what cherished family prejudices they had betrayed by then.'

It's a nice story, and might have elements of the truth, but if they were that shocked would they have returned after the interval and not laughed once, even during Cook's man on the park bench and the Shakespeare parody?

Alan Bennett might also have been elaborating somewhat when he describes the night Macmillan himself came to see the show. 'Peter therefore went several steps further, remarking on the Prime Minister's presence in the audience. Macmillan buried his face in his programme, and the audience out of embarrassment gradually froze.

This didn't stop Peter. On he plunged. Someone with less confidence would have been guided by the atmosphere.'

This, of course, is Bennett transferring his own embarrassment on to others. Presumably Macmillan knew or had been informed that he was being impersonated in the show, just as Harold Wilson visited *Mrs Wilson's Diary* and the Thatchers went to see *Anyone For Denis?* An old campaigner like Macmillan was used to seeing caricatures of himself every day in the newspapers, some of which he had on his wall. Unlike Margaret Thatcher, who emerged unsmiling from the Whitehall Theatre, Supermac claimed that he was highly amused by Cook's imitation, although in a TV interview with Kenneth Harris he mischievously pretended to have heard of it only vaguely. Prime Ministerial mimicking became the stock-in-trade of 'satirists' and on *TW3*, William Rushton, who actually admits to having voted for the man, made a good living out of doing Macmillan, something he still seems to be doing unconsciously. So infectious was this mimicry that eventually even Macmillan started impersonating himself.

Alan Bennett's squeamishness is also demonstrated by his views on a visit the Queen paid to the show. In one sketch he had to say the word 'erection'. 'The management asked me to delete this on the night of the Queen's visit. I priggishly refused. I cringe to think of it today. I suppose I must be one of the few people who have said "erection" in front of the Queen. I wish I hadn't. I don't suppose either of us profited from the experience.' There is little doubt that the Royal mother of three (Edward was yet to be) took the word in her stride, but from Bennett's attitude one would imagine that instead of merely *saying* 'erection' in front of the Queen he had actually *produced* one. (He later made amends by his flattering portrait of her in the second play of *Single Spies* in 1988.)

'Anyway, I am hoping against hope that one night the Royal Family will turn up and make my having to sit through this rotten, awful show every night worthwhile.' So says Dudley Moore in a sketch with (and written by) Peter Cook called 'The Royal Box', the earliest surviving example of a Dud 'n' Pete dialogue, Dud plays a man who has seen a show 497 times on the offchance that the Royal Family would pay a visit to the theatre. The lunatic number was (and is) typical of Cook's unique humour, resembling the sketches Kenneth Williams performed in *Pieces of Eight* and *One Over the Eight*.

Apart from the Macmillan imitation, Cook's other solo (they each had a couple) was his 'Sitting On The Bench' a favourite party piece he had developed from his schooldays during which he had the temerity to improvise nightly.

'His performance would often be quite dangerous, on the edge of embarrassment,' commented Bennett. 'It's simply that he has a kind of self-confidence which doesn't take account of audiences' reactions.'

No matter how much the soliloquy varied from night to night, it invariably began with 'Yes, I could have been a judge but I never had the Latin.' Jonathan Miller evoked the philosophy of his great-uncle Henri Bergson to describe Cook's monologue.

'It extracts peculiar surrealistic effects from the endless repetition of middle-class, lower middle-class clichés. What Peter produces is mechanical thinking . . . Peter's miner makes what philosophers call mistakes of category. He makes the mistake of thinking that the idea of capability is optional. He says, "I could have been a judge if only I had the Latin" . . . It is in fact automatic thinking and the humour about it is automatic thought, automatic cliché, a seizing of the superficial, and then investing it with an artificial authority and importance.'

Miller's analysis is valid, but as E B White said, 'Humour can be dissected, as a frog can, but the thing dies in the process and the innards are discouraging to any but the pure scientific mind.' Cook's character conforms to one dominant aspect of humour, the disparity between human aspiration and performance, a case of knowledge being bliss, no matter how unassimilated and misunderstood. His man on the park bench digs into newspapers and books to extract facts for facts' sake as others rummage in dustbins for food:

I am very interested in the universe – I am specialising in the universe and all that surrounds it. I am studying Nesbitt's book – *The Universe and All That Surrounds It, an Introduction*. There's not a lot of interest in this down the mine . . . If you were searching for a word to describe the conversations that go on down the mine, boring would spring to your lips. Oh God! They're very boring. If ever you want to hear things like: 'Hello, I've found a bit of coal. Have you really? Yes, no doubt about it, this black substance is coal all right. Jolly good, the very thing we're looking for.' It's not enough to keep the mind alive, is it? I said to a fellow miner the other day, I said: 'Have you heard of Marcel Proust?' He said, 'No, he must work down the other mine.'

The sketch that most people remember Alan Bennett for, and that stamped his personality on the public mind forever, was his woolly preacher giving a sermon ostensibly based on but never allied to, the particularly unpromising text. 'But my brother Esau is an hairy man, but I am a smooth man.' It then wanders into non sequitur and pompous platitudes of preachers, ending with a wonderfully bizarre analogy of Life. 'Life, you know, is rather like opening a tin of sardines. We are all of us looking for the key. And I wonder, how many of you tonight have wasted years of your lives looking behind the kitchen dressers of this life for that key. I know I have. Others think they've found the key, don't they? They roll back the lid of the sardine tin of life, they reveal the sardines, the riches of life, therein, and they get them out. But, you know, there's always a little piece in the corner you can't get out. I wonder – I wonder, is there a little piece in the corner of your life? I know there is in mine.'

The monologue is the perfect boarding point for a journey through Bennett's writings even to the very English *double entendre* that slightly mars the ending, and his acting roles.

The querulous, high-pitched, pedantic, Yorkshire-tinged voice and his bespectacled, lugubrious looks make Bennett perfect for playing dry academics and garrulous parsons. At Oxford, Bennett had considered going into the Church, 'not for any better reason than that I looked like a vicar . . . People often end up doing what the mirror tells them, and in the process whole lives are thrown away.' His love and knowledge of the Church enabled him to hit off the clergyman's empty idioms with accuracy, so that his satire is an extension of the old 'gas and gaiters' vicar beloved of Aldwych farces.

Less good was the sketch entitled 'Man Bites God' in which Jonathan Miller portrayed a trendy vicar at his dockland parish of St Jack in the Lifeboat. 'Don't call me Vicar – call me Dick – that's the sort of vicar I am!' It's the sort of piece that could sit easily in an old 'Two Ronnies' show, if it weren't so dated. But the TV 'God Slot' was a target with few bullet holes in it in those days.

Other subjects for satire were hypocritical journalists, chinless wonders at a restaurant ('I think I've got my contact lenses in back to front') and Cambridge linguistic philosophers ('Are you using "yes" in the affirmative sense here?'). All three sketches would work today with only slight changes: substitute Murdoch or Maxwell when the Fleet Street hack justifies working for Beaverbrook ('Just because my name's at the top of the column you mustn't think I have any connection with it . . . '); replace the silly businessman, guffawing in a restaurant, by yuppies; and change the philosophers to Structuralists. Part of the revue's success could also be put down to its ability to make audiences feel intelligent, something Tom Stoppard has made such a good living at for some years, to allow them to display their knowledge by laughing at references to Hegel, Wittgenstein, Verlaine, Heine and Shakespeare, as well as at Peter Cook's miner with intellectual pretensions.

The fact that capital punishment ended in Britain as late as December 1969 hasn't prevented the 'silent majority' from shrieking at the top of their voices for its reinstatement. Despite public opinion in favour of bringing back the noose, Parliament, because of its respect for the sanctity of life, continues to resist. The sketch in which Miller is a condemned man, Moore the guard and Bennett the prison governor needs no updating, although it has lost much of its sting. The best part is a typical bumptious peroration from Bennett comparing having 'six of the best' at school with capital punishment.

Bennett: You don't want to be cooped up for life.
Miller: Yes, I do want to be cooped up for life.

All four performers had been too young to participate in the war, but grew up with the reality of it and with the myths about it perpetrated by the movies. The older generation had fought, suffered and died in it, and the myths were necessary to sustain them. But unlike the knight who survived battles because he was told by a sorcerer that his sword was magic and would protect him, later to discover that the sword was mere base metal, they refused to throw the myths away when they no longer needed them. Over fifteen years after the war, it did not seem inappropriate to make fun of the stiff-upper-lip approach in the piece entitled 'The Aftermyth of War'.

Cook: War's not going very well, you know.
Miller: Oh, my God!
Cook: We are two down, the ball's in the enemy court. War is
         a psychological thing, Perkins, rather like a game of
         football. You know how in a game of football ten men
         often play better than eleven?
Miller: Yes, sir.

Cook: Perkins, we are asking you to be that one man. I want
you to lay down your life, Perkins. We need a futile
gesture at this stage. It will raise the whole tone of the
war. Get up in a crate, Perkins, pop over to Bremen,
take a shufti, don't come back. Goodbye, Perkins. God,
I wish I was going too.

Miller: Goodbye, sir – or is it *au revoir*?.

Cook: No, Perkins.

Peter Cook's unsmiling face, patrician features and clipped upper-class accent, the antithesis of his park bench character, made him perfect to take off the kind of officer seen in countless war films, fictional and documentary. By 1961 this type of picture, usually starring Jack Hawkins, John Mills and Richard Todd, was very much old helmet. *The Goon Show* had already made fun of the self-righteousness, artificiality and class snobbery in those wartime dramas, and mocked the military in the character of Major Bloodnok (created by Peter Sellers) who invariably replied to any greeting with 'How dare you accuse me of robbing the regimental cashbox!' Spike Milligan, whose father had been a sergeant major in the Royal Artillery, explained that 'The Goons gave me a chance to knock people who my father and I as a boy had to call "sir". Colonels. Chaps like Grytpype Thynne with educated voices who were really bloody scoundrels . . . It was cowards charging everywhere with guns.'

Knowledge of the later work of Peter Cook and Alan Bennett allows one to spot their personal contributions to the text of the 'Aftermyth Of War' sketch. Typical of Cook was the above while Bennett's reminiscent and literary vein comes out in the section, 'I'll always remember that weekend war broke out. I was at a house party in Cliveden with the Astors and we sat around listening to the moving broadcast by Mr Churchill, or Mr Chamberlain as he then was . . .' This gentle takeoff of 'Home Service' memoirs was expanded in his first play, *Forty Years On*.

The hand of Jonathan Miller, who has not really developed a recognisable comic voice since, is evident most strongly in the Shakespeare lampoon. Called 'So That's The Way You Like It', it was the ensemble sketch which pleased most people: philistines took it as an attack on the boring old bard, while more sophisticated members of the audience saw it as a parody of traditional productions of the history plays. Yet at the time the standard of Shakespeare productions had seldom been higher, with new directors such as Peter Brook and Peter Hall making their mark, the latter having been appointed managing director of the Shakespeare Memorial Theatre at Stratford-upon-Avon, soon to get the Royal seal. At the Old Vic from 1953 to 1958 there had been Michael Benthall's splendid 'Five Year Plan' to stage all 36 of Shakespeare's plays in the First Folio, which included Richard Burton's *Hamlet* as well as John Neville in a white shirt and jeans as the Prince of Denmark, the first 'I was a teenage Hamlet'.

Miller says that 'I was interested in lampooning productions of Shakespeare, not because I had a burning indignation against them but because I just wanted to get them right.' He got his chance to do so as a stage director eight years later, although it is significant that he has never tackled any of the history plays except the 'quietest' and most introvert of them all, *Richard II*. Miller's only connection with the plays has been as producer of the BBC Bardathon in which his sole contribution was *Henry VI* in its three parts, under the direction of Jane Howell. The reason is Miller's lack of interest in battles, and his still finding the many names risible.

Get thee to Gloucester, Essex. Do thee to Wessex, Exeter.
Fair Albany to Somerset must eke his route.
And Scroup, do you to Westmoreland, where shall bold York
Enrouted now for Lancaster, with forces of our uncle Rutland,
Enjoin his standard with sweet Norfolk's host.
Fair Sussex, get thee to Warwicksbourne.
And there with frowning purpose, tell our plan
To Bedford's titled ear, that he shall press
With most insensate speed
And join his warlike effort to bold Dorset's side.
I most royally shall now to bed,
To sleep off all the nonsense I've just said.

J M Barrie once said, 'I know not whether Bacon wrote the words of Shakespeare, but if he did not it seems to me he missed the opportunity of his life.' The *Beyond the Fringe* team took that opportunity brilliantly, and some of the lines could easily be inserted into a play or two with nobody being any the wiser, even perhaps, 'Oh, saucy Worcester, dost thou lie so still?'

Jonathan Miller's two monologues in the show depended more on his lanky, loose-limbed movements and staccato delivery than on spiralling absurdity of text. On paper, they smack a little of the literary and even of very amusing after-dinner speeches, rather in the manner of Gerard Hoffnung. They were, however, forerunners of the sort of personal absurdist tales that stand-up comedians of the 1980s, such as Jasper Carrot, Ben Elton and Billy Connolly like to tell.

The first, 'The Heat-Death Of The Universe', was a tall tale of tall Miller's attempts to buy a pair of second-hand trousers from the London Passenger Transport Board Lost Property, and fantasising on how it came about that 400 pairs of bright blue corduroy trousers had been lost on trains. 'Porn Shop', the second of his solos, started with 'Some years ago, when I was a medical student, I became rather interested in the shops that one finds down the Charing Cross Road in London.' Questioning the owner of one establishment that sells 'the sort of book that one has to glance at *en passant*, about who buys books on flogging, he is told that 'on the one hand there's your medical students like yourself . . . After all, perversions are in your curriculum aren't they, sir? . . . On the other hand, by far the largest cag'atry, I'm sorry to say, sir, is your straight warped!' The man, and the piece, concludes with his cure for such perverts: 'A sock in the face and a kick in the arse and whip 'em to death.'

Ironically, it was Miller, the only one of the four to give up performing altogether, who got the best reviews. Tynan singled him out and he was also Hobson's choice as the best on stage. In the essay-style tradition of James Agate, his predecessor on *The Sunday Times*, Hobson, 23 years Tynan's senior, wrote that 'Mr Miller has the misfortune to be a Cambridge man. Had he come from Oxford, I should have called him a genius. He is not a windmill, he is not a crocodile; he is not (or at least not quite) an albatross; he is not even a philosopher. But there is something of all these in him . . . He glides, he skips, he elongates, he lopes and he acts . . .'

'The End Of The World', the appropriate climax to *Beyond The Fringe*, was a hilarious Cookian joke at the expense of a sect awaiting the Apocalypse on a mountain top. Cook explains in his inimitable (but much imitated) funny voice that there 'will be as 'twere a mighty rending in the sky, and the mountains will sink, and the valleys will rise and great will be the tumult thereof', and that 'there will be a mighty wind, if the word of God is anything to go by'. Dudley Moore then asks, 'And will this wind be so mighty as to lay low the mountains of the earth?', to which Cook replies, 'No. It will not be quite as mighty as that. That is why we have come up on the moutain, you stupid nit.

To be safe from it. Up here on the mountain we shall be safe. Safe as houses.' 'And what will happen to the houses?' 'Well, naturally, the houses will be swept away . . .'

This sketch was just as funny eighteen years later during *The Secret Policeman's Ball*, the Amnesty International comedy gala held at Her Majesty's Theatre, recorded on film by Roger Graef. Then the above exchange took place between Cook and Rowan Atkinson (product of Oxford revue). When Atkinson, almost rivalling Cook in the 'Ministry of Silly Voices', asks the question about the wind rather incomprehensibly the first time, Cook replies, in what sounds like an ad lib, 'You're speaking too softly for the human ear which is what I'm equipped with.'

VIII

Most great comedy teams thrive on physical and personality differences. Tynan saw Miller as 'gawky and angular with large feet and carrot-coloured hair'; Cook as a 'well-kept minor poet, all lanky elegance and clearly as shy as they come'; Bennett 'has spectacles, flaxen hair and the beginnings of a lantern jaw'; and Moore is a 'smaller young man, with dark eyes and twinkling dark hair'. Not much has changed in succeeding years except that grey has taken over from carrot in Miller's hair and flecks Moore's dark 'Beatle' cut; but Bennett has kept both grey and lantern jaw at bay. Cook, however, now looks more like a *major* poet and 'lanky elegance' has gone to pot.

During the long run of *Beyond The Fringe* it was inevitable that their personality differences would become even more marked. Bennett felt that he was the 'edgiest person on stage – the one who didn't look as if he ought to be there. I felt that I was more an observer than a participant. I often felt the audience disliked me – "Oh, *he's* come on again." ' Miller would get restless more quickly than the others and become careless about his performance when he felt the audience was not responding as warmly as they should. This irritated Moore, who would always give his all, no matter what the house was like. Cook was the most at ease on stage but was more liable to throw the others with improvisation. In fact, the unbecoming 'unprofessional' conduct of attempting to 'corpse' one another was a way of alleviating the boredom of six evenings and two matinées a week, for over a year, in the West End.

At one performance, during Cook and Moore's 'Royal Box' sketch, Bennett ambled on and took a seat on the empty third chair. 'The first time I did it they just became helpless and couldn't get on with the sketch. Then, gradually they got used to the situation, though I didn't do it every night. . . Sometimes Jonathan would come on as well.' These are the sort of 'in' games that are lost on audiences. Corpsing, artificially or naturally induced, sometimes marred the Dud and Pete duos in the *Not Only . . . But Also* TV series from 1965 and was an unfortunate part of Spike Milligan's act. Miller feels that 'in most shows, if the actors do start to break up and giggle on stage, the audience becomes very hostile indeed. But actually, they went along with us more and more – the more we laughed, the more they enjoyed it. I think this was partly because they knew that the show belonged to us entirely.'

While *Beyond The Fringe* was at the Fortune Theatre, Alan Bennett was commuting in a chauffeur-driven Rolls three times a week between London and Oxford where he was still a tutor in medieval history, and Jonathan Miller continued to work as a pathologist. When asked how he could combine medicine with the theatre, he replied, 'My patients can wait. They're all dead.' Peter Cook had been busy setting up and running The Establishment satirical nightclub in Soho, where Dudley Moore would dash after the evening performance in order to play jazz until three in the morning and then, more often than not, take one of his female fans back to the small flat in Kilburn High Road which he had rented from band leader John Dankworth.

The flat, which had a rather vulgar bar with bamboo posts up to the ceiling, had a sea of Dankworth's band scores piled up in one room. There was virtually no furniture, so Dudley would sleep on a saggy put-you-up sofa. As there was only one blanket, he used his winter coat, the buttons of which were hanging by threads, as an extra cover. He never went to the laundrette, so that every time he wanted a clean shirt he'd go out and buy one at Marks and Spencer. Eventually the room that was full of scores became a room full of dirty clothes as well until a girl-friend of his took four car-loads of washing to the laundrette in her Mini.

In the same year, 1961, Moore wrote the music for *The Owl And The Pussycat*, the first ballet by Gillian Lynne, future choreographer of *Cats*, and later the two of them collaborated with Keith Waterhouse and Willis Hall on a revue called *England, Our England*. Dudley was living at the tempo of one of his fastest piano solos and as a result, in the month in which the show was celebrating its first anniversary, he collapsed backstage with exhaustion during the interval of a Saturday matinée. Understudy Robin Ray, who eventually replaced Moore, was telephoned and rushed to the theatre to take over the second half and continued in the show for the next three weeks while Dudley recovered in the Italian sunshine of Positano.

On his way to Italy, Moore was recognised at the airport by Sir John Gielgud, who had seen *Beyond The Fringe* and been bowled over by Dudley. When told that Moore was off to Positano, Gielgud insisted on giving him an introduction to his friends Rex Harrison and his then wife Lilli Palmer, who lived nearby. When Dudley got on the plane, he couldn't resist opening Sir John's letter. It read, 'Darling Lilli, This will introduce you to the brilliant young pianist from *Beyond The Fringe* – Stanley Moon.' This 'lunatic' misnaming immediately entered the growing collection of Gielgudisms.

At around the same time negotiations were being held about a possible Broadway transfer. Both David Merrick and Alexander H. Cohen made bids. Merrick, the bigger producer and soon to be the biggest on Broadway, had done well with English plays by John Osborne, Peter Ustinov (*Romanoff and Juliet*), *A Taste Of Honey* and *Ross*. Cohen's reputation was for more intimate theatre; he had recently presented *At The Drop Of A Hat*, *An Evening With Mike Nichols And Elaine May*, *An Evening With Yves Montand* and Lena Horne in *Her Nine O'Clock Revue*. The foursome decided to go with Cohen. They would receive ten per cent of the box-office takings, whereas in the West End, according to theatrical practice, they got only six per cent, because the show was classified a musical, due to Dudley Moore's contributions.

When the idea was first mooted that *Beyond The Fringe* should continue in London with a second cast while the show was on Broadway, the four originators baulked at it. 'I, with utter arrogance ... felt that once we'd all left, nobody would come and see it,' confesses Peter Cook. Anyway, how could anyone else play 'Jonathan Miller'? Would the Macmillan impersonation be a take-off of Peter Cook's take-off? Would not anyone else other than Alan Bennett make a curate's egg of his sermon sketch? It seemed it would be as idle to have replacements as it would have been to tell radio audiences that someone else would be taking over from Tony Hancock in *Hancock's Half Hour*. But the thought of further royalties overrode artistic considerations, as long as they each also had the veto on their alter egos.

Donaldson, the producer of the show, came up with four candidates – David Frost, John Wells, Joe Melia and Richard Ingrams as Cook, Bennett, Miller and Moore respectively. Peter Cook swore that he would have to be a dead body before Frost could fill his shoes. In the year *Beyond The Fringe* opened in London Frost had appeared in and written a great deal of the Footlights Revue called, after Cook's catch-phrase, *I Thought I Saw It Move*. Many of the sketches were a copy of (or tribute to?) Cook's comic style, prompting the latter to call Frost, in one of his most withering phrases, 'the Bubonic Plagiarist'. Cook's veto was the best thing that happened to the future Atlantic-hopping TV executive and Nixon interviewer, because Ned Sherrin signed him up soon after for *TW3*. John Wells became de Gaulle, and later Denis Thatcher; Richard Ingrams became editor of *Private Eye*. Only Joe Melia (ex-Cambridge Footlights) got the part. Although a respected comic actor, he remains less famous than the three who didn't, as do the others selected: Terence Brady (who satisfied Cook); Robin Ray, Moore's erstwhile understudy; and Bill Wallis (still doing satire in Radio 4's *Week Ending*) as 'Alan Bennett'. It is not only a tribute to the new cast that the show continued to be a success, running a further four years in the West End, but to the quality of the material, proving that it had a life independent of its creators.

An even more important decision than the substitute cast was how much the very British show would have now to be geared to American audiences. The foursome instinctively felt that they would be able to make only the most minor changes and were relieved to discover that Alexander Cohen felt that when you buy British, you should serve British. Period (full stop). He knew that the Englishness would give it a built-in snob appeal, that the Americans would get 'a sort of ethnic buzz out of little bits of limey eccentricity', as Miller claimed. At least, that was the hope, as the four of them set out to go beyond the frontier.

3

BROADWAY

After a much needed rest on the luxury liner, the *France*, the four took the show on a brief tour of Toronto, Boston and Washington DC before *Beyond The Fringe* opened on Broadway at the John Golden Theater on Saturday, 27 October 1962. According to Alistair Cooke, it was 'the unhappiest date for an opening night in the most paralysed theatre week of the season'. It was the week of one of the most dangerous moments in world history when Khruschev and Kennedy 'played their game of Cosmic Chicken over Cuba', in Christopher Booker's phrase. Alan Bennett hid under a table in Dudley's apartment on the first night of the Cuba crisis. Did the others jump into paper bags? The anti-climax of 'The End of the World' sketch might have had to be altered but Broadway was spared The Bomb and got a direct Hit instead.

Alistair Cooke wrote in *The Manchester Guardian* that 'there is hardly a review this morning that is less than delirious . . . This tumult of acceptance is a puzzle to many shrewd theatre men here who deplored the quartet's decision not to adapt their material to American themes, or their strangulated tripthongs to the ears of a people to whom a vowel is a vowel is a vowel. But they make no concessions, a British trick Oscar Wilde discovered before them. In a way their success is a reprise of the old, and most popular, visiting lecturers, who pitied their audience, said so, and made a mint.'

On the following Sunday, after his initial favourable review in *The New York Times*, the critic Howard Taubman wrote a long, extremely unfunny, satiric dialogue, inaccurately reproducing British speech patterns, but welcome from a publicity standpoint. In the guise of a British Foreign Minister he complained, 'These outrageous young men respect nothing. They ridicule our glorious war effort, our Civil Defence preparations, our philosophers, our men of the cloth, our African friends in high places, our glorious Shakespeare, our nobility, our capital punishment, our TV. Even our homosexuality. Is nothing sacred?'

Despite Alistair Cooke's statement and although Peter Cook remembers that 'we hadn't altered a word' and Jonathan Miller says 'we did not change it at all', there were in fact some small adjustments for the USA. Bennett's 'Boring Old Man' rambled on about Anglo-American relations, the H-Bomb and 'that Cuban business'. He reassured Americans that Great Britain stands with the USA on 'the nuclear defence programme', and was dismissive of 'Ban the Bombers' and 'Bertrand Russell and hooligans like that, sincere though these people are. I mean I yield to no one in my admiration for Bertrand Russell. He's a great philosopher and nudist. But as a thinker, as a thinker he should stick to thinking.' Cook's Macmillan put in a bit about Kennedy regarding 'the business of Government as being a family affair'. (This must have seemed pretty feeble to those who had heard Mort Sahl's devastating lampoon of life at the White House during the Kennedy years.) Still, on the whole, it *was* a replica of the original London production and it became the chic show to see in New York. The likes of Bette Davis, Charles Boyer and Noël Coward would come backstage to meet the cast, as did John F and Jackie Kennedy. During this last meeting Alan Bennett spent the time chatting to a young man accompanying them, not realising that he was a security man there for presidential protection. He later turned down two invitations from Adlai Stevenson to dine with the First Lady at the White House because he was afraid he would be overcome with shyness. 'Monstrous behaviour,' the now less inhibited Bennett concedes.

But the lionised limeys were determined not just to bathe in the glow of New York limelight nor to let the Manhattan grass grow under their feet. Miller, true to form, told *The New York Times* that, 'When the show closes I shall return to medicine, but we may get together occasionally for limited engagements.' In fact, during the run, he did research in neuropsychiatry at the Mount Sinai Hospital in Manhattan. Bennett, the other member of the troupe who was determined to convince people that show business was no business for him, explained that 'I've set up a schedule. I'll work three hours every morning on my thesis which will become a book on the history of Richard II.' Moore, the only one of the four who had been to the USA previously, claimed that he was going to finish a musical he had begun. 'I'm going to rent a piano and find a studio. This musical is going to be my project for the season.' Cook would be busy seeking material for *Private Eye*, which had just celebrated its first birthday, and 'I'll be looking for writers and a restaurant to set up an American version of The Establishment Club'.

As we know, Miller only returned to medicine sporadically, Bennett's Richard II never graced a bookshelf and a Dudley Moore musical is yet to be written. It was Peter Cook, the youngest and most confident of the group, who seemed to achieve everything he set out to do at that time, even though . . . or perhaps because . . . he was aiming a little lower than the others.

Soon after the *Establishment* revue opened in New York, Ed Sullivan offered John Bird (who was in it) and Cook the chance to write and appear in a half-hour satirical television show called *What's Going On Here?* Miller would direct and it would be broadcast in May 1963. Bird says, 'I knew what American television was like – I knew we had no chance whatever of doing anything remotely like what we wanted to do.' But they were even more hamstrung than Bird could have imagined. Almost the first thing at the run-through was an item in which Maryland was mentioned. 'You can't say Maryland,' exclaimed Sullivan, for fear of offending viewers from that state. 'Jonathan took it fantastically seriously – he kept walking out,' recalls Bird. 'Everything became a matter of principal. But it was just hopeless, and so they paid us off.' The show was only given two airings.

II

Naturally, after almost two years together, it was hardly surprising that the 'four irascibles of the non-establishment' (Alistair Cooke) found themselves getting on each other's nerves. 'Now and again', recalls Moore, 'tensions built up between Jonathan and Alan, between myself and Alan. I remember doing a sketch with Alan, and he was very angry about the way I did it and that kind of froze us up for a long, long time. It was a display of disapproval that I was unable to cope with and I think he couldn't either.'

'In New York,' testifies Bennett, 'Jonathan and I really got on each other's nerves and it was a great relief when he left . . . I remember, fighting very hard against Peter's vaudeville exuberance, though whether I believed it would submerge any purpose the show might have or whether it was because I thought I should be swept away because I produced so little, I don't know . . . Dudley's a great mugger, he really does make the most appalling faces.'

The fact is that Moore was always trying to corpse Bennett during the Shakespeare scene, which led to the frosty periods between them. Fourteen years later, Cook, Bennett and Miller were rehearsing with Terry Jones (in place of Moore) to do the sketch for an Amnesty International benefit, when Jones was having trouble with how the lines should go. Bennett said, 'Of course, Dudley used to mug a lot. You can always mug.' Miller on the other hand suggested that Jones 'aim for Empsonian layers of complexity'.

Miller remembers something springing up between himself and Bennett during the interval one night. 'There was a round table in a sort of green room where we used to sit and eat the most disgusting institutional sandwiches which were brought up from some hideous cemetery underneath the theatre . . . and I remember tipping the table up and racing out in high dudgeon – or trying to race out in high dudgeon, because what happens is you always forget that the door opens the opposite way to the one you think it's going to.'

Peter Cook recalls having annoyed Miller one evening in Boston during the philosophy sketch when 'Jonathan's wife, Rachel, was standing in the wings with their two-week-old baby. I became a butler and brought it on and said, "Excuse me, sir, but your wife's just had this, sir, and I wondered what I should do with it." Jonathan, quick as a flash, retorted, "Oh, bung it in the fridge." He was very cross, actually; he was certain that I'd drop the baby.'

It was Miller who first began to feel more and more discontented with himself and what he was doing. Every night he went on he found his stammer, something he had overcome in his youth by talking very fast, beginning to reveal itself more and more. Strange, for someone who appears so often on the radio and TV, gives a vast number of lectures, is a talk-show or dinner host/hostess's dream, uses the telephone as a serious means of communication and could talk the hindleg off the proverbial donkey, to feel so ill-at-ease on stage. Over ten years later, he was still having the classic actor's nightmare.

'There I am standing alone under the lights. The audience is waiting, and I'm unable to say a word.' He therefore decided to leave the show six months earlier than intended. As a result, the first run was completed towards the end of 1963. Miller's only return to acting since was as Kirby Groomkirby in Peter Yates's 1964 film version of *One Way Pendulum*.

'He has the gauche ungainliness of the self-absorbed introvert. Takes himself very seriously . . . Uneasy and querulous in his rare encounters with people,' was part of N F Simpson's description of the character in the published version of the play (1960). Miller's gawky figure and idiosyncratic movements were aptly effective in portraying the demented son of Eric Sykes and Alison Leggatt, who only reacts to given signals. 'Now he has to have a little ping every time he sits down to a meal,' says his mother. The ambition of this Pavlovian creature is to teach a collection of speak-your-weight machines to sing the Hallelujah Chorus. Miller retained his affection for Simpson's absurdist play, including it in his 1988 Old Vic season.

III

A revised and updated version of *Beyond The Fringe* returned to Broadway on 8 January 1964, with Miller being replaced by Paxton Whitehead, an English performer living in America and now a familiar face in US TV sit-coms. He was physically similar, but, as the *New York Times* critic commented, 'Mr Whitehead reminds you of a man who isn't there.'

It was decided that the show should include some sideswipes at American sacred cows while retaining its predominantly English nature. Instead of Moore giving his interpretation of 'God Save The Queen' as an opener, he essayed the 'Star Spangled Banner' in an awkward manner. He also added another number to his repertoire – 'The Ballad of Gangster Joe' – a pointed pastiche of a Brecht-Weill song. (Marc Blitzstein's English adaptation of *The Threepenny Opera* had recently closed after six years off Broadway, only to be replaced by *Brecht On Brecht*, which also had a long run.) Stateside jokes included their complaining that 'it was the Statue of Liberty that started the rot' by 'letting in a lot of riffraff' and, in a rather 'I say, I say' routine:

'I gather the Negroes are sweeping the country.'
'They are, it's one of the few jobs they can get.'
'What's all this black muslin I hear they're wearing?'
'They're not wearing it, they're joining it. It's a movement – not a cloth.'
'Isn't there a lot of poverty in America?'

'Yes, there is, but luckily it's all been concentrated in the slum areas. It's beautifully done. You'd scarcely notice it.'

A worthier addition was an Alan Bennett solo called 'The English Way Of Death' in which Bennett, as a frail old Yorkshire woman, explains why cremation is the best mode of burial, even though the immediate family are never quite sure if they're getting the right ashes. 'For all you know, it might be a couple of copies of t'*Yorkshire Evening Post* they burnt up.' Always best when tapping his roots, Bennett foreshadowed his TV monologues of many years later.

'It's a pretty dreadful piece,' said Bennett in 1986, 'and death not being the subject of lively interest it has since become, the Broadway audience received it in stunned silence.'

The Great Train Robbery provided a topical sketch in which Peter Cook was able to go into a typical flight of English nonsense humour. As a Scotland Yard detective, he explains that 'I'd like to make it quite clear at the outset, when you speak of a train robbery, this in fact involves no loss of train. It's merely what I like to call the *contents* of the train which were pilfered – we haven't lost a train since 1946, I think it was, the year of the great snows – we mislaid a small one. They're very hard to lose you see, being so bulky . . .'

But the funniest sketch added to the show was one (written by Cook) that had already been seen in the Cambridge version of *Beyond The Fringe*. Called 'One Leg Too Few', it concerned the unlikely situation of a one-legged actor (brazenly tackled by Moore) auditioning for the film role of Tarzan. (This running one-legged joke would be used again in *Not Only . . . But Also, Behind The Fridge* and, by this time worn rather thin, in the 1977 movie disaster, *The Hound Of The Baskervilles*.)

Cook: Well, Mr Spiggott, need I point out to you where your deficiency lies as regards landing the role?

Moore: Yes, I think you ought to.

Cook: Need I say without over-much emphasis that it is in the leg division that you are deficient.

Moore: The leg division?

Cook: Yes, the leg division, Mr Spiggott. You are deficient in it to the tune of one. Your right leg I like. I like your right leg. A lovely leg for the role. That's what I said

when I saw you come in. I said, 'A lovely leg for the
role.' I've got nothing against your right leg. The
trouble is – neither have you. You fall down on your
left.

Moore: You mean it's inadequate?

Cook: Yes, it's inadequate, Mr Spiggott. And to my mind, the
British public is just not ready for the sight of a one-
legged ape man swinging through the jungly tendrils.

Writing about *Beyond The Fringe* Mark II, *Newsweek* found that 'the days of the show's satirical leadership were over' and that the 'original vitriolic radicalism' had become 'diluted by a jolly spirit of comedy – highly literate and broadly humane'. *Saturday Review* thought that 'polite and gentle insanity is the essence of [its] method, which seems to destroy reluctantly rather than deliberately'.

As 1964 drew to an end, so did *Beyond The Fringe* for its four begetters (although the show itself continued at the Mayfair Theatre in London until September 1966). They returned from New York to a madly swinging London, which had been given a push by them before their departure. Since the revue 'first fell upon London like a sweet, refreshing rain on the tenth of May 1961', as Michael Frayn wrote, there had sprung up all the icons of that heady era, including *The Sunday Times* colour supplement, James Bond movies, *Z Cars*, *TW3*, Christine Keeler, the Beatles, the Rolling Stones, *The Avengers*, Mods and Rockers, Carnaby Street and the mini-skirt; a 'naughty, gaudy, bawdy' world in which our four sensitive, cultured, satirical heroes would find dominant roles to play.

PART TWO

Before
Beyond The Fringe

'Undergraduates owe their happiness chiefly to the
fact that they are no longer at school ... The
nonsense which was knocked out of them at school
is all put gently back at Oxford or Cambridge.'

Max Beerbohm, *Zuleika Dobson*

4

MEDICINE

It would not be surprising to anyone who has read Lewis Carroll to discover that May Week at Cambridge University takes place in June. The first Footlights May Week Revue, in 1883, contained the hit number 'The Cambridge Boating Song', a 'hearty', mocking ditty ending with the chorus:

> At some wretched panting fellows
> I shout and screech and bellow –
> Bow, you're hurrying, Two, you're late,
> Three, you're bucketing, Nine, sit straight,
> Six, your back's out ever so far,
> What a set of consummated muffs you are!

The tone and the targets (college rituals, pompous professors, silly students and passing fads) hardly changed for the next 70 years or so. From the 1920s, the Cambridge Footlights turned the Cam into Camp, occasionally setting it on fire. Because women were not admitted until 1957 (after one aberrant revue in 1932), young men would have to drag themselves up, not too much of a bind for those for whom slipping into petticoats was a welcome escape from masculinity. In 1925 the *Daily Sketch* ran an article called 'The Girl Men Of Cambridge' in which it complained of the many 'soft, effeminate, painted, be-rouged youths' to be found at the university. Nine years later, *Granta* satirised the latest revue called *Sir or Madam* in lines beginning:

> I am a Footlights fairy, so in terse
> But not too polished couplets, speak in verse.
> You wish to join, Sir? Are your tastes aesthetic?
> Have you long hair, or do you use cosmetic?

Although the Footlights always attracted a fair number of homosexuals, there were those who were only 'posing as somdomites'. But, whatever the sexuality of the participants, the nature of the shows – the cross-dressing, the airy fairy numbers and the bright bitchiness of the humour – could not but gain them 'nancy' notoriety. Yet, as Eric Idle, the 1965 President, has pointed out: 'If it were nothing more than gilded youths dressing up as women then you could hardly be blamed for thinking of the Cambridge Footlights as an effete collection of privileged wankers. It has from time to time been just that, but collectively it is far more than that. In fact it has proved a durable training ground for people who have gone on to become excellent in their own right.'

Among those who emerged from the Footlights were Jack and Claude Hulbert; Norman Hartnell (in his own gorgeous costumes as Kitty Fenton in *What A Picnic!*, 1921); Cecil Beaton (also in drag as Princess Tecla in *The Gyp's Princess*, 1923); comedians Richard 'Stinker' Murdoch and 'Professor' Jimmy Edwards; pretty Phillips Holmes (the future Hollywood star, killed in the war in 1942); elegant actor Hugh Latimer; Julian Slade (lyricist and composer of *Salad Days*); Julian More (of *Grab Me A Gondola* and *Expresso Bongo* fame); the playwriting twins Anthony and Peter Shaffer; newsreader Richard Baker; and conductor Raymond Leppard.

II

The tall, red-haired Miller made a great impression on his contemporaries at Cambridge when he came up to St John's in 1953 to study medicine. Michael Frayn, who had just come up after National Service, most of it spent in the company of Alan Bennett, remembers meeting this 'grand, extremely famous figure walking barefoot in the street with his friend Eric Korn'. The political columnist Neal Ascherson writes that the most shocking remark he heard at university, when being harangued by a student 'built like an Anglepoise lamp', was 'The main function of the central nervous system is to exclude the majority of impulses coming into it.' For Ascherson, this meant the end of the cult of sensibility: 'Real sophistication lay not in feeling more – but in feeling less! . . . "Jonathan's Law" or "Lex Miller" suggested that . . . I would do myself an injury if I tried to care about everything and everyone.'

Miller's father Emanuel had started as a neurologist and then became a psychiatrist of some reputation, one of the first to deal with child psychology in England. It seemed only natural that his son, like a good Jewish boy, should follow in his footsteps. However, the father-son relationship was not a particularly comfortable one and Jonathan developed a serious stammer, which he overcame by speaking very rapidly. Any vestigial guilt he has about abandoning science for the arts derives, in a great part, from the hopes his father invested in him. Peter Cook believes he feels guilt because 'He had a very early-established feeling planted in him by his family that medicine was what was worthwhile.' The Millers' own three grown-up children, Tom, William and Kate, have opted for the humanities rather than the sciences; Tom is a photographer, William manages an independent film company and Kate is a sales rep of a graphic-design shop. According to George Melly, they 'project a certain wary amusement common to the offspring of famous fathers'.

The Miller grandparents and great-grandparents had come from Lithuania to Britain in the 1860s, settling in London, where Jonathan was born on 21 July 1934. Grandfather Abram Miller had been in the fur trade but Emanuel himself broke away from the family business when he went to Cambridge in 1909, where he was taught moral science by Bertrand Russell. After World War I, during which as a neurologist he had studied the effects of shell shock, he set up the first child guidance clinic, in the East End. Among his other achievements were the founding of the Institute for the Scientific Treatment of Delinquency and the publication of a number of books including *Types Of Mind And Body* and *Neurosis In War*. Interestingly, he was also a talented sculptor, painter and art connoisseur.

Jonathan's mother Betty, née Spiro, went to St Paul's and University College, London. She became an accomplished author, publishing her first novel when she was nineteen and later moving away from fiction into biography, especially of eminent Victorians such as Tennyson, Browning and Samuel Butler. She was the niece of the French philosopher Henri Bergson. Biology was the background to Bergson's philosophical thought and he was also the author of the famous essay on 'Laughter'. Certainly Jonathan has what his great-uncle called, in his masterpiece *Creative Evolution*, the *élan vital* running through his veins.

During the Second World War, Emanuel was an Army psychiatrist so the family moved from one military hospital to another. Miller remembers: 'There were strange, long-delayed train journeys in the middle of war-time England. We would be pushed into hot summer sidings while troop trains rattled by three platforms away. I don't think I was a very happy child, but I look back on childhood with tremendous longing for those endless sunlit days.'

Emanuel, though not a believer, had felt certain obligations to Judaism. Jonathan has related an easily interpretable dream his father had of being pursued through the Uffizi by the Michelangelo Moses, its great stone feet crashing behind him, and throwing down the tablets of the law after him.

'I am Jewish in the residual sense of only half belonging,' says Miller *fils*. 'I deeply distrust Israel and Zionism and I have a loathing of all monotheistic religions.' In other words, as he claimed in *Beyond The Fringe*: 'In fact, I'm not really a Jew. Just Jew-*ish*. Not the whole hog, you know.'

III

At Cambridge Miller refrained in his freshman year from joining the Footlights, preferring to spend his time as a member of the History of Science Society and the Apostles. The latter group had begun in the nineteenth century as a secret club which elected its own members, who wrote and read essays to each other once a week.

'It was a very important part of my life when I was at Cambridge. I used to like going every Sunday night to Morgan Forster's rooms and reading papers. We discussed things and formed friendships there. It wasn't like the Freemasons. There were no rituals. There was no commitment to some metaphysics. All we did was discuss ideas. Being a member also helped in the seduction of girls. One would say, "I'm an Apostle, get your knickers off!" '

A great influence on the undergraduate Miller was the American philosopher and ex-physicist Norwood Russell Hanson. 'He had a tiny room at the top of a rather perilous wooden staircase in a yard just behind the Corn Exchange. There we would sit knee to knee over a wavering, warbling gas fire, discussing Wittgenstein, who had died the year before and had left behind this atmosphere of intense pursuit into the nature of meaning and words. In this room there hardly seemed room for both of us and this enormous explosion of ideas.' But the *élan vital* in him broke away from these learned activities and from the serious task of getting through exams, compelling him in his second year to appear in a 'Poppy Day' revue put on in the St John's bicycle shed. There he performed one of the monologues that had made his fellow schoolboys laugh.

Miller's repertoire at St Paul's had been in the main mocking take-offs of radio personalities, rather surrealist monologues and an ability to imitate accurately the sound of chickens. In the sixth form, he and his friend Michael Bacharach had contributed to a BBC radio programme called *Under Twenty Parade*; billed as 'John Miller', he and Bacharach mocked announcers, newsreaders and weathermen.

In the audience on Poppy Day 1954 was the President of the Foot-lights, Leslie Bricusse, future composer and lyricist of such musicals as *Stop The World I Want To Get Off*. He had appeared in the previous year's revue, *Cabbages And Kings*, which Richard Mayne in *Granta* described as the Footlights 'still doing what's expected of them, perpetuating for a score of nostalgic journalists their frothy undergrad-uate legend of ease and negligent wit'. Bricusse persuaded Miller to take part in that year's Footlights Revue, *Out Of The Blue*.

A Darwinian observer of the revue form might have noticed that *Out Of The Blue* had sprouted the beginnings of wings. It turned out to be the first Footlights Revue to get a run in the West End since the 'thirties and instead of being totally absorbed by the happenings and obsessions within Varsity walls, its satire ventured, albeit gingerly, out into contemporary society with sketches on the colour bar and the German economic miracle, and there was a topical calypso. Yet, according to Miller, 'There was still an awful lot of stuff with people walking around in blazers and flannels and boaters, and singing songs about Proctors . . . and punts, and things of that sort.'

His own contribution consisted of two monologues: 'Down Under', a typically physical one-man documentary on Australia; and 'Radio Page', a rehash of his lampoon of announcers from his schooldays. He also played the Village Idiot in a sketch entitled 'Truly Rural' and was Brutus in 'Rome On The Range' as well as a few smaller bits. Among the cast were Bricusse, who directed and co-wrote the sketches, music and lyrics; future Liberal politician John Pardoe; and Frederic Raphael (who turned his memories of Cambridge in the 'fifties into the 'tele-vision novel' *Glittering Prizes*).

Out Of The Blue opened at the Phoenix Theatre for three weeks in July 1954, Miller's London debut. The show came as a surprise to most critics who generally received it warmly, some of them even resisting the damning phrase 'undergraduate humour'. Most significantly, Harold Hobson of *The Sunday Times* devoted almost all of his review to praising Miller and as a result he had offers from theatrical managements dangled in front of him, all of which he turned down, announcing, not for the last time in his life, that he was giving up the theatre to concentrate on medicine. Perhaps his epitaph will be 'I finally left the theatre'.

His studies at St John's were nonetheless interrupted, or rather alleviated, by a few more stage appearances at Cambridge and a further sally into the West End. Miller's only straight acting role at Cambridge was as Troubleall, the madman in the Dramatic Society's production of Ben Jonson's *Bartholomew Fair*. (Co-incidentally, Dudley Moore was in the same play a few years later at Oxford in the part of Nightingale). Playing Troubleall suited Miller because it requires the actor to run on from time to time to disrupt the action, and run off again. It was the sort of thing Miller convinced himself he did in the revues. 'I just did my bits and got out.' This gave him the sense that he was never really part of the company. As some people leave their bodies to science, he occasionally lent his double-jointed body to the theatre.

Apart from Miller, the 1955 Footlights Revue, called *Between The Lines*, had among its cast: Peter Woodthorpe (who made his professional stage debut in the same year in Peter Hall's production of *Waiting For Godot* at the Arts, London); John Pardoe again: Julian Jebb: and Rory McEwan (later a well-known folk-singer). In London it opened at the now-demolished Scala Theatre on 28 June for three weeks, and again Miller got all the reviews. Bernard Levin called him 'a genius', a description that Miller has never actively discouraged, while *The Daily Telegraph* headlined its brief review, 'Danny Kaye of Cambridge', a tag somewhat less congenial. Miller admits to having been a great admirer of the manic American comic (whose film career was beginning to slide in the mid-1950s) when he was about thirteen. To explain the comparison, he says, 'I had an antic element to my performance, because I capered around and looked peculiar, and had red hair and a long nose.' However, the most successful of Miller's monologues in the revue (actually performed in the Broadway production of *Beyond The Fringe*), was his imitation of Bertrand Russell discussing a visit in Cambridge to the rooms of G E Moore.

'It typified the extremely arctic and detached form of discourse that took place at Cambridge,' he explains. 'It was really just a pastiche of

Russell's memoirs.'

> I had popped across and knocked on the door. 'Come in,' he said. I
> decided to wait a while in order to test the ethical consistency of
> his proposition. 'Come in,' he said once again, a trifle testily, I
> thought. 'Very well,' I replied, 'if that is in fact truly what you
> wish.' I opened the door accordingly and went in. And there was
> Moore, sitting by the fire, with a basket on his knee. 'Moore,' I
> said, 'have you any apples in that basket?' 'No,' he replied, and
> smiled seraphically, as was his wont. I decided to try a different
> logical tack. 'Moore,' I said, 'do you then have *some* apples in that
> basket?' 'No,' he said, once again, leaving me in a logical cleft
> stick, so to speak, from which I had but one way out. 'Moore,' I
> said, 'do you then have *apples* in that basket?' 'Yes,' he replied,
> and from that day forth we remained the closest of friends.

Hardly Danny Kaye material but the sketch went down so well that
he was asked to repeat it in 1955 in the unlikely setting of ITV's
immensely popular *Sunday Night At The London Palladium* compèred
by Tommy Trinder, all the more remarkable in that the author of
Principia Mathematica had not yet emerged fully into popular consciousness as the leading anti-H-bomb campaigner in Britain of the
early 1960s. Over twenty years later Miller repeated his party piece
at the Amnesty show he directed at Her Majesty's Theatre, for an
audience most of whom were too young to remember Russell's
squeaky tones, and was again easily persuaded by Melvyn Bragg to
do it on the radio in March 1989.

IV

During the run of *Between The Lines* Miller also took part in a radio
programme called *The Man from Paranoia*, subtitled 'A Thing for
Radio', which told the story of a Cambridge don who owns a singing
goldfish. As a further supplement to his income he appeared, with
Rory McEwan, at a late-night cabaret run by Clement Freud (another
future Liberal MP) in the space which later became the Royal Court
Upstairs. Fortunately these were summer activities and didn't interfere with his medical studies, and Miller came down with a first in
1956, the year of his marriage to Rachel Collet.

They had met at Cambridge and he had encouraged her to change her studies and take up medicine. Today she is a greatly respected and extremely busy GP, dealing mainly with women at a health centre in Kentish Town. George Melly describes her as 'the best, perhaps the only, partner for her mercurial, driven husband. She has a quiet, musical voice tinged with detached amusement, moves easily, radiates warmth and competence. Her own career preserves her from being drawn into the vortex of Jonathan's frenetic activity, and yet she knows everything he is up to.' John Wells feels that 'Jonathan has a very good double act with Rachel, in that Rachel manages him and is probably the only person who gets away with teasing him. She is the only person who isn't on thin ice with him.'

V

The next three years of Miller's life were spent as a research postgraduate at University College, London, where he obtained an MB and BCh. His ambition was to do neuropsychology: 'I was interested in higher disorders of brain function. I wasn't interested in the lower end of the nervous system.' But during that period, from all accounts, his performances in two hospital revues left audiences in stitches.

When the innovative TV magazine programme *Tonight* started up in early 1957, Miller was one of the first of the bright young men to be asked to appear on it. Alasdair Milne, future Director General of the BBC and one of the instigators of the programme, recalls in his book *D. G.* that 'Dr Miller's participation in *Tonight* was shortlived. Each Saturday morning, for a few weeks, Grace Wyndham Goldie [the producer] convened a meeting to thrash out the past week's work with the *Tonight* production team. I think it was on the third Saturday that she found grievous fault with Jonathan's performance a couple of nights earlier. A hilarious turn, in highly questionable taste, where he impersonated Nelson fumbling for the fatal bullet inside his waistcoat. It was no help that Jonathan, at the time uncontrollable in terms of studio discipline, had lurched past the cameras in his enthusiasm and so disappeared from view altogether for a while.'

At the same time, the overworked and underpaid doctor was pleased to make regular appearances on a radio programme of music and comedy called *Saturday Night On The Light* (the Light Programme being the forerunner of Radio 2). Some of his material on these broadcasts derived from the sketches that he and Michael Bacharach had performed on *Under Twenty Parade* some years before – on the principle of 'waste not, want not', a great deal of pre-*Beyond The Fringe* material by all four 'Fringers' was conserved and recycled over the years. When the Saturday radio show became *Monday Night At Home* (still on the Light, not on the Home Service), Miller contributed a further twelve sketches. So he was not exactly the dedicated medical man lost in his researches, the theatre behind him, when John Bassett, like the 'Person from Porlock', made his visit to the casualty department to ask Miller if he would take part in the 1960 Edinburgh Festival revue.

5

LANGUAGES

The year after Jonathan Miller came down, Peter Cook arrived at Pembroke College to read French and German literature. The budding satirist kept his writing and performing talents under a bushel in his freshman year and didn't even approach the Footlights.

'I felt the Footlights was a tremendously élite club – I was too bashful even to consider applying for it,' he commented. Never known for his shyness, his timidity towards the Footlights may be explained by the sudden difference in status he felt between being top dog at Radley College, an exclusive public school, and being a first-year student at Cambridge. It may also be put down to the fact that he thought the all-male 1958 revue *Springs To Mind*, 'a load of rubbish'. Considered 'predictable, unexceptional, amiable' by the *Cambridge Review*, it featured Joe Melia and Bill Wallis, Timothy Birdsall (who would find fame in *TW3* during his brief life), Geoff Pattie (incipient Tory minister) and Fred Emery (future *Panorama* reporter). All was to change in 1959 when Peter Cook made his entrance.

Cook was on 17 November 1937 in the genteel Devon town of Torquay, the son of a diplomat who had spent some time as a colonial officer in Nigeria. When Alexander and Margaret Cook returned to England they became active in the local Conservative Party. Peter was once described by a friend as having inherited 'the lordly mien of the forest bwana, stiff upper-lipped at the news that the natives were restless'. Cook has often regaled his friends, against their better judgement, with racist stories about his father in Nigeria. One of the least offensive tells how an incoming politician at independence presented the outgoing Mr Cook with a book as a token of his esteem; when he opened it, he found it bore a 'remaindered' stamp. In the light of these anecdotes, the liberal intentions of the black politician sketch (written by Cook) take on a slightly different tone.

Among Cook's juvenilia was 'a completely Nazi treatise on how the 'unintelligent working class' should be sterilised. People say I've got more reactionary in my old age, when in fact I've moved to the left from my very solid Nazi position at the age of sixteen!' In this adolescent respect for things colonial and right-wing, he was merely part of the public school ethos, reflecting that of the boys' ruling class parents. He looked all set for a conventional upper-middle-class existence, something in the City or the Civil Service, but he was saved by his innate sense of humour. The stiff upper-class upper-lip became effective in his comic career and helped him to adopt that superior tone used by Macmillan and politicians of his kind.

II

Unlike many other budding comedians, Cook did not need to be funny as a defence against bullying or mockery, although he did feel that 'If you were pretty funny then, on the whole, people didn't hit you'.

It was at Radley that he first developed his park-bench philosopher, later known to the world as E L Wisty. The character and voice were based on a man called Mr Boylett who, while serving at High Table, would make cryptic remarks such as 'There's plenty more where that came from, if you get my meaning.' Cook remembers Boylett used to say strange things like 'I saw a stone and I thought it might be valuable because I thought I saw it move, so I hoped to sell it.' His mimicry of the poor man had his fellow pupils rolling in the classroom aisles and 'I thought I saw it move' became a catchphrase which Cook carried with him to Cambridge.

Like almost every youngster at the time, Cook was a devotee of *The Goon Show*. When it began modestly in 1951, as *Crazy People*, nobody could have estimated the programme's influence on British humour. The anarchic and surreal gags and the stretching of English speech patterns to comic extremes sank so deeply into the psyches of adolescents of the 1950s that they are still perceptible today, and certainly they resurface from time to time in the work of the four 'fringers'. Perhaps *The Goons* had a greater effect on Peter Cook than on the others because he was still at school at the height of its popularity, while Miller, Bennett and Moore were already at university. Playgrounds of state and public schools everywhere echoed throughout the 'fifties with the voices of Eccles, Bluebottle, Grytpype Thynne and The Cruns. Grown men, for years afterwards, greeted each other with 'Hee-lo dere' and untranscribable Neddie Seagoon and Bluebottle shrieks.

'I used to go sick every Friday to listen to *The Goon Show* in the sanatorium – there was a sort of understanding between me and the matron,' Cook recalls. Under its spell he wrote a script and sent it to the BBC. He received a letter back saying that it was a good copy of *The Goon Show* and encouraging him to write something more original. He did have several short items accepted for the 'Charivaria' section of *Punch*. African and jazz influences were noticeable in one of his first pieces, *Black And White Blues*, a musical put on by the Marionette Society for which he wrote the words in rhyming couplets. It concerned a Salvation Army jazz band which went out to Africa to convert the natives. He also wrote a play about Martians landing in England and behaving more normally than the people of suburbia, and sketches in school revues 'which mainly took the piss out of the masters'.

At Radley, the adult Peter Cook can be seen in miniature, the lines of character and career already more boldly drawn than was noticeable at the same age in Miller, Bennett and Moore, who found far more room for development. Cook's reminiscences of his schooldays sound like an updated version of *Stalky and Co.* and seem to echo the title of the 1940s school farce, *The Happiest Days of Your Life*.

'I had a marvellous time at school during my last three years. A group of people, all of whom were friends of mine, became prefects by default. We'd always thought that a lot of the rules were ridiculous so, when we came to power, so to speak, there was a silent revolution. We didn't say anything; we just did not enforce any of the really stupid rules like the ones about buttons. In your first year all your buttons had to be done up, in the second year you could have one button undone, in the third year two, and when you became a prefect you could undo all your buttons and walk over certain bits of grass. We also abolished beating altogether.'

Before he gained his position of authority Cook had been caned by prefect Ted Dexter, the future England cricketer, for drinking cider at Henley Regatta. 'I've followed his career with interest but I haven't thought of a good way of getting my own back,' says Cook. During the final year, 'I had a life of complete luxury. I had two fags, and breakfast in bed. I used to go to the pictures and fish for trout in the lake. And I organised bootleg games of soccer because football wasn't allowed.' He has been a football fan ever since, becoming an ardent supporter of Tottenham Hotspur – but despite all the laughter, fun and games, he still won a scholarship to Cambridge.

A year's National Service would normally have followed after he left school in 1956. However, when he was much younger he had been allergic to feathers and although he had grown out of it, the note was still on his medical record. On coming up for his medical he was asked by the doctor if he would sneeze in a barrack room full of feather pillows. He replied 'Yes', forgetting the allergy and reckoning that everybody sneezed at one time or another. He was promptly declared unsuitable for the army.

'I told them, "If there's an emergency you will get in touch, won't you." ' Presumably if war came down to a pillow fight, Cook would not have been much use.

Having a year to wait now before university and as he was to read French and German literature, he took himself off to France and Germany, initially to Tours University to attend a French course.

'I think my parents tried to make sure that my first hesitant sexual manoeuvres took place outside the country. It was a very good plan, but unfortunately I didn't meet with much success. Interesting remarks like *"Je suis un étudiant anglais"* didn't seem to get the girls going in quite the way I had hoped.' Some years later when asked by *Playboy* how he had lost his virginity, he replied: 'At what end?' Cook's tour gave him a taste for nightlife, especially satirical nightclubs, and the idea to set up a similar establishment in London was hatched. 'For a long time my major fear was that somebody would do the obvious and start it before me.' Five years later nobody had.

III

While the egg of modern British satire was still waiting to be fertilised, one of its four fathers was being seduced by the 'Theatre of the Absurd' and the 'kitchen sink' dramas derived from *Look Back In Anger*. Samuel Beckett, who transcended the 'Absurdist' label to generate his own eponymous adjectives, had already by 1958 had London productions staged of *Waiting For Godot*, *Endgame* and *Krapp's Last Tape*. Eugène Ionesco's *The Bald Prima Donna*, *The New Tenant* and *The Chairs* had also been put on. These writers had obviously influenced N F Simpson and the young Harold Pinter, and something of them must have rubbed off on to Peter Cook, just as *The Goons*

(The Radio of the Absurd) had at school.

One of future RSC director William Gaskill's first London productions had been N F Simpson's debut play, *A Resounding Tinkle*, in a Production without Décor at the Royal Court in December 1957. Convinced that this full version was 'unplayable', he staged it a few months later at the Court as a one-act play, sharing the bill with the same playwright's *The Hole*. John Bird, who had gone up to King's in 1955 to read European drama, decided to stage the complete play at Cambridge and asked Gaskill up to see that it could be done. Bird, whose greatest claim to fame was to be his imitation of Harold Wilson on TV's *Not So Much A Programme More A Way Of Life* in 1964, cast the future mimic of Harold Macmillan in the part of Bro Paradock. Opposite Cook, whom Bird thought was the funniest man he had ever met, was Eleanor Bron, a Newnham modern language undergraduate, as Middie Paradock. (She made her name with Bird in the same TV programme.)

The Paradocks are a suburban couple who complain that the elephant which has just been delivered to them is much bigger than the ones they usually have:

> *Middie:* Tell them to come and collect it.
> *Bro:* And be without an elephant at all?
> *Middie:* We did without one the year we had a giraffe instead.

When someone comes to the door to invite Mr Paradock to form a government, he says, 'How can I start forming a government at six o'clock in the evening?'

Gaskill was impressed by the production and invited the company to the Royal Court for a Sunday evening performance. On the strength of the production, Bird was asked to become Assistant Director at the Court, but before taking up his new post he was prevailed upon to stay on at Cambridge in order to direct the 1959 Footlights revue.

IV

With the experience and confidence gained by his role in the N F Simpson play, Cook finally decided to audition for the Footlights. His park-bench 'I thought I saw it move' monologue impressed the President Adrian Slade, younger brother of Julian, and he was in.

If the 1954 and 1955 Footlights Revues with Jonathan Miller had been breakthroughs in the sense that they got to the West End and were noticed by the heavyweight critics, the 1959 show differed from all others, before or since. Called *The Last Laugh*, it was set in an underground bunker where scientists await the outcome of an experiment that may bring about the destruction of the world. Geoff Pattie, future Tory MP and Under Secretary of State at the Ministry of Defence, was in the cast, performing a monologue as a DIY expert giving instructions on how to make your own coffin. In fact, the show followed hard upon the largest and most publicised CND Easter rally since the campaign had begun two years before, attracting almost 50,000 people to Trafalgar Square. Jimmy Porter in *Look Back In Anger* had expressed what was taken to be the credo of post-Suez youth. 'There aren't any big, brave causes left.' Now young people were finding causes by the score, the first of which was nuclear disarmament.

Cook was in 13 of the 28 numbers and co-wrote 10 of them, including an E L Wisty monologue, with the nuclear theme forming a somewhat tenuous link between sketches. There was a lampoon on Scott of the Antarctic, a frozen sacred cow of the British, called 'Polar Bores'; a POW film pastiche anticipating the Fringe sketch 'Aftermyth Of War'; 'For Fox Sake' was a satiric piece on the 'unspeakable in full pursuit of the uneatable'; and 'Wex Side Story', a parochial parody of *West Side Story* (then packing them in at Her Majesty's Theatre in London) in which the feuding gangs were 'The Dukes', representing aristocratic Cambridge, and 'The Grads', the meritocrats living on grants. According to Julian Slade, up at Cambridge to see his brother perform, Cook 'made a stunning impact'. His comic voices, especially for his tramp character, were taken up by undergraduates. Eleanor Bron, the sole female in the company, remarked that 'Peter Cook's influence became nightmarish – I began to think we couldn't speak any other way.' Bamber Gascoigne, an undergraduate at Magdalene, already with a West End revue behind him, recalled in his preface to *From Fringe To Flying Circus* his discovery of 'the first superstar since Jonathan Miller' to arrive on the Cambridge revue scene: at a Footlights dinner in October 1959 the President proposed a loyal toast. 'The Queen, we all intoned, the Queen, the Queen. But the President was not done. He mumbled on, with the dreadful deadpan intensity which would later be known as the trade mark of E L Wisty. "And all who sail in her," raising his glass again in an excess of loyalty.'

Apart from the revue's sharper satirical content, another departure from the 'jolly boating' type show was its ten-piece modern jazz group accompaniment under the direction of Patrick Gowers, who also composed most of the music. (Twenty-seven years later, Gowers wrote the score for Cook's film *Whoops Apocalypse*.) The set was designed by the extremely talented and darkly handsome Timothy Birdsall, whom millions came to know from his weekly appearances on *TW3*, where he did lightning cartoons on topical subjects; it came as a great shock when he died of leukemia in June 1963 at the age of 26.

The opening night at the Arts was a disaster. The show ran almost four and a half hours – the theatre manager had to go backstage towards midnight to tell them to bring the curtain down – some technical effects, such as back projection, went wrong due to lack of rehearsal time and a Footlights first night was greeted with the rare sound of boos. It was certainly not the frivolous fare May Week audiences were used to. The local paper was predictably sour about it but Alistair Cooke, who happened to be in Cambridge at the time and wanted to show some American friends a typical Footlights Revue (which *The Last Laugh* was not), wrote a long, positive piece in *The Manchester Guardian*. Granted, the performance had settled down after the first night. He wrote: 'The whole show is acted with never a fumbling line or gesture, and since it is inconceivable that a dozen undergraduates can appear as fully-fledged professionals, the only inference is that in Mr John Bird, the club has a broth of a director. In fact, if the West End does not soon hear of John Bird, Patrick Gowers, Geoff Pattie and Peter Cook, the West End is an ass.'

Another admirer of the show, and more important to the *Beyond The Fringe* saga, was William Donaldson, not long down from Cambridge. He bought the script of *The Last Laugh*, changed the title to *Here Is The News* and much of the writing, and cast it with professionals including Sheila Hancock, Lance Percival, Valentine Dyall, Richard Goolden, Robin Ray, Henry McGee, Cleo Laine and the stripper Kathryn Keeton (who married Bob Guccione, the *Penthouse* owner). The complex sets were by Sean Kenny. John Bird again directed, and also got sole writing credit, with additional material by N F Simpson, Eugène Ionesco, Ken Hoare and Andrew Sinclair. A far cry from the Cambridge revue, it opened in August 1960 at the New Theatre, Oxford, the nearest it got to London. It didn't help that some of the billboards erroneously renamed the show *Here Is The Nose*.

Sheila Hancock, in her autobiography, writes that she got 'the angriest reaction from an audience I ever had . . . The audience had good cause, mind you.' Donaldson, out on a limb, said, 'I think it was sensational, and if it had come to London, *Beyond The Fringe* wouldn't have had any impact at all.'

V

Oxford-educated up-and-coming theatrical producer Michael Codron had seen *The Last Laugh* at Cambridge and asked Cook to write sketches for a West End revue called *Pieces Of Eight*. It opened at the Apollo Theatre in September 1959, and among the eight performers were the high camp duo of Fenella Fielding and Kenneth Williams. It was billed as having sketches by Peter Cook with additional material by Harold Pinter, Sandy Wilson, John Law and Lance Mulcahy. Pinter, at the time, was only marginally better known than Cook; his first full-length play, *The Birthday Party*, had been performed in April 1958 at the Lyric, Hammersmith, where it found little favour and fewer audiences. He, like Cook, also contributed a number of sketches to the revue *One To Another*, in July 1959 at Hammersmith.

Pieces Of Eight brought Peter Cook to Shaftesbury Avenue; the now professional undergraduate acquired an agent and revelled in the success of the show. 'I loved that revue – it was Old Fashioned Revue, which was eventually killed by *Beyond The Fringe*. I found nothing wrong with it,' he says. His contribution to *Pieces Of Eight* was the strongest element in the show, which ran for 429 performances. The funniest sketch (resurrected in 1976 for the Amnesty show, performed by Cook and John Fortune) had Kenneth Williams bringing his impish personality and everlasting vowels to bear on an irritating little man in a railway carriage who encourages his reluctant travelling companion to guess what he has in the box he is holding. Williams was also seen as a man who complains that he would have some impact on the world if he drank less and if his name had been Mark Over Grangely which, his wife reminds him, is exactly what it is.

With the plaudits of Shaftesbury Avenue ringing in his ears, Cook was elected President of the Footlights in his final year at Cambridge, during which he presented a revue called *Pop Goes Mrs Jessop* directed by John Fortune (under his real name of John Wood). The inconsequential title referred to a Britannia-like woman who is persuaded by the assembled company in the opening and closing numbers to emit a 'pop'. Among the cast was an extremely ambitious 21-year-old called David Frost. In a skit on a NATO meeting, he played a German delegate opposite Cook's French representative. Frost, a clergyman's son reading English at Caius, has said of his arrival at Cambridge in 1958: 'I got there at five o'clock and I felt perfectly at home at six.' The programme notes refer to him as 'the first Caius-man to edit *Granta* under a pseudonym. A brilliant mimic, freeman of Beccles and intimate of the great.'

Unlike the previous year's revue, dancing with themes of death and destruction, *Pop Goes Mrs Jessop* was described by Cook as 'entirely frivolous'. Frivolous or no, it revealed him in exultant form as writer and performer and featured sketches that reappeared over the years under different guises and in different locations. Most typical was 'Interesting Facts' in which Cook as the ultimate bore regales his interlocuter with every irrelevant and trivial fact he has come across.

First Man (Cook):	I'm extremely interested in all facets of human life, including you. Tell me, are you a mariner?
Second Man:	No, I'm afraid not. I'm an architect.
First Man:	Oh, I see. I only mentioned that you might be a mariner so that I could lead the conversation round to an interesting fact that I've accumulated. It pertains to the codfish, that's an ocean dwelling creature.
Second Man:	Yes, I've heard of the cod.
First Man:	Yes, it's quite an interesting fact that the codfish relies almost solely for protection on blending with the natural seaweeds amongst which it lives . . .

He then goes on to give the man the benefit of his knowledge of eagles, the Chinese and grasshoppers, prefiguring the 1980s when books of lists pandered to a kind of listomania and games like 'Trivial Pursuit' made 'trivia' a marketable word. In another sketch, 'Ducks', Cook is a manic duck trainer: 'It's quite a triumph, not like winning the war, but quite a triumph, I mean these ducks are completely under my control, eating's second nature to them now!' There was also a satiric scene on Civil Defence, a variation of which cropped up in *Beyond The Fringe*, and one about four Welsh coalminers attempting to discover in the darkness which of them is Anglo-Indian, also performed by the famous four at Edinburgh.

Despite all the time he devoted to the Footlights and writing sketches for the London theatre, Cook managed to put in just enough academic work to gain a BA.

'I got my degree by stealing Eleanor Bron's notes,' he commented. 'I toyed with the idea of going into the Foreign Office, but I don't think the Foreign Office toyed with the idea of my joining them.' The fact is that with his father's influence, his languages and old school ties, there would have been little to stop him entering the diplomatic service had he wanted to. But the bright lights of show business beckoned, especially after *Beyond The Fringe* became such a success. A month before that hit the Fortune Theatre, the follow-up revue to *Pieces Of Eight*, called *One Over The Eight* (it had a cast of nine, including Lance Percival and Sheila Hancock) opened at the Duke of York's Theatre. Once more Kenneth Williams starred, doing justice to Peter Cook's fantastical sketches. He played a peace marcher who provokes a fight with his fellow demonstrators, and a man complaining to his wife about how the war had 'held him back'. Williams made the line, 'The war clouds were looming' into (writes Sheila Hancock) 'The war clouds were leoooming. Blooming great war clouds. Leooooming on the horizon. Leoooming . . .' and so on. Sheila Hancock's best moment was as a landlady with one dingy room to let who has so many rules and hatreds that nobody would be acceptable to her as a tenant. Cook again got the top writing credit with 'additional material' by John Mortimer, Lionel Bart, N F Simpson, Carl Davis, John Bird, Stanley Daniels and Steven Vinaver. The show ran for over a year, so that the name of Peter Cook was emblazoned outside both the Duke of York's and the Fortune throughout 1961, his *anno mirabilis*.

6

HISTORY

Aside from the dreaming students and spires and the quail's egg myths perpetuated by *Brideshead Revisited*, Oxford had a more radical tradition than Cambridge. At least, it produced more 'class rebels', despite its rival's penchant for educating single spies and double agents.

Among the New Oxford Group, the generation that preceded that of the mid-'fifties to which Alan Bennett and Dudley Moore belonged, were Kenneth Tynan, Tony Richardson, Kingsley Amis, John Wain, Lindsay Anderson, Peter Brook, Anthony Wedgwood Benn, Anthony Crosland, Jeremy Thorpe, Ned Sherrin, Donald Baverstock, Alan Brien, Robin Day, Philip Larkin and Paul Johnson, the majority of whom had been to public school.

Despite the nominal opening up of Oxbridge to grammar-school boys by grants, the percentage of working-class students has not risen substantially over the years. Working-class Leeds in 1934, where Alan Bennett was born in a back-to-back on 9 May, and the sprawling housing estate in the dreary district of Dagenham in London where Dudley Moore was born on 19 April a year later, were not the most pleasant of places. Bennett's father, Walter, was a butcher and although the fact that both he and Moore managed to get behind the moss-covered walls and walk across the ancient quads of Exeter and Magdalen Colleges respectively may seem to indicate that the age of meritocracy had arrived, the exceptions proved the rule of British oligarchy. Despite the fact that Harold Macmillan announced in 1959 that 'the class war is obsolete', he duly selected his government almost entirely from Old Etonians and aristocrats. The days when the working classes would become fashionable – bringing 'vitality' into the field of entertainment in the persons of Michael Caine, Albert Finney, David Bailey, Twiggy and the Beatles – and when Harold Wilson and Ted Heath (both at Oxford) emerged from 'ordinary terraced houses' to enter 10 Downing Street, were still some distance away.

Both Bennett and Moore felt what Richard Hoggart describes in *The Uses Of Literacy* as 'an underlying sense of unease when emotionally uprooted from their class.'

Bennett noticed the upper-class students' way of looking down on him when they talked: 'Only people who are so secure in their position can be insulting to everyone else.' When Alan once invited Jonathan Miller home to Leeds, he came 'expecting us to be crouched over the kitchen hob with a pot of stew'. Bennett was able to escape into Medieval History and at the same time parodied the dons, schoolmasters and clergymen of the southern English upper classes. It would be some time before he could come out of the closet of his class and confront it in his writings.

II

'We were not poor, not well off,' Alan Bennett explains. His parents, when eating out or on holiday, went to every extreme to save money, to the immense chagrin of Alan and his younger brother. Walter and Lilian Bennett were not so much role models for the boy Alan as future models for roles. He might have inherited some of his artistic nature from his father who, when not hacking carcasses, played the violin.

Bennett worked out that he and his younger brother were conceived, three years apart, at a northern seaside boarding house during August Bank Holiday. These intimidating places, pilfered for jokes by generations of stand-up comics, were where Mum and Dad Bennett and the kids stayed on their holidays.

'We didn't actually board but took our own food. Screws of tea and packets of sugar and tins of corned beef cushioned by shirts and socks and bathing costumes . . . So when we were on holiday there was no romance about the food; we ate exactly what we did at home.' He remembers that, in a café, his parents would order a pot of tea for two and the token cake, then Mrs Bennett would furtively unwrap a parcel of bread and butter brought from home under the table, creating in the young Alan the 'fear of discovery, exposure and ignominious expulsion'. As a result, the fear of eating in public, a neurosis that doesn't seem to have acquired a name, stayed with him until well into his twenties.

Parents in their natural habitat are acceptable, but take them out of home and they are in the world's spotlight which the child reluctantly has to share. In all 'upwardly mobile' children there is an element of Pip's embarrassment at Joe Gargery's inability to know where to put his hat in *Great Expectations*. When Alan was about fifteen, his parents graduated from boarding houses to hotels. As he explained in very Pip-like terms: 'Arriving at the hotel, like leaving it, was fraught with anxiety as there was the question of The Tip. Dad would have his shilling ready before he'd even signed the register and when they'd been shown up to the room would slip it to the porter, as often as not misjudging the moment, not waiting for his final departure but slipping it to him while he was still demonstrating what facilities the accommodation had to offer. So the shilling came as an unwelcome introduction. Once the porter had finally gone, my parents' apprehension gave way to huge relief. It was as if they'd bluffed their way into the enemy's headquarters.'

The anecdote, related in his first TV documentary, called *Dinner At Noon*, broadcast in August 1988, may very well be true, but it is amusing because most of us have been guilty of social gaucherie in our time. More than likely it was the sort of situation Bennett himself must have experienced later. Was there not an element of having bluffed his way into the enemy's headquarters when the working-class boy entered Oxford?

III

The sensitive lad was rather bright so his parents had great hopes of his being accepted at Leeds Grammar School when he was eight. Unfortunately he failed religious studies, seemingly because he added an 'e' to the name of Job, knowing it to rhyme with 'probe': it seemed illogical that anyone could have called their son J.o.b. A vicar, chairman of the grammar school governors, thought otherwise and turned Alan down, and he therefore went to Leeds Modern School. There might have been an element of revenge on this clerical gentleman in his sermon sketch from *Beyond The Fringe*.

However, Bennett was very religious between the ages of fifteen and eighteen and even after he had left the North continued to go to the church in the village where his parents lived for many years. As a youth he was a member of the Crusaders, an evangelical Bible class for grammar-school boys held on Sunday afternoons in the parish room of a Congregational church in Cumberland Road, Leeds. It has now been turned into a design partnership but 'I never pass that road or look up at those windows without regretting the blighted years when I went there Sunday after Sunday.'

'I don't think I was funny at school, really,' he says. 'I was quite acid and probably sour and unpleasant.' But he admits to having been always attracted by contrived, far-fetched puns and especially enjoyed *Take It From Here* on the radio. 'I remember Jimmy Edwards sitting down and eating some soda scones. Then he said, "I shouldn't have eaten them soda scones so late; they make me disconsolate." ' (You'd probably have had to be there.) He also confesses wanting to stop laughing during a George Formby film in Leeds, because the strain was so painful.

IV

Because Jonathan Miller was studying to be a doctor, and both Peter Cook and Dudley Moore failed the medical, Alan Bennett was the only one of the four to do National Service. While the rest of his platoon was sent to back up the American 'police action' in Korea, he was selected for the Joint Services Russian Course in late 1952.

'It was a cushy number, if ever there was one,' he says, despite having had to study around twelve hours a day. The object of the course was to train soldiers to be Russian interpreters: after preliminary training in Surrey, a year was spent at Cambridge and then a further six months in Bodmin, Cornwall. At Cambridge, the non-uniformed officers stayed in barracks but attended the School of Slavonic Studies every day. On the same course was Michael Frayn, who became good friends with Bennett, and they both wrote and performed in service revues. It was at one of these that Bennett created a pompous provincial cleric who used military terms in his sermon, a predecessor of his most famous man of the cloth. The revues were really the beginnings of both Bennett's and Frayn's writings. 'I can't recall what the sketches were about,' says Bennett. 'I imagine they were full of private jokes about the Russian course, and depended for their reception upon the audience being drunk or otherwise well-disposed.

Michael Frayn, later a notable adapter/translator of Russian plays, claims that Bennett was far better at Russian than he was. 'There was a lot of mutual mockery,' he remembers. 'Even when we meet today, we are slightly cautious with each other, as we are reminded of the fact that we used to mock each other's ambitions.' When Bennett went up to Oxford and Frayn to Cambridge in 1954, they corresponded for a while. Frayn still treasures some of Bennett's long, illustrated letters written on lavatory paper, which he hopes one day to exhibit.

Bennett, who had gained a place to read history at Sidney Sussex, Cambridge, decided to work instead during his National Service for a scholarship to Oxford and went up to read Medieval History at Exeter College. Although Oxford did not have the revue tradition established by the Footlights, it did have 'smokers' (small college revues) at which Bennett enjoyed making people laugh. His star turn was the absurd sermon but he did other things, like imitations of the Queen's Christmas speech full of 'my husband and I' jokes. (The funniest of these, besides the original herself, was Stanley Baxter's version many years later, in which the camp TV floor manager insists on saying 'Cue Queen'.) John Wells first saw Bennett at a smoker in which he did a piece about an atomic scientist who had a device in a paper bag: 'I thought it was infinitely better, much better worked, much more intelligent than anything I was doing.'

Living on the same staircase at Exeter was Russell Harty, a greengrocer's son from Blackburn, Lancashire, with whom Bennett struck up an immediate friendship which lasted until Harty's death in June 1988. They put on a concert together at college, and Harty later lived at Giggleswick in the Yorkshire Dales not many miles from where Walter and Lilian Bennett retired. (Alan paid for them to move out of their terraced house in Leeds, when he started making money from his writing.) Alan and Russell once joked that when they too were old and decrepit, they would set up an old folks' home for themselves and their friends, which they would call 'Wit's End'.

Many years later, when the two friends, both famous, were returning to London from Walter Bennett's funeral in Clapham, North Yorkshire, they found themselves missing the last train back from Lancaster. Harty asked the stationmaster if there was anything he could do to help them, while Bennett hid red-faced behind a luggage trolley, embarrassed by such boldness. The stationmaster arranged for the Royal Scot to make an unscheduled stop there. 'When Mr Bennett – grand lad, isn't he? – comes back, you two stand at the end of the platform. I'll bring her in for you. You two jump on. Don't say nothing to nobody.'

'If one had to point to the quality that distinguished Russell throughout his life, it would be cheek,' Bennett said at Harty's memorial service. A good example came in 1955 when the young undergraduate suggested inviting Vivien Leigh to tea when she was playing at Stratford-upon-Avon. 'She'd never come,' said a sceptical friend. But she did. Vivien Leigh came to Harty's room at college, where she had tea and scones, and chatted for over an hour to Russell and a few other admiring students.

In September 1957, Harty and Bennett set off for a holiday in Venice. 'He was doing his shy best to hide an extraordinarily well-received first-class degree,' Harty wrote. 'Mr Bennett's degree did little to help us when we arrived in that romantic setting. Sure, the full moon shone over the Piazza San Marco. Sure, an orchestra played Beethoven's Eighth Symphony. Sure, we stood, in proper awe, at the majesty of what I now consider a vulgar overstatement. Then, when we got back to our lodging, we had troubles. He had dropped his styptic pencil down the washbasin, and I had fused the electric lighting with my razor. The honourable lady of the house patiently accepted our hesitant explanations and a placatory bunch of red roses. She was not, obviously, in the habit of being soft-soaped by students. She therefore doubled the food and halved the price.' Some time after they returned to England, Bennett to research and Harty to prep school teaching, Harty invited his Oxford friend to a staff party 'and with a burst of uncharacteristic showmanship he performed a sermon which he had written at Oxford. I say, "a sermon". I mean "*the sermon*" which now hangs like a leaden pectoral cross round his neck.'

V

The smoking concerts gave Bennett a taste for revue but he had no serious acting ambitions, steering clear of the renowned OUDS (Oxford University Dramatic Society) and the Oxford Experimental Theatre Club, unlike his university contemporary Dudley Moore, who did straight acting. Performing also helped him to gain a little more social confidence but there were subtleties that escaped him, and there remained a residue of his childhood fear of eating in public places. Once, invited out to dine at the Randolph Hotel by a very austere supervisor, Alan ordered scampi, a dish he had never tried

before. 'Ah!' said his snooty host, 'The food of the commercial travel-
ler!' On another occasion, when Bennett was junior history lecturer
at Magdalen College, he found, at his first dinner at high table, that
the batwing of his BA gown was trapped under the chair. Too shy to
stand up and release it, he waved away one delicious dish after
another, finally attracting the attention of a don sitting next to him. 'If
you're a vegetarian,' he boomed. 'I'm sure they'll make you something
special.'

Bennett stayed on as junior lecturer to do research into the retinue
of Richard II from 1388 to 1399. 'I wasn't very good at research, very
slapdash . . . I never got a fellowship and I don't think I ever would
have done.' He recalls that after the only paper he ever gave, the
chairman asked for questions. 'Total silence. Not a single one, until
an undergraduate at the front leant forward and whispered, "Could I
ask you where you bought your shoes?" '

He did very little theatre during those postgraduate years before
going to the Edinburgh Festival in 1959 with the Oxford Theatre
Group revue called *Better Late*. It was written by Stanley Daniels but
Bennett did some of his own material. Somehow the sermon sketch
didn't fit in with Daniels's scheme and it was not included, but on the
last night Bennett arranged with the technicians to allow him to do
his spot without telling Daniels.

'It was an unforgivable thing to do,' he admits, 'and there was a
tremendous row about it, but it was a great success.' He was back at
Edinburgh the following year with *Beyond The Fringe*.

7

MUSIC

Dudley Moore spread himself much wider at Oxford than did Alan Bennett. An organ scholar at Magdalen or academical clerk, as they are referred to, he had to play at the 500-year-old chapel and at daily services in the cathedral but in contrast he made a name for himself as a jazz musician, and an entertainer in revues, smoking concerts and May Balls, as well as by writing music for plays and appearing in a number of OUDS productions.

'The only theatre I'd been to before Oxford was *Bless The Bride*,' he said. Now he sang the title role of *Orpheus In The Underworld*, was Autolycus, the rogue, in *A Winter's Tale* and wrote the incidental music for *The Birds*, in which he warbled a pastiche of a western ballad in a dangerously high falsetto and in which some of the characters were take-offs of Macmillan, Eisenhower and de Gaulle. Less characteristically, he was Enobarbus in *Antony and Cleopatra*. (Alan Bennett was in the audience at one performance.) As an undergraduate in 1958, nascent theatre critic Michael Billington remembers seeing Moore as Nightingale, the ballad singer, in an open-air production of *Bartholomew Fair*, 'strolling across the sward crying "Apples, who'll buy my lovely apples?" He then took a sample bite out of the fruit, registered amazement and continued on his way shouting "Pears, pears, who'll buy my lovely pears?" ' Moore also did a show with Prunella Scales, a young actress at the Oxford Playhouse (one day to be Bennett's Queen in *Single Spies* at the Queen's Theatre) and also performed at Clement Freud's restaurant at the Royal Court.

Anthony Page, a fellow undergraduate at Magdalen, directing *The Changeling*, asked Dudley to portray the deaf mute, a spidery figure that scuttled around playing the violin, and to compose and record the music for the play. It was through this production that John Bassett met Dudley for the first time, as it was Bassett on trumpet who accompanied Moore on the organ.

Bassett ran the jazz band in the Union cellars and persuaded Dudley, who had had little experience of playing jazz, to play the piano at the Saturday night dances. As a long-time jazz fan and a naturally gifted musician, however, he picked it up very quickly and went from strength to strength. Bassett's band got bigger and bigger – there were sixteen to twenty musicians in it at one stage – and it was much in demand. They played at college dances which Bassett refers to as 'basically snogging sessions for undergraduates', debs' dos and at the Architectural Association Carnival, which had taken over from the Chelsea Arts Ball as being *the* place for students to romp. The carnival lasted from 8 p.m. to around 7 a.m. and cost 30 bob a double ticket. There were eight bands, five dance floors, two theatres and a multiple-screen cinema. Professional jazzmen like Tubby Hayes and John Dankworth used to come and sit in on the sessions and quickly recognised Dudley's talents. It seemed as if Dudley, as in the Yeats poem, was plucking 'the silver apples of the moon, the golden apples of the sun'. But there were still shadows in his life that this brightness could not dispel.

II

Dudley Moore was born in Charing Cross Hospital on 19 April, 1935, to Ada Moore (née Hughes). Her father had been a faith-healer and writer of books on Christian Science. Ada needed all her religious faith when her son was born with his feet turned inwards. At two weeks, he had the first of many operations but he remained with a club foot and a left leg almost two inches shorter than his right.

According to Leslie A Marchand's biography of Lord Byron, the poet's club foot 'caused him throughout his life much bodily suffering and mental agony, and . . . probably did more to shape his character than it will ever be possible to calculate'. Dudley spent the first seven years of his life syphoned off in hospital beds and wheel chairs. 'I had special boots, and – just like Rumpelstiltskin – the only way I could express my rage was by stamping on the floor until it collapsed and gave way. It was my leg on to which I projected all my feelings of inadequacy and self-loathing.' As it was during the war, and as neither Dudley nor his elder sister Barbara were evacuated, he was sometimes the only child in a ward full of screaming, wounded soldiers.

'I despised any sort of friendliness from a very early age. I used to get wheeled into the operating theatre and told things like "Now you are going to see a Mickey Mouse film," and I used to say whatever was the equivalent of "Oh, for fuck's sake, I'm going to have an operation." It was as if they were looking down on me.' Yet the few genuine shows of affection Dudley remembers vividly. When a nurse came to tuck him up in bed once, she asked if he wanted her to kiss him goodnight. 'I said "No," then she said "Okay" and walked away. I was terribly frightened and alone, and I shouted after her, "Yes," and she came back and kissed me. I will never forget her.'

Dudley was conscious from a very early age of the guilt his mother felt for his defects and of the cloud of religiosity that hung over the house. His father, John Moore, an electrician on the railways since his boyhood, was a strict Anglo-Catholic.

'He was very shy, very gentle, very sweet,' recalled his son in 1979, eight years after his father's death. 'I would have liked to have known him better. I always regret never really spending any time with him. If he were alive, I'd whip him off to the pub and ask him about this, that and the other. I've still got his watch. But he taught me not to be very forthcoming. My parents were frightened about being alive . . . There was always the fear of what the neighbours would think, and the usual desire to be respectable.'

However Ada, who played the piano after a fashion, got Dudley to take piano lessons. So when he wasn't in hospital he was practising pieces from a volume of Victorian melodies and was soon good enough to entertain his family and guests. When he started to read Bach scores, he says it was like reading a detective story, because he couldn't wait to see what would happen over the page. 'I used to hop around to the local library and get music out, sometimes two to three times in an evening. I would take it home and have these magical black and white notes come to life under my fingers,' he says. Later, as a schoolboy, he used to wander down to a music shop in Ilford, and buy music sheets of George Shearing, Fats Waller and Errol Garner.

At the age of eight, he had learned to play the organ, and also sang in the local church choir. Although he found the experience of being in church 'very comfortable and enjoyable' and thought of becoming a choirmaster, he turned his back on religion. When he was eleven, Dudley was awarded a scholarship to attend the Guildhall School of Music at Blackfriars (It did not move to the Barbican Centre until 1978), and there for the next eight years he studied the harpsichord, organ, violin and musical theory and composition for four hours every

Saturday morning. At the Guildhall, he composed his first orchestral work, appropriately entitled 'Anxiety'.

He was bullied constantly at Dagenham County High School and had to endure being called names like Hopalong Cassidy. As a result he turned to clowning to protect himself – the classic case of the comedian being born out of adversity. 'I used laughter as a safety valve, both for myself and as a defence against others. I remember the exact moment when it happened. I was about twelve and in an English lesson and I thought, "I can't stand this any longer," and I summoned up my courage and made some silly remark that made the children look round and laugh. I could see them thinking, "Did that come from him?" I was a very solemn sort of pompous boy and I was treated rather warily or gently by the masters which, of course, didn't endear me to the boys. The sight of them actually smiling at me was a new thing and I wanted to keep them doing that, to get their approval.'

III

After completing his schooling, Moore applied for a music scholarship to Cambridge, but was so nervous he failed the interview. On the day he faced Oxford dons at Magdalen College chapel to demonstrate his prowess on the organ, he was obliged to bind a woman's high-heeled evening shoe onto his left foot, to enable him to reach the pedals. (He later had a special boot made with a two-inch platform.) He was accepted and went up to Oxford in October, 1954.

At Oxford, Moore felt 'dwarfed by the social ease of the people who'd come from public schools. Everybody seemed to be very suave and smooth and assured. They thought I talked funny – funny strange, not funny – and I regarded them the same way. I couldn't stand the sound of their voices – they seemed so in charge of themselves. So I tried to imitate them. My vowels still got to Dagenham very easily.'

Despite his popularity as a jazz pianist, actor and revue artist, Dudley still had inhibitions about his body; 'I felt especially at a disadvantage with women.' This sounds strange from someone who seems to have had more beautiful women in his life than you can shake a stick at, but Moore has always been crushed between Orpheus and Eros, the twin gods of his life.

Dagenham County High School was co-educational, although the girls had different playgrounds and physical education was done separately from the boys. At home, sex was considered obscene and wasn't discussed at all. In typical comically exaggerated terms, Moore says, 'I once asked my mother what "cunt" meant, and she fell off her chair, wet her knickers and one tit fell out, so I realised there was something wrong about asking her anything to do with sex. I was scared stiff – no pun intended – although what a wonderful expression for juvenile erections. I thought bolts of lightning threatened to come out of the sky.'

The idea of sex caused torment and pleasure to vie for dominance within him. 'I did a certain amount with a French girl when I was about sixteen . . . She came to me with some contraceptives that she had taken from her father's drawer, and I thought, shit, he must have counted them, he must know they're missing. I refused to use one, much to her chagrin. We had this peculiar toe-in-and-out-of-the-sea relationship. I remember a few other times with girls, but again I didn't want to leave it there for more than a microsecond because of the dangers, not only from pregnancy, but from God.'

At the age of 22, Dudley finally lost his virginity, to an actress from London he met at an Oxford party. They made an arrangement to spend the night together, Dudley nervously booked a room at a hotel and waited for her at the station. 'She was supposed to get there at midnight, but she arrived at five a.m. on the milk train, so I was sitting on this bloody platform freezing to death . . . We finally got to this hotel and we went into the bedroom and we got into bed and – I don't think it was particularly colourful or colourless . . . I think it happened maybe one more time, but it was a limited experience for both of us.' The future Hollywood sex symbol's propensity to speak about his erotic experiences justifies Jonathan Miller's view of him as 'libidinous, childlike, goatlike . . . the embodiment of some peculiar mythical satyr'. But instead of playing the Pan-pipes, Dudley's fingers hit the keys of the piano, shook the chapel with his organ and stroked the strings of the violin with his bow: the first sight John Wells ever had of Moore at Oxford was of 'a tiny figure dressed in the motley of Autolycus, walking up an avenue of trees playing a fiddle'.

IV

The attractions of the stage and the dance band took Moore away from his books and in 1957 he only gained a BA Second. 'He certainly could have got a First,' said his tutor Dr Bernard Rose, 'but he wasn't a terribly conscientious academic musician. To get a First you really have to devote yourself to it.' Nevertheless, Moore stayed on at Magdalen another year to get his Bachelor of Music.

'My tutor offered me his position at Queen's College dependent on my getting a first-class degree,' says Dudley. 'It would have matured into a fellowship over a small period of time. This would have been an ideal job in many ways; being organist and choir master of a college and then finally a don in music.'

In June 1958 Magdalen held a Commemoration Ball at which Johnny Dankworth's Band was the principal attraction. Around midnight, Dudley sat down at the piano and dazzled the assembled company with jazz and a Beethoven pastiche. Cleo Laine, who was singing with her husband's band, turned to Dankworth and said, 'Next time I need an accompanist, that's the boy for me!' (Twenty-four years later, Dudley landed the job accompanying Cleo on a record of songs called *Smilin' Through*.) Dankworth told Moore then that if ever he had a vacancy in his band he would think of him but he knew that the Vic Lewis Orchestra needed a pianist. When he got to London, the newly graduated BA B.Mus. (Oxon.), playing piano at the Café des Artistes in the Fulham Road for ten bob a night, went to see Vic Lewis at his flat just off Russell Square. Lewis, a little cockney Jew, not much taller than Moore, recalls that Dudley called him 'sir'. 'Don't call me sir, I'm only a jazzman.' 'Very well, sir,' replied Dudley. He got the job with the band at £40 for three sessions a week, touring the country, but found it rather hard to suppress his instincts to show off his pianistic talents and become just a 'chorus boy' backing the star instrumentalists.

Despite the shattering effect that rock 'n' roll had had on the youth of the Western world since 1956, when kiss-curled Bill Haley and his Comets rocked around the clock and Elvis Presley warned people against stepping on his blue suede shoes, big bands were still in demand for dance halls and concerts, although their popularity was waning, threatened as they were by the Coffee Bar culture and the Traditional Jazz revival. In 1958 an arrangement between the Musi-

cians' Union and the American Federation of Musicians was negotiated, thus ending a 22-year ban on big bands crossing the Atlantic
in either direction. The first Anglo-American exchange took place
between the bands of Stan Kenton and Ted Heath (not the Balliol
organ scholar, sailor and future PM), and the second brought Count
Basie to Britain while Vic Lewis went over to the States for two months
in February 1959. Whatever comment one can make about who got
the best of the bargain, or coals to Newcastle, it allowed Moore to pay
his first visit to the country he was to make his home.

The band toured only the East coast, playing mostly army bases
and naval hospitals on Long Island, Connecticut, and Massachusetts.
Dudley pounded away for the sum of £100 a week (more than double
his salary in England) and also found time to write a score for the
OUDS production of *Coriolanus*. (Among the walk-ons in the cast,
which had Patrick Garland in the title role, were Richard Ingrams and
Michael Billington.) 'Dudley Moore's music arrives in gradual packets
from various Connecticut dance halls,' reported *Isis*, the undergraduate magazine. When the tour ended, Vic and Dudley stayed on in New
York for a while after the band returned home.

Lewis had made a decision to wind up his orchestra in a few months
to become an agent. His first client would be Dudley Moore. Dudley
auditioned for the Jack Parr and Ed Sullivan TV shows but got 'don't
call us' responses. Nevertheless, when Lewis left for England, Dudley
decided to stay behind at the YMCA feeling it would do his musical
education no harm to live for a while in the country where jazz was
born. Unfortunately, it was also the country where thousands of jazz
musicians were born and they all seemed to be looking for jobs in
New York. He did manage to get some work when he joined up with
a trio to play at the Village Vanguard, a Greenwich Village nightclub,
and at the Duplex, where Ahmet Ertegun of Atlantic Records caught
their act and offered them a recording contract. But Dudley, who was
beginning to feel homesick, and whom Vic Lewis wanted back for his
band's final tour, declined the offer, and flew back to England.

After a brief stint with Lewis, he joined the Dankworth band. 'I was
a bit nervous about playing behind the soloists, because at the time I
was on a terrific Errol Garner kick. I played in his style even when
the other musicians were trying to make a chorus and they felt it
was impossible to solo against me,' Moore remarked. But Dankworth
allowed him his head and he became a featured soloist. While still
playing with the band, he formed the Dudley Moore Trio with bass

player Hugo Boyd, a young architect Moore had met through John Bassett in Oxford, and Derek Hogg on drums. At the same time, he wrote the music for two new plays at the Royal Court Theatre, John Arden's *Sergeant Musgrave's Dance* and N F Simpson's most successful absurdist play, *One Way Pendulum*. For this he arranged the Hallelujah Chorus for 100 speak-your-weight machines. He was also profiled in an edition of *Monitor*, the prestigious BBC TV arts programme, a double-header in which Dudley was seen as an up-and-coming young jazz pianist in one half of the broadcast in contrast to his exact contemporary Peter Maxwell Davies (now Sir Peter), the 'classical' composer, in the other. Both justified *Monitor*'s faith in their future.

Moore remembered that 'Peter lived in a very ascetic set of circumstances, having a sort of pipe organ in the loft of a barn. This contrasted amazingly with my own fairly vulgar life of an existence on the Kilburn High Road in a small flat surrounded by milk bottles, old record sleeves, everything on the floor, my dad's old overcoat used for a blanket and my desire to play in jazz clubs. I think to a great extent the film was incomplete. Neither Peter nor myself would aspire to such a monochrome version of ourselves.'

Moore found his class unconsciousness in music and especially in the unélitist jazz. Now he would also enter into the swing of the 'classless' 'sixties with his Beatle haircut, his fast cars and his dolly birds. In addition, he ventured out into the world of cabaret, teaming up with Joe Melia, a former Footlighter, for a number of cabaret appearances including the swanky *My Fair Lady* Ball at the Savoy Hotel, where they were painfully billed as 'The Moore The Melia'.

Dudley's solo act was a mixture of one-liners, amusing anecdotes and pianistics including pastiches of the great composers, a sophisticated turn that fitted some venues better than others. One Manchester club proved a low point: he had to follow wrestlers and strip-tease artistes. 'No-one warned me what a dive it was. So after the strippers went off, I came out and did a brilliant satire on Schubert *lieder* and the operas of Benjamin Britten,' Moore recalls in horror. 'Obviously I bombed miserably.' Luckily it was not long before he received a call from Bassett asking if he was interested in taking part in a little revue at the Edinburgh Festival.

PART THREE

After
Beyond The Fringe

.

'For what do we live, but to make sport for our
neighbours, and laugh at them in our turn.'

Mr Bennet in *Pride And Prejudice*
by Jane Austen

8

DR JONATHAN AND MR MILLER

If one were surveying the terrain of Jonathan Miller's career, aside from the gushing hot spring of *Beyond The Fringe*, any large-scale map of his public life would be dominated by his work for the stage.

In July 1962, just before the quartet journeyed to Broadway, George Devine (pronounced Deveen), the enterprising and perspicacious artistic director of the English Stage Company at the Royal Court Theatre, asked Miller to direct one half of a John Osborne double bill entitled *Plays For England*. The English Stage Company had been formed in 1956 'to stage and encourage new writing'. Living up to this pledge, Devine presented a multitude of new works by British writers in the nine years he was at the Court, and simultaneously launched the careers of new directors such as John Dexter, Tony Richardson and William Gaskill. The company's first outstanding success had been Osborne's *Look Back In Anger*, as significant a scalpel on the face of British theatre as *Beyond The Fringe* was five years later.

Osborne was 27 when his play opened on 8 May 1956, almost the same age as Miller when Devine decided to offer him the job of directing *Under Plain Cover*, (The other half of the bill was *Blood Of The Bambergs*, a weak satire on the press and royalty, directed by John Dexter.) *Under Plain Cover* was a Genet-esque piece in which a young couple (Anton Rodgers and Ann Beach) never stray from their home but dress up in order to play a variety of masculine/feminine roles – doctor-patient, master-maid – illustrating the proposition that an anal-sadistic relationship need not preclude love. 'This is perhaps the most audacious statement ever made on the English stage,' claimed audacious Kenneth Tynan in hyperbolic fervour. However, it proved a landmark in British theatre only in one way: it was Jonathan Miller's professional debut as a theatre director.

Why should George Devine have given him the job? Miller believes he was chosen because no one else agreed to direct the play or 'because presumably it had a slightly satirical edge to it, he thought "Let's get one of those satire boys to come into it" – like trying to get a specialist plumber'. Osborne, only five years older than Miller and fresh from the triumph of his sub-Brechtian play *Luther*, was 'not only a very well established playwright but also a cult figure in post-war theatre . . . I was never tempted to take the work and re-fashion it in my own image'.

Miller, who belongs, on the whole, to the only-good-playwright-is-a-dead-playwright school of directing, was perhaps not altogether surprisingly inhibited by the acerbic presence of the author who came to rehearsals every three or four days and who 'resisted cuts as a Christian Scientist resists surgery'. But: 'It was a pleasant way of passing the time before going to America, and I discovered I could direct, I could hear how the lines should be spoken although there were still some skills to be learnt along the way.' It would be another six years before he had the next opportunity to direct a play in England.

It was in the USA that Miller first really cut his teeth as a director. He had met Robert Lowell, the New England poet, towards the end of 1963, after Miller had left *Beyond The Fringe*, and discussed the possibility of putting on Lowell's *The Old Glory*, an adaptation of two stories, *My Kinsman Major Molineux* by Nathaniel Hawthorne and Herman Melville's *Benito Cereno*. But in December 1963 Lowell was committed for the second time to the Institute for Living, a psychiatric hospital in Hartford, Connecticut and it was not until some six months later that Miller was installed in a small studio upstairs from the Lowells' New York apartment at West 67th Street, to prepare the production. He was able to have regular but not always fruitful conversations with the author, who had never written for the stage before. Lowell would ask Miller to sit up 'a little bit later at night, and then later and later' and would become 'hectic and slightly impatient' if he was refused. The poet, in his less lucid moments, would come up with things like: 'I've got this new act. The widow of Sir Walter Raleigh comes on with her husband's decapitated head in her hands, blood streaming from the neck. I guess you could do that with ribbons.' Lowell also came to almost every rehearsal, although Miller writes that 'I never succeeded in hearing answers that elucidated exactly what he intended.' In fact, it was Miller's production that helped elucidate to the author, if not to the audience, what his intentions were. Lowell saw the plays as 'allegories of modern America', but for the tyro director their chief attraction was that they escaped what he saw, and continues to see, as 'the dead hand of contemporary naturalism'.

A glance down the arm-length list of Miller productions reveals hardly any plays that could be defined as naturalistic, and after his association with Osborne and Lowell, fewer than half a dozen by living playwrights.

'I don't do more contemporary plays because you have to do a very heavy reading of scripts,' he says. 'You have to cultivate the company of writers you admire. You do it to the exclusion of classical theatre. I've committed myself to being a custodian of a museum.'

My Kinsman Major Molineux tells of a youth's search for his first cousin, a governor of a New England colony, only to find his kinsman hated and reviled by the people. He learns to make his own way in the world, without relying on the spoils of colonialism. *Benito Cereno*, the longer of the two plays, concerns a mysterious encounter between an American sailing ship and a Spanish vessel filled with Negro slaves. Captain Delano goes on board the Spanish ship with the aim of bringing help and succour to the crew and their ailing captain Cereno. Miller felt 'The play shows that American benevolence, because of its assertive virtuousness, tends to bring violence in its wake'. When it was revived in England (at the Mermaid in 1968), without its original companion piece, it was seen as an allegory of the Vietnam War, mistakenly in Miller's view. However, this was an understandable interpretation since Lowell had headed marches against the war, was an active supporter of the Civil Rights movement during the period, and in fact actually stated that he wrote the play with that in mind.

The Old Glory opened at the American Place Theater in New York in November 1964. The *New York Times* critic found *Major Molineux* 'a pretentious arty trifle . . . staged in a series of mannered postures and movements as if they were choppy segments of an animated cartoon'. But in *Benito Cereno*, 'Mr Miller appears to relish every atmospheric and theatrical opportunity'. In January 1965, *Cereno* alone was transferred to the Theatre de Lys in Greenwich Village for a reasonable off-Broadway run. Of the London production, Lowell admitted that 'the reviews were lousy. There were a lot of complaints about it being too short.' The English critics did find the 90-minute 'opera without music', and without an interval, too stylised for their tastes. Irving Wardle of *The Times* felt that 'Opera and melodrama are

---

not really comparable idioms, and Mr Lowell gets the worst of both.'

Three years after *The Old Glory* in New York, Miller's association with Lowell was resumed at the Yale Drama School with a production of the poet's 'imitation' of Aeschylus's *Prometheus Bound*. Robert Brustein, Dean of the school, told Lowell's biographer, Ian Hamilton, that 'the two men complemented each other strangely. Lowell taciturn and soft-spoken, mournful and reserved; Miller dynamic, convivial, hyperactive, marvellously funny, a cascade of anecdotes and insights always pouring from his lips'.

Some time before, Lowell had published *Imitations*, a collection of foreign poems regenerated into English rather than translated or 'made new', in Pound's phrase. Lowell had clearly moved on from his stated position of 1963 when he had felt that Greek tragedies by Aeschylus and Sophocles 'are so different [from an English cultural tradition] that you could hardly think of even the attempt to imitate them, great as their prestige was'. His attempt to do so, in 1967, presented Miller with a thorny problem. The play had Prometheus, played by Kenneth Haigh, creator of Osborne's Jimmy Porter, tethered to a rock on a Caucasian mountain top throughout, not the most exciting prospect for either audience or actor. Miller, who feels 'It is invariably true that nature looks atrocious on stage,' found an alternative setting, an example of the ingenuity that colours most of his subsequent work. With the designer Michael Annals, he planned a setting that would suggest the rock without representing it. The 'action' took place in a ruined Renaissance courtyard with Prometheus on a small pedestal in the middle of the theatre's pit, a device which conveyed his imprisonment on the rock without completely limiting his movement. However, it still didn't do enough to disguise the static nature of the play.

The opening night on 9 May 1967 was an unusually glittering affair for the Yale Drama School Theater, attended as it was by David Merrick, Robert Motherwell, Stephen Spender, Philip Roth, George Plimpton and Susan Sontag, and other assorted eggheads. They greeted the play as politely as guests would a meal at a friend's that did not really satisfy.

Some critics complained about Miller's decision to set the Greek tragedy in a ruined seventeenth century castle, with the hero dressed in knee breeches and leather jerkin; others were unhappy with Lowell's treatment of the original, which he had extended by a third. One outspoken Yale professor claimed it was a mistake to have turned

Prometheus into 'a mumbling victim of radical intellectual anxiety'.

When the production turned up at the Mermaid in June 1971 (also with Kenneth Haigh), the setting was reduced to a bare grey platform, a stool and bucket as if it were a cell in which Prometheus languishes as a political prisoner. His constant references to his rock and chains (of which there was no sign) disconcerted a number of critics. *Prometheus* again failed to catch fire, and most of the audience were Morpheus Bound. The play worked much better a few months later when Miller directed it with Haigh, and Irene Worth as Io, on Radio 3, radio being the least passive medium where audiences are pleased to listen to words and provide the action themselves. 'Doing this on radio is a marvellous opportunity. There is a certain austerity in sound and not fussing with decor and scenery,' commented Miller at the time. 'I am allowing the play to speak for itself, with the minimum of effects. It would be like doing Shakespeare on ice to introduce a lot of sound effects.'

Before dealing in the rarefied atmosphere of Lowell's *Prometheus*, Miller had had 'a disastrous experience' with the workings of American commercial theatre, this particular example being a comedy by Lee Minoff and Stanley Price called *Come Live With Me*. 'I wanted to make a hit and a lot of money,' Miller admits. 'At the time it was a nightmare, but it was one of the comic episodes in my life which I would never have done without. Re-writes in smoky hotel rooms in New Haven and Philadelphia.' He resigned out of town as director 'for reasons of personal and family business', according to the producer. When the play, directed by Joshua Shelly and starring TV comic, Soupy Sales, opened on Broadway in January 1967, Miller was billed in the programme as 'production associate', The *New York Times* commented that, 'No one behaves as if there'd ever been a director on the premises.' Needless to say, it flopped.

II

Just after his first collaboration with Robert Lowell, Miller landed the prestigious job of fronting the BBC TV arts programme *Monitor*, which had been in the genial and capable hands of Huw Wheldon for five years. Again, as with the Royal Court offer, he was handed a job for which he seemed to have little qualification. He had appeared in the first issues of the breakthrough daily news programme *Tonight* in

1957 but had made few appearances on TV since. 'I am amazed at my rashness, knowing as little as I did about TV. But there are great advantages about being an amateur. You don't know the rules. I was impatient with what I had previously seen on the arts and wanted to see what would happen when fresh air blew through the studio.' His confrontation with the wonderful world of American television in *What's Going On Here?* in 1963 had been a less than edifying one. Naturally, Miller came to *Monitor* knowing that there was, in the days before deregularisation, a vast difference between a big American commercial TV network and the state-run public-servicing BBC – the men from UNCLE *vs* Auntie. But in the 'sixties the old lady had extensive cosmetic surgery, donned a mini-skirt, changed her name to the Beeb and started to swing with the times. By the autumn of 1964, when Miller stepped into Wheldon's shoes, *TW3* had already come and gone and the BBC was launching *Not So Much A Programme* . . . to prove that satire was still alive and biting.

There are few of the two million regular viewers of *Monitor* between 1958 and 1964 who can listen today to Dag Wiren's 'Serenade for Strings' without recalling this mostly traditional but often controversial, stimulating and, above all, educative arts programme. Few things are more potent than a signature tune, cheap or otherwise. As there were only two TV channels at the time and no video, the nation watched most of the same things at the same time, and the Punch-profiled Wheldon, for all his seeming naivety, fumbling speech and bumbling exterior, or because of them, was a much-loved national institution. Miller was the exact opposite. He spoke rapidly, gave the impression of being in command and never pretended any ignorance on any subject. In 1964, *The Observer* wrote perceptively that Miller was 'one of the few "bright young men" to receive the full blast of the publicity machine, who still seems capable of development as an individual and of meaningful work . . . he is, of course, an intellectual, but – English rarity – still in touch with feeling'. Nevertheless, from the first programme, an unwieldy and unWheldon but 'with it' discussion with Susan Sontag, *the* definer of 'camp', Miller's sojourn on *Monitor* is generally regarded as catastrophic.

'The English are prepared to tolerate the arts as long as they are perpetuated by tweedy figures living in farmhouses,' he says. 'The idea that it might take place in Manhatten lofts is unthinkable. I remember that pontifical, pipe-smoking Yorkshire twerp, J B Priestley, condescendingly saying "*Monitor* has settled down on the corner of

42nd Street and 7th Avenue." ' Wheldon didn't think *Monitor* was Miller's 'cup of tea': 'What he likes is the enormous relevance of the classics.' The problem was that in a country that loves to typecast people it was disconcerting to see a 'funny man' getting all 'artsy fartsy'.

'In England, if anyone does more than one thing, he is classed a dilettante,' says George Melly, jazz singer, art historian and critic. 'But someone who spends his whole life boring the arse off the world with one nail they keep hammering, is taken more seriously.' Melly recalls a visit to Belgium for the twenty-minute film he made with Miller for *Monitor* on René Magritte. 'The neatness of the painter's house aroused Jonathan's scepticism. He suggested that through the back of the closet lay another room, where, in complete squalor, the Magrittes lived their real life, coupling frantically in a dishevelled bed full of sausage-roll crumbs with a half-empty bottle of Dr Pepper stuck on top of a cupboard containing an unemptied chamber pot.' Unfortunately, none of this surreal fantasy was contained in the piece, which Melly feels 'wasn't particularly well-filmed . . . I looked at a rough cut and saw that all the words were with the wrong images. I helped with the editing, because Jonathan made it and then sort of drifted away.'

Monitor was killed off a few months later and Miller was charged by the public and critics with its murder. In 1970 the accused explained to Joan Bakewell and Nicolas Garnham, with an element of soothsaying in his vision of the video age and of the coming acceptance of 'Talking Heads', how he saw his stint on *Monitor*:

'My main difficulties were divided into two groups; one, as it were, purely institutional and the other technical. The institutional difficulty was associated with the fact that I inherited a programme that already had a reputation, and therefore an expectation of a certain sort on the part of its audience, and I violated that expectation. Secondly in terms of pure technique, there were things I thought could be done on that medium and they could not be done . . . relatively complicated ideas could not be put across. This is something which print will always have over TV, until TV is, in fact, simply a private viewing box with private controls which allows you, simply, to run the tape backwards and forwards . . .

'There is also the dogma within TV that it is boring to transmit ideas . . . If someone simply sits in front of a camera and talks and tells you things and points things out with his finger, it is somehow not TV. It is as if they had in their mind that somewhere, by common consent, there was a Platonic ideal of TV from which all other actual practical forms of TV are, more or less, deviations, of which they are replicas . . . I rather like to see people sitting in front of a TV camera and talking. As you no doubt know, the idea of the talking head is anathema to most TV people. It seems to me that the talking head is the best sort of head there is, and the head, in general, is the most interesting thing we have really, and it is best to talk through it . . .' Actually, as he told Michael Parkinson in 1978, his own stutter made introducing *Monitor* 'an assault-course over nets and ponds of consonants'. In 1977 Miller returned to BBC TV with a vengeance (literally?) when he presented *The Body In Question*, becoming one of the most famous talking heads in the business. In 1982 he sat fifteen great thinking heads down in front of the camera and let them talk in a series called *States Of Mind*.

In fact, Miller has over the years become a familiar inhabitant of the 'global village' (Marshall McLuhan's definition of TV), happy to put on productions of Shakespeare, travel round the world interviewing musicians in *Four Virtuosos (sic)* and take part in chat shows. Interestingly he has never admitted a love for the medium. In his first book, *McLuhan* (1971), he spent much of its 133 pages demolishing the message of the Canadian guru of the mass media:

'It's a bit heavy-handed but it's original in that I identified the connection between McLuhan's technological jargon and his deep commitment to Catholic conservatism. I became more and more impatient with his misuse of technical terms.' Taking him to task for his deification of television, Miller (a humanist scientist) claims that McLuhan (a Catholic agrarian) ignores the destructive features of TV:

'The alienating effect is magnified by the fact that the TV screen reduces all images to the same visual quality. Atrocity and entertainment alternate with one another on the same rectangle of bulging glass,' he wrote. 'Comedy and politics merge into one continuous ribbon of transmission. It is hard to see how ordinary village life can survive under such conditions, let alone that of a global village.' The book, which made McLuhan see red also, according to *The Times* critic, 'takes apart the logical fallacies of McLuhan's use of clever paradox, exaggeration and analogy . . . but fails to account for the stimulating impact of McLuhan's volatile if unreliable showmanship'. Five years previously, McLuhan had been interviewed by Miller for *Monitor* but 'he was so boring' it wasn't broadcast.

III

After the *Monitor* debacle Miller wrote an episode on Anne Hutch-
inson for TV New York's *Profiles In Courage* in 1965 and in the same
year produced and directed *The Drinking Party*, a splendidly subtle
and radiant rendition of Plato's *Symposium*, for the BBC. The memorable *Alice In Wonderland* film commissioned from him by the BBC
was shown at Christmas 1966.

No one who has read *Interpretations of Alice* or *The Annotated Alice*
would have been shocked by Miller's Pre-Raphaelite post-Freudian
'interpretation' of Carroll's masterpiece. *Alice* has been under analysis
since the 'thirties and placed in a literary line that includes Dickens,
Chesterton, Kafka and Nabokov. It was after Miller had seen Orson
Welles's overblown film of *The Trial* that he felt he could transfer
Carroll's book to the screen:

'My determination to go on with the project was reinforced by my
recognition that Alice was a precursor to Joseph K,' he wrote. 'In both
novels the protagonists find themselves involved in a legal process
whose accusations remain obscure. The overwhelming impression of
Carroll's novel is that *people had been talking about A* . . . ' (Actually,
the famous first line of *The Trial*, in the translation by Willa and
Edwin Muir, is: 'Someone must have been telling lies about Joseph K,
for without having done anything wrong he was arrested one fine
morning.') By the time Miller had the revelation that there was a link
between Lewis C and Franz K, it was already common currency in
Carrollian criticism. He also made the discovery 'that I could only
succeed with *Alice* if the film realised the characteristically disjunctive grammar of dream'. To film *Alice* as a dream, which it is, would
of course merely be to use the disjunctive grammar of the cinema,
which Cocteau once defined as 'the dream we all dream together'.

What did provide *Alice* with a new party dress was Miller's recognition that it was an individual dream dreamt by a Victorian child,
and a collective one by Victorian society, filtered through 1960s sensibility. The exquisite use of Ravi Shankar's music on the soundtrack
was a brilliant stroke. (Shankar, at that period, was already rather
bemused to find himself a renowned figure in the pop world after he
had taught the sitar to George Harrison of the Beatles.) Miller's vision
was enhanced by his decision to turn his back on the Tenniel illustra-
tions, engraved on most readers' minds, and to strip the anthropomor-
phised animals of their disguises, revealing them to be Victorian

adults seen through the child's eyes. After all, Carroll does not make a great distinction in tone or style between creatures such as the Caterpillar and the March Hare and humans like the Queen of Hearts and the Mad Hatter. In the book we see the human in the animal: in the film we see the animal in the human.

Although Miller turned to the 'hallucinatory realism of the Pre-Raphaelites' rather than to Tenniel, the crisp black-and-white photography and the physical appearance of many of the characters, particularly of Leo McKern in drag as The Duchess and Ann-Marie Mallik in the title role, are reminiscent of the original drawings. Miller was reunited with Peter Cook (the Mad Hatter) and Alan Bennett (the Mouse) – Dudley Moore appeared as the Dormouse (here played by Wilfred Lawson) in a dull 1972 movie – also irresistibly cast were Peter Sellers (the King of Hearts), Wilfred Brambell (the White Rabbit), Michael Redgrave (the Caterpillar), John Bird (the Frog Footman) and John Gielgud and Malcolm Muggeridge as the Mock Turtle and the Gryphon, two elderly gentlemen strolling on the sands. (Eric Idle made a brief, uncredited appearance.)

The film was originally intended to be screened during the Christmas holiday but Huw Wheldon, then Controller of Programmes at the BBC, announced that he deemed it unsuitable for children under the age of twelve and that it would be transmitted on 28 December 9.05 p.m. thereby causing the Puritan Brigade, who condemn anything on TV that is not suitable for a child, to attack it unseen. Miller added fuel to the fire by talking about Freud and Kafka, nothing more likely to make the eyes of the English public glaze over, as well as seeming to support Wheldon's decision for a different reason. 'I spent eighteen months working on it and I was not going to have it wasted on a lot of little kids at 5.30 in the afternoon,' he told the press. As *Alice* is one of the few childhood classics that is read with even greater satisfaction in maturity, it seemed logical to make an 'adult' version that could nevertheless still appeal to children, instead of the other way round. 'In the past hundred years we have thought of *Alice* as a charming fairy story,' explained Miller, 'but there is an enduring melancholy, which outlasts fun. It reveals the silent fears of growing up.'

The idea of tampering with a childhood classic caused choleric correspondence in *The Times*, which meant rumblings in the Home Counties. Writing from deepest Hampshire, the playwright William

Douglas Home complained about liberties taken with classics. However, a few weeks later, he wrote *The Times* another letter:

> Sir, Having seen *Alice in Wonderland* last Wednesday night, I am now prepared to prostrate myself in sackcloth and ashes at Jonathan Miller's feet, provided that Huw Wheldon joins me there. For he it was who led us all astray. By his pre-production warning, he created a situation similar to that which would arise if the managing director of Harrods were to issue a statement warning younger children against visiting the toy department. Naturally, furious parents like me would dash off furious letters to you, Sir, only to find on visiting the store later without younger children, that, apart from a shortage of playing cards, mushrooms, hookahs, teapots, pigeons and other livestock, it was much the same as ever, if a little less exciting, for these reasons. For apart from having mistakenly tried to make sense out of nonsense, Jonathan Miller's only sins are sins of omission. His integrity, which I confess to having doubted after the Huw Wheldon warning, remains virgin white, nor can one fault his brilliance or his taste. If he should tackle *Peter Pan* next year, may I suggest he casts Huw Wheldon in the role of Tinkerbell. Then we could keep control of him!

On the whole the critics were favourable and when *Alice* was shown on TV in the USA the *New York Times* said it was a 'widely different and often magnificently inventive interpretation of the Lewis Carroll classic'. In the same month as its original transmission, the BBC announced that Miller's contract with them had expired.

IV

It is surprising that a man with such a visual flair has only flirted sporadically with film since making *Alice*. 'Almost all film-makers who've worked on TV feel they haven't really made a film until it's been shown on a screen in a cinema. I was speaking to some American film executive when he said, "Well, have you made any films, Jonathan?" and I said "Yes, I've made five television films" – and he replied "Oh, yes, television films, but how about *film* films?"'

A couple of years before, when *Beyond The Fringe* was coming to the end of its New York run, the four 'Fringers' had written an outline for a film to be called *The Curious Gentlemen* – an Edwardian comedy of manners – but the project was aborted due to producer Sam Spiegel's insistence on controlling the screenplay. In 1967, Miller made a documentary called *Scotch* for John Walker and Sons and returned to the BBC as a freelance to make a version of the M R James ghost story, *Oh, Whistle And I'll Come To You, My Lad* (the film's title left out the 'My Lad') for the *Omnibus* slot. Miller expunged the ghost and treated the tale as a Freudian case study in suppressed homosexuality. His next short film for TV, six years later, was *Clay*, based on the James Joyce story.

Miller's only 'film' film, *Take A Girl Like You*, was a screen adaptation by George Melly of Kingsley Amis's 1960 novel of the same name, shot and completed at Shepperton for Columbia Pictures in 1969, but released in early 1971. It concerned a twenty-year-old North Country schoolteacher's determination to preserve her virginity in a swingingly permissive London. When asked the reason by her would-be lover, she replies 'Because.' Although not exactly *Measure For Measure* nor something with which Miller, who claimed to be an admirer of Bresson, Welles and Olmi at the time, could feel much personal involvement, he protested that he found the plot an interesting one: 'The fact is that virginity and its surrender is a somewhat existential issue,' he said, giving it his best shot. 'When someone decides to change their status and go from a virgin to a deflowered girl, they're actually making a decision about choosing a character for themselves. The moment at which the body is enjoyed by someone else is a moment, in fact, of great gravity and it's not actually as trivial as we make out.'

Obviously the thought of making a feature film for a big American studio had its attractions beyond the purely artistic, but Miller and Melly found it an uncongenial experience, and they were soon at odds with Columbia and with producer Hal Chester. 'I did it because I thought it was a marvellous opportunity for doing a piece of social realism of the fifties. Instead, the stupid producers wanted to update it because they thought the fifties were out of date. They knew nothing about England and were only interested in making money out of the Swinging 'Sixties craze . . . There were also tremendous pressures on us to make it more sexy. I shot a necking session with both people fully clothed and they made me do another shot with the man stripped to the waist. We wanted an awkward seduction scene with two girls in their poky flat, which would have been realistic and rather funny; but we had to make it a big house by the river. I was endlessly bullied to put in scenes we didn't want: "You've got to open it out. You're not making TV here." '

Melly feels that it's more Hal Chester's film than anyone else's. 'He was an old-type Hollywood man who bullied us unmercifully. I'd write dialogue and he'd say "Where's the beat?" I had to rewrite the bloody thing because I was desperate for money. The marriage of Chester and Jonathan was strange. Hal wanted more tit, Jonathan more art. I think he buggered both our chances – of me being able to write a screenplay again and Jonathan being asked to direct a full-length feature.'

The film, starring Hayley Mills (daughter of Sir John), Oliver Reed (nephew of Sir Carol) and Noel Harrison (son of Rex) plus Sheila Hancock and John Bird, contributed in a minor way to the death throes of Swinging London. Audiences and critics remained as unfulfilled as the men trying to bed Hayley. John Russell Taylor in *The Times*, wrote: 'The characters never begin to exist . . . To make matters worse, Mr Miller, as well as being noticeably ill-served by his continuity girl or editor or both, has elected to treat this light, rather silly social comedy as strong drama such as might make a meaningful statement on the human condition. Needless to say, it doesn't, and the film as a whole leaves one mystified as to why anyone thought it a good idea in the first place.'

No wonder Miller never returned to the arena of the Big Picture, although he did express a wish to film 'in a mogul-free world' a typically wide range of material: Kafka's *America* (since made admirably by Jean-Marie Straub), the novels of Svevo (which he was reading at the time of his *Merchant Of Venice*), and much of Dickens, especially *A Christmas Carol* – 'one of the first modern examples of psychotherapy'. Nearly twenty years on, at the Folio Society's Literary Dinner Debate, Miller was found vigorously proposing (and winning against Frederic Raphael) the motion, that 'Good literature is too substantial to fit through the lens of camera.'

In August 1963, after Miller had left *Beyond The Fringe*, he was guest film critic in four issues of *The New Yorker* while Brendan McGill was on vacation, ably demonstrating that had not more lucrative or more satisfying projects come his way, or if he could have accepted the existence of a refuse-collecting mole which is the life of a film critic, he could have made a living at it. He reviewed *The Great*

Escape – 'It seems strange that the Germans should be the constant foe, since this sort of masculine nostalgia is very Teutonic'; *The Leopard* – 'An expensive and unnecessary confidence trick that relies on the audiences having read the book'; and *The Nutty Professor* – 'A pictorial supplement to Richard Hofstadter's *Anti-Intellectualism in American Life*' in which he was able, unlike most Anglo-Saxon critics, to give Jerry Lewis the consideration he deserves and found the picture 'very funny'. 'Like Lenny Bruce, Lewis elicits favour by exploiting his schlemiel's licence to ape the heroes and villains of the youthful community.'

Yet Miller would never claim to be a man of the cinema. 'I have always been exhausted by all the bullshit you have to endure in order to get a film going. You can actually parley the film into existence for eighteen months. In eighteen months I would have done six stage productions.' Even in the theatre, he shows an impatience with the mechanics of the medium and would undoubtedly find tedious the day-to-day film-making grind of set-ups, lighting, takes and cutting. But that is not all. Miller professes to be far more interested in the way the brain receives images than in what it receives. At a lecture at the National Film Theatre in December 1988 he analysed the nature of cinematic movement or the pictorial illusion of it. It was a scientific rather than an aesthetic approach to the art. (The lecture was expanded into an *Equinox* programme for Channel 4 in 1989.) The audience was invited to watch an extract from *Vertigo* without any reference to context, aesthetics, character or plot but to see the effect the sequence has upon our perception of space and movement, and how the eye and brain are able to make sense of them, even when much other information is withheld.

When pressed by a member of the audience, itching to get back to more conventional NFT preoccupations, to name his favourite films, Miller reluctantly volunteered three that meant something to him: Disney's *The Reluctant Dragon* – he remembers the effect of the colour on his seven-year-old mind; *A Matter Of Life And Death* ('which I suppose is a rather silly film'); and then revealed that he was a *The Third Man* freak, having seen it umpteen times and visited the places in Vienna where it was shot. At the Café Mozart he asked one of the waiters, who appeared in the film, who among the cast he recalled seeing at the café. 'Zere vos Orson Velles und Carol Reed . . . und . . . und . . .' The man hesitated, trying to remember. 'Oh, und zere vos a sird man . . . '

V

Despite constant threats to return to medicine Jonathan Miller began his career proper as a theatre director in 1968, and has maintained it almost without a break for twenty years, becoming an important part of English theatrical life. He began modestly, away from the spotlight of London, at the Nottingham Playhouse with three classics: *The School For Scandal*, *The Seagull* (by another doctor-artist) and *King Lear*, the first play in a long preoccupation with the Bard.

Stuart Burge brought Jonathan in as associate director as soon as he was appointed Artistic Director of the Playhouse. Miller was 'extremely stimulating for the company, because he entertained them and his enthusiasm was infectious,' says Burge. 'I remember coming into the Green Room one day and it was rather like a doctor's surgery, with the members of the company all lined up with their ailments. He was very generous about that.'

In those days the London critics used to travel up to Nottingham and on the opening night of *School For Scandal*, Miller did the unheard-of thing. Before the curtain went up he gathered the scribes around him in the foyer and explained his concept of the play to them. His idea was to do away with 'our chocolate-box view of the eighteenth century – fans, minuets, lace handkerchiefs, lorgnettes and grand living ... people had to put up with draughty, badly furnished houses.' The cast largely had regional accents because 'it's very difficult to know what the English accent was in the eighteenth century. But there certainly wasn't any Edith Evans precision elocution, that's just a theatrical thing.' True to his Hogarthian vision, Lady Sneerwell was bald beneath her wig, and had an incurable cold; Lady Teazle's maid was pregnant and everybody was more unpleasant than usual. This approach to Restoration and eighteenth-century comedy was not new, but it was rare.

King Lear was staged with the minimum of properties and effects, influenced by Miller's memories of the Berliner Ensemble's *Mother Courage*. The production provided a firm frame for 58-year-old Michael Hordern's Lear, 'a very foolish fond old man'. An ingenious stroke was the casting of Frank Middlemass as the Fool, almost the same age as Lear: 'I see them both as old men – mirror images of folly, distinguished from one another only by their social station,' explained Miller. 'A foolish old king shadowed by a wise old fool.' (He has followed this conception even unto his 1989 Old Vic production of the play, although Eric Porter's king seems less of a fool, and the fool less of a sage.) Hordern played Lear twice again for Miller – on TV in 1975, when he was 64, and in 1982, at the age of 71. The Nottingham production of *King Lear* visited the National Theatre at the Old Vic in 1970 where Miller was to become an Associate Director.

The years 1969 and 1970 saw Miller on a non-stop Bard binge, directing no fewer than five Shakespeare plays, while knocking off *Take A Girl Like You* at Shepperton. In March 1969 he went back to his *alma mater* to direct a Cambridge undergraduate *Twelfth Night*, then *Lear*, followed by two of his most acclaimed productions, the late nineteenth-century *The Merchant Of Venice* at the National Theatre and the colonialist-conscious *The Tempest* at the Mermaid. In October 1970 he directed *Hamlet* for the student Oxford and Cambridge Shakespeare Company (or OCSC) at the Arts, Cambridge (later transferring to the Fortune in London for three weeks). This, according to Michael Billington, then second-string critic on *The Times*, confirmed 'Miller's status as one of our most intriguing contemporary Shakespearean directors'. Innovations in the production, which featured 22-year-old Oxford undergraduate Hugh Thomas in the title role, had the Ghost and Player King doubled, Osric silently shadowing Claudius throughout, and the play opening with Claudius's first speech to the court.

Miller, conscious of the encrustation of tradition that gathers quickly upon the classics, realises the need constantly to clean them up and keep them fresh. It is also true that artists, though long dead, continually change with the times. The main attraction of Shakespeare for Miller, besides the obvious one of indisputable dramatic greatness, is 'not that there is a central realisable intention in each play that we still continue to value, but because we are still looking for the possibility of unforeseen meanings . . . I may start with dry conceptual diagrams, but I never understand a piece until I listen to people speaking it.'

It was Kenneth Tynan, then Literary Manager of the National Theatre, who had persuaded Laurence Olivier to employ Miller to direct *The Merchant Of Venice*. One day, while making *Take A Girl Like You*, Miller got a message at the studio to say that Laurence Olivier was on the phone and wanted to speak to him.

'I thought it was Alan Bennett or Peter Cook. Anyway a hoax. I came to the phone and heard this voice saying, "Dear boy . . . This is Laurence Olivier here . . . Joanie wants to do *The Merchant Of Venice* and would love you to direct it." No question of him acting in it, no mention of that at all. "I would love to," I managed to say and I mentioned doing a nineteenth-century version. He said, "Whichever way you want to." '

Miller's idea came out of 'my hearing certain speeches, in my mind's ear, delivered in a way that was incompatible with a sixteenth-century setting. As a director I often respond negatively to a precedent and, in this case, I recoiled from the sentimental radiance that actresses bring to Portia's famous mercy speech ... In my mind's eye I saw Portia leaning impatiently across the table to say, "The quality of mercy is not strained" as if having laboriously to explain what should have been self-evident to someone too stupid to understand. This dispute was too ugly to be argued out in public. The courtroom disappeared and was replaced in my mind by a rather drab Justice's Chambers. When I reached this point, I began to realise that it would be an impossible location for the sixteenth century, but I did not want to set it in a modern era where all the twentieth-century notions of anti-Semitism would overwhelm the play.'

The 79-year-old Olivier, in his book *On Acting* (1986), remembers it rather differently. 'First of all I wanted to find a setting for *The Merchant Of Venice* which would give dignity and austerity. I hit upon 1880–5, that period when the Victorians had found their maturity. Tall hats and frock coats, a time of clean and polished fingernails. Fortunately Jonathan and my other associates agreed with my vision.'

Once the time shift had been decided upon, Miller, as usual, looked across to other arts for inspiration, in this case, photographs of Venice taken by the Count de Primoli at the end of the nineteenth century, and the novels of Adriatic mercantile life by Italo Svevo. He also saw the relationship between Antonio (Anthony Nichols) and Bassanio (Jeremy Brett) in terms of Oscar Wilde and Bosie, 'where a sad old queen regrets the opportunistic heterosexual love of a person whom he adored'. The central dilemma, however, as in all productions of this problematical play for late twentieth-century audiences, remained the portrayal of Shylock.

'Olivier began with the idea of being a grotesque, ornamentally Jewish figure and bought himself very expensive dentures, a big hook nose and ringlets. With the exception of the teeth, in which he had invested such a large amount of money that I did not feel justified in asking him to surrender them, he gradually lost the other excrescences,' Miller relates. Olivier wrote, 'I was determined to maintain dignity and not stoop physically and mentally to Victorian villainy. Not for me the long, matted hair, invariably red, the hooked nose and the bent back . . . That image of Shylock I had always seen as a caricature and an easy way out, not only making mock of the Jewish race but also of Shakespeare himself.' Shifting his attention away from the nose, Olivier then concentrated on the mouth. 'I had teeth made that totally altered the shape of my face. They pulled my mouth out and pushed my upper lip forward. Suddenly there he was, my Shylock. Months of sitting and staring at noses that didn't exist, and there it was all the time. The mouth was the thing . . . So I had my new teeth and immediately I felt right. My only concern was that Jonathan Miller might take one look and confiscate them. But I think he was so relieved that I hadn't put on a false nose, he willingly let me keep them.' Although Olivier claimed more credit for the conception of the production than warranted, he did give Miller credit here. 'Slowly he made me see myself as others saw me. He wanted to help me out of it. I'd made a mountain out of mannerisms and had ended up impersonating myself. It's a habit that old actors fall for very easily. Miller opened my eyes and made me look in the mirror again.'

The updating bore fruit in making Shylock less offensive to Jews by making him almost indistinguishable in dress and looks from the ship-owning Antonio; Merchant and money-lending Banker tied together by their positions in a greedy philistinic society. Of course, the line 'You call me misbeliever, cut-throat dog, And spit upon my Jewish gaberdine' is slightly meaningless when uttered by a clean-shaven Shylock in morning suit, gold spectacles, top hat and carrying a silver-topped cane. But the character gains in pathos because he is brought low from an ostensibly assimilated and initially dignified position.

There were some amusing perversities, like having Lorenzo (Malcolm Reid) played as a pipe-smoking bore whose unpoetic rendering of 'The moon shines bright. In such a night as this . . .' sends Jessica (Jane Lapotaire) to sleep, and the very funny casket scene which has the Prince of Morocco (Tom Baker) resembling a negro minstrel. Joan Plowright, the *raison d'être* of the production in the first place, was a splendid, forthright Portia, playing opposite her husband for the fifth time. It was the last of Olivier's great stage performances and the first of the best of Miller's productions.

Purists aside, most critics found the production stimulating, although qualifications abounded. Rather revealingly, the *Plays And Players* reviewer Peter Ansorge commented that 'Olivier's Shylock isn't a Jew, but an actor with a Jewish director up his sleeve. For this reason the rehearsals . . . may have been more engaging to watch than the actual performance which, to my mind, reveals just a few pale flickers of meaning borrowed from an original luminous conception.' This complaint was one that would dog Miller for most of his career. Critics' views, like those of some people about having a baby, have often found the conception more enjoyable than the result.

Miller had first met Olivier informally at parties after *Beyond The Fringe*. As Miller recalled in the book *Olivier – In Celebration* in 1987, 'He saw the show and was, I suspect, slightly irritated by our Shakespeare sketch. He had sat in a box and it got backstage that he was not conspicuously amused. My first professional contact with him was when Ken Tynan edited a TV programme called *Tempo* which was commercial TV's answer to *Monitor*. With his wonderful flair for what is fashionable, Tynan had asked us to do a regular satirical spot. In the opening programme there was a pastiche of C P Snow written by Alan Bennett, a high-table scene of people drinking, wearing gowns and so forth, and bandying conversation about. On the same programme Larry was being interviewed by George Harewood about the opening of Chichester. We were on first but we began "corpsing". There were two takes, three takes, and Larry was obviously amused by the fact that the young lads couldn't do it. By the fourth take we could see him getting more and more impatient at these dreadful amateurs. It took something like twenty takes before we got it right, by which time he was thoroughly nettled, if only because we'd kept him waiting so long.'

A few years after *The Merchant of Venice*, Miller gave an interview about Olivier for Logan Gourlay's book *Olivier* in which he was fairly negative and indiscreet about the Great Actor. It was sent in page proof to Lady Olivier for her approval, and she was distressed by the interview and phoned Miller to tell him. Only then realising that his words might have been wounding, he paid £700 to the publisher to have it removed from the book. Miller never directed Olivier again and has only worked once more with Plowright, in *The Taming Of The Shrew* in 1972 at Chichester.

VI

Twenty-eight years separate Jonathan Miller's two productions of *The Tempest* but the basic concept remains the same. The guiding principle came from the 1956 Otto Mannoni book, *Prospero And Caliban*, which used the master-servant relationship of the play as the archetype of the colonial experience. Interviewed before the 1988 version at the Old Vic, Miller foresaw what the 'whingeing critics' were going to say: 'They'll all say, "Oh, this is what he did before." But thinking in these fields has matured and expanded in those two decades, and I need to amplify and improve on the ideas I had then.' Like Karajan repeatedly recording Beethoven symphonies over the years, Miller regards some of his productions of classics as 'unfinished business' and has continued to reproduce them in the light of new experience.

Both in the 1970 *Tempest* at the Mermaid and in the later one, the idea of making Prospero a 'paternal white imperial conqueror' and Caliban and Ariel black native people, 'the rightful inhabitants of the island', seemed to spring naturally from the play itself without having a scheme imposed upon it. As it happens, most theatre critics, whom Miller likes to call 'invertebrates', had been slouching spinelessly in the stalls for so many years that many of them did react the second time round as he had predicted. Yet there were audiences, who weren't around in 1970, who came fresh to this interpretation of the play, even more than did the director.

Inevitably the slant on the work was altered by the different casts except for Rudolph Walker, who repeated his West-Indian-accented Caliban, age making him a nobler savage. (Walker had also appeared as Babu, the slaves' leader, in Miller's production of *Benito Cereno* in 1964-5.) Graham Crowden's Prospero was less sympathetic and therefore closer to the Mannoni coloniser than Max Von Sydow's glowing but tortured personality, surrounded by the aura of Ingmar Bergman's films. Norman Beaton played Ariel as 'a Patrice Lumumba figure, a French-speaking, Sorbonne-educated, fly-whisk-wielding, ironic, well-spoken figure, obedient rather than servile, who was constantly and ironically pressing for his liberty, and waiting only for the moment when the white master will disappear to take control himself'. The ending, not in Shakespeare, has Ariel picking up his ex-master's broken staff and mending it in order to take power. Caliban remains enslaved, except that he will kiss a black foot instead of a white one. This worked even less well in the 1988 *Tempest* because Cyril Nri's Ariel was an altogether lighter, more puckish character, whom it is difficult to imagine in an authoritarian capacity.

In a sense, this Millerian ending can be taken as paternalistic and reactionary: one justification for colonialism has always been the idea that the colonising nation, however unjust the situation seems, will do a better job of running the colonised country than the indigenous population, a view often uttered by the South African regime, whose view of the blacks as children has automatically and conveniently kept them from growing or advancing. But the director is also suggesting the cyclical Viconian view of history, a belief he takes McLuhan to task for holding, in which actual progress is impossible. Despite certain conceptual weaknesses in both productions, a strong colonial parable emerged without obscuring the ethical theme of forgiveness and reconciliation. More importantly, the Mermaid production gave the first intimation that Miller might make an opera producer, not only because of his antipathy towards naturalism but for his 'musical' approach to the work. The similarities in themes and characters between *The Tempest* and *The Magic Flute* have been pointed out by, among others, Sir Michael Tippet: Prospero-Sarastro, Papageno-Trinculo, Ferdinand-Tamino, Miranda-Pamina and, even more in Miller's production, Caliban-Monostatos.

VII

In October 1970 Jonathan Miller announced that he was returning to medicine: 'After *Danton's Death*, which I'm doing for the National Theatre in the spring, I shall just direct something I particularly want to now and then, in the vacations.'

Earlier in the year Miller had become a member of a study group at the Royal Society, investigating the nature of human expression: what hand movements are, what eye movements mean, the reasons why people smile or laugh at a particular moment. From 1970 to 1973 he became a Research Fellow in History of Medicine at University College, London, where he was to be found in a small room, eight hours a day, poring over tomes on Mesmerism, phrenology and spiritualism. He believes that in such 'crank subjects' can be seen the 'grass roots of psychoanalysis'. All this was to form the basis for a book he hoped to write on nineteenth-century medicine. Nearly two decades later, Miller, who has a couple of dozen box files full of material on Mesmerism in his home, has yet to write it.

'I find writing quite hard,' he admits. 'There is no substitute for organised written thought. I suppose I'm frightened of having to confront it.' The fact is, he has himself been mesmerised by the bright lights. Like the hero of Graham Greene's *Ministry Of Fear*, he is drawn irresistibly to the fête, 'a helpless victim to the distant blare of the band and the knock-knock of wooden balls against coconuts'. As Miller says, 'There is an air of carnival and festivity that is attractive.' Medicine did not cure his addiction to theatre and he continues to need his 'fix'.

During the years at UCL, Miller did try to cut down on his theatrical activities. He had already committed himself to *Danton's Death* in 1971 but his only other production of the year was *Julius Caesar* for the Oxford and Cambridge Shakespeare Company. In 1972 he confined himself to *School For Scandal* and *The Taming Of The Shrew* in England, and *Richard II* at the Ahmanson Theater in Los Angeles with Richard Chamberlain. With the student company, as Miller was later to find at Kent Opera and with the National Theatre's shoestring touring Theatre-Go-Round, he felt able to take more risks when less money was involved. Again prowling the art galleries for a painter who would provide a strong visual base for a production, Miller found that De Chirico's architectural surrealism coincided with his image of *Julius Caeser*, an attempt to 'reconcile in one format all the conflicting themes – Roman antiquity, the Renaissance and the faint implications of modern Italian Fascism which I did not want to make explicit but to hint at'. He did not think, however, that 'modernising and presenting it as a play about a totalitarian state is either justified or interesting'. (One of the most famous and acclaimed twentieth-century productions of the play was by Orson Welles in 1937, set in Nazi Germany.) Miller offers an Adlerian power dream, opening, not with the crowd scene but with a frozen tableau of Caesar, a cigar-smoking grandee in a white suit giving orders to his henchmen. But the lack of political or social context did diminish much of the play's vitality and passion, with the mob being reduced to a speechless, humming, masked crowd, and the characters to puppets.

This manoeuvring of characters as marionettes of history was also manifest in his National Theatre production of Georg Büchner's *Danton's Death*, adapted and translated by John Wells. The set (by Patrick Robertson) was a sinister museum with a series of oblong, gauze cases containing costumed decapitated models. As the central conflict of the play revolves around the passionate pragmatist Danton and the cold dogmatist Robespierre, and is clearly on the former's side, a coolly analytical Robespierrian production defeats the purpose. Charles Kay was a chillingly persuasive Robespierre but Christopher Plummer was a rather miscast Danton, both physically and emotionally – he lacked the complexities of character brought out by Patrick Wymark and Brian Cox in two other productions. Perhaps too Miller himself was miscast for the difficult but often extraordinary play. However, John Barber in *The Daily Telegraph*, thought it 'beautiful to look at, finely acted', and concluded that 'Dr Miller's farewell production is his masterpiece.'

Miller's 1972 approach to *School for Scandal* did not differ markedly from his Nottingham Playhouse production a few years before. Again it was set in Hogarthian squalor, with all the gilt stripped from the gingerbread. This time he had the National Theatre's money to lavish on the seediness and a stronger cast, including Ronald Pickup and John Shrapnel as the Surface brothers, Paul Curran as Sir Peter, Denis Quilley as Crabtree and, way down the list, Maureen Lipman in a small part as a maid. Apparently, during rehearsals, Quilley was having some trouble in capturing his reprehensible character. Miller was able to set him on the right track by saying, 'Think of Ned Sherrin.' This anecdote is repeated graciously by Sherrin himself.

At Chichester, Miller tackled *The Taming Of The Shrew*, the first of three goes at it, two on stage, one on television. Like *The Merchant Of Venice* and to some extent *Measure For Measure*, *The Shrew* contains cultural values that the modern liberal theatre-goer finds unpalatable, usually overriding the universality and timelessness always attributed to Shakespeare. It is this very problem that attracts Miller to the play. Eschewing a contemporary feminist interpretation, he tried to look at the play on its own terms, recognising the 'Tudor social ideas of the function of the woman in the household without agreeing with them'. The prevailing view, reflected by Shakespeare, was that 'It is meet that our English housewife be a woman of great modesty and temperance as well inwardly as outwardly. Inwardly, as in her behaviour and carriage towards her husband, wherein she shall shun all violence of rage, passion and humour, coveting less to direct than to be directed, appearing ever unto him pleasant, amiable and delightful ... ' (Gervase Markham 1615). In fact, seeing Kate (Joan Plowright) converted to the values of her society by finally submitting to Petruchio (Anthony Hopkins), a close-cropped grizzled Puritan squire, is more likely to evoke the audience's assumed consensus feminism than if she seems aware of an injustice, or gives in to him with irony.

VIII

Despite complaining that the three productions in 1972 held up his research work at University College, as well as delaying a monograph on Sir Charles Sherrington, 'the Darwin of neurology' and, of course, his book on Mesmerism, Miller asked Peter Hall, when he took over the National Theatre from Laurence Olivier in November 1973, if he could join the company as an associate director. Although he had spent some six months, on and off, writing over half of the Sherrington book and its impending publication was announced, he got badly blocked and it was never completed. 'Partly because it was too difficult. I would have had to write a text book on elementary neurology before I could go into the details of neuropsychology as they existed in 1906. There was a difficulty of getting it all in.'

In April 1973 therefore, Miller, with Harold Pinter and John Schlesinger, was appointed associate director at the Old Vic, joining Michael Blakemore (an associate since 1971), Laurence Olivier and Peter Hall (co-directors until Olivier's retirement). Hall noted in his diary, at the first meeting of them all, that 'a great deal of Guinness and champagne was drunk as a celebrating ritual. Larry was very pleasant, if a little over-humble; and the baroque fantasies of Miller's conversational style were occasionally checked by Harold Pinter saying "What do you mean?" or "Would you mind saying that again?" '

While Miller optimistically awaited the call from Hall or Olivier to direct his first National production under his new contract, he took on a couple of plays; *The Seagull* at Chichester and John Marston's *The Malcontent* at the Nottingham Playhouse. His second shot at the Chekhov was more mature than his first attempt at Nottingham four years before. Penelope Wilton (Masha), Robert Stephens (Trigorin) and Irene Worth (Madame Arkadina) were allowed ample room to develop their characters in a non-fussy production, the setting on the open stage consisting of back projections. At Nottingham, a town where 'I thought I'd be happy to live until they started to foul it up', the rarely done Marston tragi-comedy, written in 1604 for the children's company at Blackfriars, was given a farcical slant, taking its cue from John Wells's adaptation. Derek Godfrey was a fine Malevole, the deposed and banished duke who returns to Genoa in disguise to watch the widespread cuckoldry, but the stylised production, with much use of *commedia dell'arte* masks and white faces, over-refined Marston's already self-conscious play. It was at Nottingham that Miller first worked with the designer Patrick Robertson and performers like Penelope Wilton and Peter Eyre (both in his 1989 *King Lear* at the Old Vic), to whom he has been extremely loyal over the years.

Now everybody held their breath to see what exciting things Miller would do at the Old Vic, but they had to hold it beyond human capability. First, like a teenager given a moped before being allowed a motorbike, he was permitted towards the end of 1973 to take a £500 production of *Measure For Measure* on the road as part of the National Theatre's Theatre-Go-Round. Miller thought it 'one of the best productions I have ever worked on . . . It was a wonderful experience, the atmosphere was intense and companionable without any sense of self-importance as we all knew we had nothing to lose and everything to gain.' Financial restrictions dictated costumes and scenery – the main set consisted of a row of doors taken off a building site – and the period was shifted from Renaissance Vienna to Freud's Vienna, more effective in the dramatic than in the comic parts.

At the beginning of 1974 the theatre bug had bitten deeper through Miller's thin skin. Hall notes that over dinner one night 'He went on talking until one o'clock about play after play. At this moment in his life he wants to direct everything. He said with engaging frankness, "Only time stops me from doing ten productions a year." ' But Miller directed only two further productions for the National, not enough to satisfy his Rabelaisian craving to absorb and display the world's drama.

Neither Beaumarchais's *The Marriage Of Figaro*, in a new English version by John Wells, nor Peter Nichols's *The Freeway* can be put down as a success. The former had incidental music composed by Carl Davis (who has since helped revitalise silent film classics by writing new scores for them); choreography by Eleanor Fazan, the director of *Beyond The Fringe*, and a cast that included Derek Godfrey as Count Almaviva, Gemma Jones a much younger Countess, and Gawn Grainger and Nicola Pagett as Figaro and Susanna. It included the joyous *Vaudeville* at the end, usually omitted in the frequent French productions of the play.

After the first preview, Hall wrote in his diary, 'A dreadful evening. Granted it was the first time the actors had met an audience. But since I saw rehearsals, the comic business has grown and the seriousness has been entirely lost. The whole play comes over as a charade with comic bagpipe music. I talked to Jonathan, who seemed very worried. I urged him to go back to his beginnings – his original conception – to make the play clear and hard. Trust the play, not the jokiness. And cut down on the bagpipes.' After the first night Hall noted that 'Jonathan has cut a lot of nonsense, and tightened and hardened things considerably. There is now a joy in the actors which does communicate to the audience. But the serious dialectic of the piece is not there. If it were, the play would be funnier. Apart from a scene where Figaro shaves the Count and one feels the imminent presence of steel at the aristo's neck, there is virtually no conflict. Above all I am bewildered by Jonathan's direction. He's an enigma, whose work I like and dislike in equal measure. That, I suppose, is talent. The great shout of pleasure that greeted the end of the play proves that we have got away with it. But getting away with it is not much satisfaction.'

Certainly not much satisfaction was given to or gained from the critics, who, while finding intrinsic interest in the enterprise, did not fully appreciate some of the humour, mistaking the broader social satire of Beaumarchais's *folle journée* for Da Ponte's more compassionate but less subversive libretto. 'I always get mixed reviews. There would be something wrong if I met total approval,' Miller says.

In the case of *The Freeway*, the first play by a living playwright that Miller had directed since his work with Robert Lowell, he says: 'I knew it was bad and everyone had a right to say it was rotten. I shouldn't have chosen it.'

Nichols was present at almost every rehearsal, 'so that whatever I introduced was subject to his criticism and I was very careful in this particular case not to let my imagination run riot. The possibility of this happening was limited by the much more detailed readability of the social details written into the play.' The play's two-hour traffic concerned a gigantic tailback more than 80 miles long on the freeway of the title. Waiting for it to clear are a working-class couple (Paul Rogers and Irene Handl) and a peer and his old-fashioned mother (Graham Crowden and Rachel Kempson). Despite the fine cast of veterans and a striking set by John Bury (a large, gleaming caravan), this ponderous parable met with a cool reception. Miller resigned from the National in the spring of 1975 with some acrimony.

In *Subsequent Performances* Miller wrote, 'I came up against a form of executive ambition on the part of Peter Hall which I found totally impossible ... the endless discussions about what we ought to be doing in the theatre were too boring. I do not think the theatre is important enough to bear such bureaucratic scrutiny. For me, what is attractive about the stage is contained in the name of what it is we do: it is a play and is playful. But suddenly it became an institution that was grandly self-important. The committee approach became too engrossed in its own deliberations.'

Like Alice in the White Rabbit's house, Miller felt cramped and uncomfortable at the National Theatre under Hall. One of the first things he suggested at a creative meeting was for the door of Peter Hall's office to be taken off the hinges, so that he could be accessible to all and sundry. This was greeted as if Miller himself were unhinged. At another meeting Miller proposed that he should do an all-male version of *The Importance Of Being Earnest*. He was sharply opposed in this by Harold Pinter, defending the writer's corner: if Wilde had wanted the women's roles to be played by men, he would have said so, a fruitless argument that could extend to any updating of a classic, and nothing really to do with the value or otherwise of the idea. ('If Shakespeare had wanted to set *Julius Caesar* in Fascist Italy, he would have said so.') In 1967 the National had put on a successful all-male *As You Like It* which was fallaciously claimed to be as played in Shakespeare's time, though the 26-year-old Ronald Pickup's Rosalind was hardly the unbroken-voiced unbearded boy of Elizabethan theatre. Whether seeing Cecily portrayed by a man in skirts, or changed to Cecil, would have added to the play is a matter for conjecture, but as Miller writes, 'The validity of any idea can emerge only when it is tried out, and the one way a director can justify himself is by seeing if a production works.'

Peter Hall, who claimed to be neutral in the argument, though *Earnest* in *travesti* was never put on, commented that he recognised something of himself in Miller's anger at not being able to do what he wanted: 'A desire to be an outsider in any organisation, to be the victim of authority, and to use that victimisation to collect sympathy and to go one's way.' The importance of the *Earnest* episode is that it aggravated an already soured relationship between the new Artistic Director and Miller. 'I didn't get on with Hall,' Miller says. 'I couldn't bear his discourse. I thought he was a vulgar philistine. He was starstruck. He was excited by Schlesinger because he had directed movies, and Pinter because he was a millionaire. Blakemore and I were unglamorous workhorses.'

In November 1980 the Hall-Miller feud surfaced again in an article in *The Sunday Times* entitled 'The Grizzled Cherub', written to celebrate Sir Peter's 50th birthday. In it, Hall says that the attack on him by Miller and Michael Blakemore, when he took over from Laurence Olivier, was spurred on by the late Kenneth Tynan and encouraged by Olivier himself: 'My mistake was to try to keep two of Olivier's people, for continuity, who both thought they should have got my job. That was a grave error,' Hall confessed. 'Miller said to some of our actors recently "It must be awful to wake up each morning and find that you're Peter Hall." Well, it isn't. Jonathan is very paranoid. But I was a useful target; it always happens if one has some power.' In a letter to the paper the following week, Miller wrote: 'The suggestion that my criticisms were encouraged by the late Ken Tynan is even more absurd. I saw Mr Tynan once or perhaps twice before his death and since the poor man was fighting for what little life was left in him, he had neither the energy nor the interest to ghost the campaign which Sir Peter suspects . . . I've never had the slightest interest in running a large theatrical institution. I do not expect justice from Sir Peter Hall, but he would do himself a service by recognising that sustained opposition is not necessarily prompted by base or self-seeking motives.'

The soft-spoken, rather avuncular Sir Peter Hall claims to bear Miller no ill will and is genuinely puzzled by Jonathan's animosity towards him. 'I really cannot understand why in interview after interview he continually feels the need to revile me. I can only think that it is something deep in his psychology that dates from his schooldays. There was really no need for him to resign from the National Theatre, although I don't think Jonathan is a natural collaborator, or that he enjoys being in any situation where he cannot have his own way.'

Miller was never asked back to direct another play for the National while Hall was in charge and he continues to feel the same way about large artistic institutions. He scorns Covent Garden, although he has not been asked to direct there. The gossip is that his name has come up at meetings but that the consensus has been that he is 'too lightweight and undisciplined'. He has done one production at Glyndebourne (*The Cunning Little Vixen*) and has only worked once (*The Taming Of The Shrew*, 1987) for the Royal Shakespeare Company. However, a hatred of institutions did not prevent his taking on the 1980-1 BBC Television Shakespeare season or the artistic directorship of the Old Vic, returning, this time, as captain not boatswain of 'a small sailing vessel, not a luxury liner'.

Miller did direct *The Importance Of Being Earnest* in March 1975 at the Greenwich Theatre, while unemployed by the National and before resigning from it. He cast from both sexes and now thinks the all-male idea was a bad one; he professes a distaste for this play, and others, in which 'people speak in epigrams'.

The 426-seat Greenwich Theatre put Miller in the position where he is happiest – at the helm – and provided him with a refuge from the politics and back-biting at the Old Vic. His season there placed *The Seagull*, with virtually the same cast and production as at Chichester, beside *Ghosts* and *Hamlet* under the generic title of *Family Romances*. Miller explained: 'In each play you have a young man who has a different moral and spiritual problem as a result of a mother either losing or overthrowing her husband and entering into a relationship with another man keenly resented by the young hero. This right-angled triangular relationship of the son, mother, lover, plus absent father means that the young man is prevented from realising and fulfilling his proper erotic relationship to a lover of his own.'

The juxtaposition of works with a common or tangential theme is more often seen at the National Film Theatre than in the theatre: previous examples were the Marlowe-Shakespeare couplings of *Edward II* with *Richard II* and *The Jew Of Malta* with *The Merchant Of Venice*. There is much to be said for it, as Miller's season demonstrated, because it gave the plays a different resonance. Irene Worth played Madame Arkadina, Mrs Alving and Gertrude; Peter Eyre was Konstantin, Oswald and Hamlet; Nicola Pagett was Masha, Regina and Ophelia; and Robert Stephens Trigorin, Pastor Manders and Claudius.

Irene Handl, who had been in *The Freeway* at the National and had tried to get her part made larger, was asked by Miller to play Lady Bracknell in his Greenwich production of *The Importance Of Being Earnest*, an unusual choice of a lovable character actress who had made her name as a chirpy cockney in many of the Boulting Brothers films, although she had played Miss Prism in a television production. As Miller has always liked to 'respond negatively to a precedent', he thought of Handl because she was a far cry from the imperious Edith Evans. There were problems during rehearsals in trying to get Handl to find the right tone until Miller, in desperation, hit on the idea of essaying the role with a German accent – after all, many of the aristo-crats and even Queen Victoria had married Germans. It worked in a remarkably fresh way, with the famous line coming out as 'A handbeg!' It also resulted in the cutting of Lady Bracknell's lines on the respectability of the German language. This incurred the wrath of John Peter in *The Sunday Times* who thought that the idea was as painful 'as having Algy played by an Eskimo'. *The Financial Times* critic, B A Young, commented: 'It's almost impossible not to enjoy *The Importance Of Being Earnest*, but you can rely on Jonathan Miller to try and stop it.'

There was a proposal to couple two Shakespeare plays, *Measure For Measure* and *All's Well That Ends Well* under the generic title of 'Bed Tricks' (both use the same medieval device of a substituted bedfellow) at the Greenwich in 1975, but only the latter was performed. 'In this production,' wrote *Sunday Times* critic Harold Hobson, 'Mr Miller refrains from any attempt at brilliance. The splendour of courtly life is represented only by a bench and an empty stage.' The solemn and simple staging (and Penelope Wilton's Helena) brought some veracity and sincerity to one of Shakespeare's most synthetic and unpleasant plays.

In the following year he directed *The Three Sisters* at the Cambridge Theatre. 'I reacted against the genteel approach, trying to make the work much coarser and more comic,' Miller claimed, and Janet Suzman, who played Masha, said 'Jonathan decided that the best way to approach the characters was through laughter. It became a play of serious hilarity.' Strangely enough, although it was bitterly comic, and the text was edited down somewhat, the stylised production moved at a leisurely tempo that sometimes presumed that slowness and atmosphere were synonymous. But there were richly nuanced performances against sets that were Austerity 1976.

IX

Around the mid-1970s the allure of directing plays was beginning to diminish for the artistic grasshopper. He had found another part of the magic garden to play in. Over the next decade Miller directed five times as many operas as stage plays. He was asked to direct his first opera in 1974. *Arden Must Die*, based on the anonymous late sixteenth-century play *Arden Of Faversham*, was the first opera by the contemporary British composer Alexander Goehr. Born in Germany in 1932, the son of the conductor Walter Goehr, he is now professor of music at Trinity Hall, Cambridge.

The work had been premiered in Hamburg seven years previously and now the New Opera Company was to give it three performances at Sadler's Wells, and thought that as Miller had done Elizabethan theatre, he would be an interesting choice as director. The opera, based on the libretto of Erich Fried (who died in 1988), told of the murder of Thomas Arden, ex-mayor of Faversham in Kent, by his wife and her lover. For some reason unknown to the composer, Miller decided to set it in late Victorian times. Miller explains that he thought there was something Dickensian about it but Goehr, who 'would sooner trust my kidneys to Jonathan than an opera of mine again', felt that Miller didn't really understand the music. 'For example, in the opera there is an attempted murder. But that is in the orchestra. Jonathan didn't hear it. Whereas the director in Germany, a follower of Brecht, understood that. Neither did he understand what singers need. Most of them are arseholes and need to be given much more. They don't want concepts, they want to know where to stand.'

The director, on the other hand, had 'an enormously thrilling time' working on his first opera and loved working with a living composer. Goehr, however, could not have been much heartened by Miller's views, expressed before the performances of *Arden*, that 'The performing arts have been dogged by a sort of hideous pedantic romanticism about the obligation that we owe to the author or to the originator of the work. We owe him nothing at all.'

On the whole, the critics greeted Miller's entry into opera with raspberries rather than with trumpets, finding that the production lacked dramatic impact. 'Where was the enormously imaginative understanding of character and the inventive stageplay to be found in Dr Miller's *Merchant Of Venice* (for example), where his ability to recreate a work in his own, often revealing terms?' asked *Opera* magazine. In Goehr's opinion, 'He didn't let his very warm and personal talents go into the production.' The opera, influenced by Brechtian *Lehrstück* methods, is a package of closed forms which needs to be done in a very stylised manner, whereas the flatness of Miller's production killed it off, in the memory of those who saw it.

Undeterred by these mainly negative reactions, the small, subsidised, touring Kent Opera (founded in 1969) decided to take Miller up and in their company he flowered into one of the most commanding, controversial and celebrated of opera producers in Britain. Miller began to regard Kent as the only safe home for a director: 'It specialises in works that have been over-produced in an effort to make their moral diction more audible by taking the din out of them,' he proclaimed. 'A lot of operas, kidnapped by the grand houses, have been de-natured by magnification. There is far too much Zeffirrealism.'

His seven productions for the company between 1974 and 1982 were all by composers who weren't around to carp at anything he did. The first was *Così Fan Tutte*, which he claimed he had always wanted to do but 'not having proved myself in opera there was no chance of doing it for a big company . . . with a small budget . . . your feel your imagination is released'. It was the start of a sequence by the team of Miller, Roger Norrington (conductor), Bernard Culshaw (designer) and Nick Chelton (lighting designer) which, according to the critic Michael Ratcliffe, had 'a harmony, pattern and logic to it equalled only by his work on the BBC Shakespeare'. Miller certainly did most of his best work with Kent Opera, where it is easier to take an opera as a workshop vehicle and readily communicate your ideas to young singers willing to respond to them.

Most people remember the staging of *Così* for what it didn't have rather than what it did. There was no Bay of Naples or Vesuvius, nor was there much Rococo in evidence. In fact, Miller saw the third and last Da Ponte-Mozart opera of 1790 as a Neo-Classical work, 'something elegant and precise, like the Jane Austen of *Mansfield Park*'. Financial restrictions also had something to do with it. Miller responded to an observation in Robert Rosenblum's *Transformations In Late 18th-Century Art* that 'late eighteenth-century artists squashed the action into a shallow rectangle that lay parallel to the picture plane . . . we created a back wall similar to those curtained-off back walls you find in the paintings of David . . . I used a wall pierced by two classical doorways, which again emphasised the symmetries of the entrances and exits so that it was almost as if the characters were coming and going like figures in a weather vane.'

He also brought *Così* forward beyond the date of its setting and composition, an attempt to move it away from 'apfel-strudel comedy' into a less frivolously perceived period. Other reasons of his for temporal transpositions have been, in the most simple terms, to increase the relevance of a work for a contemporary audience (*Tosca* set in Fascist Italy) or to strip off the patina of tradition (the non-Japanese *Mikado*), the sort of exercises that have been readily accepted, save by artistic fundamentalists, for over half a century.

A further incentive to update an opera, more contentious in the reasoning than in practice, is the need to bridge the discrepancy between the composer's music and the period in which it is set. Miller has expressed his irritation at the 'implausibility' of mid-nineteenth-century romantic music being heard at the mid-sixteenth-century court of the Gonzagas in *Rigoletto*. The theory is, if you can't change the music, set it in the period of its composition, which he did at Kent. The company, however, rejected the idea of placing the action in Al Capone's Chicago of the 1920s – but seven years later, Rigoletto, Gilda *et al* found themselves set in Little Italy, New York in the 1950s at the Coliseum. If this became common practice there would be more 'plausible' productions of *Electra* set in the Greece of 1909, *Turandot* in the China of 1926 and *Moses Und Aaron* in the Israel of 1957.

Of course, the majority of operas take place in an era that predates the style of music or singing used and Miller is meticulously selective in what he chooses to update. He feels that in most nineteenth-century operas 'the director is relieved of the obligation of considering the punctuality of the setting' because 'composers and librettists dealt rather carelessly with the past. The anchorage of the work to the period in which it's said to happen is loose and very provisional anyway. The past is simply a sort of Madame Tussaud's – other elsewheres.' However, no matter what the dialectic behind Miller's productions, the proof is in the putting on. Rodney Milnes, the opera critic, found the Kent *Rigoletto* to be 'Jonathan Miller's first indisputably great staging. The up-dating to time of composition worked: the immediacy of the action and the emotional quirks behind it were horribly direct . . . The first night was an occasion I shall never forget.'

The same year saw Miller at Glyndebourne, for the first and only time, directing the 1975 Festival's opener, Janacek's *The Cunning Little Vixen*. As in his TV *Alice* he rejected the 'pantomime cat' type costumes for the animal characters in favour of stylised nineteenth-century peasant clothes, cleverly avoiding any cute *Bambi* or Beatrix Potter association. This resulted in greater poignancy, without any loss in the humour or anthropomorphic points. There was also a clever use of back projections which altered dimensions according to the size of the humans and animals in front of it. Of this episode, Miller said later, 'I know it was a fairly contemptible business. I don't mean doing the opera, but for that particular audience. However, the working conditions were ideal.' (The ubiquitous Miller directed a well-received revival for Frankfurt in 1977.)

On his return to Kent Opera the following year, he tackled

Monteverdi's *La Favola D'Orfeo* (The Legend Of Orpheus), known simply as *Orfeo*. 'I'm attracted by very hieractic and artificial operas,' Miller
says. The production, managing to conjure up the epoch in which the
opera was written, the conducting of Norrington, an expert of the music
of that period, and a clear English translation, allowed one of the earliest
of performed operas to communicate with today's audience. To visualise
it, 'I had to think of a painter or painters from the same period who
represented the antique. Poussin was the artist who came to mind . . .
Both use very restrained and formal structures to express a preference
for a passionate stoicism.' Not wanting to utilise blown-up reproductions
of Poussin, he asked Daniel Lang, an American landscape painter, to
copy the painting of 'Orpheus and Eurydice', 'knowing perfectly well
that someone as original and creative as Lang would automatically
introduce his own perspective in a twentieth-century rendition of Poussin', What emerged was Poussin 'abstracted', Xeroxed several times
and transformed on to revolving periactoids or 'Toblerones', as Miller
explained to a lecture audience at Sotheby's in relation to the production.

In order to help the singers and dancers imitate the gestures of the
figures shown in the paintings, a copy of Anthony Blunt's great work on
Poussin, *Catalogue Raisonnée*, was kept in the rehearsal rooms as a
reference – 'or, as we learned to call it after his arrest, the *Catalogue
Traisonnée*'. Is this dubbing with hindsight? As Blunt's espionage activities were only made public three years later, such a contemporary joke
would indicate that Miller had inside information. Could he have been
the fifth man?

Over the next few years Kent Opera had the advantage of Miller
bringing his intelligence and his painterly eye to bear on *Eugene Onegin*
(1977), *La Traviata* (1979), *Falstaff* (1980), and *Fidelio* (1982). For the
latter, he went to the war paintings of Goya, particularly the 'Caprichos'
and 'Disasters Of War'. Nick Chelton, the lighting designer, says that
'Jonathan taught me to look at paintings and I spent hours studying the
peculiar light of Goya's drawings and etchings.'

X

'The filming of the thirteen-week series of *The Body In Question*
[shown from November 1978] was enormous fun,' Miller said, plug-
ging the programmes on Michael Parkinson's TV chatshow. 'It took
me to a lot of places which I always wanted to go to. There is a very
extraordinary magic carpet feeling about writing anything for the

BBC – you find yourself writing a line about some place and suddenly you're there and it's almost like the Midas touch – be careful because you find yourself writing about places which you normally wouldn't wish to go to, and you suddenly find yourself conveyed there whether you want to or not; you're bound and gagged and deposited in the middle of Africa or somewhere so that in that sense it has been extraordinary.'

This sort of glorified epidiascope lecture had made academics like Dr Jacob Bronowski and Sir Kenneth Clark, working in the Judeo-Christian tradition, as much household names as TV comedians or today's soap-opera stars. They were concerned with popularising, exploring and eulogising Western Civilisation; with themselves acting as trusted ciceroni. Miller joined their ranks with his fantastic voyage through the body and the advances in scientific medicine that keep it going. For the none-too-squeamish lay person – Miller performed an autopsy on-camera – the doctor proved a magician who eliminated mystery with a wave of his elongated expressive fingers and banished old wives' tales at a flourish. What emerged was Miller as an instructive and humorous entertainer, at home in a subject for which he felt no apologies were needed. His strong belief in modern or conventional medicine has made him intolerant of those who seek remedies elsewhere. On the open-ended TV discussion programme *After Dark* in 1988 he defended the orthodox view passionately, swallowing up anybody who disagreed with him: 'Speaking as an atheist, I find your amorphous views blasphemous. Blasphemous in the rejection of a scientific body of evidence built up in the last fifty years.' In fact, it emerged that he thought homeopathy wasn't even worth rejecting, it was the people who believed in it that he couldn't stomach.

His fame magnified ten-fold by the TV camera, Miller returned from *The Body In Question* to dissecting the heart and soul of Mozart, Verdi and Shakespeare. While cohabiting happily with Kent Opera, he managed a few other opera productions on the side. The main rival for his attention was the English National Opera at the Coliseum, which was to become his second home and where he had more resources to realise the concepts in his mind's eye. *The Marriage Of Figaro* marked his debut at the ENO in 1978, the first of nine productions at the Coliseum. Miller must be one of the few directors to have staged both the play and the opera of *Figaro*.

Miller's movements in that period were rather in the nature of a character in a Feydeau farce dashing from one room to another in a hotel to satisfy different occupants unaware of each other. In late 1980 he was rehearsing *Falstaff* for Kent Opera in the morning, *Arabella* for the ENO in the afternoon, then going down to the BBC to supervise a couple of plays and direct one or two himself for the Shakespeare TV season. He would also find time to appear on chat shows, as well as popping up on the radio arts programme *Kaleidoscope* . . . and he gave interviews to any hack who managed to catch up with him.

The marriage of Miller and the ENO began well with *The Marriage Of Figaro* in 1978, the first of nine productions he did at the Coliseum. It was intelligent and convincing despite a tendency to explain things that are clearly being articulated in the music. One example will suffice. In the introduction to 'Porgi, Amor', when the Countess laments her lost love, her children are brought in. She kisses them good night sadly and sings on, as if her maternal attention to them is one reason the Count has tired of her. This upset many critics, including Alan Blyth in *Opera* who, pulling out the old 'good doctor' routine that drives the director into apoplectic invective, wrote in his otherwise favourable review that 'as a medical man, Jonathan Miller will understand my saying that the scene was "an excrescence on his production".' The children were expunged in later revivals.

Although *The Turn Of The Screw* (1979) takes place in a large house, Britten's eerie, claustrophobic chamber opera works much better in a small one. But the sheer forcefulness of the piece and Miller's lucid and uncluttered staging, though often posed and static, generally overcame the vastness of the Coliseum. The country house is seen as a back-projection in front of which is a glass-panelled arena where the battle for the soul of an innocent takes place; it was a shock to discover that automatic sliding doors were already in use in the nineteenth century. The decision to present the ghosts not as rarefied apparitions but as flesh and blood characters in the Governess's (and our) eyes, provided a greater threat but slightly lessened the complexity of her neurotic psyche.

Miller told the cast of *Falstaff* (1980) at one of the early rehearsals to 'Just goof it around,' and explained that 'Fun is not just a bit of business. Fun is the frivolous demonstration of the truth.' Although *Falstaff* is an ensemble opera for great voices, which Kent Opera lacked, and the sets seemed to suffer from budgetary considerations, fun and serious games carried the work. Money was not a problem with his *Otello* (1981) which, according to more than one critic, 'looked like the Cyprus branch of Habitat', but it was a very respectful production that allowed tenor Charles Craig to sing his first *Otello* in English.

There is a rumour that Miller arrived at the first rehearsal of *Arabella* (1980) and announced 'I've just heard the music. Not very good, is it?' The first collaboration between Miller and the ENO's Music Director Mark Elder nearly had the last Strauss-Hofmannsthal collaboration transposed from the Vienna of the 1860s to the late 1920s. As Miller explained, 'There is a certain irony in the fact that *Arabella* was written at the time when the sound of the goosestep was just beginning to be heard.' The fact that there is no sound of the goosestep in the music, and that the composer and librettist had purposefully set out to write a 'throwback' opera reminiscent of *Der Rosenkavalier* did not seem to worry him. If he had updated it the production would have suffered, in reverse, from exactly the discrepancy between setting and music that he had sought to rectify in his first *Rigoletto* production.

When Miller came to do what turned out to be his most celebrated, popular and successful production – the 1982 'Mafia' *Rigoletto* – he was able to put into practice what he had preached a few years before at Kent Opera. 'I noticed how consistent the plot was with something that could have taken place in another Italian community where people had absolute power of life and death over others, namely the world of *The Godfather* and the Italian Mafia. Since the music of the nineteenth century continues to be played and is influential in the Italian communities of the twentieth century, it seemed much less anachronistic, and a perfectly obvious and effortless transposition.'

Even before this *Rigoletto* played at the Metropolitan in New York it was found to be 'patently offensive to the Italian-American community'. However, with its sets out of Edward Hopper, the Duke of Mantua turned into a Godfather ('Duke') and singing 'La donna è mobile' to a jukebox; the production was an offer that the public on both sides of the Atlantic couldn't refuse. However, confining *Rigoletto* to only one element of society, a purely criminal one, does diminish the political force of Verdi's opera in which the Duke, who exerts such power, is the head of the state. Also, as Miller himself recognises, by placing it in 1950s New York, a setting that seemed remarkably at ease with the libretto (translated by James Fenton) and the music, another inconsistency was created – a linguistic one. 'I was tempted to recommend the use of recognisably American idioms, but the conductor [Mark Elder] resisted these changes in the belief that they would clash with Verdi's music. In the end we agreed to disagree and seeing the production after several revivals I still have serious misgivings about this discrepancy.' In his worrying about 'discrepancies' and 'inconsistencies' in an art form whose very nature is based on 'discrepancies' and 'inconsistencies', Miller often sounds like the expert on chairs who criticised a lamp because it couldn't be sat upon.

XI

In the hyper-active years between 1979 and 1982 Miller also launched a *Flying Dutchman* at Frankfurt, one of only two Wagner operas he's done, and jetted to St Louis, Missouri to direct his second *Così Fan Tutte*. In this he used his knowledge of Mesmer to introduce the magnetic bucket at the end of Act One. Miller explains that the twelve-year-old Mozart's *Bastien and Bastienne* 'was performed in Mesmer's garden. This evidently left an impression, and here is a back-handed tribute to his original sponsor that must be treated seriously if it is not to become an excuse for a lot of facetious theatrical horseplay.' An American critic found that Miller's production brought out the 'more introspective, serious and passionate aspects of this glowing score'.

This three-year period also included the British TV Bardathon, for which he was overall producer, and two returns to the 'legit' theatre with *She Would If She Could* at the Greenwich and his 'farewell' production, *Hamlet*, at the Donmar Warehouse in August 1982. The former, a rarely performed George Etherege Restoration comedy, involves the randy adventures of two young men about town, and two dissolute old men, all of whom have the seduction of two young ladies in their sights. Miller's stylised, pacy production showed some influence of his opera experience.

Out of the eleven plays in the BBC Television Shakespeare Miller directed six (*Troilus And Cressida, The Taming Of The Shrew, King Lear, Othello, Timon Of Athens* and *Antony And Cleopatra*), Jane Howell two (*The Winter's Tale, Henry VI*), Elijah Moshinsky two (*All's Well That Ends Well, A Midsummer Night's Dream*) and Jack Gold one (*The Merchant Of Venice*). The critic Shaun Sutton expressed the general view when he wrote that 'Miller made Shakespeare on TV exactly what it should be – fine actors delivering lines of genius in conditions of absolute clarity.' The series did spotlight some brilliant performances and illuminated much of the verse. Most of the visual style and settings derived from the Old Masters, which studio lighting brought to life not merely as *tableaux vivants* but as a lived-in space. Stuart Burge remembers meeting Jonathan in the lift of the BBC while Miller was filming *King Lear*. 'Every frame a Caravaggio!' the director exclaimed with supreme satisfaction. Sometimes this became rather self-conscious; often Miller's tendency to 'nudge-nudge' took over or became, as the title of the Amnesty show would have it, *A Poke In The Eye With A Sharp Stick*. His *Troilus And Cressida* least threatened blindness: the soldiers wore uniforms derived from German Gothic paintings of the sixteenth century, but khaki-coloured: 'The effect was that the cast looked like officers out of *M*A*S*H* . . . I even went to the extent of having pin-ups on the wall of Ajax's tent, and showed a large, very rubbed out pin-up photograph of Cranach's Eve.'

The play that opened the season was *The Taming Of The Shrew*, with Sarah Badel in the title role and the unexpected casting of John Cleese as Petruchio. 'I chose him because I had seen him in various guises in Monty Python and spotted a vigorous stock there, without any leaves or flowers but highly suggestive of what might develop when planted and nourished with a classic text. I was interested in the irritability he showed in the character of Basil Fawlty but there are also strange sympathetic depths in the man that I thought could be usefully applied to the character of Petruchio.' Another member of the cast, one not usually associated in the public mind with classical drama, was Bob Hoskins who played Iago to Anthony Hopkins's Othello, although his previous roles had included Richard III and Touchstone. For Miller he represented 'the rough army sergeant, the puritan trooper at Naseby and the mischief-making fairy-tale dwarf – a primal trickster like Rumpelstiltskin'. In the long dialogue between 'the more fair than black' hero and the 'black' villain, the director used an extremely effective long take of over twenty minutes without a cut, with the camera moving stealthily around, sustaining the tension.

The Bard on the box was applauded; at the Coliseum, he had been triumphant with his 'Mafia' *Rigoletto*; and his Goya-esque *Fidelio* was praised at Kent Opera (the rehearsals of which were filmed for Channel 4). Miller was quoted with reverence almost daily in the press and appeared as a TV personality. On another level, he conducted the *States Of Mind* interviews on BBC2, also published in book form. The fifteen 'psychological investigators' he interviewed were George

Miller, Jerome Bruner, Richard Gregory, Daniel Dennett, Jerome Fodor, Stuart Hampshire, Norman Geschwind, George Mandler, Rom Harré, Robert Hinde, Clifford Geertz, Ernst Gombrich, B A Farrell, Thomas Szasz and the sole woman, Hanna Segal. It certainly made for stimulating television, 'talking heads' though they were, and Miller proved that in order to be a good listener, it is also necessary to be a good talker.

In the latter half of 1982, Miller backed into the limelight again by announcing that he really was giving up directing, once and for all, and returning to medicine. This was taken seriously in the world of art and fulsome farewells appeared in the press. In his review of the farewell *Hamlet*, John Barber in *The Daily Telegraph* wrote: 'Miller has announced his intention of quitting the theatre. But on my knees, Dr Jonathan, *please*, Dr Jonathan, don't let your talents leave the stage.' If Miller's only reason for his valediction was to bring a critic to his knees, he succeeded. Robert Cushman in *The Observer* was more sceptical: 'Jonathan Miller may believe in quitting while he's ahead. That could explain his announcement that after *Hamlet* at the Warehouse he will direct plays no more. But I'll believe that when I don't see it. We've been here before.'

Miller's closet production in the 244-seat studio theatre, stripped to its bare essentials, concentrated the mind wonderfully on the text. But the more facetious end of the critical fraternity seemed disconcerted by Anton Lesser's lack of height as Hamlet – 'Half-Pint of Denmark' (*Time Out*) and his resemblance to a flatulent, bearded TV comedian – 'Kenny Everett without the jokes' (Milton Shulman, *Evening Standard*). More controversial was Miller's treatment of Ophelia's madness, not in the traditional interpretation 'of the boards' but as genuine dementia. It is true that some of Kathryn Pogson's tics, such as trying to stuff her fingers into her mouth, made some of her lines inaudible, but the gains were greater than the losses.

XII

Perhaps as a sort of farewell present for having done the state some service, Jonathan Miller was awarded the CBE in the 1983 New Year's Honours List. 'I accepted it in a moment of great weakness. I was flattered, because I was recognised. If I had refused it, I would have had to go through the elaborate process of keeping secret both the appointment and the denial. I suspect Alan Bennett has been offered it and turned it down.'

His second retirement was as shortlived as the first. Medicine is not something you can just drift back into, and his re-entry into the medical world was not as easy as he had hoped. If you've been away from science for some years, things change, and then you're a dinosaur: 'It didn't work. I was older. I'd already become ill-at-ease in anything other than the easy bohemian life you lead in the theatre. I was competing with young men who were hungrier and more eager. I'd grown lazy. There is a sort of sloppy disordered conviviality about the theatre which is not there in medicine. You're free at times of the day when most people are working hard.' The idea that those who work in the theatre lead an 'easy bohemian life' may be seen as an affront to those dedicated workers in the field and may reinforce the view, held by many in the profession, that Miller is a dilettante. The paradoxical claim that this workaholic is lazy also finds echoes. It is true that the nuts and bolts business of rehearsing bores Miller rigid. Once he has had long discussions with the cast, and the original concept has been developed and tried out with adjustments, he starts to lose interest and wants to move on to something new and challenging. It is as if his considerable *élan vital* would be used up on the banal. Miller's mind, like champagne, cannot be wasted on the everyday. He has been seen sitting like the Image of Melancholy at a run-through. During the rehearsal of the Beaumarchais *Figaro* at the Old Vic he remarked to John Wells and Carl Davis, 'How is it that I can remove an appendix but I can't get an armchair off the stage?' A lot of rehearsal time is taken up with brilliant monologues, as memorable and as stimulating as the play he is working on but which only go some way to helping the actors. Wells remembers that at a lunch break during rehearsals on *Danton's Death*, a member of the cast asked him, apropos of nothing, how a telephone worked. Miller's description had everybody round the table riveted, an interlude far more fascinating than what they did in the afternoon. After most rehearsals, the company will sit around and listen spellbound to a Miller discourse. He is, like Dr Pangloss in Voltaire's *Candide*, 'a professor of metaphysicotheologicocosmonigology'.

For an actress like Janet Suzman, the myriad of ideas on offer in a Miller production lend insights into the role and the play. When Miller asked her to take on the title role in *Andromache* at the Old Vic in 1988, she found his exposition on the link between Racinian tragedy and Newtonian physics irresistible, something that might have put many another actress off. However, few actors or singers can resist the educative experience of working with Miller. Suzman, who has only acted for him twice, finds that he makes the rehearsal room 'a cosy, friendly, accessible place, rather like a nursery'. Another impression given is that the rehearsals are like a series of lectures in preparation for the performance/examination, which the performer is expected to pass without assistance. There is a story of an actor, nervously making up on the first night, who felt he had been given very little help during rehearsals and who hoped for some lead or comfort when Miller entered his dressing-room. All the director had to say to him was, 'God, how I hate first nights!' His own vast reservoir of knowledge often cuts down his need for extensive preparation before rehearsals or before lectures. Fellow opera directors have commented that Miller doesn't understand the tough graft of long, long hours needed to be put into preparing an opera. In other words, the reason he is seen to be able to do so many things is that he spends less time doing them, whether out of speed, prior knowledge or laziness is open to question. He certainly rejects the theory of the 'alchemy' produced by long rehearsal periods: 'If you know what you are doing, you can get it done in five weeks.' However, there were rumblings at the ENO towards the end of his stint there that he was not even spending that amount of time on rehearsals, but was here, there and everywhere else.

Retirement ended in 1983 and the first beneficiary of Miller's return to the Arts was Scottish Opera, with *The Magic Flute*. In his determination to get away from the pantomime aspect of the opera, an essential part of its perennial charm, he set it in a huge library reminiscent of the Biblothèque Nationale, in which Tamino, a young student, falls asleep over his book (like Alice) and dreams a fairy tale of The French Enlightenment or, as Miller says, 'The Sleep of Reason that brings forth Monsters.' The Three Ladies were three Habsburg dowagers, the Queen of the Night was 'a representative of that world of obscurantist Jesuitical Catholicism without having her literally embody the Empress Maria-Theresa' and 'Sarastro was no longer a berobed bore but a bewigged eighteenth-century gentleman, an aristocratic mason.' Papageno became a gamekeeper figure in breeches and gaiters derived from Meissenware ceramic figures rather than a 'Tweety-Pie dressed in blue feathers, walking with his toes turned out and pretending to be a bird'.

This was one of those characteristic productions by someone who has thought very hard about what he is doing, has come up with extremely interesting notions, but which failed to ignite on stage. What *The Magic Flute* gained in gravity and historical context it lost in fun and magic; and the library, like the one at Gormenghast Castle, limited illumination and action. Miller's pre-production eloquence is sometimes self-defeating in that by describing what he had in mind and the multifarious connections he has made, greater expectations are raised than can ever be satisfied on stage. Opera critic Nicolas Kenyon once said that opera houses should hire a competent director to put on the works and the programme should read 'After a wonderful idea by Jonathan Miller'.

The artificiality of the genre of opera is heightened when translated to television but paradoxically it works better when this element is played up rather than damped down. Miller's splendid 1985 *Così Fan Tutte* succeeded not only because Mozart's most intimate major opera takes place in one enclosed space, but because the production was able to strike a balance between the realism of the image and the artificiality of the substance. *The Beggar's Opera* is far more intractable as TV fodder, as Miller found when he attempted it for the BBC in 1984, especially when let down by would-be actor and pop-star Roger Daltrey as Macheath. John Gay's ballad opera of 1728 was built around the rogues, thieves and harlots about Newgate prison, spoofing the accoutrements and aristocratic trappings of the contemporary vogue of Italian opera and politicians of the day. It was an age of satire and Gay's wry look at an 'acquisitive society' was one of the things that attracted Brecht to it, and Miller too for that matter. 'Rather than filming a stage version,' writes Miller, 'I staged a version in a studio, but even so I do not think it was successful. *The Beggar's Opera* is undoubtedly at its best when staged in its rightful environment, the theatre.'

XIII

For his first production at the ENO since his 'megahit' *Rigoletto* (which made over a million pounds and for which he received £9,000), Miller completed his Da Ponte-Mozart trilogy with a *Don Giovanni* that took audiences and critics aback by being set in Spain during the conventional period. During early rehearsals Miller and Mark Elder got quite carried away toying with the idea of changing the ending by putting the epilogue at the beginning before the overture, to function rather like a pre-credit sequence in film, but decided against it.

Giovanni was portrayed as a young rake (Cherubino grown up?) not as an ageing one with a death wish but although it was good to see a young, virile and handsome seducer, it was difficult to believe that he had time for the thousands of conquests noted down in Leporello's catalogue, unless he was a mythomaniac. Also, one can more easily accept an older man as representative of the *ancien régime* beginning to lose his grip and ready for hell's fires. The gloss on Donna Anna's character suggested that she was really more than usually in love with her father, offering a reasonable explanation for her obsessive revenge, while boring old Don Ottavio was seen as a man with a foot in the next century who respected the law. Many found this production of the *dramma giocoso* (gay drama, in a past sense) rather too gloomy, but the effective revolving brick wall sets and the costumes all in black and grey created the shadowy atmosphere of a world in which Giovanni could believably operate.

Miller's next new production at the Coliseum could not have been more of a contrast. *The Mikado* was approached from the point of view that it was a very British, un-Japanese pantomime. 'It's a potty-training opera. Look at the words, all potty training,' he observed. 'Nanki-Pooh, Pooh-Bah, and Yum-Yum.' To avoid the absurd spectacle of presenting English singers with 'knitting needles through their hair', Miller decided to set it in a Grand Hotel in England in the late 1920s and early 1930s. 'I don't like Gilbert and Sullivan,' he admits. 'I thought you'd have to get away from that dreadful English Archers amateur village hall sort of shit.' Stripped of its *Japonaiserie*, the operetta was revealed more plainly to belong to the English nonsense tradition of W S Gilbert's *Bab Ballads*. This time, instead of the spirit of an Old Master from the National Gallery inspiring the staging, the production was pervaded more by a compendium of movie references, from Jack Buchanan musical-comedies (which Miller had screened for the cast) to Marx Brothers films. Katisha became a Margaret Dumont figure and Ko-Ko's entrance was pinched directly from Groucho's in *Duck Soup*. The Mikado, huge in a helium-filled suit, was based on Sydney Greenstreet (associated with the 1940s!).

The role of Ko-Ko, whose 'little list' aria contained topical jokes at each performance, was given at first to ex-Python ex-Footlights member Eric Idle (followed later by ex-Goodie ex-Footlights member Bill Oddie) and by Dudley Moore a few months later at the Los Angeles

Opera in March 1987 in an ENO co-production with Houston Grand Opera and the LA Music Center. On the whole, although it was unusual for Miller in being a somewhat camp production, the evening was one of 'innocent merriment', even if it had all been done before in *The Boy Friend* with less 'inconsistent' music. The South Bank Show TV film of the rehearsals shows everybody giggling a lot and enjoying themselves immensely, especially the director, who collapses on the floor laughing at his own jokes. Audiences seemed to find it equally entertaining, especially those who could never stomach the D'Oyly Carte productions.

If *The Mikado* went down well on both sides of the Atlantic, Miller's *Tristan And Isolde* for the Los Angeles Opera was 'a nightmare . . . It was something I should never have done in the first place. I was chosen long after David Hockney was chosen as designer. He was the centre-piece of it all. I was nothing more than an estate agent showing people round the property. It was a disaster.' The reason is clear. Miller needs to work in a small unit from the outset, formulating a concept with a designer and people who know him. The *Tristan* was merely an unfolding of Hockney's magical Pre-Raphaelite designs; anything that seemed to indicate production didn't happen, the singers merely performed as they had done in other productions of the opera. It was also difficult for a 'leader' like Miller to play second fiddle to the even more famous Hockney.

Miller's professed antipathy to Wagner could not have made him the man for the job. Wagner is one of the few subjects which finds Miller in deep water, waving his arms to give the impression of swimming not drowning. 'He nauseates me,' Miller says. 'Partly with being Jewish [!], I suppose, and I can't bear synthetic mythology. It's like Tolkien. The only way to do *The Ring* today would be to do it like *Star Wars*.' (There had been productions of the Tetralogy as a space opera long before the release of the juvenile movie.) In 1973, a year before he made his debut as an opera director, Miller saw his first Wagner production, when taken by Peter Hall to *Siegfried* at the Coliseum before they had found each other out. 'He said to me afterwards that he had had an absolutely fascinating experience, and he could say without hesitation that he would never do it again,' wrote Hall in his diary. Yet the more Miller intellectualises his hatred for the Wizard of Bayreuth, the more convinced one becomes that his reaction is an emotional one. Wagner creates complex reactions, never more so than in Friedrich Nietzsche, who repudiated his youthful worship of the composer with neurotic fury: 'Speaking psychologically, all the significant traits of my own nature are presented as belonging to Wagner,' he wrote in *Ecce Homo.*' 'The juxtaposition of the most lucid and fateful forces, a Will to Power such as no man has yet possessed, reckless spiritual courage, an unlimited capacity to learn without any corresponding diminution of capacity for action.' It is not too fanciful to find some echo there of Miller's own nature. More down to earth, Karen Stone, an ENO producer who has revived some of Miller's productions, believes that the long-drawn-out duets and scenes do not suit Miller's personality as does the immediacy of Mozartian numbers or Puccini scenes, which are very reduced and tight, offering a great deal in a short time and allowing his mind to spring into action. At least *The Flying Dutchman*, Miller's only other Wagner production, is a story with a series of events.

Miller followed the *Mikado* updating with *Tosca* set in Italy under Mussolini, a far more obvious idea. Neither was it the first time this had been done: a few years previously Anthony Besch had placed *Tosca* in Fascist Italy for Scottish Opera. No matter. The opera fits snugly into the time shift without betraying Puccini and even increases its dramatic impact by taking place in a social and historical context recognisable to modern audiences. Unlike the 1950s updating of *Rigoletto*, it becomes a more active political piece by tearing away the falsely romantic. Whereas we may all assume that life was brutal in 1800, the torture of Cavaradossi becomes more perturbing when closer to the present day. (Miller, as a long-time member of Amnesty International, is aware of this.) It could also be argued that just as the Mafia bosses might have listened to Verdi on their jukeboxes, so the sentimental melodramatics of Puccini's music would be just the kind of music to please the ear of the Fascist Scarpia.

The production, which arrived at the Coliseum in January 1987, had first been created the previous summer for the Teatro Communale in Florence as part of the Maggio Musicale, with Eva Marton in the title role. In Italy the right-wing Christian press had attacked it because, by being set in 1944, it equated the Pope with Hitler. On the other hand, many of the chorus had actually lived through the epoch depicted. Miller had asked them to come on to the stage very simply and quietly and to think back on those moments of personal tragedy, and sing with that emotion. As a result, the chorus at the end of Act I was a genuine statement of feeling instead of the usual chattering group. Because of the living memories of the period, Marton, who had given more than 200 performances in different productions, stated that this was the first time she was really terrified of Scarpia.

During rehearsals for Act II, an idea was mooted that Tosca should set fire to Scarpia's filing cabinet but the pyrotechnics required soon put paid to that. There was also a discussion between Miller and Eva Marton's surgeon husband as to how it would be possible to stab someone in the back through to the heart – it's a little confusing to the lay audience when Scarpia sings, after being stabbed in the back, that he was stabbed in the heart. Sometimes being a doctor has enabled Miller to convey illness, madness and death, the staples of nineteenth-century Italian opera, in a clinically accurate manner: the dying consumptive Violetta in his rather realistic *La Traviata* for Kent Opera in 1979 is a vivid example.

Miller often enlists the support of the cast in any production that strays significantly from the norm. Much of the concept of the *Tosca* hung on Roberto Rossellini's 1945 Neo-Realist film, *Rome, Open City*, so a screening was arranged for the cast. They started off complaining that it would be better to spend the time rehearsing than watching a film, but ended up being very moved by it and understanding completely why Miller had wanted them to see it. Miller's method is to send people to art galleries, bring in drawings, diagrams or books to give performers a better understanding of the way he sees the work, as usual making connections. All this is more important to him than blocking scenes. He is not punctilious about where someone should stand or how many paces forward they should take. It is the psychology of the scenes that concerns him.

Miller points to the library in his Camden Town home. 'It is like a spectrum that runs imperceptibly from one subject to another. Pure neurology on one side, history on the other, but it runs through cognitive psychology, social psychology and anthropology. I believe that the world hangs together. Put a book on neurology beside one on medieval art, you'd think there is nothing to connect them. They belong to the same world. I've never felt the "Two Cultures". Discontinuity of knowledge is an artefact of bad education.'

XIV

When Miller first entered the Coliseum he was under the benevolent protection of Lord Harewood. On first collaborating with the music director, Mark Elder, he talked grandiloquently of the 'producer-conductor relationship' being 'a kind of Gothic arch with both sides leaning together and supporting each other'. Elder quipped that as the producer was the taller of the two, he would have the advantage. By the end of Miller's stay with the ENO, the arch was a Gothic ruin.

The run of opera productions at the ENO ended with *The Barber Of Seville*, which opened in November 1987. Thereafter Miller announced that he would never direct an opera in his own country again. 'I'm so pissed off with having to swallow the diet of criticism from English opera critics. I make no money out of it and I get pissed on. I just don't like being written about by these people.' A great deal of critical urine was expended on *The Barber*, much of it with good cause. Taking as his starting point that the opera has its roots in *commedia dell'arte*, a perfectly respectable view, he failed to sustain it sufficiently. For example, Dr Bartolo is not the usual *basso buffo* but an oppressor who, after all, does keep Rosina under house arrest – but is also asked to conform to the comic notion of Pantalone, the deceived husband/guardian. Not only was there an uneven clash of styles but, as a *Guardian* headline proclaimed, it was 'a *Barber* shorn of laughter'. However, Rossini's effervescent masterpiece remained indestructible.

In Miller's demonology, theatre critics are placed just below opera critics in the scale of malevolence. 'They are like the Wizard of Oz, booming through the public address system of their papers. The dignity of the organ outweighs the intelligence of the opinion. There is a sort of invective that has been aimed at me, ever since I started directing – "too clever by half", "the good doctor" – by the anti-intellectual critics. The cheap journalistic world of Jack Stinker and Irving Weasel that consider it either an anomaly or an impudence or a pretension. The hostility comes from a sort of mindless envy, a mindless determination that no one can possibly know that much. I'm tired of being described as a jack of all trades by people who are jacks of none. It's not that I know so much, it's just that they know so fucking little. The people with whom I spend most of my time are not impressed by or envious of the scope of my mind, because the scope of their minds is exactly the same. There's nothing remarkable about what I do. In France or the USA, I'd be regarded as not very talented. I can't play an instrument. I'm not very good at maths and I can't paint very well. There are lots of people who can do all these things.'

As critics are used to dishing it out, they should be able to handle brickbats themselves. But Miller's scorn sometimes extends to audiences who are 'preconditioned by critics to sit on their hands if they have been assured they are in the presence of a failure, but if they have been told it is a success there will be thunderous applause at the end of a mirthless evening'. Of course, there are those who, when asked if they like a play, reply, 'I don't know. I haven't read the reviews yet' but few people purposefully go to see things they have been told are failures and even the most brainless audiences would recognise a mirthless evening if they saw one.

From 1976 to 1986, while mainly concentrating on opera and being showered with praise or with piss for his pains, Miller had given spineless wonders of the theatre critics' fraternity only intermittent chances to have their say. Four years after his farewell *Hamlet* he returned to the theatre with Eugene O'Neill's mammoth *Long Day's Journey Into Night*, the first American play he had directed since Robert Lowell's *Prometheus*. 'I've been out of the theatre for a long time,' he told an American interviewer in *Vanity Fair*. 'Being shut out of the National Theatre because of my row with Peter Hall and not being able to go to the Royal Shakespeare Company because it's a closed shop had the effect of turning me towards opera. But I found I missed being able to play around with the inflections and intonations of language. Music gives you this impermeable membrane where you can actually press through and alter shapes of words, but one can't get direct access to them. Music surrounds the words.'

As the O'Neill play is considered to be the The Great American Tragedy it is usually played in the USA, according to Miller, as if ponderousness equalled profundity. 'Actually, the genre of the play has been mis-identified. It is not epic, but something that really happened, remembered by O'Neill with urgency.' In order to liberate it from tradition, Miller had it played in a more realistic, conversational manner with a consistent use of overlapping dialogue. This not only made it a shorter day's journey (by around 60 minutes, though it still ran over three hours) but made it a more immediate, powerful and often even amusing family drama. One could argue that O'Neill is not a naturalistic playwright and that all his plays are free verse dramas, *Strange Interlude* being the most overt of them. But Miller's production had its own inner rhythm and worked to perfection. Much of the success was due to the American cast, led by a white-maned Jack Lemmon. 'I could have been a great Shakespearian actor,' says Lemmon as James Tyrone . . . and you believe it.

The play marked Miller's first return to Broadway since *Beyond The Fringe* over twenty years before. On the whole, the New York critics were not convinced but it then successfully transferred for a season at the Haymarket Theatre, London and was filmed by the BBC. In 1987 he made another return to his 1960s past by putting on a play at the Royal Court Theatre, the scene of his first job as a professional director and where he had played in cabaret. The work, another of his rare excursions into contemporary drama, was *The Emperor*, adapted by Michael Hastings from the book by the celebrated Polish journalist, Ryszard Katuscinski, on the decline and fall of Haile Selassie of Ethiopia. The cast of six actors, led by the extraordinary Jordanian, Nabil Shaban, a small, disabled man in a wheelchair, delivered their interlocking accounts of the end of the emperor's reign straight to the audience against Richard Hudson's effectively symbolic set of strange doors and spyholes. Miller, who likened this trenchant tragi-comedy to an oratorio, said 'We've made no attempt to dramatise the scenes because it is not about that. It is about language.' He was in his element working with an intimate company in a very small theatre. (It had started at the Royal Court Upstairs before moving downstairs to the larger theatre which could satisfy the demand for seats.) In order to pay for the set, Miller gave his fee to the theatre.

Then came his only production to date for the Royal Shakespeare Company at Stratford. Strangely, the company of the Bard had not asked the producer of the Bard to work with them before and have not asked him back, despite the huge success of *The Taming Of The Shrew*. Given Miller's penchant for returning to Shakespeare plays he has done before, reworking and redeveloping them, it was only natural that he should tackle this problematic play once again. This time Katherina (Fiona Shaw) was a neurasthenic, crop-haired intelligent girl, never a shrew but jealous of her father's love for Bianca, who turns out to be the real shrew when she gets the man she loves. 'We cannot act or see Shakespeare today as the Elizabethans and the author did but we can take into account that our perception is a modern one without rewriting the plays to make them contemporary,' Miller says. The rough-hewn Petruchio (Brian Cox) goes about his business of brainwashing and subjugating his wife because society expects it of him, and because it is kind to be cruel. When, in the 'goods and chattels' speech, Petruchio refers to the Bible, Kate has to accept it, and her last speech is played straight and solemnly, and listened to in the same way.

XV

In 1987, Canadian entrepreneur 'Honest' Ed Mirvish, the executive director of the Old Vic who had bought the theatre five years before, offered Miller the post of artistic director and he returned as master to the historic theatre, which he had left when Peter Hall was running it for the National. Ed Mirvish and his son David, who had spent £2.5 million on buying and renovating the theatre, then footed the bill for a further £500,000 for the season. 'Ed is very supportive,' says 'Honest' Jon Miller. 'I try to persuade him that his investment, in the absence of an Arts Council grant, is not so much a loss as a subsidy.'

Remembering Peter Hall's 'bureaucratic set-up' and closed-door policy, Miller made his office at the Vic open to everyone. 'They drop in without knocking, sit on these couches, talk to me and relax. I cannot make a private telephone call. Everyone who comes here says what a nice place it is to work in and wants to come back. It's the opposite from the National Theatre which has never been a home for anyone . . . People like this cosy common-room set-up where everyone knows everyone, including the stage staff. They all know me as well as they know each other. There is no question of a steep hierarchy or of having to make an appointment to see me.'

In his first season, which could have been called *Beyond The Canon*, he put on a series of challenging productions, deciding to direct five out of the seven plays himself. 'At a time when our theatre reeks of caution, I applaud the wild eclecticism of Jonathan Miller's Old Vic season. All the same, in directing five out of seven shows, Dr Miller is taking on too much,' wrote Michael Billington in *The Guardian*. For Miller, the repertoire was 'the kind that would be taken for granted in most other European capitals. The whingeing critical fraternity, of course, call it "eclectic", which is a posh word for the fact that they've never heard of it.' Aside from the obligatory Shakespeare, a transfer from Scottish opera of Leonard Bernstein's Broadway operetta *Candide* and a resurrection of N F Simpson's absurdist comedy of 1959, *One Way Pendulum*, the four other plays had seldom, if ever, been performed in England. Neither the biggest success nor the biggest flop of the season was directed by Miller. The former, Alexander Ostrovsky's *Too Clever By Half* (a title some people have stuck on to Miller), was directed by Richard Jones, a young opera director whose work includes operas with Opera North, Kent Opera and the ENO. This, his first major production of a straight play, was a brilliant feat of ensemble playing that Miller was not able to get from his own productions. (Jones returned for the second season in 1989 with Feydeau's *A Flea In Her Ear.*) At the other end of the success barometer was *The Tutor*, Brecht's adaptation of the Lenz novel directed by Angelika Hurwitz of the Berliner Ensemble. 'My fault,' says Miller. 'I'd seen it in Vienna ten years ago, and liked it, but it didn't mesh with English actors.'

Miller's own productions (and the season) kicked off with Racine's *Andromache* in a plain iambic translation by his friend Eric Korn (Craig Raine was chosen first but opted out). Given British audiences' and critics' aversion to or ignorance of classical and neo-classical tragedy, it was a bold step. There were the predictable reactions. Sheridan Morley, giving the game away in *Punch*, considered it 'user-unfriendly to those of us with an abiding terror of eventually being found dead of boredom in the stalls of the *Comédie Française*'. Others, hearing the word 'culture', reached for their pop guns by variously evoking the names of Harpo Marx, Jack Benny, Lon Chaney and Frankie Howerd; and nervous titters were heard in the audience as if there was a law forbidding laughter in the theatre when things are not clearly labelled 'comedy'. It was an example of English audiences' lack of familiarity with the stylised, formalised language of Racinian tragedy breeding contempt. Apart from some jarring but intended verbal anachronisms – a misguided attempt at approachability – the tragedy of unrequited love moved powerfully, in two unbroken hours, towards its inexorable conclusion. The cast, led by Janet Suzman as the eponymous heroine and Penelope Wilton as Hermione, negotiated the text, and a dangerously raked set, with aplomb.

The sublime gave way to the ridiculous with Miller's second production, *One Way Pendulum*. The first night saw a nostalgic public reunion of 'Fringers', ex-members of the Establishment club (two of whom, John Bird and John Fortune, were on stage) and a smattering of Monty Pythons. The 'farce in a new dimension' itself was a nostalgic delight, with Richard Hudson's set of the Groomkirby suburban living room, in which the Carrollian trial is held, reflecting the 1950s. Despite being rather too much like a series of lunatic revue sketches laid end to end, the superlative cast kept up the hilarity for most of the evening. Nevertheless it was perceived as a comedy relic, and audiences barely reached an average of 50 per cent: on one night it played to 65 souls.

It was an education for most people to see George Chapman's Jacobean tragedy *Bussy D'Ambois*, not performed since 1650, but it too failed to arouse the curiosity of the Great British Public. On first looking into Chapman's play, one was struck by the remarkably rich language, strong political themes and thunderous theatricality, none of which came across very convincingly in Miller's underpowered and undercast production, set against an austere single set, with the characters in costumes of browns and black. It was proof that what was needed at the Vic was a permanent company of players, with star actors.

Interest naturally centred round the casting of the giant of Swedish theatre and cinema, Max Von Sydow, as Prospero in *The Tempest*, Miller's reworking of the Mermaid Theatre production of 28 years before. 'Why me?' was the Swedish actor's reaction when Miller asked him to do it. 'Do you have to cross the river to fetch water when you have so many wonderful actors in England?' Von Sydow came with the aura of the classic Ingmar Bergman films still clinging to him and brought the authority and warmth of his personality to bear on the scientist-artist-director figure (a familiar character?). The critics, however, pounced on the fact that he had 'a wretched attack of first night nerves', so that his extended solo at the beginning 'seemed as though it would stretch till the crack of doom', and 'his command of the lines and the Shakespearean music is extremely unsteady'. There is always a risk in casting a foreigner (and even an American) in Shakespeare in England, where there is a kind of proprietorial attitude to the Bard. What the critics failed to see was that although Von Sydow may have forgotten some of his lines (on the first night), he never forgot his part.

Miller's roller-coaster first season at the Old Vic ended with Bernstein's much-fiddled-with *Candide*, first seen on Broadway in 1956. The history of this musical, rather like Voltaire's view of history in general, is 'nothing more than a picture of crimes and misfortunes'. But that would require a book on its own for those fans interested in the ups and downs, rewrites and rethinks of the work. Suffice it to say that the Miller-John Wells effort (originally for Scottish Opera) was generally considered the best of all possible productions.

Despite an attempt to make the show as Voltairean as they could,

Broadway kept crashing in. It was neither light enough for a musical, nor profound enough for an opera. There were pleasant enough pastiche numbers and good lyrics, though 'What a day for an auto-da-fé' is not one of them. Miller, a man who is most passionate when talking about the Enlightenment, whom one could see round a table talking to Pope, Rousseau, Dr Johnson and Voltaire, admits that 'One has to reconcile the bitterness of Voltaire's amusement with modern requirements for straightforward entertainment. You can't make it that serious.' As a result, *Candide* finally gave audiences at the Old Vic something they had been deprived of throughout the season – good middlebrow entertainment.

There was no doubt that the Mirvishes would keep Jonathan Miller on as artistic director for another, less ambitious Old Vic season; this time with four plays, compared with seven in 1988, two of them directed by Miller. Shakespeare is always good box office and the 1989 season began with Miller's fourth attempt to scale the heights of *King Lear*.

The play-goer, walking to the Old Vic from Waterloo station, would find it difficult not to notice, unless he or she decided not to, the groups of vagrants, beggars and homeless people huddled in the portico of St John's church like a dark scene from Piranesi, or in the city of cardboard boxes in the subway under Waterloo Bridge. Obviously, Miller's constant walks to the theatre through this Thatcherville impinged on his social consciousness. In a *coup de théâtre* in Act 3, Scene IV 'before a hovel on the heath', Miller transports the nightmarish vision of the 'houseless poverty' outside the theatre on to the stage, therefore when Lear prays for 'poor naked wretches, whereso'er you are', the well-heeled audience knows exactly where they are to be found. As Michael Ignatieff writes in *The Needs Of Strangers*, quoted in the Old Vic programe, 'The heath is both a real place and a place in the mind. It is what the human world would be like if pity, duty, and the customs of honour and due ceased to rule human behaviour. It is the realm of natural man, man beyond society, without clothes, retinue, pride and respect.'

For Miller 'the heath, where the anonymous sufferer exists, is not something that lies outside the bounds of the city. It actually has its fingers infiltrating into the very centre of our own life.' This, then, is an inner-city *Lear*, a stark tragedy of the disinherited. Grey brick walls enclose the action, fog and darkness constantly enshroud and imprison the characters. No blade of grass is to be seen. Sometimes the murkiness and the deafening storm, portrayed by billowing black curtains, lessened visual and aural clarity, but the strong cast (not always the case in previous Old Vic productions) served the production well. Remaining with his concept of the Fool as Lear's contemporary, Miller shifted the daughters' ages to keep up with his own (54). Because Lear is over 80, it seems more appropriate that his offspring should be getting on a bit, and Regan and Goneril (Frances De La Tour and Gemma Jones) were seen not as fairy-tale monsters but as two middle-aged women struggling to cope with an aged parent. Sixty-one-year-old Eric Porter's Lear was passionate, vigorous and rich-voiced, though hardly the 'infirm and weak' man he calls himself. On the whole, the critics and public were generous in their praises. King Jonathan retained his crown at the Old Vic.

XVI

As yet, to take an Olympian view, Jonathan Miller has made no major contribution to medicine nor has he written an important scientific, philosophical or psychological work. He became known as a performer in a watershed revue over a quarter of a century ago and has hardly appeared on stage since. In the 'sixties he made a few television films, of which one, *Alice In Wonderland*, is remembered fondly by those around at the time, and his only feature film was mediocre. His widely-seen and acclaimed series, *The Body In Question*, put him in the Dr Bronowski, Kenneth Clark, David Attenborough class of expert TV pundits and popularisers. That was over a decade ago, and wasn't followed up. As a talk show guest, he is as wide-ranging and as amusing as Peter Ustinov and Dame Edna Everage. He is much in demand on the lecture circuit in Britain and the USA because of his omnivorous mind and the ability to give tongue to his febrile thoughts in a witty, provocative and challenging manner. Perhaps one could argue that there are many university lecturers around who are his intellectual equal or superior on their specific subjects, and some (though not many) as entertaining. If there is one area where he is to be taken seriously, it is that of stage direction. Yet whatever the trend, whether away from or towards 'producer's theatre', plays and operas will always be considered, first and foremost, the province of the playwright and composer, the actor and the singer. Directing for the stage is like writing on water; with very few exceptions, there is no theatre equivalent of a Luis Buñuel, Federico Fellini or Jean Renoir. Miller has not earned the international reputation that has accrued to Giorgio Strehler, Patrice Chereau, Jean-Pierre Ponnelle, Götz Friedrich and the three Peters – Stein, Sellers and Brook. Nevertheless, he would sit comfortably in a list that includes John Dexter, Bill Bryden, David Pountney, David Freeman, Deborah Warner, Richard Jones, Nicholas Hytner, Richard Eyre and the four Peters – Hall, Bogdanov, Wood and Gill.

He is a bold type, more than the sum of his parts; a scourge of the middlebrow, an unabashed intellectual. Jonathan Miller's cornucopian knowledge and energy, his ability to make connections between the arts and sciences, between the arts themselves, between life and science, between life and the arts, make him a welcome, cherishable rarity in the predominantly philistine air of these isles where the love of ideas is the love that dare not speak its name. For Miller, it is natural to believe in *Zusammenhängen*, the coherence of things. He only *seems*, like the Stephen Leacock horseman, to be riding 'madly off in all directions'.

'There is little accommodation in England for the possibility of two lives. You can't do theatre and medicine, but you can be what one is not embarrassed to call an intellectual in France. The idea of a commitment to the life of the mind is something characteristic of European life. In England, it's thought pretentious, spreading oneself too thin.' Therefore if he were sent to France, his intellectualism, to paraphrase the Gravedigger, 'would not be seen in him there; there the men are as intellectual as he'. If one were to divide intellectuals, as one did Thatcher's original cabinet, into dries and wets, Miller would be a wet. His passion often allows his tongue to run rashly ahead of his brain in a manner that takes one aback. But in his work he is not passion's slave; rather, he uses passion to do his bidding. Sense and sensibility, never sentimentality, are the hallmarks of a Miller production, a reflection of the man himself.

Most critics are unable to divorce their reviews of his work from their knowledge of Miller the man. Music critic Ronald Crighton once remarked that Miller has no visual sense at all and that his own shambling physical quality, his stumbling, long-limbed manner is reflected in his productions in ways he didn't intend. Clive James reviewing *The Body In Question* in *The Observer*, typifies this attitude, writing that Miller is a prisoner of his own versatility: 'It has been said that Miller is a Renaissance man. Certainly he has the gifts. But really it was intensity of effort, rather than universality of range, that characterised the men of the Renaissance. Even at their most fiercely competitive they were ready to leave some departments of knowledge and achievements to be taken care of by others.'

Testimonials from his friends establish Miller as 'a warm and wonderful host'; 'very exhilarating company'; 'the breadth of his references is breathtaking'; 'more brains and more energy than most people.' From the man himself: 'I'm faster off my feet and wittier than most other people.' All this accepted, there are some reservations. 'He cannot take the mildest criticism'; 'he is unbelievably thin-skinned. Anyone who doesn't meet him with anything less than unqualified praise is immediately an enemy'; 'one has the feeling that out of his vast store of energy, eighty per cent goes into conversation, twenty per cent into his actual work'; 'he is nine out of ten times wrong, but when he is right he is brilliantly right'; 'he hates humanity. He has no idea of doing anything for his fellow men. He doesn't feel that anyone achieves anything that way.'

Jonathan Miller would share Jonathan Swift's feelings: 'I have ever hated all nations, professions and communities, and all my love is towards individuals . . . But principally I hate and detest that animal called man: although I heartily love John, Peter, Thomas and so forth.' Certainly he is capable of Swiftian vituperation. He once described Peter Hall, with inexplicable venom, as being 'like a ball of rancid pig's fat rolled around the floor of a barber's shop at the end of a busy day,' and Bernard Levin as 'a huge tongue on legs'. Yet witness him with people to whom he is sympathetic or whom he considers his intellectual equals: sharing *States Of Mind* with a group of renowned 'psychological investigators' or frowningly trying to get to the root of musical genius by questioning virtuosi and getting 81-year-old Nathan Milstein's response, 'I'm sorry. You vant to know everything nobody know.'

Miller continues to want 'to know everything nobody know'. In *Ivan*, a moving documentary made for the *Horizon* series for BBC in 1984, Miller and Ivan Vaughn, a lecturer in psychology seriously afflicted by Parkinson's disease, explored and explained the illness in an enlightening and humorous manner. As President of the Alzheimer's Disease Society, he brings his prestige and knowledge of the subject to the research to find a cure and, coequally, the cause. He was the sympathetic presenter of a series called *Who Cares?* on BBC2 in May 1989, which looked at cases of relatives having to give the disabled constant care. 'I did the programmes partly because I felt guilty; about twenty years ago I was not very caring at all when my mother developed Alzheimer's disease,' he says. The answer to the question, Who Cares? is – Jonathan Miller. Despite the melancholy clouds and sudden storms, he has what Nietzsche described as *La Gaya Scienza* (joyful wisdom), 'that union of singer, knight and free spirit'.

According to Schopenhauer, 'Genius holds up to us the magic glass in which all that is essential and significant appears to us collected and placed in the clearest light, and what is accidental and foreign is left out.' Many of Miller's productions aspire towards this condition and very often achieve it. A Jonathan Miller production, whether it comes off or not, is never routine: there is always an informed intelligence behind it. Whatever the temptation, 'run of the Miller' is not a joke one can make easily about his work. He lives very much by the credo he imputes to Shakespeare, who wrought changes upon antiquity 'not because he arrogantly supposed their stories to be smaller or thinner than his own imagination but because he realised that one of the tasks of art is to overthrow the tyranny of time and to recreate a universe within which the dead converse at ease with the living'.

9

THE SINGLE SPY

In July 1962 at the Royal Court, while Jonathan Miller was directing
Under Plain Cover, Alan Bennett was playing the Archbishop of Canterbury in the other half of the Osborne double bill, *The Blood Of The
Bambergs*, before going to New York in October with the original cast
of *Beyond The Fringe*. Returning to London in 1964, he played the
Rev. Sloley-Jones in a revival of Ben Travers's 1925 farce *A Cuckoo In
The Nest*, in which John Osborne himself played a role. It began to
seem as if Bennett's revue performance of the cleric would condemn
him to playing men of the cloth for the rest of his life: if anyone
envisaged a future for him, it might have been as a character actor in
British comedies, a sort of bespectacled Derek Nimmo.

Like the Englishman in the Eartha Kitt song, Bennett took his time.
The gust of *Beyond The Fringe* blew through the West End and
deposited Jonathan Miller on the box as art guru and director; Peter
Cook, the satyr of satire, exposed follies at his nightclub and through
the pages of *Private Eye* and later joined Dudley Moore, who was
making a name for himself as a jazz musician, in the 'funny, funny,
funny' (one of the TV show's catchphrases) *Not only. . .But Also*. Whatever happened to the fourth member of the team?

On his return from America in 1965 Bennett re-entered academic
life for a while, continuing research for his book on Richard II and his
days were spent in the Public Record Office, poring over parchments.
For some time, according to John Wells, 'He had had the sense of
having fallen from grace by having slummed it with showbiz people.'
Research was a kind of penance, so when Ned Sherrin asked him to
write and perform some sketches for the satirical show *BBC3*, Bennett
was only too pleased.

'I got into the way of writing occasional sketches with John Fortune
and John Bird. We would meet towards the end of the week [the show
went out on Saturday evenings] and try to knock out a script,' recalls

Bennett. 'I had a contract which allowed me to withdraw if no satisfactory idea emerged. I wasn't used to working to such a tight schedule or to performing live on TV, but I got to enjoy it. I was also well paid – by the minute, I remember, which gave one the incentive to pad it out.'

Sherrin calls the contract he made with Bennett 'whimsical': 'Alan would meet Bird and Fortune . . . and see if the spirit moved him. If it did not, he went home, and the other two, perhaps with Doug Fisher, improvised without him.' What Bennett remembers about the sketches was 'We would make enormous detours in order to fetch in the most terrible jokes and puns.' Bennett's own appearances were usually as donnish types in monologues, although he did also play a variety of roles in *My Father Knew Lloyd George*, a splendid-looking television film (broadcast in December 1965) conceived by John Bird, directed by Jack Gold and largely improvised by the cast, made up of John Fortune, John Bird, Eleanor Bron and Bennett. It was a witty, complicated political farce about a Charles Dilke-like scandal.

A few years later, in 1971, Bennett wrote and performed a spoof account of a visit to Bernard Berenson's villa in Florence: 'Berenson recalled Proust rushing down the Boulevard Haussmann, cramming cake into his mouth, and shouting Thomas Hood's "I remember, I remember" at the top of his voice. I wanted to know more . . .' Not the sort of humour one gets very often on television these days, where the comedians' frame of reference is usually the frame of television itself. One of his funniest and most typical solos (which was to reappear virtually unchanged in *Forty Years On*, his first play) was a description of a literary party given by Virginia Woolf, a lady he seems always to find good for a laugh or two:

> Of all the honours that fell upon Virginia's head, none I think pleased her more than the *Evening Standard* Award for the Tallest Woman Writer of 1933, an award she took by a short neck from Elizabeth Bowen, and rightly, I think, because she was in a very real sense the tallest writer I've ever known. Which is not of course to say that her stories were tall – they were not. They were short.

Bennett gradually developed into a master of monologue and the sketch form. Television proved particularly suited to his intimist talents. Most of all he sharpened his teeth and his writing in his own

TV comedy series, *On The Margin*. Six 30-minute programmes were broadcast weekly on BBC2 from 9 November 1966. Each show consisted of sketches, a straight reading of a poem (favourites being John Betjeman and Philip Larkin) and a film clip of old music-hall artistes. One running sketch was called 'Life and Times in NW1' (Bennett was living in Chalcot Square, NW1), which satirised the antics of 'trendies' Nigel and Jane Knocker-Threw, played by Bennett and Yvonne Gilan.

Nigel: It is perhaps the most beautiful experience in all the world – and also the most nauseating. I remember when Jane was having Belinda I was in rather a quandary because the night she started having the pains there was this repeat of a Ken Russell film on, and I'd missed it the first time. Just a question of priorities, really. I watched the film. Well, I mean – you know, we were going to have more kids, and it's not every night you can see a Ken Russell film.

Today the reference to Ken Russell seems culturally inapt, but at the time Russell was known for the fresh approach and visual flair he brought to mini-biopics of composers on BBC TV, before becoming a gaudy and flaunting feature film director.

Bennett also 'camped it up' as the proprietor of an antique shop, a more subtle companion piece to Kenneth Williams's and Hugh Paddick's Julian and Sandy on radio's long-running Kenneth Horne shows. In one sketch he apologises for keeping a customer waiting by saying 'I'm so sorry. I was just stripping a tallboy.'

Customer: (pointing at old money box) That's not an antique. They had these when I was a boy.
Bennett: Oo, you said it, dear, not me. (Picks up a chamber pot) Have you ever thought of going in for these? I think that this is Worcester.
Customer: What is it?
Bennett: Well, it's an eighteenth century breakfast cup, is that. I mean, in the eighteenth century they used to have these great big breakfasts – I mean, none of your two prunes and a Weetabix – so they had such big cups. (Picks up an old policeman's truncheon.)

	Do you know what they're using these for nowadays?
Customer:	Well, I know one thing – it's not teapot stands.
Bennett:	Oo, get in the knife box, you're too sharp to live.

Other episodes, still remembered and quoted with affection, included a 'film profile' of a best-selling novelist from Barnsley, now living in the South of France and retracing his roots. He explains that the reason he lives on the Mediterranean is because 'the blue of the sea reminds me of the blue of coal-miners' eyes as they come up from the pit'; critics earnestly discussing a play called *Yes, We Have No Pyjamas*, a *Monitor*-type item on Kafka's underpants; and a group of stoics contemplating 'a real slap-up do' of beans. Jonathan Miller joined his erstwhile stage partner in an ancient Roman sketch, and they also played a couple of queenish actors in the BBC canteen. One of the monologues that had an after-life was archetypally Bennett, his pedantic, posh voice attempting to dictate a telegram over the phone.

. . . I want to end it if I may: NORWICH. Norwich, yes . . . well, it's an idiomatic way of saying 'Knickers off ready when I come home.' You see, it's the initial letters of each word. Yes, I know knickers is spelled with a K. I *was* at Oxford, it was one of the first things they taught us. And in an ideal world it would be KORWICH, but I don't think it carries the same idiomatic force.

Alas, *On The Margin* must remain forever a pleasant memory, never to be seen again, because the BBC, in an act of vandalism, wiped all the recordings. Still, one advantage of the show's disappearance from the face of the earth is that those who saw it all those years ago will never have their enthusiasm dimmed by a revisit.

II

While Bennett was working on his TV series (for which he was nominated Light Entertainment Personality by the Society of Film and Television Arts) he was busy putting together sketches that he thought would make up a literary revue. He would include the Virginia Woolf monologue from *BBC3* and one on Lawrence of Arabia, and gradually they came together within the framework of an end-of-term school play. Originally titled *The Last Of England*, it was first offered to the

The four new West End
satirical sensations of 1961 pose
in Regent's Park.

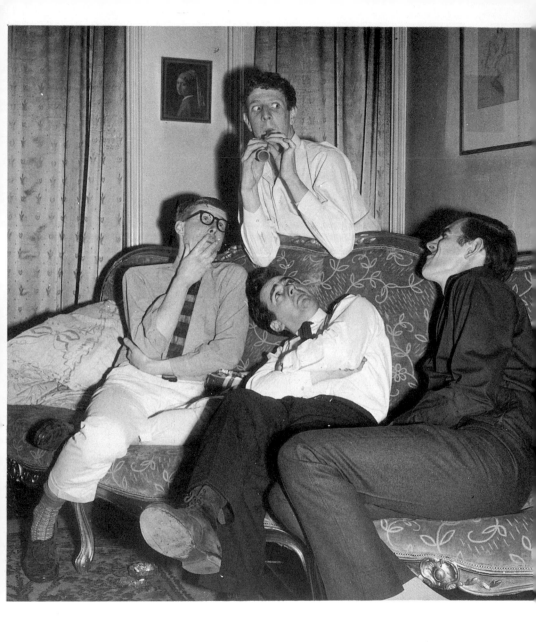

A break in rehearsal for the cast in
their Edinburgh flat before the opening of
Beyond The Fringe at the 1960 Festival.

'Right, I'll get this. No, I insist,
this one's on me. Drinks are on me. Drinks on me.'
The 'Bread Alone' sketch from *Beyond The Fringe*.

The undergraduate
Jonathan Miller
in the 1955
Cambridge Footlights
Revue
Between The Lines.

Jonathan Miller, in his only screen role, as Kirby Groomkirby,
teaches speak-your-weight machines to sing the Hallelujah Chorus
in the 1964 Woodfall Production of N F Simpson's *One Way Pendulum.*

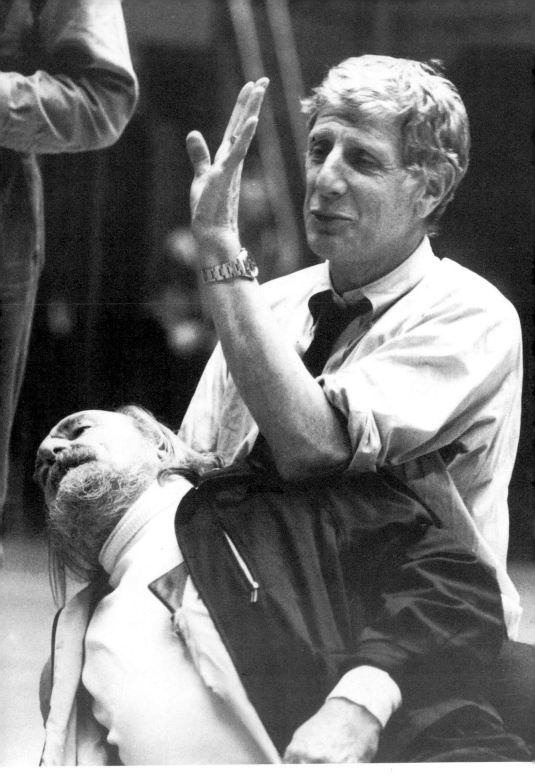

Jonathan Miller rehearses
Eric Porter in the title role of the
1989 Old Vic production of *King Lear*.

ALAN BENNETT, 1961.

(left) Alan Bennett taking over the role of Mrs Swabb in 1974 in *Habeas Corpus* at the Lyric Theatre. (Seen here with Mike Carnell as Mr Purdue.)

(below) Alan Bennett as Anthony Blunt in *A Question Of Attribution*, the second half of the *Single Spies* double bill at the National Theatre in 1988.

DUDLEY MOORE, 1961.

(above) 1958: John Bassett (*far right*) goes over a score with his Oxford Jazz Band which featured pianist Dudley Moore (*second right*). (below) Dudley Moore and Tuesday Weld in September 1976, exactly a year into their five-year marriage.

Peter Cook, 1961.

(above) Dud'n'Pete swap wisdom during the 1965 Royal Command Performance.
(below left) Derek and Clive obviously thinking and/or doing something obscene.
(below right) Peter Cook parodies the judge's summing-up in the Jeremy Thorpe
trial during the 1979 *Secret Policeman's Ball*.

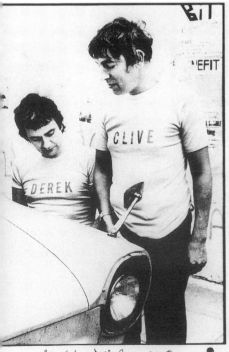

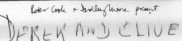

At Regent's Park Zoo, 1961.

National Theatre in 1968, who turned it down – in fact, it took 20 years before he was performed there. One day, when Bennett went out to the Post Office in Camden Town, he found it closed but theatre director Frith Banbury happened to be passing, and Bennett asked him if he had a stamp. They got talking and as they strolled up Primrose Hill, Banbury, whose name generally conjures up for the cognoscenti a picture of french-window revivals, told him he was about to go into rehearsal with Dodie Smith's 1938 family saga *Dear Octopus*, at the Haymarket with Cicely Courtneidge and Jack Hulbert. Bennett replied that he had just written a play much of which referred to the 1930s. Banbury said, 'The trouble with doing these period pieces is that people think the 'twenties was everybody doing the Charleston in short skirts, and the 'thirties was only Munich and Hitler and all that. You get the impression that the periods were nothing more than one or two salient fashions. In fact, people still did the usual things they do nowadays.'

About three weeks later a script was pushed in at the front door of Banbury's elegant house near Regent's Park Zoo. It was called *Forty Years On*, with a note attached saying: 'See page 80.'

'I turned to the page and found the observations I had made to Alan on Primrose Hill, but written in a far more amusing manner.' (These lines were subsequently cut.)

Banbury read the play, loved it and invited Bennett round for a drink and a chat. Bennett was rather disconsolate. 'Oh, I don't know how I'll ever get it on,' he moaned. 'It has this enormous cast of schoolboys.' Banbury immediately put him in touch with Toby Rowland, managing director of Stoll Theatres.

'With what seemed to me at the time great presumption,' Bennett noted in the diary he kept of the production, 'Rowland sent a second draft to Sir John Gielgud.' When Bennett met Gielgud (at Rowland's house in Smith Street) Sir John, when he got round to speaking of the play, started 'straight in on what is wrong. This disconcerts me, particularly since his first target is the 25 boys we have decided on as the minimum requirement for the school. He would like none at all; they will fidget, they will distract, surely cardboard cut-outs would be better?'

This depressed the novice playwright but at a second meeting, over lunch at the Ivy, 'Gielgud is reconciled to the boys, and agrees to do the play.' Bennett's diary entry for 9 July 1968 reads:

'Yesterday and today are spent auditioning boys at Her Majesty's.

When I first arrive at the stage door I am put at the end of the line. Since we had advertised for boys of 15-18 this flatters me, until I see that many are considerably older and seem increasingly so as the day draws on: by the time five o'clock comes round I would not have been surprised to see Lewis Casson walk out on to the stage.'

But they managed to find two dozen excellent boys, one of whom, George Fenton, who played Tredgold and the guitar, later composed the music for a number of Bennett plays. Another, Keith McNally, became a firm friend. McNally owns the Odeon restaurant on 145 West Broadway, New York, in which Bennett invested. 'I don't get anything out of it except free meals,' Bennett comments. It is an establishment over which he feels rather proprietorial. Ned Sherrin remembers sitting in the Odeon a short while after it opened. 'Alan happened to be there and caught me looking round as if I was looking for a waiter. He came up to me like a maître d'hôtel and asked "Is anything wrong?"' Since then McNally has branched out into the highly successful Café Luxembourg and Nell's nightclub, into which Bennett has also put some money.

Although Frith Banbury would dearly have liked to direct *Forty Years On*, it had already been bespoken by Bennett's Oxford buddy, Patrick Garland, who had worked with Bennett on one programme in a TV series called *Famous Gossips*. (He had also known Dudley Moore at Oxford, and had been assistant to Jonathan Miller on *Monitor*.) The music for the show was adapted by the American-born Carl Davis, who later composed the incidental music for Miller's *The Merchant Of Venice* and *The Marriage Of Figaro* at the National Theatre. Julia Trevelyan Oman, who designed the production, later was responsible for the sets for the Miller *Merchant* and his TV *Alice In Wonderland*. The Casa Nostra of the Theatre is relatively small.

Forty Years On, the play that 'seemed to me much closer to what I wanted to do in the theatre than *Beyond The Fringe* . . . a half-way house between revue and theatre', opened at the Apollo Theatre in November 1968. Aside from Gielgud as the headmaster of the Old School (in both senses), the cast included Alan Bennett as Tempest, a junior master and Paul Eddington as Franklin, a housemaster. Another of the boys was Anthony Andrews, who in another decade would make his name as Sebastian Flyte in the TV adaptation of *Brideshead Revisited*.

Albion School for Boys is a microcosm of English society, 'a valuable site at the crossroads of the world'. The end-of-term show sets out to be anti-*Cavalcade*, Coward's Union Jack-wrapped pageant, but ends on a note of regret for a passing England, a melancholy valediction to a vanishing age. Throughout, parody turns to eulogy, mock patriotism becomes the real thing, and *vice versa*, a conscious ambivalence as Bennett himself realised. He noted in his diary on Armistice Day: 'I listen to the ceremony and as I sit typing this I hear the guns rumbling across the Park at the start of the Two Minutes' Silence. I find the ceremony ridiculous and hypocritical and yet it brings a lump to my throat. Why? I suppose that was what I was trying to resolve.' Bennett says it was his way of 'trying to shed the burden of the past', but he had only shifted it on to the play-goer.

Also running through the play is the seemingly never-ending English obsession with the never-never land of public schools (this time seen by an ex-grammar school boy). Plays, books and films feed the public's insatiable desire for the sex, sadism, sport, snobbery and spies at these establishments. No matter. Bennett's debut play was really an excuse for a series of hilarious revue sketches in which the humour ranges from the low to the high, from the corny to the epigrammatic. Which is which must remain a matter of personal taste.

There is no doubt that he has a penchant for the pun (said to be an indication of immaturity), for non-sequiturs and for double entendres: 'When a society has to resort to the lavatory for its humour, the writing is on the wall.' 'It's the end of the world, Nursie. They are rolling up the maps all over Europe. We shall not see them lit again in our lifetime.' And of T E Lawrence: 'There was something feminine about his makeup, but his was always so discreet. But can one ever forget him, those china blue eyes, that boyish, almost girlish figure and that silly, silly giggle. The boys at his school had called him Tee Hee Lawrence, and always at the back of his hand or the back of his mind there was that ready snigger.' The lantern-slide lecture on Lawrence verges on a music-hall turn and then moves on to scintillating Oscar Wilde pastiche with Bennett's variation on 'All women become like their mothers. That is their tragedy. No man does. That's his,' becoming 'Every woman dresses like her mother. That's her tragedy. No man ever does. That's his.' In the confirmation class sketch, the teacher (Bennett), hands straying, warns a boy to keep his private parts private, an echo of an earlier line: 'I don't seem to be able to put my hands on the choir's parts.'

One of the great strengths of the first production was Gielgud's marvellous bewilderment and what seemed genuine outrage at the proceedings around him, symptomatic in a sense, of the 64-year-old Gielgud's first plunge into post-Osborne drama. Perversely, Irving Wardle's review in *The Times* did not mention him once!! (Bennett was unhappy when Emlyn Williams took over from Gielgud after ten months, and blamed him when the box-office started to slip.)

When the play was revived at the Queen's Theatre in August 1984, directed again by Garland, Paul Eddington had been promoted to Headmaster. Although he exuded chalk, he lacked Gielgud's ability to give the impression of being somehow detached from the show but attached to the school. Stephen Fry, a bright new 27-year-old comic talent, shone in Bennett's old role in various guises, including Lady Bracknell and Lady Ottoline Morrell. If the earlier production had seemed out of touch with the seething student movements of 1968, sixteen years on, in the harsher 1984 world of Big Sister, it seemed rather quaint but was still very funny.

Forty Years On brought Bennett fully into the limelight again, where he joined Miller, Cook and Moore, who had never been out of it. The play was given a 'special' award by the *Evening Standard* and the Variety Club of Great Britain named Bennett the 'most promising star of 1968'. In a speech at the *Evening Standard* award ceremony, Frankie Howerd, who had been rediscovered by Peter Cook and Co., joked that he hated Alan Bennett as he was not only talented but young with it. Howerd was 47, Bennett 34.

III

It was three years before a second play by Alan Bennett, always a slowish writer, reached the West End. *Getting On*, originally entitled *A Serious Man*, was his first attempt at a well-made play and starred Kenneth More. The 57-year-old More was a little too old for the part (originally meant for Alan Bates) of Labour MP, George Oliver, 'a man of about forty, rather glamorous once, now a bit florid, worn, running to fat'. The plain-speaking, three-times married, golfing actor, who looked perfectly at home in the cockpit of a plane or standing on the bridge of a ship, clearly had little affinity with the shy bachelor playwright, who looked perfectly at home in a library or lecture room. Trouble brewed from the beginning, when More refused to say certain lines he felt his public would not accept, despite Bennett's protestations that the play would be 'disembowelled'.

More wrote in his autobiography, 'I can't say I got on as well with the author as I should like to have done. We were polite to each other, and I admired his ability, and of course, still do, but somehow we just did not hit it off. This situation stemmed from an incident that happened in Brighton before we brought the play to London. I went into Mona Washbourne's dressing-room just before we were due to open, and found her in tears. "Alan's just been in and reduced me to nothing. Now I feel completely lost." To me this was the most disgraceful thing to do to any artiste when he or she is about to appear on stage. I went at once to see Patrick Garland, the play's director, and told him what had happened. "Pat," I said, "you have got to get Alan Bennett out of this theatre tonight, otherwise I'm not going on." I can't do that, Kenny," he said. "He's an old chum. We were at Cambridge together." ' This reported comment by Garland seemed to confirm the actor's suspicion of the so-called Oxbridge Mafia, no matter that he got the name of the university wrong. However, Garland took More's threat to leave the show seriously, and Bennett was barred from the theatre, not such an unusual occurrence for a writer. Frith Banbury, who had directed More in his favourite role, Freddy Page in Terence Rattigan's *The Deep Blue Sea* (1952), comes to Bennett's defence:

'Alan felt that Mona was making the part [of More's slightly bohemian mother-in-law], much sweeter than it should have been, and told her so. He dislikes sentimentality and sweetening up in any form. I'm sure he was artistically right. Anyway, it's easy to reduce actors to tears. I should know. Alan is not the sort of person who would do so intentionally. I've never seen him shouting at anybody.' Given Bennett's fondness for elderly ladies, it seems inconceivable that he was deliberately cruel. It is the case, though, that he was going through a particularly difficult emotional period, and this may have made him more tetchy than usual. Without Bennett's presence in the theatre, and without his permission, the play, according to its author, had been 'clumsily cut', reducing its serious content and turning it into 'a complacent light comedy with sad and sentimental moments.' Even with the cuts restored, however, the play makes a similar impression to that given by the form in which it was originally performed.

Getting On opened at the Queen's Theatre in October, 1971 to mostly good reviews. Irving Wardle of *The Times* found it a soft-hearted, 'deeply English work' and commented: 'It is no slur on the funny men of ten years ago that they are not so funny as they used to be. Satire is generally a young writer's trade, and from Angus Wilson to Michael Frayn there seems to come a point where they have decided that it is better not to raise a laugh at all than to do so cruelly.' *The Observer's* Helen Dawson wrote, 'Bennett's writing is often bravura: there are lines which are good jokes, there are lines that are belly-laughs, there are passages of nostalgic enthusiasm and, suddenly, he can bring you close to tears. He is unafraid of sentiment and therefore quite unsentimental.'

Although it does contain a fair amount of Bennett-esque themes, variations, and language ('If I had my time over again I wouldn't have daughters, I'd have geraniums'), this is one of his least personal works; a Simon Gray play, through which Bennett is struggling to get out. One doesn't feel that he is really involved in this middle-class home (designed by Julia Trevelyan Oman) or with the cynical leading character and his marriage. The political views of the play's Labour MP and his 'friendly' Tory MP rival, are rather caricatured and the young people are unconvincing. They carry the accoutrements of their generation, they talk of communes, 'good vibes', wanting to do nothing, and are ignorant of Captain Oates. But the play does introduce Bennett's first overtly homosexual character in the part of Brian Lowther, the Tory MP, played by Brian Cox. It was still fairly unusual on the West End stage to find a 'normal' stiff-wristed homosexual (the word 'gay' had not yet become current), although Simon Gray's *Butley*, which had opened a few months before, had Alan Bates living with a young man and John Schlesinger's film that year *Sunday, Bloody Sunday*, centered around both Peter Finch and Glenda Jackson suffering exquisitely as they lusted after the same vapid boy.

Another Bennett theme that emerged was the obsession with bodily (or private) functions and decay. 'There are still people who stink, did you know that? They sit there on the other side of the table in Sam's airless little office and they stink of muck and squalor and filth and despair.' This obsession was pushed more to the foreground in his next play *Habeas Corpus*.

Getting On received the *Evening Standard* award for the Best Comedy of 1971. Accepting the statuette, Bennett told the story of the gardener who, having lovingly reared a marrow, found at the local horticultural show that he had been awarded the prize for the best cucumber. 'The panel will have to be careful. Next year the award for Best Comedy will go to *Long Day's Journey Into Night*.'

IV

In the 1960s a new species of respected writer emerged in Britain – the TV playwright. In the previous decade, in the USA, television had already become a medium in which serious writers could explore more interesting themes away from the gigantic pressures of Hollywood and the box-office requirements of Broadway. Ironically, the one-eyed monster, the movies' arch-enemy, provided Hollywood with some of its best screenplays of the era, from the pens of Paddy Chayefsky, Rod Serling and Reginald Rose. In Britain Clive Exton, Alun Owen, David Mercer, Harold Pinter, Charles Wood, Alan Plater, Dennis Potter and John Bowen served the two main TV play slots; ITV's *Armchair Theatre* and the BBC's *Wednesday Play*. Only Plater and Potter continued writing as prolifically as ever for the box into the 'seventies and 'eighties and their one serious rival in this area, apart from Mike Leigh, is Alan Bennett.

TV and Bennett make the perfect marriage between medium and messenger. Had he been writing before television, he could have written radio plays for the Third Programme or scripts for Ealing Comedies, or for Will Hay, or even George Formby. Nowadays, although the British film industry, helped by the advent of Channel 4, has allowed Bennett the occasional shot at a screenplay, he remains best known for his contribution to television drama. Since 1975, he has written only three full-length plays and two one-act plays (one derived from a TV play) for the stage and two screenplays. He has had 23 plays screened on television.

There is something unpretentious, intimate and homey about the nature of television. It flickers and chatters away happily in people's homes all across the country. One could imagine the inhabitants staring at their surrogates on the screen as they might stare into the electric coal fire or sometimes at their unbelieving reflections in the mirror. The diminutive, democratic and domesticated television set suits Bennett's diminutive, democratic and domesticated plays. As Clive Hodgson has written, 'Other writers may choose the great themes of Life and Death; Bennett is content with the everyday matters of – well, life and death. His concerns *are* everyday, and they *do* matter. He counts out the small change of life on this tiny island with care and compassion.'

Despite the wide audiences and acclaim his television work has brought him, Bennett feels that his theatre work is still more important to him. Television continues to struggle for acceptance as an art form against its big brothers, the stage and cinema. TV's availability makes it seem like tap water to the theatre's wine. Just as a director of television films is not considered a 'real' film director until he has made a 'film' film, television playwrights need to write a 'play' play.

'It's the thing I can't do,' says Bennett. 'Or the thing I find hardest to do, because I think of it as permanent, probably. I think of a stage play as closer to a finished work of art.' But nowadays the best of TV plays are published and respectably preserved between book covers (all of Bennett's are), as well as having the advantage over stage plays in that they can be seen again at the push of a remote control button. Productions of stage plays are partly erased from memory.

A Day Out, Bennett's first TV play, was a first in other ways. It was his first work set in the North of England and it marked the beginning of a long collaboration with director Stephen Frears. Frears and Bennett had met in 1964 at the Royal Court, where Frears was assistant director and Bennett was appearing in *A Cuckoo in The Nest*. Frears, born in Leicester in 1931 entered films in the mid-1960s as assistant to Karel Reisz, Lindsay Anderson and Albert Finney on *Morgan*, *If* and *Charlie Bubbles* respectively. It was to Finney that Frears had brought the screenplay of his first feature, *Gumshoe* (1971), written by Neville Smith. The film gave Finney one of his best roles as a Liverpool bingo caller swept into a Chandler-esque drama. Its mixture of reality and imagination and its references to *film noir* put *Gumshoe* ahead of its time. It was thirteen years before the 'promising' director made a second feature film. In the meantime, he ploughed the less glamorous field of television, directing eight of Bennett's plays, and produced others.

A Day Out was to have been directed by Patrick Garland, but due to the temporary rift between the old Oxford chums over *Getting On*, it was given to Frears at the BBC. He remembers the play as being only seventeen pages long, very slim, and sketchy. It had been inspired by one of Bennett's large collection of old photographs – a formal group portrait of a cycling club. The play's title refers to an outing in the countryside of the Halifax cycling club in the summer of 1911. Bennett had merely written 'they go somewhere'. Their destination became Fountains Abbey (a now oft-visited landmark in Bennett plays).

'The actors spent a great deal of their time trying to make their parts bigger', says Frears. 'I liked the play because of its mood.' The cast included Northern club comedian Paul Shane, later of *Hi-De-Hi*, in his first role; Brian Glover; David Waller; Anthony Andrews and Virginia Bell, tall Virginia Woolf's great-niece. Bennett had had the same kind of indulgent Technicoloured lyricism in mind as he had seen in Bo Widerberg's *Adalen 31* (1969) about a 1930s strike at a paper mill. Happily, Frears opted to make it in black and white, partly because it is easier to eliminate anachronistic details that way and partly because it was closer to the period photographs that engendered the film.

V

Habeas Corpus, Bennett's third stage play, is reminiscent of Joe Orton's posthumous farce *What The Butler Saw*, which had been at the Queen's with Ralph Richardson in 1969. Bennett was an admirer of Orton's work and his play, too, has a farcical structure. During rehearsals, Bennett realised that he had used the word 'farce' twice in the text and promptly cut both mentions out. Nevertheless, the mood is established quickly by the leading character. 'The longer I practise medicine the more convinced I am there are only two types of cases; those that involve taking the trousers off and those that don't.'

Habeas Corpus has a fair amount of trousers down and skirts up, although Bennett claimed never to have written *anything* to do with sex until his father's death in 1974, which he felt also released him to write more about his Northern background. Michael Billington, in *The Guardian* saw the play as 'a gloriously vulgar but densely plotted farce that is a downright celebration of sex and the human body.' Actually, it was rather more of a wake than a celebration. Dr Wicksteed: 'They troop in here with their sore throats and their varicose veins. They parade before me bodies the colour of tripe and the texture of junket. Is this the image of God, this sagging parcel of vanilla blancmange hoisted day after day on the consulting-room table? Is this the precious envelope of the soul?' (Notice the upper-class doctor's comparisons of the body to working-class food that he would never eat.) And later: 'We're all pigs, pigs; little trotters, little tails. Offal. Show me a human body and I'll show you a cesspit.'

Like *Getting On*, the play is about the onset of middle age and the intimations of mortality. 'It is at the core of both plays,' said the 39-year-old Bennett, 'although I feel much younger now than when I was really young. What I regret is the time wasted in the past and perhaps that regret is at the heart of *Habeas Corpus*. I'm often in the depths of gloom and yet I still make jokes.' There are jokes aplenty in the play, rather too many are in fact, as jokes rather than witty lines in a play are a bad sign. The best were those of a linguistically nonsensical variety, with its shades of N F Simpson and Peter Cook and the moronic delivery of Spike Milligan's Eccles.

> *Connie* (the doctor's sister): It's no use. Look at my legs.
> *Mrs Swabb* (the cleaning lady): Very nice legs if you ask me. There are people running around with no legs at all, who'd be more than happy to have yours.

And . . .

> *Mrs Wicksteed:* Of course, I've known for years our marriage has been a mockery. My body lying there night after night in the wasted moonlight. I know now how the Taj Mahal must feel.

And . .

> *Canon Throbbing* (a celibate): How old are you, Connie?
> *Connie:* Thirty-three.
> *Throbbing:* What a coincidence!
> *Connie:* You're not thirty-three.
> *Throbbing:* No, but my inside leg is.

And . . .

> *Throbbing:* Then I had to get my skates on for Evensong.
> *Wicksteed:* Evensong on ice? The Church must be desperate.

More doubtful however, are the topical jokes ('I feel like Jan Masefield.' 'No dear, Jayne Mansfield.' 'No. Jan Masefield. She was a girl in the front row at school. Actually, it was the second row but it looked like the front row.') And the facetious jokes ('Isn't that the doorbell?' 'Let's not jump to conclusions. It could be the man next door taking his first tentative steps on the xylophone').

Joking apart, the play cleverly manipulates the stereotypes of farce through a fast and furious (and angry) *danse macabre*, gently raging against the dying of the light, far more entertaining and penetrating than the even more punnilinguistic 'intellectual farces' by Tom Stoppard – *Jumpers* and *Travesties* – that appeared the following year. Directed by Ronald Eyre, it opened at the Lyric Theatre in Shaftesbury Avenue in May 1973 with Sir Alec Guinness in the role of Dr Arthur Wicksteed. Guinness remembers Bennett saying to him that he hated *Great* acting. One of the most subtle of actors, Guinness definitely does not belong to any *great* school of acting; his secret is to steal scenes without being caught. Revealingly, the reserved Guinness is very much at home playing extrovert figures like the lascivious Arthur Wicksteed. (The play is full of suggestive names – Throbbing, Rumpers and Shanks.) Also cast were Margaret Courtenay, Phyllida Law, Joan Sanderson, Andrew Sachs and John Bird. The role of Mrs Swabb was played by Patricia Hayes, everybody's favourite cleaning woman.

When *Habeas Corpus* opened, Bennett remarked that 'Now the play is on, I feel bereft and out of the family . . . When it's all over you realise once again, what a lonely business writing is. You have to spend so much time by yourself. Probably I'm more gregarious than I think; probably I really enjoy being in a group. Perhaps I should have taken one of the parts myself and so stayed with the family.' That's exactly what he did. During the run in 1974, in the midst of a writer's block, Bennett dragged up successfully to take over from Patricia Hayes. He could have played the part of the Canon, but was 'fed up with playing clerics'. When *Habeas Corpus* was performed at the Martin Beck Theatre in New York in 1975, it featured Donald Sinden, Rachel Roberts, Celeste Holm, Richard Gere (before film stardom) and June Havoc as Mrs Swabb. The rare meeting of a Bennett play and Broadway was not a particularly happy one. Of the influential New York critics, only the expatriate Clive Barnes of *The New York Times* liked it, thereby laying himself open to accusations of being partisan.

VI

For *A Day Out*, Bennett's debut TV play, he had ventured North and into the past. *Sunset Across The Bay*, broadcast in the BBC *Play for Today* series in February 1975 and directed by Stephen Frears, was set squarely and surely in present-day Yorkshire. It tells of an elderly couple (Harry Markham and Gabrielle Daye) who move from Leeds to a retirement flat in Morecambe Bay. In the end the old man dies of a stroke, and his widow will presumably join others like her, killing time until time kills them.

'I didn't have to work at the dialogue – it's all there in my upbringing,' Bennett says. 'I'm sure too that some of the reluctance I felt at first stemmed from the fact that many other writers are mining the North Country seam.' But he mined a different seam from Northern writers such as David Storey, David Mercer, Alan Sillitoe and John Braine, whose work had shaken Southern complacency in the 1960s in novels, on stage and on the large and small screens. They had revealed the deep political and social differences in this 'Divided Kingdom', whereas Bennett explores the cultural and linguistic aspects of the county of his own childhood and adolescence. He takes particular pleasure in the eccentricities of speech and behaviour of the elderly or middle-aged lower-middle class, derived from his observation of his parents and a cluster of 'aunties'. *Sunset Across The Bay* was the first of his plays to draw directly upon his own life, family and background.

There was a time when Bennett kept a notebook and would write down things he overheard on buses or in waiting rooms or shops – a single spy collecting evidence for a play. 'One does hear extraordinary dialogue,' Bennett told Paul Bailey on Radio 3 in 1988. 'My mother's in a home near Weston-super-Mare. I went to see her, and she can't speak any more. But the old lady next to her is very garrulous and she talks and talks and talks. She said, "They keep telling me I ought to have been a Trappist nun. I don't want to be a Trappist nun. My dad kept Friar's Balsam in the medicine chest but that's as far as it went." It came out absolutely like that. It was so perfectly constructed, with the point at the end of the joke.' Ten years before on ITV's *Russell Harty Plus* . . . he had read out some of his eavesdroppings: 'I thought that was a fellow in a raincoat bending down – it's two sheep.' 'I see the President of Romania's mother is dead – there's always trouble for somebody.' Unlike the jokes in his stage plays, which seem to come from the author not the characters, those in his television work are part of the idiom of the Doreens, the Maureens and the Winnies, and the way in which they see life.

In his published introduction to two of his television plays Bennett writes; 'People, by which I mean television producers, imagine northern speech simply as standard English with a dirty dishcloth accent, and northern women as southern women who can't speak properly. They're not. Northern women are another species. They have come down by a separate generic route and like the Galapagos turtles (whom some of them resemble) they have developed their own characteristics and attitudes . . . Social distinctions are subtle and minute. There are advantages to be drawn from status, however lowly . . . It's social climbing, albeit very much on the lower slopes. I was once on the top of a tram in Leeds with my aunty. We were passing Wellington Road gasworks. She laid a hand on my arm. "That's the biggest gasworks in England," she said. "And I know the manager." ' Bennett also recalls day trips to Morecambe from Leeds during which his mother would make a remark like, 'Oh look, there's that Mr Thornton. He used to be an inspector on the trams.'

But between his hilarity at remarks picked up by his sensitive antennae, and his own jokes, he reveals a wistful, melancholy streak. 'I tend to go from silly jokes to quite high seriousness in quite a short space of time,' he says. 'But I'm afraid my life's like that, I do go from frivolity to seriousness very quickly.'

Robert Hardy, who replaced Alec Guinness in *Habeas Corpus*, said at the time, 'He's obsessed with long afternoons. I have to say that phrase at least three times in the play, and you have to keep treading a very thin line between comedy and tragedy.' Bennett is one of those writers whose world we enter willingly as an audience but which we would loathe to enter in reality. Like many of his characters, he shares a sense of foreboding and gloom. Thoughts inevitably lead to old age, disease and dying, to the old-age home, the hospital and the cemetery, places to which his TV plays continue to return. *A Little Outing* (1977) was to an old people's home; a hospital was the setting for *Intensive Care* and for *Rolling Home*; *Our Winnie* took place in a graveyard (all 1982). These capsule lives of 'people of no importance' manage to be stimulants and depressants at the same time, forcing ostrich-like audiences to raise their heads from the usual sit-coms and soaps.

Patricia Routledge had a long career in musicals and the classics before Bennett inducted her into his world. Their first collaboration was *A Visit From Miss Prothero*, directed by Stephen Frears for the BBC in January 1978, the first of the plays to have been filmed in a studio. Routledge, as the eponymous Miss Prothero, descends upon the retired Mr Dodsworth (Hugh Lloyd) in the cosy living-room of his semi-detached house. After a short while she destroys his illusions by 'bringing him up to date' on the people with whom he worked. To the credit of the two-hander, it is difficult to quote lines out of context because the characters are so rounded and complete. As Bennett says of northern women, 'Bare words on the page cannot convey the rhythms of their speech or the nuances with which they invest it' and this applies especially to the Birkenhead-born Routledge's delivery and timing. Miss Prothero is, as Mr Dodsworth calls her, 'a bad, boring bitch' but like most of Bennett's 'monstrous regiment of women' she is seen with pathos and humour, despite the slightly patronising tone he often adopts towards his characters. Aside from their little snobberies, it is the apparent paucity and poverty of other people's pleasures, be they evening classes, hang-gliding, romantic novels or ballroom dancing, that are the butts of his scorn.

VII

Before Bennett embarked on his series of six plays for London Week-end Television in the 1978-9 season, he returned to the theatre with *The Old Country*, which opened at the Queen's Theatre in September 1977 and again starred Alec Guinness, this time as a Kim Philby figure, in exile in Russia. It begins in what seems like the depths of the English countryside, with a middle-aged couple pottering about in the garden and Elgar in the background. Then, gradually, one realises that it is not a cottage in England but a dacha outside Moscow. The deception is kept up for an inordinately long time, but this kind of surprise can only work, if at all, on the opening night or if audiences come without any pre-knowledge.

Part of the play's discourse is that the character of Hilary (like Burgess in Bennett's later play, *An Englishman Abroad*) is living in a parody of the England he remembers whereas his visiting brother-in-law Duff, writer-lecturer, on the board of the Arts Council, Covent Garden and many other organisations, only sees contemporary England, its decline in the arts, architecture and 'the loss of the elm'. Both of them are men of the past and the play is peppered with enough nostalgic references to make you sneeze. Regret is expressed over the demise of the lending library at the Army and Navy Stores, and of Gamages, Pontings, trains from Kemble to Cirencester, and Lyons Corner Houses; at changes in church services; etc., etc. In other words, it is no crime to have betrayed a country that has betrayed itself. It is also littered with epigrams of a Stoppardian nature: 'In England we never entirely mean what we say, do we? Do I mean that? Not entirely. And logically it follows that when we say we don't mean what we say, only then are we entirely serious.'

'I'm not really interested in espionage at all. I wrote it in order to get some view of England from a distance,' Bennett explains. 'I mean, it says nothing about Russia. Neither does *An Englishman Abroad*. In a way, these plays, and also *Forty Years On*, are all attempts to stand back and look at England and express my ambivalent feelings about it. In a way, the character in *The Old Country* is based on someone like Auden, not Philby.'

The conventionally constructed play (though french windows exist only notionally in it), contains its share of rather awkwardly contrived meetings, especially one between Duff and a young man who proceeds to blackmail him over an alleged homosexual incident. But Alec Guinness's dry delivery and perfect timing enabled him to ride Bennett's winged hobby-horses with consummate ease.

VIII

The *Six Plays* on LWT had first been offered to the BBC who agreed to do only three of them, one a year. That wasn't on. The sequence of plays (actually telefilms), shown over six weeks, put Bennett in the forefront if not the *avant garde* of television playwrights and in terms of television drama were a considerable achievement. This despite the fact that films made for the small screen are usually saddled with the slightly derogatory tag of 'miniaturist'. It is regarded as especially damning for a critic to compare a feature film with 'something made for television' – a common criticism – but most telefilms suffer less in the cinema (witness the Alan Bennett season at the National Film Theatre in 1984) than many feature films do on television. Of the six, four were directed by Stephen Frears, one by Lindsay Anderson and one by Giles Foster. Since then, Frears has hit the 'big time' on the big screen.

The plays range far more widely thematically, spatially and stylistically than the second half-dozen plays Bennett wrote for the BBC in 1982 and are, on the whole, less pessimistic. The author himself narrates the story of the 35-year-old sexually repressed Polytechnic teacher (Neville Smith) in *Me, I'm Afraid Of Virginia Woolf*, which ends with his joyful bursting out of the closet and final acceptance of his nature when he falls for a male student, to the strains of 'I'm In Love With A Wonderful Guy' from *South Pacific*. Frears says that when they put the orchestral version on the soundtrack it didn't work: 'The lyrics [sung by Mitzi Gaynor] made it overt and very funny.' Up to this climax, the dullness of provincial town life is captured in all its ghastly detail – draughty classrooms, streets and canteens, the poor man having to listen to his haranguing, gossiping mother (Thora Hird) and having to satisfy his girlfriend (Carol Macready), to whom he is not attracted. In one scene, he reproaches his mother for calling him Trevor.

'You're in the outside lane before the pistol goes with a name like Trevor. It's not Trevor Proust, is it? Trevor Sibelius? Lenin, Stalin, where would they be if they'd been called Trevor?'

This does not faze his mam at all.

'Well, what about Mrs Beaver's son? He's called Trevor. He's the North Western Area Manager for Kayser-Bonder. Trevor hasn't stopped him getting to the top.'

Like Trevor, Lee (Henry Man), the Chinese waiter in *Afternoon Off*, is also cut off from his environment but in this instance it is a linguistic and cultural barrier that separates him from the inscrutable English. In a poignant, picaresque tale peopled with a collection of Bennett types (Thora Hird crops up), the ingenuous and initially cheerful oriental embarks on his quest round Hartlepool for a girl he was told to contact, equipped only with her name, Iris, and a box of Milk Tray for her. Bennett himself has a brief cameo as a man in the office of a factory confusing Lee even further: 'She was in despatch. She had a big mauve jumper. Her mother had a duodenal ulcer. They had a caravan at Skipsea.' Frears says the action was shifted to Hartlepool on the West Coast because 'I was fed up with shooting in places like Morecambe. In fact, I discovered that Hartlepool was the most haunted town.' As with most of the six plays, the location is not a backdrop to the action but a participant, relating strongly to the characters' emotions. Bennett's own acute awareness of his environment comes through in these works. He was chairperson of the Civic Society in Settle, where his parents lived, in an attempt to do something about the destruction of the countryside and the redevelopment of towns.

'You can't go on wringing your hands forever. I used to say I'd like to live in Blackburn or Halifax, somewhere like that, but not now, they've been so messed about. But you can't keep on going around hiding your eyes from things. I sometimes think I should go and live in Centre Point or the Barbican. In the middle of somewhere so unpleasant that whatever they did, they couldn't make it any worse.'

Morecambe is the setting for *All Day On The Sands*, directed by Giles Foster. This combines the writer's own childhood memories of holidays at the Lancashire seaside resort with the doleful reality *circa* 1979. The pretensions of the Miramar Guest House attempting to bring a touch of the Riviera to its clients are mordantly satirised, and the family's agony at trying to keep up a front and hide the fact that the father has just been made redundant is sharply observed and played.

Bennett had written *One Fine Day* a little earlier than the others in the series. Most of it takes place in an empty high-rise office where an estate agent, who has been unable to let the property, decides to camp out. The characters, milieu and the limited amount of dialogue make it rather uncharacteristic of Bennett's work, neither is there hair nor hide of an elderly Northern woman. It is also unusual in that it features Irish 'sit-down' comedian Dave Allen as the estate agent, finding reality and himself in the unreal situation. For director Stephen Frears, it was a breakthrough.

'The world changed for me with *One Fine Day*,' he says. There is a fluency in the camerawork and a spatial dimension that exceeds his previous work: it is the most cinematic of the sequence of plays.

On a much smaller scale, shot in a studio and set in an office in Harrogate, was *Doris And Doreen* (renamed *Green Forms* for publication), a kind of companion piece to *A Visit From Miss Prothero*. It is a quick-fire double act for Prunella Scales and Patricia Routledge as two office clerks choking on red tape, green and pink forms, preconceived opinions and business jargon. Place names like Newport Pagnell, Cleveleys, Mablethorpe and Bispham, and proper names like Angela Barlthrop, Mr Swithinbank and Mrs Henstridge clutter their conversation not in themselves funny except on the lips of these two ladies. Their jobs seem to be threatened by the coming of a Ms Dorothy Binns, who has left a 'trail of redundancy' wherever she's been. Bennett captures the way the trivia of office life take on important dimensions for those whose empty lives they help fill: 'Office life has always fascinated me, I don't know why, because I've never worked in an office myself,' he states. It crops up again some years later in *The Insurance Man*.

Out of the handful of plays one stuck out like a sore thumb. Television critics who were generally warm to the series, were considerably cooler towards *The Old Crowd* but their bile was aimed not so much at the author as at the first-time TV director, Lindsay Anderson.

'It needed Lindsay Anderson . . . to bring out a quality in Alan Bennett's writing which had hitherto lain dormant – crass stupidity,' Clive James smirked in his *Observer* column. 'Previously Bennett had been the helpless, shackled prisoner of his wit, sensitivity and insight. Secretly he was crying out for someone to spring him loose, so that he could set about doing what the real, committed playwrights do – i.e. make large, vague and hectoring statements about Bourgeois Society, of which they know little, and the Human Condition, of which they know less . . . If Anderson had brought nothing but his talent to the job, the show would have been over in five minutes . . . The whole enterprise has been very instructive . . . The chief lesson to be learned is that even a writer as intelligent as Alan Bennett can fall prey to the delusion that solemnity equals seriousness. Only a lurking desire for respectability could have led him to deliver his work into the hands of Lindsay Anderson.'

Anderson, at Oxford in the 1940s with Tony Richardson, John Schlesinger and Kenneth Tynan, had gained attention as a harsh critic himself in *Sequence*, an influential quarterly film magazine between 1946 and 1952. He then made his name at the Royal Court Theatre and as part of the movement called Free Cinema in the late 'fifties, before directing his first feature, *This Sporting Life*, in 1963. There is still something touchingly 'sixties about his films, relics of the satire boom of the period made by an 'Angry Old Man'.

'Lindsay talked too much about it *(The Old Crowd)* beforehand,' said Bennett. 'He puts people's backs up.' Before it was shown, London Weekend claimed that it had cost a quarter of a million pounds, unprecedented for a taped studio production, and Anderson announced that it would 'destroy the myth of the television play by being anti-television'. Anderson was determined to 'alienate' (not only in the Brechtian sense) the audience by revealing this as a TV play – we see the crew, monitors, the three-walled set, etc.; at one moment it goes into black-and-white and back into colour. The story dealt with a house-warming party held, in an almost completely empty Edwardian mansion in trendy Islington, for a number of affluent guests, including Jill Bennett, John Moffat, Isabel Dean, Frank Grimes, Cathleen Nesbitt and Rachel Roberts, who busily display their social etiquette while civilisation collapses around them. Much of Bennett's stylised, absurdist dialogue retains echoes of reality but unfortunately, though an often fascinating experiment, the whole enterprise is too self-conscious and suffers in comparison with that master of such anti-bourgeois surreal parables, Luis Buñuel – to whom Anderson pays open homage.

IX

Apart from the hullabaloo over *The Old Crowd*, Bennett's TV plays were held in esteem, and his four stage plays, each with a big star, had had respectable runs in Shaftesbury Avenue and made him a fair amount of money. The word 'flop' was not in his CV. His next play, *Enjoy*, would put it there.

Up to 1980, Bennett had reserved the North of England for television and the South for the stage, as if small people's small lives in small Northern homes fitted more easily on to the small screen. The London theatre was too posh for all that. It was the domain of the public school in *Forty Years On*, with its undaunted references to Virginia Woolf, Bertie Russell, Stephen Spender and Julian Grenfell; an Edwardian mansion in London suburbia inhabited by an MP in *Getting On*; the consulting room of a private physician on the south coast in *Habeas Corpus*; and the Russian dacha housing an upper-class English 'traitor' in *The Old Country*, all traditional West End fare. *Enjoy*, which opened at the Vaudeville Theatre in mid-October 1980 starring Joan Plowright and Colin Blakely, was set in 'the last back-to-back in Leeds'. Neither the critics nor the public took the title as an invitation and it closed seven weeks later. During rehearsals, according to Plowright, who played Blakely's wife, Bennett 'used to lie on his back in the stalls groaning a lot, but I think he was fairly happy with the way it went during our trial fortnight in Richmond. We only lost two old ladies and they walked out during a matinée. You never know with Alan's plays until you get them in front of an audience what they're going to be like.'

Enjoy was unveiled in the same week as Howard Brenton's potent parable of colonialism, *The Romans In Britain*, which caused a storm of protest, its portrayal of a homosexual rape leading to the prosecution of the director, Michael Bogdanov, by Britain's moral watchdog, Mrs Mary Whitehouse. (The case was won by the National Theatre.) Some of the language and situations in the Bennett play, although mild in comparison with the Brenton, provided further evidence of the moral decline of the country, causing worthy citizens to write to *The Times* from the Home Counties. The metropolitan reviewers took Bennett to task for aesthetic rather than ethical reasons.

'Too slow, too fussily written and too much a comic anthology of working-class attitudes and bromides,' was John Barber's opinion in *The Daily Telegraph*. B A Young in *The Times* disliked the 'rather condescending jokes' such as 'Linda is quite at home in hotels, she can choose from a menu without turning a hair.' But the play seemed to hit a raw nerve in James Fenton of *The Sunday Times*, who found that Bennett's 'own nausea and self-accusation is presented on stage; the son who swears to his mother that he will never put her in a home turns out to be a playwright; the museum for which he has destined his mother is none other than this play. The overall result is sentimental, embarrassing and bad; bad from a combination of strong talent and little faith in the value of art. It is true that there can be something unpleasant in the actual act of turning one's relatives into art – but nobody is obliging Mr Bennett to be a playwright or to be that kind of playwright. I felt most strongly that the problems raised in this play, and its awful self-accusations, should have been resolved by the author before the work reached rehearsal.' Fenton might not have liked the result, but playwrights from Ibsen and Strindberg to O'Neill and Tennessee Williams have presented their 'own nausea and self-accusation' on stage, though seldom as amusingly. The best notices went to Plowright and the worst to the playwright.

The starting point for the flawed play had been Jeremy Seabrook's *What Went Wrong?* – 'a very good book about old-style trade unionism and the Labour movement', according to Bennett. Ms Craig (obviously Philip Sayer in drag), a wordless social worker, calls on an elderly couple, Wilfred and Connie Craven (Blakely and Plowright). 'Her' silence allows Bennett to exploit one of his favourite devices, the monologue. The characters could only come from one pen. There is a sour description of Leeds, a deeply depressing view of old age, a suspicion of social workers as a class, a vulgar daughter, a transsexual son and a nice line in non-sequiturs: 'Who says I'm your daughter, anyway?' ' 'Course you're our daughter. I bought you those slippers.'

Joan Plowright's husband, Lord Olivier, rode to the defence of the play in the letter columns, calling it 'a dazzlingly brilliant work and we know that dazzling brilliance is often blinding to some critics'. He went on to say that 'Mr Bennett does his simple duty as a playwright and artist in writing of human nature as he recognises and shrewdly observes it for the better understanding in human nature of itself.'

His wife was no less fulsome. '*Enjoy* is about love and death and cruelty and age and hypocrisy and forgiveness and language and the twentieth century and things like that. It's also very funny.'

X

In 1982 Alan Bennett came up with another cluster of six television plays, this time for the BBC. In some of Bennett's plays, mention is made of a parent whose son or daughter 'is not quite right'. *Our Winnie*, directed by Malcolm Mowbray, brings one of them into the foreground. Winnie (played by Sheila Kelley) is a mentally retarded woman on a visit to her father's grave with her mother (Elizabeth Spriggs) and her aunt (Constance Chapman). The familial affection and the recognition of Winnie's sexuality is undeniably moving. The mother and aunt are created through the idiosyncracies of their conversation, but Bennett is, as so often, less sure with younger people. Certain contemporary phrases seem to the author to be part of the deterioration of the English language when it is mere linguistic nostalgia on his part. He seems to find amusing and distressing the fact that the school subject of Nature Study has become Environmental Studies and that the lower middle-classes should be going in for things like Sub-Aqua. ('He's gone overboard for Sub-Aqua.')

The retired couple (Hugh Lloyd, Thora Hird) in *Say Something Happened* have a son 'not right' and a daughter whom they proudly claim to be a top executive's secretary. They are visited by a young, jargon-mouthing social worker (Julie Walters) in her first 'interface situation', who has come to help them but ends up being helped. 'I've no experience of social workers, and I slightly feel they have a bad deal in what I write,' says Bennett. 'I don't want to take the attitude of *The Sun* or *Daily Express* of thinking of them as these monsters, but I think I write about them because they're agents in interfering and directing people's lives, and in that sense they keep cropping up, but then so do clergymen, whom I also have a very ambiguous attitude towards.' Ambiguity is something Bennett thrives on. It also prevents him from coming down strongly on one side or another in his plays. As he sniggers at his characters, so he weeps for them; as they are condemned so they are praised.

What are we to make of Miss Schofield in the first of his TV monologues, *A Woman Of No Importance*, directed by Giles Foster?

As Bennett points out, 'Miss Schofield is a bore. But to have her in full close-up, retailing in unremitting detail how she borrowed the salt in the canteen, takes one, I hope, beyond tedium.' She is one of those lonely women, like Miss Prothero, Doris and Doreen, who have spent their lives in an office where the petty squabbles, manoeuvring for position and daily contact has offered a substitute for family life and meaningful existence. The tremendous presence of Patricia Routledge forces the spectator's (and Bennett's) initial superiority to be replaced by deep affection for this pathetic creature wasting away from an unspecified disease.

Mr Wyman (John Barrett), a retired bricklayer in a geriatric ward in *Rolling Home*, endures the visits of his well-meaning family in virtual silence, reserving his conversation for a young male nurse (David Threlfall). Wyman's two contrasting daughters, not without guilt at putting their father in an institution, are preoccupied with their own lives. Molly (Pat Heywood), middle-aged and married, talks repetitively of her children's achievements at getting life-saving medals and doing indoor rock-climbing, while Val (Maureen Lipman) is a buyer for a clothes shop: 'Off to Harrogate next week, Dad. My annual jaunt. Northern Fashion Show.' Their petty lives are held to be absurd against the universal absurdity of the old man's death.

Intensive Care is what Bennett takes to hit the right tone, whether it be voice or atmosphere in the journey towards self-fulfilment of Denis Midgely, a 39-year-old schoolmaster, waiting in the hospital for his dad (a retired plumber) to die. The fact that Bennett himself plays the central character necessarily gives the play an autobiographical tinge. Bennett is so present in all his TV plays that it's difficult to believe that he had as yet appeared only briefly in one of them. He had first found fame as a performer in his own material and his face has somehow become a familiar one, despite his relatively rare appearances. Bennett disagrees. 'I've got an anonymous face, so I'm not easily recognised,' he once said. 'The biggest risk is that people might think I'm David Hockney.' In *Intensive Care*, directed by Gavin Millar, Bennett as Midgley and Thora Hird as his Aunt Kitty sit side by side keeping vigil, two of the most famous bespectacled faces on TV, apart from the Two Ronnies.

'You wouldn't think they'd have curtains in a hospital, would you? You'd think it wouldn't be hygienic,' says Aunt Kitty, looking around critically, jumping from one subject to the next. Midgley takes his glasses off when he gets into bed with the night nurse (Julie Walters), during which time his father dies. 'It's a pity you weren't here, Denis,' says Aunt Kitty. 'You've been here all the time he was dying. What were you doing?' 'Living,' he replies. When it was suggested that Bennett play the leading role, he hesitated, thinking he'd be too shy to go to bed with Julie Walters. 'Then I thought, "That's no reason for not doing it." So I said I'd do it and then I had to audition for the part.'

The plight of an under-educated, unemployed sixteen-year-old boy (a rather older-looking Ian Targett) underlies *Marks*. The title refers to school marks, character marks, stretch marks and the tattoo mark of 'Mother' the youth has put on his arm. The tattoo causes his mam, deserted by her husband, to react violently.

'Writing on your body. You can't even spell and you go writing on your body.'

The bitterness and desolation of the characters, tempered by their humour, counterpointed by Bennett's own irony, make for an effective piece of social realism. There is, however, an unexpected and uncomfortable end to the tale. The last scene, set some years later, shows the boy naked on a bed while a voiceover explains that 'When he looked at the tattoo it did always remind him of his mother, though not in the way it had been meant to. He remembered only her anger and her grief, and how she had wept to see him spoiled. In that sense the tattoo had served its purpose. It was a badge, an emblem. A mark that he was hers. It was as if she had engraved it herself.' Then a man strokes his tattoo, saying 'Tattoos always turn me on.' The relation is made between the mother's hold on him and his homosexuality.

There was an overflow of themes, characters and situations into these half-dozen plays from the short-running *Enjoy*. Mention is made of the opening of a hospital ward or a visit to an Old People's Home by a minor royal personage, an important highlight in the residents' existences, these institutions being held as the worst places in which to spend one's last days. (As a student, Bennett had spent a couple of vacations cutting the grass at Leeds crematorium, witness to the perfunctory passing parade of countless unimportant lives.) Leeds is seen as a spoiled city with 'precincts', in which unfeeling social workers, relatives and nurses intrude upon people's lives. There is a preponderance of 'old-fashioned' names like Wilfred and Doris. It might have been of some amusement to Bennett that a young actress in *Marks* was named Tracylynn Stephens.

In 1969 *TW3* supremo Ned Sherrin had set up a film company for whom Bennett wrote a screenplay provisionally titled *Parson's Pleasure or The Vicar's Wife*, a comedy in the Ealing manner which centred round a sexy young woman's plans to kill her elderly parson husband by exhausting him to death, in bed and out. The script was offered to Peter Sellers, who turned it down, presumably because he had suffered a heart attack just after marrying Britt Ekland, some years his junior. Unlike the vicar's wife, the film was never made. Around 1972 there was serious talk of Bennett writing the screenplay for *A Handful Of Dust*, directed by John Schlesinger, but the whole project was considered too expensive by producers.

Nearly fifteen years later, Alan Bennett was sitting on a Yorkshire hillside watching his first feature film, *A Private Function*, being shot, the punny title of which is a typical Bennett or English joke: *vide* also Peter Nichols's *Privates On Parade*. On this same moor, many years before, Bennett had seen his aunty scattering his uncle's ashes while he remained, embarrassed, in the car. He remembered that his mother had spread greaseproof paper on the kitchen floor because the urn, which had spent the night before in their house, seemed to her in some mysterious way unhygienic. Heaven knows what she would have thought of having an incontinent pig in her house, the central comic situation of Bennett's farce.

This piggy element came from the director, Malcolm Mowbray, whose cousin had kept an unlicensed pig in the days of post-war rationing. The film is set in 1947, when Bennett, the son of a butcher, was thirteen.

'The butcher down the street from us was on the fiddle, and one of his customers was a stipendiary magistrate who was known to be hand-in-glove with him. The people on the council did well out of the black market, and so did the police chief. My dad didn't. I wish he had in a way. He used to be sat at the table at night looking at the ration books and worrying about making the meat go round.'

The plot concerns a mild-mannered chiropodist (Michael Palin), whose social climbing wife (Maggie Smith) will do anything to get invited to the small town's exclusive banquet to celebrate the forthcoming marriage of Princess Elizabeth to Lieutenant Philip Mountbatten. The foot doctor finds himself involved in the flourishing black market after kidnapping a pig to provide his family with a decent meal but which the local bigwigs want to consume at their private function. It was no coincidence that *A Private Function* appeared not long after another Royal wedding and that greed is the prime driving-force behind the class-ridden society depicted. 'I don't know what we fought the war for,' someone says.

The film, plainly in the satirical fable Ealing tradition of *Passport To Pimlico*, not only recaptures the days when people went to any lengths to circumvent the strict food rationing but lifts the lid on the crassness of the British class system. The gradations and nuances of class are beautifully caught by the cast, from Denholm Elliott's smarmy upper-class Dr Swaby (who thinks nothing of sending slightly dotty pensioners to the nearest asylum) and the porcine accountant Richard Griffiths, who falls in love with the doomed pig, to Bill Paterson's 'little Hitler' from the Ministry of Food. Palin, whom Elliott calls a 'festering bunion-scraping little pillock', and Maggie Smith, desperate to be accepted at coffee mornings, never put a foot wrong. Despite suffering from budget restrictions and cuts, the 'Pig Film', as Bennett liked to call it, was a notch above most British comedies of the 1980s.

XII

Although Bennett's admiration for Kafka had revealed itself briefly in *On The Margin*, the name of the great writer from Prague was not, in 1986, one that sprang naturally to mind in any discussion on the writer from Leeds. Yet his plays have sometimes had the glib and over-used adjective Kafka-esque affixed to them (whose haven't?), and one can see that Bennett would have an affinity with the grim humour and soulless societies of the mind of Franz Kafka, a man psychologically isolated from his environment.

'I do feel for Kafka. A very moving personality,' he says. 'Other people have lives, and I sit at home and write or sit at home and look out of the window. I go to Marks and Spencer largely, that's my day. I felt that when I was a child and I still feel like that now.' (That is, of course, when he isn't on location or playing nightly on the West End stage.)

Whereas the author of *The Trial* was used as a spark in *Kafka's Dick*, he was more of an inspiration for *The Insurance Man*, the shorter, and better, play. The former, which opened at the Royal Court Theatre in September 1986, studies how far a biographer is justified in probing into his subject's life and going against the subject's wishes, as Max

Brod did by not destroying his friend's novels as instructed. A chastening experience for any biographer in the audience to hear himself called 'yet another of those academic blow flies who make a living buzzing round the faeces of the famous'. Kafka (Roger Lloyd Pack) metamorphoses from a tortoise kept by a Leeds insurance clerk (Geoffrey Palmer) and his wife (Alison Steadman) after Max Brod (back from the dead) has urinated on it. The literary revue sketch, much favoured by Bennett, is here expanded and some jokes have a distinctly familiar ring to them: 'T S Eliot is an anagram for Toilets.' There was more self-plundering from the short-lived *Enjoy*: the senile, incontinent old man who must be given a memory test and talks of having 'had fifteen men under me' when he was in work, a phrase Bennett has found amusing enough to repeat in three plays.

He also uses the final, superfluous scene in Heaven to settle some personal linguistic scores. Heaven is a place where nobody says 'hopefully' or 'at the end of the day' or 'at this moment in time', or 'we're in the presence of a God situation here'. Apart from Virginia Woolf, who crops up again, among the 'heavenly' inhabitants are 'camp' Hollywood stars Carmen Miranda and Betty Hutton, incongruously paired with Bertie Russell and Ludwig Wittgenstein. Someone says 'Talk of the Devil, here comes God,' and Kafka concludes, on arrival, that 'Heaven is going to be hell.'

The Insurance Man, first shown on BBC TV in February 1986, was set in Pre-World War I Prague (shot mainly in St George's Hall, Liverpool). The director Richard Eyre, now artistic director of the National Theatre, said that Bennett's script looked like spotted dick: 'It was typed on very thin paper with notes in a calligraphic hand stuck on to bits of tissue paper, and it's a kaleidoscopic script . . . Bennett and Kafka meet *Alice In Wonderland*.'

The story concerns Franz (Robert Hines), a young man who has caught a skin disease for which he blames his job in the dyeworks. In order to 'seek compensation for his condition' he visits the industrial accident insurance company where he is interviewed by the claims assessor, a Mr Kafka (Daniel Day-Lewis), who does some writing on the side. Bennett called it 'a mirror image of *The Trial* in that this boy tries to find his way through bureaucracy to get some kind of justice'. Bennett and Eyre managed what few have done in meeting Kafka and his world head on; they have recaptured his style and spirit, as well as commenting on it.

XIII

'I don't want my biography, or a bit of it, written,' Alan Bennett wrote to this 'academic blow fly' to express his suspicion of this book. 'Forgive me – it's a kind of reticence which isn't in any way modest. I just don't want to be pinned down . . . This isn't to say you shouldn't do it . . .'

In *Kafka's Dick*, he himself had explored some of the ethics of biography and its inevitable intrusion into other people's lives. He had already dramatised an anecdote involving Guy Burgess in *An Englishman Abroad* but when he agreed to write the screenplay of *Prick Up Your Ears*, adapted from John Lahr's life of Joe Orton, he entered fully into the biographical arena, where many a reputation has been picked clean. The film ends with Peggy Ramsey (Vanessa Redgrave), Orton's agent, and John Lahr (Wallace Shawn), visiting the tiny Islington flat where Kenneth Halliwell, Orton's lover, had killed Orton and himself. It is now occupied by a newly married young couple. The husband says to them, 'Have you seen enough?' Bennett writes that this echoes 'my own ambivalent feelings about gossip and biography, and about Orton himself'. At least, as far as his conscience is concerned, Bennett only transmuted the already very public story of Orton's life and death into a film script and further distanced himself by the device of having John Lahr interview people in the process of his research for the book.

At the time of writing his book, John Lahr (son of Bert Lahr, the Cowardly Lion in *The Wizard Of Oz*) offered the screen rights to Stephen Frears. He and Bennett had gone their separate creative ways after the *Six Plays* for LWT although they saw each other as friends, since Frears's ex-wife and children live opposite Bennett in Camden Town. Frears had made a return to feature films with the pretentious, Spanish-located thriller, *The Hit*, which turned out to be The Flop. Bennett feared Frears had developed a taste for action and helicopters, not in the Yorkshire writer's line at all, but then came *My Beautiful Laundrette*, in which Frears dealt delicately and amusingly with the love affair between two boys, a Pakistani youth and a skinhead.

Although as personalities, the promiscuous extrovert Orton and the monastic introvert Bennett were as unlike as one could imagine, there were similarities. Orton's upbringing and family background in Leicester in the late 'thirties and 'forties approximated to Bennett's own in Leeds. They had both become famous in 'Swinging 'Sixties'

London and both were playwrights who pricked up their ears at any linguistic idiosyncracies. In *Loot*, Orton's most perfect play, there is much in his special brand of anarchic humour and puncturing of the gentility and snobberies of the stifling lower middle-classes that is recognisable in Bennett. Seemingly meaningless lines that make sense within the context, like 'I might have been a redhead today if you had been an accountant' or 'Even the sex you were born into isn't safe from your maraudings' could have come from Bennett. Orton once said that he 'developed a mocking, cynical way of treating events because it prevented them from being too painful'. One wonders what he would have written in Thatcherite Britain. In some ways the gentler, less subversive Bennett has carried on Orton's verbal comedy and heightened realism.

Bennett says, 'I feel I wouldn't have liked him. And I don't think he would have liked me. I feel the intensity he had and the single-mindedness and the determination to succeed. I find that's rather alienating.' However, in *Prick Up Your Ears*, the sort of smutty pun that appeals to Bennett, the two playwrights met most happily across the years. With suggestions from Frears and Lahr, Bennett wrote five or six drafts before he got it right.

'My initial attempts to turn the book into a film were heavy-handed and clumsy. To begin with Orton's life was unevenly documented . . . I admired his plays, but I had mixed feelings about the man. I took sides with Halliwell.' The first American producer to see a draft 'wanted an English *Cage Aux Folles*' and 'One Hollywood producer who saw an early draft of the script said that he saw no problems so long as Orton was made an American; oh, and he should of course be heterosexual.' Apocryphal or not, these stories explain why the film was British-made (much of it shot in Croydon) and why Joe Orton was not played by Tom Cruise but by an eerily convincing Gary Oldman, fresh from his role as Sid Vicious in *Sid And Nancy*.

Anyone who has read the Orton Diaries, edited by Lahr, might have wondered how the catalogue of 'cottage' visits and the '*mille e tre*' Arab boys Orton had in Tangiers could be translated to the screen without it toppling into pornography. The answer was merely to suggest them by a few representative, somewhat reticent, scenes – a group of Moroccan youths in decorous white djellabas romping on the beach, with no sign of the poverty that led them to be exploited by Westerners such as Orton. What comes across is nostalgia for the dawn of the new Elizabethan age (Orton and Halliwell have sex for the first time during the Coronation TV transmission), for the Festival of Britain, the freedom of the 'sixties and a pre-AIDS world. Bennett skilfully extends the real-life *A Star Is Born* plot into his own territory to include Julie Walters as Orton's mother, other members of Orton's family ('I never thought such things went on in Leicester') and a landlady ('Idle curiosity's never been my strong point').

The most successful sequences of the film were those of the 'marriage' between the bald failure Kenneth Halliwell (a rather too charismatic Alfred Molina) and the perky, sexy, talented Joe Orton in their claustrophobic flat. The relationship was seen by Bennett as 'a marriage between a wife who bears all the burden of the heat of the day and pushes her husband until the point where he becomes successful – at which point the first wife is often discarded and the second one comes along. We didn't just want to make it a gay film.' The marriage analogy is rather obviously stated by showing Lahr and his wife under some strain. The need to explain and underline mars the climax when Halliwell, ironically having achieved posthumous fame, delivers a monologue to the mirror before he kills his lover.

The gay community was generally favourable to the film's portrayal of homosexuals, dissenting voices typified by a letter in *Time Out* which expressed the fear that 'The film's happiest audience must be homophobes who believe gay men are either pervert anything-fuckers that hang around sordid public lavatories or psychotic murderers . . . Homophobes love connecting homosexuality with self-loathing.' In fact, both Orton and Halliwell are depicted as perfectly at ease with their homosexuality (a rare thing in films). The real theme is closer to that of *Amadeus*, with it examination of the jealousy of the mediocre for the great.

On 5 June 1988 Alan Bennett and other stars took part in a benefit show organised by openly gay actor Ian McKellen to protest against the iniquitous Clause 28 (which legislated against the 'promotion' of homosexuality). Bennett told the audience: 'I was telephoned by Ian McKellen and asked whether I would be prepared to have a piece of my work performed alongside that of Oscar Wilde, W H Auden and Noël Coward. So I said it was an interesting list. Then he came straight out with it. "Are you a homosexual?" he asked. I said that it was a bit like asking a man crawling across the Sahara whether he would prefer Perrier or Malvern water.'

Like Orton, the two other real-life characters Bennett has dramatised, Guy Burgess and Anthony Blunt, were homosexuals. The homosexual and the spy, living a lie (perhaps) and hiding a secret, share a sense of not belonging to the society around them. When they happen to be homosexual spies, they are double agents in more senses than one. But the interest for Bennett was not in their sexuality (an essential factor in any *serious* study of their personalities), nor so much in their spying activities (for which they owe more of their notoriety), but in the related act of disaffection and their roles as opters-out. As in *The Old Country*, the double bill *Single Spies*, consisting of *An Englishman Abroad* and *A Question Of Attribution*, is a vehicle for commenting directly on England, for Bennett has never written anything that does not with the possible exception of *The Insurance Man*.

It was during the run of *The Old Country* in 1978 that the seed of *An Englishman Abroad* was planted in Bennett's mind. As he writes: 'Friends and well-wishers would come round after the performance, often with reminiscences of Philby and his predecessors, Burgess and Maclean. One of these was Coral Browne who told me of her visit to Russia with the Shakespeare Memorial Theatre in 1958 and the particular incidents that make up *An Englishman Abroad*. The picture of the elegant actress and the seedy exile sitting in a dingy Moscow flat through a long afternoon listening again and again to Jack Buchanan singing "Who stole my heart away?" seemed to me funny and sad.' Browne's extended anecdote was turned into a funny and sad television film for the BBC five years later, with the 69-year-old Australian-born actress convincingly playing her 45-year-old self and Alan Bates impeccable as Burgess. It was directed with unaccustomed wit, style and intelligence by John Schlesinger, with whom Bennett enjoyed working. 'It's three parts gossip to two parts work with John. When I first started I thought: "Surely you can't get much done like this?" But you can.'

Most people who knew Burgess agree that although Bates was not physically like him, he and Bennett captured the character of the man. 'I find it difficult to get worked up about Burgess as a spy partly because he was such a funny man,' says Bennett. 'His friends, like Arthur Marshall, said that he had people in gales of laughter. I know most people think that was not an excuse but I'm afraid I do think so.' The humour, including some sparkling one-liners, comes from a combination of the 4 B's, Burgess, Browne, Bates and Bennett.

A snow-bound Dundee did a good job as a stand-in for Moscow, though most of the film consists of interiors. The final image has Burgess in his new Savile Row suit, sent to him by Coral Browne, carrying an umbrella and crossing a snow-covered Muscovite bridge to the strains of 'He Is An Eng-lish-man' from *HMS Pinafore*. The irony, more heavily present in *The Old Country* and seen in the titles of both works, is that separation from the homeland makes the political exile become more and more English. In fact, he longs for an England that no longer exists, the England of Lyons Corner Houses, unspoilt countryside and cities without 'precincts', the England that Bennett himself dreams of. Therefore, the exile can never return home because home no longer exists, it is frozen in the time zone of his childhood. In a sense, Bennett's 'Spy Trilogy' is his most autobiographical work and he admits to having put some of his own sentiments into Burgess's mouth: 'So little, England. Little music. Little art. Timid, tasteful, nice. But one loves it. Loves it. You see I can say I love London. I can say I love England. I can't say I love my country. I don't know what that means.'

Some of the physicality of place was inevitably lost in the sly adaptation of *An Englishman Abroad* for the stage, which opened at the National Theatre in December 1988. There was also a slight diminution in the casting. Alan Bates was able to suggest the dissoluteness and faded charm of Burgess more than Simon Callow, a lighter, more ebullient personality, although much humour and pathos survived. Of course, it was impossible to repeat the dream casting of Coral Browne, then looking after her ailing husband, Vincent Price, in California, but Prunella Scales made a fine substitute. Miss Browne did find time to come over to England and see the production and soon after her visit she wrote to Bennett, complaining about her ersatz self. Something must be done about Prunella Scales' clothes; she would never have dressed like that. 'Like that', only noticeable to those with an eye for such things, was the refusal of Ms Scales, an animal rights campaigner, to wear genuine fur. Coral Browne, whose mother's maiden name was Bennett, is notorious for her acid wit. She told Alan that a Hollywood writer had said to her that he had enjoyed *An Englishman Abroad* on TV, but didn't think the writing was up to much. She replied, 'Listen, dear, you couldn't write "fuck" on a dusty venetian blind.' There is a story of her ringing up the box-office of a theatre for two tickets for the opening night of Charlton Heston in *Antony And Cleopatra*. The assistant told her that the house was completely full. 'I don't mind if the seats are not together,' Coral said. 'I'm sorry, madam, there are no seats available.'

'Well, I'm sure you'll find two. I'm Coral Browne.' 'It makes no difference who you are. We have no seats,' insisted the clerk. 'But I'm married to Vincent Price.' 'I don't care who you're married to, the house is full.' Finally, Coral Browne gave in. 'Okay, give me two seats for *after* the interval,' she replied.

Bennett directed the first play of *Single Spies* himself and appeared amusingly in the tiny part of a rather camp tailor. He didn't particularly want to direct but did it 'because I know the text pretty well and how it should sound'. In the second play Bennett is never off stage in the part of Anthony Blunt, his first major role in the theatre for fourteen years. 'We used to rehearse *Englishman* in the morning and *A Question Of Attribution* [directed by Simon Callow] in the afternoon and I was always relieved when we got to the second, when I was only acting and didn't have to make any decisions. I find it quite unnerving that people are looking to you for a decision, which I'm not good at. On the other hand, now we're playing it, I have to sit through *Englishman* waiting to go on and by the time I'm ready I'm a jelly. I'm so nervous. So I wish I was on at the start, as it were,' he told a radio interviewer just after the opening.

Bennett plays Blunt in the line of the dry-stick dons he used to take off in the 'satire' days. There is a moment in the play, when Blunt gives an illustrated lecture, which takes one back to *Beyond The Fringe* and *Forty Years On*. The play concentrates on the cat-and-mouse game between a bluff Scots MI5 officer (Callow) and Sir Anthony Blunt, soon to be revealed as the 'Fourth Man'. A central scene, and the one that got all the publicity, is when queen meets queen, the first in any play in which a current Queen of England appears as an important character.

The scene has HM walking in unexpectedly on the Surveyor of her pictures while he is removing a Titian from the wall for cleaning. The painting is used as a metaphor for the subject of treachery, fakes, deceit and art. Hidden behind their discussion is the feeling that the Queen knows Blunt is a fake. Though starting off as a clever and subtle conceit, the play becomes rather obvious and ponderous before the end.

'I often just write things on spec and I wrote a scene between Blunt and the Queen. Just as a kind of exercise,' Bennett says. 'Then I thought I would look to see whether there was a painting which one could centre it around. That's when I started looking through the catalogue of the Royal Collection and came across an article on the "mystery" of a Titian painting. And once I had come across it, I felt I had to write the play, and if I didn't someone else would.' While Bennett was writing it he happened to talk to Stephen Frears on the phone. Frears, as it happened, had had an idea for a film in which there would be a scene involving a meeting between the Queen and Tony Benn, then a Labour minister. When Frears mentioned this, Bennett screamed down the phone that he was writing about the Queen already and nothing must be said to anyone about it.

Prunella Scales is as near as can be to what the public thinks and wants to think the Queen is really like. She bears a striking resemblance to the monarch and had been wary of playing the role at first: 'In many ways, it seemed tantamount to blasphemy.' It is said that many British citizens literally dream of meeting their monarch. Here the audience shares in a collective dream. She is the National Mum, royal and, at the same time, just like us. Again, Bennett has proved that he understands the English psyche more than most writers. If one did not know him for a serious artist, one could accuse him of knowingly combining the twin indulgences of the English – royalty and espionage – for financial gain. The two plays made for an entertaining, civilised, lightweight and safe evening, the lack of a political or psychological dimension limiting the fascinating subject to the anecdotal, game-playing and parodic element. Bennett, through the mouth of Burgess, is aware that 'the average Englishman, you see, is not interested in ideas. Say what you like about political theory, and no one will listen. You could shove a slice of the Communist Manifesto in the Queen's Speech, and no one would turn a hair. Least of all, I suspect, HMQ.' It was no surprise when the plays transferred with success to the West End, appropriately to the Queen's Theatre.

Single Spies, The Old Country and Julian Mitchell's *Another Country* all dabble with the idea that there was no real political philosophy behind the espousal of communism by Philby, Burgess and Blunt, that they never went beyond the phrase 'It was the thing to do at the time.' To quote Gilbert Adair's essay on the two 'Country' plays in *Myths And Memories*, 'The effect of their plays is to confine, however prematurely, the constructive or "creative" phase of communism more or less to a single decade, to neutralise its potential contemporaneity . . . and render it, along with various other quaint isms – Fabianism, d'Annunzism, Poujadism, etc – evocatively "period", even kitschy.' Mitchell even goes so far as to suggest through the 'character' of the embryonic 'Guy Burgess', a homosexual public schoolboy called

Bennett, that turning to Marxism was merely a revenge against the upper-class bullies who were intolerant of 'the love that dare not speak its name'.

Both plays turn upon E M Forster's phrase from *Two Cheers For Democracy*, most often quoted without its first clause which puts the apolitical sentiment far more strongly: '*I hate the idea of causes* [my italics], and if I had to choose between betraying my country and betraying my friend, I hope I should have the guts to betray my country' – it is more the idea of cause than of country that Forster finds anathema. The sentiment astutely claims the heterosexual Philby character in *The Old Country*, is 'nancy rubbish . . . You only have to substitute "my wife" for "my friend" to find it's nothing like as noble . . . My friend. That's what brings in the cellos. My friend. Who is my friend? My friend is the memory of the youth half of them were gone on at school. My friend is True Love as it presents itself the one and only time in their stunted, little lives in the shape of some fourteen-year-old tart giving them the glad eye during the service of Nine Lessons and Carols. . .'

The plays do work as metaphorical links between homosexuality and espionage, where the secrecy of one echoes the clandestine character of the other. Herein lies the subtext of Bennett's plays about spies who are forced to lead secret lives at risk of imprisonment. This fear of being found out extends to other people, whether homosexuals, old people hiding behind lace curtains, afraid of being institutionalised, or women pretending to a gentility they cannot attain, all of them with secrets, secrets. They seem safe only when alone in the seclusion of their rooms, away from prying eyes; except those of Bennett's.

In answer to Guy Burgess's question in *An Englishman Abroad*, as to how Coral Browne likes Moscow, she replies, 'Loathe it. I cannot understand what those three sisters were on about.' Alan Bennett had the chance to see for himself in May 1988 when he and five other writers (Sue Townsend, Timothy Mo, Christopher Hope, Craig Raine and Paul Bailey) were sent by the Great Britain-USSR Association on a goodwill visit to the Soviet Union.

Bennett was the only Russian-speaking member of the delegation, although 'He was hesitant to speak it to begin with, but soon found courage, and could often be heard chatting to the hotel staff and to our excellent guides,' wrote Paul Bailey, who shared a suite of rooms with Bennett at a Moscow hotel.

As Sue Townsend reported in a *Guardian* article, the trip was punctuated by a great deal of giggling and sniggering, not exactly Arthur Miller travelling for PEN. In the Ukraine, at a lunch given by the Writers' Union, 'The conversation at Messrs Raine's, Bennett's and Bailey's end of the table had turned to sex,' she wrote. 'Their laughter attracted the attention of the wife of the chairman of the Lvov Writers' Union. I said, "They are talking about sex." "Oh," she said, "all says, little do's." Quite a devastating remark from such a mild-looking woman.' It was during their visit that Kim Philby died. Unfortunately, Bennett and the others were not able to attend the funeral, to which they were invited, because they had previously arranged to fly to the Ukraine. It would have made some poetic sense, Bennett at Philby's funeral.

XIV

The screenplays (*A Private Function* and *Prick Up Your Ears*) and the spy and Kafka plays of Alan Bennett, although obliquely personal, are not as centrally Bennett-esque as his television work. Other writers can claim equality or superiority in the territory of feature films; Graham Greene and John Le Carré have gone more profoundly into the psychology of espionage; and Kafka, in various forms, has been a literary shuttlecock since the 1930s. What Bennett can claim as his own is the immortalisation of the lonely, elderly woman. Although specifically Northern – in cultural attitudes, place and speech patterns – she has a far wider familiarity in any society which has abandoned the extended family.

It is in the television monologue, hitherto not the most enticing or common of forms, that Bennett has reached his peak. Many TV films can happily be shown in cinemas; many TV plays could be put on almost unchanged in the theatre; other TV monologues could transfer well to the radio. Bennett's six monologues, however, first broadcast on BBC1 from April 1988 under the generic title of *Talking Heads*, are essentially televisual. Directed in a stylistically consistent manner by Bennett, Giles Foster and Stuart Burge, they consist of various short scenes or 'acts' punctuated by George Fenton's subtle music, in which the single person is placed in a dramatically important relationship to a particular interior, all designed by Tony Burrough. The subject dictates the form: loneliness is best described by a single figure in a room, talking silently or aloud to themselves. The principal material is the face of the performer. Within the structured story of each monologue lies a double narrative – a subjective one told by the unreliable narrator or the soliloquiser, and an objective one which points up for the camera or the audience the character's reality.

Bennett had experimented with the television monologue, as distinct from the one-man sketch directed at an invisible but present audience, in *A Woman Of No Importance*, one of the most acclaimed of his six BBC plays of 1982. He wrote *Talking Heads*, which 'I wanted to call *Dull Lives* but I didn't think that would pull in many viewers', specifically for the five actresses who performed in them.

'I didn't write the one for myself. When we were actually starting rehearsing I said to Stuart Burge, who directed it, "Couldn't we get Michael Gambon to do this?" I don't think I'm an actor, really. I'm never desperate to act. I enjoy doing it. But it's like a holiday, generally. I don't feel it's like work. And that makes other actors cross, quite naturally.' Burge says he had to act as umpire between Bennett the actor and Bennett the playwright. Occasionally, the actor would say, 'God, what a terrible line!' and the writer would also criticise the actor.

In *A Chip In The Sugar*, Bennett plays Graham Whitaker, a middle-aged man 'married' to his 72-year-old mam. He is relatively content until she meets Frank Turnbull, an old flame from her past. 'I didn't know you had a past,' Graham protests. Through Graham's eyes we see Frank as a vulgar little man stealing his only companion, and leaving him alone with his gay magazines. Mother and son are 'happily' reunited when Frank is discovered to be married already. The only male monologue fits in perfectly with the five others because Graham is 'an old woman', in popular terminology.

Patricia Routledge as Irene Ruddock in *A Lady Of Letters* is desperately lonely after her mother's death and spends her time spying on the neighbours and writing off letters of complaint to all and sundry, until she is arrested for some written with her poison Platignum pen. In prison she finds a new lease of life, her 'first taste of freedom in years' – she is less lonely. Like *A Chip In The Sugar*, this play literally has a happy ending – 'happy' is the last word uttered. But any happiness found in these 40-minute one-handers can really only be defined as diminished melancholy.

If Doris, a 75-year-old widow with a pacemaker, living alone in the house with the ghost of her dead husband, Wilfred, were moved to an old folk's home, she would sing 'I am un-h-a-p-p-y,' despite the fact that in her own house she is only visited by Zulema, a home help ('Home hindrance', Doris calls her). The title of Doris's story, *A Cream Cracker Under the Settee*, refers to Zulema's slapdash attitude to cleaning. Thora Hird plays Doris – a 'museum name' like Lilly, Madge and Mabel, not given to girls nowadays – who resists the blandishments of the municipal departments to move her to a home, choosing to die alone rather than call for help. This is Bennett as close to Beckett, another master of the *memento mori* monologue, as he has ever come.

Soldiering On is Muriel (Stephanie Cole), another widow, this time an upper-middle-class one with a favourite son, Giles, and a mentally disturbed daughter, Margaret; the sort of woman with attitudes, accent and slang all old-fashionedly genteel, who might have been taken off by Joyce Grenfell. She says, 'I think I'll just drag our brogues on this one,' and talks of 'the tele box'. But Giles is a bounder who loses most of her money for her, and her late husband quite likely caused the daughter's mental breakdown. Bennett manages with pinpoint accuracy and a mixture of admiration and antipathy to turn the distressed gentlewoman into almost as touching a figure as her even more distressed lower-class sisters. Neither a Muriel nor a Doris can easily come to terms with losing a partner.

One of Susan's problems – Maggie Smith, un-madeup, unmannered and well cast as the alcoholic wife of a trendy vicar in *A Bed Among The Lentils* (directed by Bennett) is the very fact of her partner. Like the mummy's boy, the town gossip and the charity-bazaar lady, the vicar's wife is a staple of British comedy which Bennett proceeds to subvert. Susan's sexual life with her husband is described as 'rare and dessicated conjunctions' – then she finds joy in the arms of Ramesh, a young Indian shopkeeper. One of the set pieces is an E F Bensonian description of the floral arranging round the altar, during which the vicar's wife, after quietly drinking the communion wine, falls down and hits her head. The scene is so vividly narrated one feels that if ever the BBC fell on hard times, they might prevail on Bennett to write a succession of monologues and save on large casts and sets, with no real loss of viewing pleasure.

The funniest of the six, *Her Big Chance*, features Julie Walters as Lesley, a struggling small-time actress who gets a role in a German skinflick being made on location in Lee-on-Solent. 'Travis is supposed to be a good-time girl, though you never actually see me having a good time, just sat on this freezing cold deck plastering on the sun tan lotion.' The play is cruelly accurate at depicting the tattier end of the industry which Lesley cons herself into believing is art. Perhaps her complete lack of self-awareness is unconvincing: hers is the youngest head of the six portraits, and the only one which has a patronising attitude heaped upon it.

It is clear that of all the men and women on Bennett's stage, his finest characterisations are of the sixth and seventh ages. He has an affinity and empathy with the old and he is able to project himself forward and towards them. The fear of infirmity, senility, decrepitude and death (Bennett is a self-admitted hypochondriac) is faced by personifying them, staring them in the face.

Maggie Smith, Patricia Routledge and Thora Hird were nominated for BAFTA Best Television Actress awards in March 1989. Thora Hird won. 'That says more about Alan than about me, love,' stated Thora. 'I just don't know how a young, single gentleman can have such insights. He makes you know what he's talking about without spelling it out, without using the words. He's just brilliant.'

XV

Alan Bennett is extremely well-off; he lives in a large, comfortable home in a pleasant part of London. But in order to get to his front door one has to edge round a rather unlikely dormobile in his driveway. In the early 1970s, not long after he moved into his house in the exclusive Gloucester Crescent opposite Jonathan Miller, a vagrant old lady came to live in the street in a decrepit, rusty, squalid van, without water, electricity or sanitation. The residents began to complain about her disfiguring presence, the health authorities were unhappy about it and wanted to institutionalise her, the police were called in to tell her that she couldn't remain. Bennett became so disgusted by her persecution, as he saw it, that he got a few men to push the van into his driveway. When he knocked on her window to ask if he could help her in any way, he was told to 'fuck off.' Gradually, however, he won her confidence, brought her clean water, went shopping for her and got an electric cable into the van. One day the whole vehicle collapsed, with no roof left on it. Bennett bought her a new van and there this 'eyesore' sits, blocking the York Stone patio, in front of the elegant mid-Victorian house, a constant reminder of poverty and old age.

This is one person-to-person cause that Bennett has taken up rather than the larger issues, although he often gets angry with the Thatcher ethos, anger which aggravates a duodenal ulcer already worsened by a drug prescribed for an inflammatory knee condition. Bennett has sounded off in private and in letters to the press about the destruction of the environment, the deterioration of the cities, the dismantling of TV, the Official Secrets Act and the cuts in education and the health service. 'When my Dad died I left BUPA. I'd always been a member. But the NHS were marvellous to him,' he said. Although these preoccupations are not central to his plays, they do lie just beneath their transparent surfaces. For some reason he feels unable to write an overtly political play: 'It's not cowardice, something I'm scared of doing. It would just be a bad play . . . My thoughts are very naive, which is why I'm not a political writer. I can only do what's under my nose.'

Another person-to-person cause that surfaced in October 1988 was Bennett's anger at the way the gutter press had treated his oldest friend, Russell Harty, during the last days of his life earlier that year. Bennett was the chief orator at a memorial service given for Harty at St James's Church, Piccadilly. After Ned Sherrin, Sue Lawley, Penelope Keith and John Birt, deputy director-general of the BBC, had all given readings, and Diane Langton had sung some Stephen Sondheim songs, Bennett stood up to make his address to an audience that included Melvyn Bragg, David Frost, Frank Muir, Lord Snowden and the nurses who had attended Harty in hospital.

'Russell had never made a secret of his homosexuality but he had not been a crusader . . . With the gutter press systematically trawling public life for sexual indiscretions, he knew he was in a delicate position. So when in March last year *The News Of The World* set him up, then broke to an unstartled public the shocking news, Russell thought his career was over.' Bennett went on to describe how reporters 'infested his home village for more than a year, bribing local children for information about his life, forcing their way into the school, even trying to bribe the local vicar'. He explained how the vilification in the press for his homosexuality drove Harty to over-work, making him more vulnerable to hepatitis when it came.

'He thought it was AIDS and of course the press hoped it was AIDS . . . Russell, with his usual lack of consideration, was dying of the wrong disease . . . Now, as he fought for his life in St James's Hospital, one newspaper took a flat opposite and a camera with a long lens was trained on his ward. A reporter posing as a junior doctor smuggled himself into the ward and demanded to see his notes . . . One saw, in the tireless and unremitting efforts of the team at St James's, the best of which we are capable, and in the equally tireless, and rather better rewarded efforts of the journalists, the worst.' Bennett reached his conclusion. 'Some of you may think that these kind of recriminations are out of place at a memorial service and certain it is that Russell would not have approved. Had he lived, he would have gone on going to Mr Murdoch's parties and doing his column for a Murdoch newpaper. The world is like that. Or at least, England is like that.'

It was one of the rare times at a memorial service when a speaker received a standing ovation from the entire congregation.

XVI

Look in most companions to the theatre or studies of international modern playwrights, or even in books on the British theatre, and you will see Alan Bennett seldom or only marginally mentioned. His plays are not translated to any significant degree, nor are they very often revived. In the 21 years since his first stage play, *Forty Years On*, Bennett has written five full-length plays and two one-acters for the theatre; two of these, *Enjoy* and *Kafka's Dick*, had ignominiously short runs. It could not be said that even his best plays advance the theatre in any way, either in terms of ideas or of style: *Forty Years On* is a series of revue sketches disguised as a play; *Habeas Corpus* is too Orton-influenced; *Getting On* and *The Old Country* are conventional, well-made plays. Among contemporary British playwrights – let us include Harold Pinter, David Hare, David Edgar, Edward Bond, Howard Brenton, Caryl Churchill and even 'playboys of the West End' like Alan Ayckbourn, Peter Shaffer and Tom Stoppard – Bennett seems a minor figure. He only makes rare appearances as an actor, and then in only two role-types – upper-class pedants like Lord Pinkrose in *The Fortunes Of War* and Anthony Blunt, or repressed lower-middle-class Yorkshiremen typified by his *Talking Heads* monologue. Among the arbiters of taste, television is still culturally and intellectually suspect. Very few of the world's leading playwrights have written for the box, and if so, only rarely, whereas the bulk of Bennett's writing has been for this mass medium, this parasitic poor relation of the arts.

Nevertheless, if one had to judge which of the four 'Fringers' had fulfilled themselves most in their own terms, one would have to point to Bennett. He has created a solid, instantly recognisable body of work, an *oeuvre* of considerable merit. The character of the man and the work seem inseparable. The mixture of anger and calm, superiority and humility, subjectivity and objectivity, tragedy and comedy, reticence and boldness, the Oxford scholar and the butcher's son from Leeds, are all present in his plays. It is the gentle shift from one mood to another and the ability to reconcile opposites, that are his stylistic strengths. Because the substance of his major work is that of minor lives, it is on television that they are best examined.

'My wife has no sense of place,' says Hilary in *The Old Country*. 'To her one spot is very much like another. It matters to me.' The sense of place distinguishes Bennett from most of his contemporaries. He can use the vaudeville comedian's joke of only mentioning the name of a town, say Cleethorpes, to get a laugh, but makes it funnier by setting it in a realistic context, related to the character's life and expectations. The further one travels from the immediate area, usually West Hartlepool or Morecambe, the more prestigious one becomes. The old couple in *Say Something Happened* judge their daughter's success on the number of places she goes to. 'Margaret goes all over. You'd be staggered if I told you her itinerary.' We know where everyone comes from and where they're going, where they live and where they die.

Bennett country is situated in a Northern corner of England, usually hidden away from tourists and omitted from most literary maps. It is no country for young men. It is an incontinent continent where the dying old and the unfulfilled middle-aged struggle to retain some dignity in undignified circumstances, and try to make themselves heard when nobody is listening and nobody cares. They deceive themselves and others but deception is the only thing they have to soften disappointment. Yet Bennett gives them just enough self-awareness to allow them to be laughed *with* as well as *at*. It is this balance that alleviates the gloom.

Dinner At Noon, Bennett's incisive and witty 1988 documentary, is as close as he has ever come in public to direct autobiography. It made the critic of *The Observer* squirm in embarrassment as Bennett 'sat in the foyer of a Yorkshire hotel and dissected British attitudes to class by ridiculing (once again) his deceased parents'. As a matter of fact Bennett's mother Lilian was still alive at the time, in a home, unable to recognise her sons: 'She's quite cheerful. She used to suffer depressions, but as the memory has gone, the depression has lifted . . . It's called Alzheimer's Disease now, but my grandma's memory failed, my mother's did, and I haven't got one even now'.

It was from his mother that Alan had learned the finer gradations of the class system. She would talk of people being 'better class', 'well off', 'nicely-spoken', 'refined', 'educated', 'genuine' or the ultimate condemnation – 'common'. She believed strongly in the saying, 'if you want to get ahead, get a hat,' and had a variety of them, which she wore on all occasions. Lilian also always used a strainer when pouring tea, something which was thought to be rather posh.

Bennett's mother's sisters were more outgoing and ambitious. 'One of my aunties worked in a shoe shop in Leeds. This was in the days when there were still grand stars touring the country and Ronald Colman came in one day and she said, "Have I the pleasure of serving Ronald Colman?" and he said, "No". Oh, it was *dreadful*. I was only a tiny child when I heard her telling this story but I sensed that some terrible humiliation had been done to her. I'm not sure that she did.' It is his mother, who 'was unconsciously funny', and the various aunts of his childhood, who loom largest in his plays for the small screen, set in lower-middle-class Yorkshire.

'Northern women's lives are slung between three poles; dirt, disease and the lavatory,' he told his friend Russell Harty on ITV in October 1977. 'It is funny but it's also sad. They batten on to illness – people always make out that their case is very interesting. "Our Clifford went into hospital and he baffled the surgeons." '

The great French philosopher and autobiographer, Roland Barthes, describes the pleasure he gets from texts which contain 'petty details: schedules, habits, meals, lodging, clothing, etc . . .', the bliss he receives 'from a singular theatre: not one of grandeur but one of mediocrity (might there not be dreams, fantasies of mediocrity?)' 'the hallucinatory relish of "reality". . . And is it not the fantasy itself that invokes the "detail", the tiny private scene, in which I can easily take my place?' His words reflect exactly the discreet charm of this most English of modern playwrights.

10

SMALL IS BEAUTIFUL

There is just a possibility that if *Beyond The Fringe* hadn't come along, nobody outside the medical profession or academic circles would have heard of either Jonathan Miller or Alan Bennett. On the other hand, both Peter Cook and Dudley Moore were already in show business, Cook having written West End revues, and Moore having composed for the theatre, played in a jazz band and performed in cabaret. Had there been no *Fringe*, and had the tinsel fairy godmother not waved her magic wand over Dudley Moore and transformed him into a Hollywood star, he still would have made a good living on the jazz circuit.

The Dudley Moore Trio, formed at the end of 1959, continued to be in demand during the run of *Beyond The Fringe*, but before the show left for Broadway, Hugo Boyd, the bass player, was killed in a car accident while on holiday in the south of France. It was a personal tragedy for Moore – Boyd had been a close friend as well as a brilliant musician. Later on the trio was re-formed but with Chris Karan, an Australian of Greek parentage, replacing Derek Hogg on drums, and Pete McGurk on bass. They can be heard on three jazz albums: *Theme From 'Beyond The Fringe' and All That Jazz* (recorded in August 1962), *The Other Side of the Dudley Moore Trio* (1965) and *Genuine Dud* (1966). The three played together for almost seven years before tragedy struck once more. Three days after Dudley's first marriage, to Suzy Kendall in June 1968, McGurk was found dead in his Putney flat from an overdose of barbiturates. His depressive nature had suffered markedly when his girlfriend had left him some months before to marry Chris Karan. Moore's marriage unavoidably heightened his sense of isolation. With talk of a jinx on bass players it was some time before the trio re-emerged, with Jeff Clyne and then with Pete Morgan on bass.

Apart from the jazz, there was Moore's talent for writing theatrical scores and film music. He had already written incidental music for two plays at the Royal Court when he was asked to provide the score for William Gaskill's RSC production of Brecht's *Caucasian Chalk Circle* at the Aldwych in March 1962. 'Gaskill didn't like anything I wrote, and kept asking me to change it. Peter Hall finally came in at the last moment and accepted what music I had, although he didn't think it was much good either,' Dudley remembers of his oriental-inspired work.

While appearing in *Beyond The Fringe* and playing with the trio almost nightly at Cook's Establishment Club, Moore joined up with dancer Gillian Lynne on two other projects. Lynne, formerly a leading dancer at Sadler's Wells Ballet, had ambitions as a choreographer. Her new career was launched when she was commissioned by the Western Theatre Ballet to choreograph *The Owl and the Pussycat*, a one-act ballet based on Edward Lear's nonsense poem. Moore was asked to provide the music and the pair were then approached to do the choreography and music for a new review entitled *England, Our England*, with book and lyrics by the authors of *Billy Liar*, Keith Waterhouse and Willis Hall. Some weeks into rehearsal with a cast headed by Billie Whitelaw, Roy Kinnear, Bryan Pringle, Alison Leggatt and Murray Melvin, John Dexter was brought in to direct after R D Smith was dismissed for continually arriving at the theatre in a state of intoxication. The revue, which was meant to reflect the life of Northern folk in contrast to that of effete Southerners, had some success during its pre-West End tour of the North, but when it arrived in May 1962 at the Princes Theatre (now the Shaftesbury), Londoners found it as difficult to swallow as black pudding. Two of the better numbers were a Flannagan and Allen-type song and a mock-patriotic finale, with Kinnear as John Bull.

Despite these inauspicious beginnings, Gillian Lynne has gone on to become one of Britain's 'hottest' dance directors for stage and screen, her biggest success being the long-running *Cats*. She told Paul Donovan, Dudley Moore's biographer, that Dudley was 'the single most important influence in my life. . . it was he who influenced me totally as a choreographer, by showing me the rhythm that is one of the essences of jazz. All my grasp of jazz phrasing I learned from Dudley. It was a tragedy that he stopped composing and became a star. There are so few people who have equal ability in both jazz and classical music.' The two of them worked together again on a jazz ballet called *Collages* for the 1963 Edinburgh Festival, though he was in New York and she in England: he recorded the music on a tape recorder and sent the tapes over. The ballet was a success and a film about it, directed by Melvyn Bragg for a pre-Jonathan Miller *Monitor*, brought it welcome publicity.

A year later, after *Beyond The Fringe* came to an end in the USA, Moore was commissioned to compose a score of incidental music for a production of Eugene O'Neill's *The Emperor Jones* for the Boston Arts Festival, effectively replacing the incessant drum beat called for by the playwright; and he also supplied some dialogue and the music, with jazz trumpeter Dizzy Gillespie, for an ingenious and amusing cartoon called *The Hat*. Dudley seemed able to turn his hand with facility to almost anything he was asked to do.

II

Although Moore kept his virginity until he was 22, he certainly made up for lost time in the 'Swinging 'Sixties', and it would be difficult, and dishonest, to expunge his erotic impulses and sexual relationships from his life and work. Despite his club foot and lack of height, or because of it, he gave the lie to the expression 'Birds nest on the highest branches'. Unlike Miller, Cook and Bennett, Moore's public persona has been directly shaped by his libido – many of his utterances relate to it – but in common with the others he gets pleasure from administering shock treatment, in his case seeming almost unable to get through an interview without some scatological expression. 'The ability to enjoy your sex life is central. I don't give a shit about anything else. My obsession is total. What else is there to live for? Chinese food and women. There is nothing else.' 'If I took cocaine, my ass would fall to the ground, my cock would explode into a thousand stars and a breast would turn into a cantaloupe – you know, the usual humdrum stuff.' 'I'm often amazed that women can get hold of those things and pop them into their mouths. I mean, they're strange-looking creatures. If it were a bar of chocolate, I could understand.' Humour continually undercuts the gravity he undoubtedly feels for the subject. Asked once if he was serious, he replied, 'Of course. Very, very serious indeed. Gosh. Absolutely. Profoundly serious. Very, very, very serious. Phew. Gosh. Golly. Fucking A-serious.'

Dudley became very, very serious about someone for the first time in 1961. She was Celia Hammond, the model who along with Jean

Shrimpton, was an icon of fashion in the early sixties. Hammond later lived with Rock guitarist Jeff Beck for 18 years, before devoting most of her time to CHAT, the Celia Hammond Animal Trust, which shows her continued devotion to cuddly things. Shrimpton was the Galatea of David Bailey; Hammond came to the public eye via the camera of Terence Donovan. The cool, 21-year-old blonde met Moore when he was performing at The Establishment, he followed up the meeting and they started an affair. During his stay in New York with *Beyond The Fringe*, he wrote her sheaves of letters and spent a fortune on trans-Atlantic calls. In 1963, Dudley was offered a large apartment in Washington Square by the actress-singer Joan Diener, who had starred in *Kismet*, while she was touring. Celia agreed to fly out and join him there for a few weeks. John Bassett was staying with Dudley at the time in one of the two enormous double bedrooms. Before Celia arrived Dudley asked him to go into his room, shut the door and listen, to check if he could hear anything while Dudley made puffing and panting noises on the bed in his own room. Bassett assured him he could feel perfectly at ease: the apartment had obviously been designed to surmount that particular embarrassing eventuality.

Unfortunately, the relationship with Celia didn't last and when, on a second visit to New York, she left Dudley to join Terry Donovan in Florida, he was devastated. It was that breakup which led him to psychotherapy for the first time. Of these initial sessions in New York, Moore recalls: 'I told him [the psychiatrist] I couldn't work. But I also wanted to find out about myself. It was pretty fascinating, though very embarrassing at times – spouting on about my hidden lust. The trouble was I couldn't shock him. He just sat there filling his pipe, observing . . . ' Moore has submitted himself to different forms of therapy right through into the 1980s. As Peter Cook commented, 'I don't know why Dudley took so long to find himself. I found him years ago.'

III

In the spring of 1964 Dudley Moore returned from the USA to England. He grew his hair long, bought a black Maserati Mistrale and settled into a bachelor pad in Mayfair's Shepherd Market, rented from his friend George Hastings, an Old Etonian advertising man. Though inwardly still terribly unsure of himself, he presented the very image of the 'sixties swinger and, as always, never lacked for work or women.

He was in fact dating two women at the same time. One evening one of them, discovering that he was about to go out with the other, came over to his flat and emptied a bottle of perfume over an astonished Dudley. A long time was spent in the bath fruitlessly trying to scrub off the scent.

The *Beyond The Fringe* team seemed to have broken up forever – four diverse talents had come together for a memorable moment, then scattered in all directions. Miller had given up performing and was busy editing and presenting *Monitor*; Bennett seemed to have been swallowed up again into the academic vortex; and Cook was involved with *Private Eye*, occasionally popping up on television. Moore displayed his range of musical skills in a programme called *Offbeat* on the new BBC2 channel, taking seventeen different roles, including Seven Singing Viennese Sisters, a lover of English madrigals and a man who falls in love with his violin. The show included two comedy spots with Peter Cook, one of them with Cook as an upper-class twit explaining how he has dedicated his life to teaching ravens to fly underwater, the other sketch with Cook and Moore as two cloth-capped cretins discussing their relationships with famous film stars.

'It was a joke that Peter has been doing for years,' Dudley explained. 'He would be on the phone talking to a friend and suddenly shout down the mouthpiece, "Goodbye for ever." Then he'd turn to whoever was in the room and mumble apologetically, "That was that bloody Sophia Loren again." '

Working on *Offbeat* was BBC director Joe McGrath, who suggested that Moore and Cook reunite for a comedy series on BBC2. *Not Only . . . But Also*, a 45-minute fortnightly show, began on 9 January 1965 and ran until 3 April. So popular did it become that it returned for a second series in January of the following year, and a third from February 1970. The 'Dud 'n' Pete' double act also appeared in five feature films, the stage show *Behind The Fridge* (renamed *Good Evening* in the USA), made a couple of hit singles and, as 'Derek and Clive', recorded three 'smutty' albums and a video. For over ten years, the duo were a national comic institution.

The programmes were structured to include a number of general sketches, one or two with a guest performer; at least one filmed item; a musical interlude with the Dudley Moore Trio; Peter Cook's E L Wisty monologue on a park bench; and a meeting between 'Dud' and 'Pete', two proletarian pillocks in cloth caps, dirty raincoats and white scarves, swapping undigested pieces of information (echoed in Mel

Smith and Gryff Rees-Jones's two idiots in profile in *Alas Smith and Jones* in the 'eighties). The shows usually began with Moore at a piano or cinema organ playing variations of the signature tune in various incongruous filmed surroundings, and ended with Dudley at a grand piano and Peter leaning against it, singing an old number called 'Goodbye-ee', rendered in an affected 'twenties manner.

Just as Alan Bennett drew on his childhood memories of adults in Leeds, transmuting them into plays, so Moore plundered some of his recollections of people from his working-class neighbourhood for the 'Dud 'n' Pete' duologues. Most of the names mentioned are of real people and, says Moore, 'I drew my own character from various, inoffensive compliant men I'd known, including myself.' If the origin of the duo was Dagenham, the inspiration came mostly from Cook: 'Peter has this extraordinary seam of invention he can draw on, an area of fantasy derived from Edward Lear and Lewis Carroll that I had no sense of before . . . I perhaps have a slightly stronger feeling, though, for the emotional content and architecture of a sketch.' Cook commented that 'Dudley can root out a lot of things from his working-class past and I can root out a lot from my basically middle-class upbringing . . . Dudley began, when we had an idea, to examine what was logically incorrect, right at the beginning. I would regard this as pernickety, and he would regard it as logical. So the writing process became slower . . . I tend to flutter off very quickly, and improvise, and ignore illogicalities.'

As in most comedy duos, there is a more dominant partner: Hardy over Laurel, Abbott over Costello, though these were reversed off-screen. However, because of Cook's height, personality and upbringing, he tended to dominate Moore *on and* off screen. 'I used to call him a club-footed dwarf,' says Cook. 'I think it was good for him. Everyone else used to pussyfoot around his problem.' Nicholas Luard, with whom Cook started The Establishment Club, has even patronisingly called Moore 'Cook's creation'. Certainly most of the verbal invention came from Cook, and he was the funnier of the two. Dudley overdid the mugging, twitching and corpsing as 'Dud' and found it hard to attain the consummate timing of Cook in the other sketches, often only scratching the surface of a character. Sometimes he seemed hypnotised by his partner but the chemistry worked most of the time, and the material was consistently hilarious.

Although they did have much in common, especially a brand of surreal humour, their relationship was founded on a certain unease.

First, one that all Englishmen feel, whether spoken or unspoken – that of class and, by extension, of accent. Moore had already suffered somewhat from Miller and Bennett's intellectual snobbery, but Cook's snobbery was of a more conventional kind: a good reason for Moore to feel at home in California where neither sort could touch him. As Michael Caine, another Hollywood emigré from London's East End, expressed it: 'When I moved to America, although I missed England very much, for about six months I was walking around thinking, "There's something here that's rather nice and I don't know what the bloody hell it is!" Then I woke up one morning with the sudden brainstorm that I hadn't been bothered by the *class* thing for months. And I thought, "That's it!" ' Secondly, despite Moore's brilliant parodic qualities on the piano and natural comic gifts, he was in *Not Only* mostly speaking Cook's lines. The long shadow of Cook was something he had to move away from before he could get closer to 'finding himself', a quest he had embarked upon in 1962 with his first session of psychotherapy. There was a deeper reason that brought tension into the relationship: jealousy and rivalry, two emotions that existed between all four of the *Beyond The Fringe* performers from the beginning and of which there are still vestiges at work.

IV

Painful as the Celia Hammond experience had been, Dudley was soon living with another English model, Cynthia Cassidy, in New York. He then had a brief fling with the actress Shirley Anne Field, whom he had met while on holiday in Italy in the summer of 1964. But the following year, during the run of *Not Only . . . But Also*, he met Suzy Kendall, a 25-year-old aspiring actress. She was 5 foot 4 inches, only two inches taller than Dudley, had long blonde hair and the kind of sought-after 'dolly bird' looks of that period. Born Freda Harrison of working-class parents in Belper, Derbyshire, she had studied at Derby Art College before moving into modelling and bit parts in films. Her marriage to a jazz musician had ended in divorce after six months and she was living in a flat just off the fashionable King's Road, Chelsea. Four months after they met, Dudley moved in with her.

A year and half later they decided to buy a house. Earnings from *Beyond The Fringe* and *Not Only . . . But Also* enabled the couple to think big and they bought a 230-year-old Georgian mansion near

Hampstead Heath, not far from Peter Cook's house. It had seven bedrooms, a walled garden and an underground running spring in the basement. Parked in the garage was his Maserati and her yellow E-type Jaguar. Dudley seemed perfectly at ease as a member of the 'New Aristocracy'. He appeared in the gossip columns, took part in chat shows, played jazz at the Cool Elephant Club (behind Oxford Circus) with his trio, cut two more albums with them, and recorded *Goodbye-ee* with Peter Cook, which remained in the sacred Top Twenty for ten weeks. A couple of years later, John Lennon, who had been a guest on their TV show, offered them a song of his originally intended for *Sergeant Pepper's Lonely Heart's Club Band*. It was called 'L S Bumblebee', a take-off of a psychedelic song. All this activity led to the movies.

In the early 1960s British cinema had made a move away from middle-class-dominated films towards more naturalistic, unpatronising movies about the working classes, such as Tony Richardson's *A Taste Of Honey* and *The Loneliness Of The Long Distance Runner*, Karel Reisz's *Saturday Night And Sunday Morning*, Lindsay Anderson's *This Sporting Life* and John Schlesinger's *A Kind Of Loving*. As the 'kitchen sink' sank in the mid-1960s, it was replaced by stultifying and superficial images of 'Swinging London', predominantly red buses and Rolls-Royces going round Parliament Square: Schlesinger's *Darling* and Reisz's *Morgan: A Suitable Case For Treatment* were as trendy-artificial as their earlier films had been trendy-natural.

John Boorman started his feature film career with a vehicle for The Dave Clark Five in *Catch Us If You Can* and Richard Lester put the Beatles through their frantic paces in *A Hard Day's Night* and *Help!*, starting the fashion for placing pop groups in various unlikely settings, using jump cuts and speeded-up motion. American capital was moving into the British film industry to an unprecedented degree, the prime example being Eon Productions, formed by the gold-fingered producers Albert R 'Cubby' Broccoli and Harry Saltzman, making a string of James Bond movies and still going strong after a quarter of a century. It was on to this conveyer-belt of modish artefacts that Dudley Moore jumped when he made his entry into motion pictures.

Ironically, the filmic 'swinging' had begun with a period piece, an adaptation of Henry Fielding's *Tom Jones* (1963). Tony Richardson and his screenwriter John Osborne transformed the great eighteenth-century mock-heroic 'novel of manners' into a simple-minded, tricksy, bawdy romp yet it not only won four Oscars but was the biggest British box-office hit ever, thus opening the way for British films to compete successfully in the world market.

Cook and Moore, leading figures in the 1960s London scene, made their screen debut in *The Wrong Box* (1966), a story set in the 1880s. It was the first time since their university days that either of them had been employed as a comedy team to perform anything but their own scripts. The screenplay, based on the black comic novel by Robert Louis Stevenson and his nephew Lloyd Osbourne, was loosely adapted by Larry Gelbart and Burt Shevelove, the American writers of the book of the musical *A Funny Thing Happened On The Way To The Forum* being filmed by Richard Lester at the same time. They were directed by Bryan Forbes, who turned the charming light classic into a leaden period burlesque. As one critic wrote, 'Rather than any real endeavour, however crude, to reconstruct the visual and verbal textures of Victorian England, the movie opted for a 'sixties romp in cod Victoriana, very much in the manner of certain Carnaby Street boutiques [e.g. 'I was Lord Kitchener's Valet'].'

Despite insensitive and gag-chasing direction, the cast, with such old hands as Ralph Richardson, John Mills, Peter Sellers, Wilfred Lawson, Tony Hancock, Cicely Courtneidge and Irene Handl, could not help but give *The Wrong Box* some comic distinction. The intricate plot, involving the attempts of an elderly man (Mills) to kill his brother (Richardson) over money, had the grandson of one of them (Michael Caine) falling in love with the niece (Nanette Newman, Forbes's wife) of the other. Peter Cook and Dudley Moore played Ralph Richardson's rascally nephews, Cook being the more dominant and scheming of the two.

Cook and Moore were not outshone by the company in which they found themselves, although they would have made more impact with better material. Some idea of the originality of the enterprise is conveyed by the first word Moore utters – 'Fu-nny', a catchphrase from the *Not Only* TV show. Dudley found the experience unfulfilling.

'I disagreed with Bryan Forbes a great deal about his approach to comedy,' he said. 'He used to act it out all the time; he used to do it for you . . . I never used to find what Bryan did too easy to follow – it was like aping movement and facial expression. . . I've seen the film a few times and I've never been able to understand quite what goes on in it – probably because I was so obsessed with the discomfort I went through when I did the film.'

When Cook and Moore started working on their second film, *Bedazzled*, the second series of *Not Only . . . But Also* – now put out on BBC 2 weekly in 30-minute slots – had come to a successful end and *The Wrong Box* had already opened . . . and flopped. This time they were to star in a script written by Peter Cook, based on an idea by Cook and Moore, with music and songs by Moore. Although shot in England, with an English cast – except for voluptuous sixties sex symbol, Raquel Welch – it was to be distributed by Twentieth Century-Fox and directed by Stanley Donen. They did not have to go to Hollywood, Hollywood came to them.

All of Donen's best films had tripped the light fantastic, especially the three he co-directed with Gene Kelly: *On The Town*, *Singin' In The Rain* and *It's Always Fair Weather*. He also directed *Seven Brides for Seven Brothers* and *Funny Face*, which starred Fred Astaire. With the demise of the Hollywood musical, Donen's career had faltered, revived briefly with two flashy Hitchcockian thrillers, *Charade* (1963) and *Arabesque* (1966), and stopped in its tracks with *Bedazzled*. Yet, despite its failure, both commercially and critically, the film was far more interesting than *The Wrong Box*, not only because Donen is a better director than Forbes but because it gave the Cook-Moore duo some chance to expand and experiment. All the same, just as Bennett's first play *Forty Years On* was a string on which to hang a series of polished revue sketches, so the structure of *Bedazzled* allowed a sketch from *Not Only . . . But Also* to be gathered up into its bulging net. In this episodic Faustian tale, Moore played a character called Stanley Moon, the name John Gielgud had mistakenly given him some years before, and in Stanley Moon can be glimpsed the Hollywood Dudley Moore in embryo – the lovable little man filled with self-doubt about his height, his sex life and his personality.

Stanley is a cook in a Wimpy bar, in love from afar with a waitress (Eleanor Bron). Too shy to speak to her, he is attempting to hang himself when the Mephistopholean figure of Peter Cook as George Spiggott (the name carried on from the ubiquitous 'One Leg Too Few' sketch) appears and offers him seven wishes in exchange for his soul.

Again, Dudley felt unhappy about his director. 'Stanley Donen wanted to make it look visually good. So there was a certain tightness in *Bedazzled*. Maybe it was just something I was projecting on to Donen. He was very amenable, but Peter and I had a slight timidity about pushing our own point of view that much.' Actually, shot in Panavision and DeLuxe colour, the film lacked any particular visual flair, something Donen usually had a-plenty. *Bedazzled* was to have been followed up with another Donen-Cook-Moore collaboration, a musical called *The Whack*, starring the comedy team as two daffy doctors, but bad box-office takings whacked the project on the head.

V

Dudley Moore was coming up to his 32nd birthday when he embarked on his most autobiographical film and his first solo starring role. He wrote the screenplay of *30 Is A Dangerous Age, Cynthia* with the film's director, Joe McGrath, and John Wells, the satirist. The latter wrote an outline and then the three of them worked over a typewriter interrupted by the producer, Walter Shenson, 'coming in rather heavily with suggestions'.

According to Wells, 'Dudley has got a very happy way of inventing dialogue, and is certainly one of the funniest of men in private life. However, there was a stage when he was first going through analysis that he thought he had to be deadly serious. Once during the shooting, he sat in the middle of a group of cameramen telling them that the reason he had trouble producing scripts was because of potty training. Nobody laughed at all, as it was done with the utmost seriousness. I think that's what Peter teased him about most, and what Jonathan and Alan think about him, that he gets too easily drawn into being profound. Whereas his great gift is not being profound; his gift is being a fantastic clown.'

The film gave ample evidence of Dudley's clownish side as well as elements of the sentimental Littlechap syndrome, brought to its nauseous nth degree by Anthony Newley in *Stop The World – I Want To Get Off*.

Moore was exposed in the spotlight as never before, without any support from Cook's lofty presence or invention. It gave him a chance to demonstrate his ability as a devastating musical pasticheur – Beethoven, Mozart, Handel and Noël Coward are mimicked – to play the jazz piano, and to indulge himself in some romantic wish-fulfilment. There is no doubt that *30 Is A Dangerous Age, Cynthia* is a very personal film, in a contextual rather than a stylistic sense. The Cynthia of the title refers to Cynthia Cassidy and not any character in the movie; his own role as Rupert Street, was named after an actual street in Soho near where The Establishment Club used to be. Rupert's inamorata is called Louise Hammond, recalling Dudley's past love, Celia Hammond, played by Suzy Kendall, his present love. There were also gags that came from his own life: 'My mother always sent me my laundry through the mail – just like Rupert's does in the film. And like Rupert's she always included a sack of lemon drops and some bread pudding in the package.' The Dudley Moore Trio supplied most of the film's music, composed by Moore and subsequently recorded. The cast included John Bird, John Wells, Patricia Routledge (all three connected in some way with Miller, Cook and Bennett) and American comedian Eddie Foy Jr.

The plot concerns a nightclub pianist whose two ambitions are to write a hit musical and get married before his 30th birthday, only six weeks away; overcoming various obstacles, he achieves both just before the end titles come up. In real life Moore has yet to write that musical, rather as Jonathan Miller has yet to write his book on Mesmerism. Marriage has come more easily to him.

The film's failure to gain critical or public approval was all the more painful because Dudley had put himself so blatantly on the line and had wanted to prove he could go it alone. The movie was another example of a British film being manhandled by American commercial interests – *vide* Jonathan Miller's *Take A Girl Like You*, also released by Columbia Pictures. (By the 1980s, when Alan Bennett did his screenplays, creativity had returned somewhat to the creators.)

'Unfortunately, after three-quarters of an hour, the film took a direction I didn't want it to take,' Moore told *Film Commentary*. 'There were too many cooks. I really wanted it to be a simple story about a man who wants to compose music. I didn't want to have a girl in it, or the fact that he wants to get married. That seemed to me irrelevant.' Columbia had other ideas and it was publicised to cash in on the 'Swinging London' image of pop stars, mini-skirts and sexual permissiveness (a word that now seems to have fallen into neglect) despite the film's whimsy and innocence having little to do with any of that. Although much of the blame should accrue to Moore, it is the director Joe McGrath who must ultimately be held responsible for the finished picture. In the same year, McGrath had been dismissed from his first film, the elephantine multi-Bond spoof *Casino Royale* although he shared the director's credit (or debit) with five others.

On 14 June 1968 Dudley Moore married Suzy Kendall at the Hampstead Registry Office, a ceremony kept secret from all but two close friends, one of them Peter Cook. The press were allowed to get in on the act after the wedding and the next morning the newspapers contained the usual spread given to the mating of show-business personalities. Suzy had made something of a name for herself, having played in *To Sir With Love*, a preachy school drama featuring Sidney Poitier, and two films directed by Peter Collinson, in which she starred: *The Penthouse*, a nasty little shocker, and *Up The Junction*, a strained attempt to return British cinema to a kind of naturalism. After *Cynthia*, Dudley wrote the music for *Inadmissible Evidence*, directed by Anthony Page, the film version of John Osborne's vituperative play. It was Page who had directed Moore in plays at Oxford (and also Alan Bennett in *A Cuckoo In The Nest* at the Royal Court). Incidentally, Eleanor Fazan, the first credited director of *Beyond The Fringe*, played a leading role in the film. Moore followed this up with another film score, working for Stanley Donen again, on *Staircase*. His music was one of the few lively elements of this dreary movie, set in London but inexplicably shot in Paris, in which Rex Harrison and Richard Burton, two safely heterosexual actors, slummed it as a couple of queens.

Pending the possibility of a third series of *Not Only . . . But Also*, which had won the 1967 Best Light Entertainment award given by the Screen Writers Guild of Great Britain, Moore and Cook came together again for two films in a row. As in *The Wrong Box*, they were cast in smallish roles among a roster of many other stars, something which suited their type of comedy. In other words, the sketch form with which their careers began.

Ironically, and tragically, *The Bed Sitting Room* only came about because of Joe Orton's murder by his lover Kenneth Halliwell in August 1967: Richard Lester had been all set to do a musical starring Mick Jagger with a screenplay by Orton when the chauffeur, sent to collect the anarchic playwright for an initial meeting, discovered the bodies of Orton and Halliwell. As a replacement project Lester quickly bought up the screenrights of a satiric post-nuclear-war play by Spike Milligan and John Antrobus and shooting began on Cobham Common in May 1968.

The fact that Ralph Richardson played the title role (!) in *The Bed*

Sitting Room gives some idea of the film's surreal, Goonish humour. A small group of people lead a precarious existence in a desolate Britain three years after the bomb has dropped. Among them are a family consisting of father (Arthur Lowe), mother (Mona Washbourne) and daughter (Rita Tushingham) who live on a Circle Line tube train; a fire guard called Mate (Spike Milligan); head of a regional government (Harry Secombe); a male nurse in drag (Marty Feldman); and Mrs Ethel Shroake (Dandy Nichols) who becomes Queen of England, being the closest survivor in line to the throne. Peter Cook and Dudley Moore play two policemen in bowler hats and macs suspended in a balloon. The most challenging part of their roles was the difficulty of performing in a balloon and their attempts to prevent it from crashing into electricity cables. Lester, shooting in sepia, created an eerie comic nightmare and one of his best films. However, it bombed at the box-office and Lester had to wait almost five years before he worked again. Although Moore was not unsatisfied with the finished product, he had, as usual, something to say about the director: 'Dick Lester never seemed to know what he wanted. He gave peculiar instructions, which were hard to follow. He wanted different opinions but rejected them all, which was very disconcerting.'

Monte Carlo Or Bust (UK), *Those Daring Young Men In Their Jaunty Jalopies* (USA) or *Quei Temerari Sulle Loro Pazze, Scatenate, Scalcinate Carriole* (Italy) was one of those hybrid creatures, the 'international' film, made under the mistaken idea that in order to gain audiences in the world market one had to cast stars from as many countries as possible. The result was the cinematic equivalent of a Eurovision Song Contest entry, another nostalgic, slapstick, inflated, all-star co-production coming after *The Great Race* and *Those Daring Young Men In Their Flying Machines*, which looked into a fantastical past of the pioneering days of automobiles and planes. Twenty cars from the golden period of 1926-9 were specially designed (all with modern Fiat 2,300 engines) for the Monte Carlo Rally of the 1920s. The principal participants were villainous Brit Terry-Thomas, German gangster Gert Fröbe and American hero Tony Curtis (who wins, naturally). Peter Cook and Dudley Moore, as two pukka British officers, Major Dawlish and Lieutenant Barrington, were amusing comic book cut-outs but the film, directed by Ken Annakin, hardly regained the wit of Ronald Searle's opening credit titles.

Only television seemed to unbottle the comic genies of Peter Cook and Dudley Moore; feature films put a cork firmly on their talents.

After going their separate ways – Cook made *A Dandy In Aspic* and Moore *30 Is A Dangerous Age, Cynthia* – they appeared together again in an ATV special called *Goodbye Again*, which had guest Anne Bancroft performing a lampoon of *The Graduate*. Then their careers went off at a tangent again, Peter starring in *The Rise And Rise of Michael Rimmer* and Dudley returning to the West End stage in Woody Allen's *Play It Again, Sam*.

VII

Woody Allen and Dudley Moore were born in the same year. Both are short, play jazz, have sexual hangups, visit shrinks and are comedians. They also began in show business about the same time: when Dudley was in *Beyond The Fringe* Woody was just starting to become known as a gag writer for big comics on American TV and as a stand-up comedian in his own right. By 1966 he was able to move into a spacious six-room duplex apartment in New York's East Side while Dudley became the owner of Bentham House in Hampstead. Woody's first film was the quintessentially 'Swinging London' comedy, *What's New Pussycat?*, the score of which Dudley was mooted to compose. (Burt Bacharach in fact got the job.)

Woody Allen's second full-length play, *Play It Again, Sam*, opened on Broadway in February 1969 starring the author. As Allan Felix (Happy Allan?), Woody incarnated a version of himself, a bespectacled, intellectual, nebbish film critic whose relationships with women are disastrous. Taking as his mentor Humphrey Bogart, who, together with an octet of gorgeous females, appears to him in his fantasies, he attempts to overcome his insecurity and sustain a relationship. It sounded just up Dudley's street; he felt he could draw on his own experiences and anxieties for the role.

Although David Merrick's London production had a respectable run of ten months at the Globe Theatre from September 1969, due mainly to Dudley's pulling power (Woody Allen had not yet gained a following in Britain), it might have had a longer one had Merrick, with the collusion of Moore, not mistakenly decided to anglicise it. Transplanting the action from the smart East Side of Manhattan to London's Swiss Cottage deprived the humour of its roots – the running jokes on psychiatry, hypochondria and old movies being lost in the slightly off-English transition. Dudley admitted that he had changed many of the jokes 'to make them more meaningful to English audiences' but had tried to retain 'that peculiarly Jewish comic gloom'. The one important difference between Allen and Moore was that Woody was New York Jewish and Dudley was London English. One is reminded when watching a Woody Allen movie of a remark John Updike makes through one of his characters who thought that 'anyone who didn't live in New York has got to be kidding!' Woody's achievement is that he has managed to get assorted goys from all over the world to appreciate the essentially Jewish-Manhattan-middle-class experience.

Most of the critics were kind to Dudley but the play was dismissed as only suitable for the 'tired businessman'. One of the most positive was *The Daily Telegraph*'s John Barber. 'Relying on the cuddly appeal of a small furry animal, Dudley Moore looks appropriately hunted and haunted. His is already a spry, twinkling performance, though it will improve as he explores the possibilities of a well-written role ... As a nice, gay little evening the comedy has much to commend it.' *The Times* thought 'Dudley Moore gives a shaky performance, occasionally venturing beyond a note of monotonous complaint to passages of precarious clowning, and conveying scant confidence in the feeble dialogue.'

While playing the sexually anxious Allan Felix deserted by his wife, Dudley was having his own marital problems. 'With Suzy, I was very repressed, very contained in myself, but I know that she knew all that was going on inside me, and didn't have to comment on it,' he told 1980s *Playgirl* readers slavering to know all about Cuddly Dudley's sex life. 'She, in a sense, let me be. She believed in her own feelings, which is something I've only just started to learn how to do, to believe in *my* own feelings.' Both Dudley and Suzy were seeing psychiatrists at the time. Neither was willing to make a full commitment to the other person. She was afraid of losing independence and he would go into long periods of silence. She claimed that he loved their five Persian cats, Charlie, Sadie, Ada (Dudley's mother's name) and two others with no names, more than she did him. In 1970 he moved out of the mansion in Hampstead (where a remarried Suzy Kendall still lives) and took up residence in a small ground-floor flat in Camden Town, not far from the houses of old mates Jonathan Miller and Alan Bennett. In September 1972, after two years of separation, Suzy was granted a divorce on the grounds of the 'irretrievable breakdown' of the marriage.

VIII

Moore's ten-year working partnership with Peter Cook meanwhile continued on its sporadic way. The third series of Not Only . . . But Also, broadcast from February to May 1970, was acclaimed and enjoyed as much as ever.

Comedy shows, whether put together like a revue or a sitcom, take up most of the screen time on TV except for rediffused cinema films, but very few manage to surface above the sea of canned laughter. Not Only . . . But Also remains one of the landmarks, along with Hancock's Half Hour, Steptoe And Son, Till Death Us Do Part, Monty Python's Flying Circus and Fawlty Towers, all justified to claim the over-used appellation, 'classic'. However, in 1971, Cook and Moore decided to go beyond the Box.

The result was a two-man stage revue, the title of which came from the doorman at Barbetta's, a New York restaurant the Beyond the Fringe cast frequented from time to time when on Broadway. He would invariably greet them, in a thick foreign accent, with 'Ah, gentlemen – Behind The Fridge.' In an unusual and smart move, it was decided to take Behind The Fridge on a preliminary five-month tour of Australia and New Zealand, where their TV show was popular. The Antipodean tour (one of the furthest out-of-town tryouts imaginable) was a great success and it also gave the duo the chance to adjust and polish the show before the London opening.

Moore enthusiastically recollected that 'When we were in Australia with this show, there were nights when I couldn't think of anything more enjoyable. It was such tremendous fun, and you came off absolutely ecstatic and jumping about the place. In New Zealand, it really hit a ridiculous pitch of enjoyment in performance. It was marvellous.' If there was occasional friction between Cook and Moore on the tour, the knowledge that they would be working together for the next year or two made them soon patch up their differences for practical as much as personal reasons. The thought that Behind The Fridge would be a four-year commitment never occurred to them.

The show, presented by Cook's agent, Donald Langdon, and directed by the cast, aided by Joe McGrath, opened at the Cambridge Theatre on 21 November 1972. Since Beyond The Fringe there had been only rare sightings of revue on the West End stage, even in its redefined form. One had been a thing called Hulla Balloo, set in a 'loo', with contributions from two young men named Andrew Lloyd Webber and

Tim Rice, which had run for a few nights at the Criterion three weeks before Cook and Moore were to open. They needn't have worried. Although there are certain genres in the arts which have great days and then fall into decline (e.g. the oratorio, verse drama, the picaresque novel, the four-movement symphony or the Western), there are always one or two examples that make an isolated impression out of their time.

The revue consisted of twelve sketches, including two which had been seen before, *One Leg Too Few* and *The Frog And Peach*. The programme was completed by three piano numbers performed by Moore and ended with the inevitable 'Goodbye-ee'. 'Hello' had Dudley and Peter as two men who have a long chat, each thinking the other knows him. In another sketch, the minute Moore plays a schoolmaster preparing to cane a recalcitrant pupil, the lofty Cook. Closer to home was an item in which Moore as a film star visits his working-class father who proceeds to explain the facts of life to his celebrated son.

Some sketches were filmed and projected on a large screen, including one of a blacked-up Moore singing 'Ole Man River' in a shower. As the makeup begins to wash off, so his voice becomes more and more English until, by the end, he is all white and sounding like Noël Coward. Expanding on his Kurt Weill pastiche from the New York production of *Beyond The Fringe*, Dudley performed 'Eine Kleine Brechtmusik' with Cook dragged up as Marlene Dietrich. Only a few attempts at topical satire – cracks about Idi Amin and Edward Heath – seemed a little off-key. In 'Gospel Truth', Moore is a reporter from *The Bethlehem Star* interviewing a Mr Arthur Shepherd, a witness at the birth of Christ at a nearby stable. When the show went to the Plymouth Theater in New York in November 1973, under the title *Good Evening*, this sketch provoked Christian fundamentalists to outrage. With a vehemence that marks their kind, of whatever creed, some expressed the enlightened desire to see Cook and Moore burn in Hell. Fortunately, there were no serious death threats nor was the show hampered by any significant demonstrations; as usual in these matters, the religious zealots only managed to create free publicity for the producers, who must have thanked God for them.

Good Evening ran for over a year on Broadway followed by a seven-month tour of the United States, ending up at the Shubert Theater in Los Angeles and gathering a Tony Award along the way. During the New York run, apart from TV appearances, they performed at

Michael's Pub, the exclusive venue where Woody Allen can some-times be found playing clarinet in a Dixieland band. As during *Beyond The Fringe* ten years previously, they were lionised wherever they went. America had re-discovered Peter Cook and Dudley Moore, and *vice versa*. The period marked a giant step on the diminutive Dudley's road from Dagenham to Hollywood.

IX

Between the tour of Australia and New Zealand and the opening at the Cambridge Theatre of *Behind The Fridge*, Moore found time to make another film, this time Cookless. Perhaps because he had missed being in Jonathan Miller's 1966 *Alice In Wonderland* for BBC TV, in which both Bennett and Cook appeared – he was too busy with *Cynthia* to bother about *Alice* – Dudley was glad to take the role of the Dormouse in an all-star British film musical version of the Carroll tale. The furry brown costume Dudley wore was emblematic of his reputed cuddliness. Actually, a couple of years before, Moore told a reporter, 'Cuddly I am not . . . I highly resent being considered as some sort of human Sooty, a plaything for doting matrons. It was an image that grew on me like fur. I now want to shave it off.'

As the Dormouse appears in only one scene, ' A Mad Teaparty', Moore had just five days to spend on the picture. With him in the sequence were Peter Sellers, as the March Hare (switched from the King of Hearts in Miller's version), Robert Helpmann as the Mad Hatter, and an overmature Fiona Fullerton as Alice. Despite the cast, including Michael Crawford (White Rabbit), Michael Hordern (Mock Turtle), Spike Milligan (Gryphon), Ralph Richardson (Caterpillar), Flora Robson (Queen of Hearts) and Roy Kinnear (Cheshire Cat), it was a pretty dismal affair, unenlivened by the sixteen superfluous songs written by John Barry and Don Black.

The movie, the only one of many films to use the book's actual title, *Alice's Adventures In Wonderland* (the sole authentic thing about it), opened at Christmas 1972 to a lukewarm reception. Moore by that time was being warmly applauded every night at the Cambridge Theatre. He appeared on TV in a BBC 'special' called *It's Lulu – Not To Mention Dudley Moore* and was the subject (or adored object) of that tendentious, trivial and treacly tribute, *This Is Your Life*.

It is no reflection on Dudley to say that only he, out of the four

'Fringers', lends himself to such treatment. (He was again the programme's victim in 1986.) Can anyone imagine Jonathan Miller being hugged by Ernst Gombrich or Alan Bennett's old driveway 'tenant' recounting her rescue by him or the staff of *Private Eye* reciting encomia at Peter Cook? *This Is Your Life* is what Gilbert Adair calls 'a trial without prosecution. Witness follows witness to testify to the defendant's charm, wit, talent and generosity . . . his unfailing good humour in adversity . . . And, as one might well predict, not one of these maudlin trials has ever ended in anything but acquittal, with the tearily grateful subject surrounded, embraced, by those who have helped to exonerate him.' Moore's 'friendly witnesses' included Peter Cook, Spike Milligan, Oscar Peterson, John Dankworth and Moore's mother and sister.

X

'The world is full of dames – all you gotta do is whistle,' says the shade of Humphrey Bogart to Allan Felix-Dudley Moore in *Play it Again, Sam*. It seemed that all Dudley had to do was tickle the ivories for girls to fall at his feet. One of them was blonde twenty-year-old Hollywood 'Teen Queen' Tuesday Weld. In November 1963, the star of *Sex Kittens Go To College* went backstage after *Beyond The Fringe* and whisked Dudley away in her chauffeur-driven Cadillac to her apartment, where they made love.

They had met briefly a couple of evenings before when she saw him 'fucking the piano' (as Moore puts it) at a New York nightclub. Ten years later they met again in New York, when Moore was performing in *Good Evening*. Tuesday had the kind of looks he was attracted to: 'I'm rather fond of prominent teeth. It's the Leslie Caron type of face that gets me. My ex-wife Suzy Kendall had that same toothy smile, flared good nose and slightly Eurasian eyes, and Tuesday's got that sort of full mouth.' (So has his present wife, Brogan.)

Since their brief but passionate encounter, both Tuesday and Dudley had married and divorced. Tuesday (born Susan) had come up the hard way. At the age of three she was already supporting her widowed mother, older brother and sister as a child model and TV performer. She suffered her first nervous breakdown at nine, was an alcoholic at ten and attempted suicide at twelve. At thirteen she made her screen debut, among The Moonglows and The Flamingos, in *Rock*

Rock Rock, made for $400 in the Bronx. In Hollywood she gained publicity as a pubescent sex kitten at Twentieth Century-Fox in *Rally Round the Flag, Boys!*, *High Time*, *Return to Peyton Place* and *Wild in the Country*, and by dating older men such as Frank Sinatra, John Ireland and Raymond Burr. Yet despite the titters her name and image used to evoke, after leaving Fox she gained a reputation as an actress opposite Steve McQueen in *Soldier in the Rain* and in *The Cincinnati Kid*; in George Axelrod's wild and wicked satire *Lord Love a Duck*; as the sexy high-school psychopath in *Pretty Poison*; and as an actress at the end of her tether in the ghastly *Play It As It Lays*, for which she won the Best Actress award at Venice in 1972. In the late 1960s playwright-screenwriter-director George Axelrod claimed that 'Tuesday's a great actress, and can become a great star because she doesn't fake anything. And the reason she doesn't fake anything is because she simply can't. She has what Mr Hemingway so brilliantly described as a "Built-in shit detector." '

Not long after their second meeting Dudley and Tuesday, like Robinson and Friday, shacked up together. About eighteen months later, Tuesday, who already had an eight-year-old daughter from her first marriage to writer Claude Harz, announced that she was pregnant. Ignoring the fact that their relationship was already rather sparky, they decided to marry, as if the blanket of respectability that wedlock is supposed to bring would damp things down. The marriage took place in September 1975 in Las Vegas. Patrick Moore was born a few months later.

Dudley Moore was now resident in the United States, making occasional forays into England to visit his mother in Dagenham, play with his Trio at concerts and at John Dankworth and Cleo Laine's Wavendon Festival, from which an album was cut, and to make a few recordings with Peter Cook. Although *Not Only . . . But Also* and their stage show had ended, their comic partnership still had some life in it.

'Derek and Clive' derived from the dirty cross-talk Cook and Moore privately indulged in. 'It's how we talk when we're alone – schoolboy smut,' Dudley explained. 'I've always been a smutty little bugger. It's like rolling in mud, except that sounds as though I think it's dirty, whereas I feel it's natural. I feel it's quite quaint that people should be shocked by orifices and excrescences.' The cover on the first record, *Derek and Clive Live*, featured sketches Cook and Moore had performed at New York's Bottom Line nightclub, and bore the warning 'This record contains language of an explicit nature that may be offensive and should not be played in the presence of minors.' As usual, this kind of caveat was misdirected; adults should have been warned that the humour would appeal principally to minors, at least to those who had reached puberty. Yet there is something liberating about this outflow of obscenities injected into a puritanical society, not only for the listener but for the performers. There seemed to be absolutely no limit which they were prepared to set; much of the material was not found 'behind the fridge' but 'in the lavatory'. It was irrelevant that there was little wit or subtlety in this verbal graffiti.

Nevertheless, philosophy, politics, sociology, religion and art are somehow discussed. Bertrand Russell is called a 'white-haired cunt', James Callaghan is an 'oily heap of shit', Lord Longford sexually arouses Myra Hindley; Christ, whose top half is divine and bottom half human, masturbates; and Picasso paints his penis in different colours. (Their targets were wild – Russell was a free soul and Picasso a true erotic artist.) Derek (Dudley) describes ejaculating over a picture of his father and pushing a Jaffa cake in his mother's 'gob' so 'her right tit fell off', and Clive (Peter) tries to break the world record for the longest trail of snot. It was all far more regressive than shocking or subversive, and naturally the records sold like condoms at an AIDS convention. They were ideal gifts for one's randy bachelor friends, for liberated couples, rugger buggers or saloon bar bores. *Derek and Clive Live* was followed by *Derek and Clive Come Again, Derek and Clive Ad Nauseam* and finally a 'very naughty and dirty' 90-minute video (cut from twelve hours) issued in 1979.

The Derek and Clive albums were the culmination of a tendency which may have started on 13 November, 1966 on the late-night satire programme *BBC3* when a stuttering Kenneth Tynan broke new ground by saying 'f-f-fuck' for the first time on British TV. The musical *Hair* had opened the day after theatre censorship officially ended in 1968, thus allowing audiences the sight of full frontal nudity, both male and female, and prompting the remark from Lord Longford that the show contained 'some moving things'. It was followed in the same year by Tynan's collection of dirty jokes and nudity, *Oh Calcutta!* Slightly to paraphrase E C Bentley:

What I like about Derek and Clive
Is that they are no longer alive.
There is a great deal to be said
For being dead.

Filmed at the Bray Studios and released in 1977, *The Hound Of The Baskervilles* was the last film (to date) which Peter Cook and Dudley Moore made together and nobody had anything good to say about this umpteenth version of the Conan Doyle story, the most famous being the 1939 first-time pairing of Basil Rathbone and Nigel Bruce.

From the mid-1970s spoof movies became popular, emerging out of film buffs' nostalgia, a camp sensibility and American college humour. They were the celluloid equivalent of MAD magazine's comic-strip lampoons of movies. Mel Brooks was one of the prime movers of the trend with parodies of the Western (*Blazing Saddles*, 1974), the horror pic (*Young Frankenstein*, 1975) and *Silent Movie* (1976), most of them used as the basis for corny vaudeville routines, TV-fodder jokes and low comedy. In 1977 alone there was Mel Brooks's Hitchcock spoof *High Anxiety*, Gene Wilder's *The World's Greatest Lover* and Marty Feldman's *The Last Remake Of Beau Geste*, all in the same crass tradition which continued unabashed into the 1980s.

The Hound Of The Baskervilles derived from a combination of this American strain and the English *Carry On* . . . pictures, those crude comedies consisting of lavatorial schoolboy jokes, a *double entendre* a line, and a string of hammy, campy actors telegraphing each jest with pursed lips, rolling eyes and a snigger. Even a 'smutty little bugger' like Dudley Moore found them 'dreadful, raucous and unfunny'. No matter how vulgar Derek and Clive had been, there was nothing suggestive about their 'single entendres' and Dud and Pete had taken English humour into new realms of absurdity.

The director chosen by Michael White, who had produced two earlier spoofs, *Monty Python And The Holy Grail* and *The Rocky Horror Picture Show* (both 1975), was the American Paul Morrissey, an admirer of the *Carry On* . . . series who had made a fringe reputation directing films from the Andy Warhol 'factory'. The titles of the first three (from 1968–71) sum them up: *Flesh*, *Trash* and *Heat*, amusing camp exercises in the best of bad taste, peopled by junkies, hookers and drag queens and all featuring beefy Joe Dallesandro as a male hustler. Not exactly the world of the nineteenth-century English sleuth.

Apart from composing the score, Moore co-wrote the script (with Cook and Morrissey) and played Dr Watson (with a Welsh accent), Sherlock Holmes's mother, Ada (Dudley's mother's name), and Mr

Spiggott, the one-legged refugee from the *One Leg Too Few* sketch which had seen service in a number of shows over the years. The rest of the cast, headed by Cook's Jewish-accented Sherlock Holmes (perhaps as a tribute to Mel Brooks), contained many who had made better contributions to British comedy in the past: Joan Greenwood, Terry-Thomas, Max Wall, Irene Handl, Kenneth Williams, Roy Kinnear, Spike Milligan, Hugh Griffith, Prunella Scales, Penelope Keith, Denholm Elliott and Jessie Matthews.

Much of the blame for this dog's dinner of a picture has been laid at the door of the director, with whom many of the performers found themselves arguing, but Cook and Moore cannot escape unscathed. It was sad to reflect that the duo so long in the forefront of comedy was falling behind and seemed to have served their term. Comedians they had inspired, such as the Monty Python team, were passing them by. The parting of the ways for Peter Cook and Dudley Moore was the final breaking-up of the *Beyond The Fringe* fraternity, excepting for rare reunions.

Another breaking-up was taking place for Dudley at the same time, his marriage to Tuesday Weld. 'I love her and she loves me but we can't live together,' he told American newspapers. 'There are problems in me that are exacerbated by marriage, a whole fragile area. I am easily deflected by lack of self-esteem. My self-esteem has always been on the droopy side, though I can usually rustle up some more later in the day.' Years later he further analysed the relationship with the acumen of one who had spent a long time on the psychiatrist's couch.

'I think resentment trickled out on all sides because I was putting myself in an arena of challenge where the pain was very tough. I wanted to bring myself out, *be* myself, but I resented the fact that I was denying who I was. Sure, there was a lot of anger and hostility . . . We didn't have a lot of calmness in our relationship. But now I realise that's not a bad thing necessarily. We were fighting for a purpose. There was nothing wrong with it. Any couple that doesn't have their spoken differences and open fights is possibly having them physically and in a more horrendous way.' It was all a perfect demonstration of Miller's proposition in the philosopher's sketch from *Beyond The Fringe* that 'there is too much Tuesday in my beetroot salad'.

The couple separated in 1978 and divorced two years later, Tuesday returning to New York with four-year-old Patrick just after Dudley

Moore had become something that, despite its diminished coinage, still has a glamorous ring to it – a Hollywood star.

XII

A portion of the American public had been aware of Moore, on and off, since *Beyond The Fringe*. The coast-to-coast tour of the States with *Good Evening* and the televised Tony Award ceremony brought more exposure. Cook and Moore had also been seen hosting a segment of NBC's hit comedy show *Saturday Night Live* and on an ABC Documentary Special, *To The Queen! A Salute To Elizabeth II*, a republic's royalist homage to the Queen's Silver Jubilee, in which they performed a sketch gently ribbing the royal family's lifestyle. All very well but none of his films had made much impact in the States, and who knew Dudley Moore in Peroria, was the movie moguls' cry.

'I started going round the agencies, but they didn't know what to do with me,' Dudley says. 'I thought I would do small parts, because I'm a little person. I'd done a Tony-Award winning show with Peter on Broadway, but it didn't seem to do any good whether you knew Tony well or not. It didn't seem to make much difference.' However, in late 1977 Moore was offered a supporting role (originally written for Tim Conway, who turned it down) in Paramount's *Foul Play*. Although it was to be his first Hollywood movie Dudley says, 'I didn't want to do that film at first. I thought it was a kind of archaic part for me. Very familiar.' The role was that of Stanley Tibbets, an orchestral conductor who leads a double life as a sex-starved would-be swinger, frequenting singles bars, and whose bachelor pad is furnished with every sex gadget imaginable.

His appearance is really a comic set-piece cameo that could easily have been excised from the film without any damage to the plot. But it was the kind of role that gets noticed and he managed to be very funny and slightly touching in it. The story was another of the many exercises in Hitchcockiana around at the time, more likely to create dizziness than *Vertigo*. Set in San Francisco, it involved a recently divorced librarian called Gloria Mundy (Goldie Hawn) who gets caught up in a plot to murder the visiting Pope during a performance of *The Mikado*, conducted by Moore at the opera house. Characters include a menacing albino, two dwarfs (both shorter than Dudley by some inches), a German 'hit' lady (Rachel Roberts), a scar-faced killer

219

and a nonchalant detective (Chevy Chase, the TV comedian in his first film lead).

Dudley's big moment comes when Goldie, fleeing the albino, ducks into 'Twosomes Bar' and suddenly lights upon his harmless-looking self at a table. 'Take me home, please,' she demands. 'My place or yours?' 'Which is closer?' 'I have a little pad just round the corner,' he suggests. Feeling safe from threat in his apartment, she is shaken to find him transforming it into a sexual fly-trap by pushing a variety of buttons. Popping out of closets are life-size plastic dolls and a double bed covered in flashing lights under a strategically placed mirror. He projects a porn movie on to a screen and strips down to his boxer shorts, dancing erotically to disco music blaring from hidden speakers. Observing the albino driving away, Goldie decides to take her chances in the mean streets rather than submit to Dudley's kinky advances. Abashed, he puts his trousers back on, and winds down.

This protracted but amusing diversion was written and directed by the Australian-born Colin Higgins, who had penned the screenplay for *Harold And Maude* (1971), a black comedy covered in the syrup of 'young at heart' idealism, and *Silver Streak*, another half-cock Hitchcock comedy-thriller. Higgins, directing his first picture, was 'very easy to work with', according to Moore. 'I had the feeling that he wasn't quite sure sometimes of what he wanted, and maybe was a little nervous of telling you he wasn't sure that what you just did was not quite to his specifications. But it's very difficult sometimes to know what you can extract from a performer and how much you'll get from him if you let him have his way.'

Foul Play was a huge success worldwide. Dudley gained a fair share of the plaudits and, as he puts it, 'sporadic supermarket recognition and spotty visibility in Mexico', as well as a house in Marina Del Rey, a chic oceanfront area of Los Angeles. It also helped him to be offered the starring role in a Blake Edwards movie called *The Ferret*.

XIII

'Psychotherapy made me alive,' claimed Dudley Moore. It also, circumstantially, helped him become a Hollywood star. Since living in LA, Dudley had attended group therapy sessions on Tuesday (significant?) of each week, later extended to a twice-weekly session when they joined forces with the Friday group.

'We sit in a circle and just chat. We have a couple of film actresses, an architect, a script supervisor, a film director, a novelist and one total non-achiever who happens also to be very rich,' Moore explained. 'When I get weighed down by the gravity of the whole thing, I make the odd joke. Then there's the therapist who listens to us and takes the money. It does seem funny to the outsider, but all these new cures and therapies come from a genuine attempt to find a way of dealing with life. I myself find it very useful.'

The film director mentioned was Blake Edwards; they had met previously at a Hollywood party where Moore was entertaining the guests by demonstrating how different nationalities throw up. The 57-year-old Edwards had started off as a radio and TV writer and had acted in five films in the 1940s. Then he wrote the screenplay for six Richard Quine movies from 1952–7. His first directorial efforts were almost indistinguishable from Quine's but it was *Breakfast At Tiffany's* (1961), a sugary version of the Truman Capote story, that made his name in the charm school of cinema of which Quine was a member. *Days Of Wine And Roses* (1963), however, was a surprisingly black, realistic portrait of alcoholism. Then Edwards's development was arrested by Inspector Clouseau in the shape of Peter Sellers, whose endless battle with inanimate objects and the English language began in *The Pink Panther* (1964) and who continued to fall about (as did many audiences) through four more slapstick movies. Meanwhile, Edwards had taken a few pratfalls himself with two pictures starring his wife, Julie Andrews; *Darling Lili* (1969) and *The Tamarind Seed* (1974).

As the *Panther* pictures had been his only successful ones in the previous fourteen years, Blake was naturally tentative about branching out again into more sophisticated territory. (So Panther-obsessed was Edwards that he pursued Peter Sellers beyond the grave by making the bizarre and tasteless *The Trail Of The Pink Panther* in 1982, maladroitly piecing together leftovers and out-takes from previous Panther movies.) He had two Hollywood projects going, a romantic comedy of adultery called '*10*', featuring George Segal and Julie Andrews; and a comedy about a bumbling Clouseau-type secret agent called *The Ferret*. Peter Sellers had just suffered a heart attack, but Blake thought that Dudley would be a perfect substitute in the role.

'I thought he'd be just marvellous as *The Ferret*,' said Edwards. 'When I discussed it with Dudley he was equally enthusiastic . . . So if the film took off – and one is always hoping for sequels – then he'd prove invaluable.' (Hollywood was becoming sequel-punchy in the late 1970s.) Moore, however, only agreed to take the role on condition that he was not forced to make any sequels, since he wanted to avoid typecasting, a forlorn hope in a commercial system that thrives on the philosophy of 'don't change a money-making product'.

As Blake Edwards's '*10*' was scheduled to be shot first, Moore took a trip to London where he enjoyed himself, put on weight, and visited his sister in Upminster and his 78-year-old widowed mother in her Dagenham council house. The fact that she still lived there has some-times provoked the accusation that Dudley is 'a mean bastard', as someone was heard to say when a picture of the house came up on the screen during *This is Your Life*. But, like Alan Bennett's parents, she preferred to stay where she had always felt at home. 'She likes living there,' Moore explained. 'She'd hate to move. She won't even come to see me in America. Wouldn't get on a plane to save her life. She gets a weekly amount of money from me, so she's well taken care of.' Ada Moore remained in Dagenham until her death in 1981, aged 81.

XIV

Meanwhile, in Hollywood, George Segal walked off the MGM studio lot on the first day of shooting, protesting at the over-abundant amount of control he felt the associate producer and his co-star, both in the person of Julie Andrews, had over the film. He had also insisted on his own wife, Marion, participating in the editing and production. Orion Pictures filed a legal action seeking damages of over $11.5 million and Segal countersued for $10 million. With a crew and cast standing by, Edwards summoned Moore to take over the romantic lead.

'George Segal couldn't do the film, so of course the first person they thought of was me,' commented Dudley. Thus, in the best *A Star Is Born* tradition, he was immediately flown to Hollywood, put on a crash diet, passed from hairdresser to tailor to bootmaker (he was given 2½ inch lifts in his shoes) to makeup man – *et voilà!* – little Dud of the dirty raincoat had been metamorphosed into Dudley Moore, Superstar.

'Isn't it incredible?' he told a reporter. 'It's something I've always wanted, but I never thought I stood a chance. This sort of thing could never have happened in Britain where I'm still thought of as a comic. Which is limiting . . . It's like starting all over again. And it's exciting. There's a big-time feeling about it all. It's funny. Twenty years ago I was just getting started in London and making a nuisance of myself and telling everyone the kind of things I wanted to do. And I was lucky. Since I've been living here I've done the same thing and now this has happened. I still can't believe it . . .' and so on.

(This last-minute replacement seemed to augur well for him, because a few days before Edwards had been about to begin shooting the original *Pink Panther* picture, Peter Ustinov walked out, and Peter Sellers was called in at the last moment.)

It is hard to believe that the role of George Webber was not written with Moore in mind. He is a successful 42-year-old composer-pianist-songwriter, living in an expensive beach house at Malibu and undergoing psychotherapy. 'They say that life begins at forty. Well they've been lying in their teeth,' says George dolefully.

' "*10*" ' really seemed to mirror my life. It was a conjunction of my personal and professional life. I came up with who I was and went with it. I felt comfortable in the role playing myself. So I decided to allow that part of myself in my work and any other vulnerabilities that might arise. I remember talking to Blake about it because I wasn't sure how I wanted to play the character, but I felt it would be better if I played it straight. He agreed and I felt fine doing it because I didn't have to put on a voice or a funny walk, which I had always done in my other work.'

Coincidentally, Moore had written an outline for Paramount about a year before called *The Joys Of Sex* on exactly the same theme. 'Everybody liked it, except they wanted to turn it into an episodic comedy like Woody Allen's *Everything You've Always Wanted To Know About Sex* . . . But I wouldn't agree to that,' he remarked.

Putting aside the very real compensation of over a million-dollar salary, the benefits accruing from increased fame and the fact that performing was his profession, it must have taken a certain amount of courage for Moore to bare himself (in two senses) in the picture. For a long time it has almost been obligatory for the leads in a Hollywood movie to take off their clothes at one point or another. Since the late 1960s, the inclusion of a nude love scene in commercial films has been as essential as its exclusion was when the Hays Code operated.

Dudley's first nude scene takes place at an orgy for which Edwards had employed a number of porno film 'actors' and 'actresses'. Despite his self-consciousness about his size (his height, that is) and his disabled left leg, Moore decided not to fake it. 'Normally, there are about six guys behind the camera, but when I peeled off there must have been about fifty of them, all waiting for me to give my all. The lighting cameraman went into hysterics. I'd have felt pretty silly standing there with a towel around me. So I took everything off. When I got home that night, I had a delayed reaction. I suddenly sat up in bed, horrified. Had I really done that?' Actually, the only bit of Dudley that is visible on screen is his bare buttocks. (A group photo of the nine men and twelve women all in the buff, posing as if for a school photo, with Dudley at the centre, fully-clothed and wearing sunglasses, is prominently displayed in his Californian home.) For obvious reasons he wears a tracksuit during the beach scenes: 'Because of my leg, the tracksuit was a funny prop in the end, a piece of wardrobe that was quite useful.'

Much more was seen of the voluptuous, statuesque body of 23-year-old blonde blue-eyed Bo Derek, who plays Moore's ideal woman, the ten out of ten of the title. There was a joke going the rounds at the time of the film's release (1979) that went: 'What is 10, 9, 8, 7, 6 . . . ?' Answer: 'Bo Derek ageing.' However cruel, the joke is accurate: since all her roles consisted of little more than just looking her ravishing self in various stages of *déshabillé*, her career dipped almost to non-existence as she passed the dangerous age of 30. Her husband, John Derek, 29 years her senior, had also seen his film career wane as he lost his 'pretty boy' looks. But for one short moment in '*10*', the display of Bo Derek in her one-piece bathing suit and Afro-plaited hair brought her international fame.

The film also helped revitalise Julie Andrews's drooping career as Moore's long-time girlfriend Samantha Taylor (naturally called 'Sam') despite not having very much to do on-screen except wait around for him to have scruples about the belle Bo and return to her for the soppy, happy ending. Yet the fact that she swears and has sex out of wedlock moved Andrews away from her wholesome, English, over-enunciating, singing nanny-governess image which had prompted Christopher Plummer to say after *The Sound of Music* that, 'Working with her is like being hit over the head with a Valentine's card.' Blake Edwards put it another way: 'Once, before I'd met Julie, some people were conjecturing about her success. I said, "I can tell you what it is. She has lilacs for pubic hair." ' It was really in her husband's next film, the bile-filled satire on Hollywood, *S.O.B.*, that Mary Poppins finally undid her starched pinafore, although the film revealed more of Edwards's sour grapes than his wife's slightly larger breasts.

Another beneficiary of '*10*' was Maurice Ravel, whose orgasmic *Bolero* is used as background music to Bo Derek's seduction of Dudley and which she calls 'the most descriptive sex music ever written'. Dudley might have been reminded of the sketch in *Not Only . . . But Also* when 'Pete' says: 'Whenever I hear Ravel's *Bolero* I think of Eileen Latimer. I can't think why I keep thinking of her whenever I hear that tune. I think it may be due to the fact that she came round to tea one day and smashed the record over my head.' The only person who didn't get much of a boost from the film was George Segal, whose career faded as Moore's blossomed.

The plot of '*10*' concerns the middle-aged George Webber who, though wealthy and acclaimed and loved by his 38-year-old singer girlfriend Samantha (43-year-old Andrews), longs for his lost youth and lusts after the newly-married Jenny, whom he follows on her honeymoon in Acapulco. When her husband David (Sam Jones) is taken to hospital with severe sunburn after falling asleep on his surfboard out at sea (a situation reminiscent of Elaine May's *The Heartbreak Kid*, 1973) and being rescued by George in a motorboat, Jenny makes love to George. He cannot rise to the occasion, she pulls his hair painfully, her braids get in his face and the love-making is interrupted by his having to put the *Bolero* back to play from the beginning, to unstick the record and say 'hi' to her husband on the phone. He returns to Samantha, an older and wiser man, realising 'There's more to life than turning on and screwing to Ravel's *Bolero*.'

Dudley, 'one of the great Anglo-Saxon heterosexual bores of all time' according to his gay lyricist partner (Robert Webber), runs the gamut from melancholy middle-aged delusion to sexually fixated lover stoned on amphetamines and double-brandies to 'elevator music' pianist and singer, while nimbly negotiating the various slap-stick situations (some crude, some amusing) with which Edwards likes to punctuate his movies. The voyeurism of the character, and consequently of the film, is hardly discounted by Julie Andrews's gentle protestations: he watches his swinging neighbour's carryings-on with 'broads' through a telescope, sneaks into the back of a church to watch a wedding, for which he gets a bee up his nose, and surrepti-tiously observes the sun-bathing Bo on the beach.

In terms of profit, the *raison d'être* for most American movies, '*10*', a mellow male-menopausal Californian comedy, was a $60-million masterpiece, having cost only $6 million to make. The reviews, although hardly rating the film as high as the leading man's assessment of Bo Derek, were mostly on the positive side and Moore won the Golden Globe Award (given annually by the Hollywood Foreign Press Association) for best actor in 1979.

'The reason Dudley does so well is that American women are finally tired of this macho stuff and prefer a man who can be tender, sweet, romantic, without being rough,' explained a producer. 'A man who needs just a bit of care.' Like the short character who 'made no secret of his height' in Alan Bennett's *Habeas Corpus*, and unlike forties 'heart throb' Alan Ladd (5 foot 6 inches), Moore never stood on a box or got his leading ladies to stand in a hole. After '*10*' he was labelled a 'heart throb' in his own right; in 1979 he was presented with the Golden Apple award as Male Discovery of the Year by the Hollywood Women's Press Club.

'In a sense being small has been my biggest asset. It helped in *Beyond The Fringe* when I was surrounded by three other guys who were over six foot two and still are as far as I know, unless osteoporosis has got them by what can only be called the backbone,' Moore said in a TV interview in December 1988. 'It was a good thing when I had to look up to Peter like that. Men who are five foot seven or eight say "Oh, I'm so small." I'm five foot two. It doesn't mean a darn thing now, but I say that now from the advantage of going through a lot . . . I feel better about myself basically. I don't want to sound boring and Californian, but it's true.'

In 1979, living alone in his house at Marina del Rey, where he played the piano, watered his plants, did most of his own housekeeping and also claimed to be having a series of 'one-week stands', Moore had immediately signed to do another picture. (The projected second film with Blake Edwards, *The Ferret*, had been rejected by the studio, who grew disenchanted with the script and the size of the budget.) Before shooting began in October on *Wholly Moses!*, he made a short visit to London to see 'dentists, lawyers, mothers, accountants and friends' and be the guest star in the then immensely popular *Muppet Show*: 'I was guest number 79. I was hoping for 69. I seem to miss all the fun.' On the principle that the Devil shouldn't have all the best tunes, God had been embodied in 1977 by the cigar-smoking vaudevillian George Burns in *Oh God!* ('It's an almighty laugh!' proclaimed the posters.) Two years later another comedy of religion, *Monty Python's Life Of*

Brian, had brought a vast amount of shekels into the box office, although some picketing Christians failed to see the joke. It told the story (in wildly anarchic Pythonian terms) of an exact contemporary of Christ who is mistaken for the Messiah and crucified. *Wholly Moses!* (1980) (originally *The Book Of Herschel*) centres on Herschel (Dudley Moore) coming across a burning bush in the desert and, not seeing his brother-in-law Moses kneeling behind it, thinks that God is addressing him. He then attempts, in the most bumbling fashion, to lead his people out of bondage. Finding his rivalry with Moses a great strain, he explodes: 'If I have to hear about the Red Sea parting for Moses once more, I'll stuff the tablets down his throat. I'm beginning to have second thoughts about Thou Shalt Not Kill.' Woody Allen or Zero Mostel might just have got away with such lines. The story is all told in flashback when a New York language professor called Harvey Orkin (actually, the name of a well-known Hollywood agent), also played by Moore, comes across the tale recounted in an ancient scroll he discovers while travelling in modern Israel.

Wholly Moses! was a curious follow-up to '*10*' in that Moore did not continue the exploration of himself as a 'straight' comedy actor but retreated into the farce of his earlier manner. It was the first film directed by Gary Weis, whose previous experience had been on TV's *Saturday Night Live*, it was produced by David Begelman, between studios, just after the whistle had been blown on his dubious financial practices at Columbia.

XV

'It's sexual voyeurism. People seem to get a curious, vicarious thrill about the sexual wanderings of celebrities,' commented Dudley Moore when the show-biz scribes and their parasitic *paparazzi* started to scent a romance between the self-confessed 'ludicrously small but extremely passionate' star and Californian-born Susan Anton, a tall (5ft 11in), slim, blonde 30-year-old model-cum-actress. 'It's quite ludicrous, yet I'm delighted they're interested as well.'

By most people's definition, the line of fame runs parallel to the line of public interest in the private life of an individual as drawn on the celebrity graph. As distinct from a mere actor, a film star has to perform in two spheres simultaneously, that of fact and that of fiction; no wonder the boundaries around them become blurred in the minds of the observers and the observed. Pursuing the biographical method with Dudley entails following a trail that takes in both the life and the work. More ink has been spilled over Dudley Moore's *amours* than over the personal life of the other three 'Fringers' put together, not necessarily because there is more to tell (though that is a factor), but because he is the most widely known. There is a danger when detailing his career that his relationships could be reviewed in the same way as his films – a series of flops and successes, long or short runs. The question, in *Variety* lingo, is 'Has it got legs?'

Susan Anton certainly had legs, and the long-and-the-short-of-it couple were perfect fan magazine fodder. 'I go *up* on Susan,' quipped Moore. The one thing Peter Cook found ironic about the relationship was that Dudley 'should choose a girl-friend who sings country and western when I know for a fact that Dud can't stand that type of music'. Dudley and Susan began seeing each other a few months before *Wholly Moses!* was being put back among the bulrushes and at a time of change in Dudley's private life. In April 1980 Tuesday Weld gained custody of their son, their mutual community property was divided and he was ordered to pay $3,000 a month in maintenance. A third marriage was not contemplated but a third starring role in a Hollwood film was.

James Caan, Al Pacino, Jack Nicholson and Richard Dreyfuss were among those who turned down the title role of the drunken, laughing, millionaire playboy in *Arthur*. 'Agents kept telling me nobody wants to see a picture about a rich drunk,' said ex-Madison Avenue whizz kid Steve Gordon, who had written the screenplay with Robert Redford in mind. When Paramount lost interest, Orion, the producers of '*10*', picked it up and offered it to Dudley Moore. Some alterations were made in the script to suit Moore's personality and 'I explained to the director that I couldn't possibly do it as an American since I spent half the time trying to get my vowels right.' As a result, Dudley never changed his English accent even when he played an American politician in *Six Weeks*. There is nothing new in that. Since the talkies began, English actors like Ronald Colman, Leslie Howard, David Niven and George Sanders played Americans, only occasionally flattening their vowels as a discordant concession. Among the handful of British actors who have made it in Hollywood in the last few decades, Richard Burton remained resolutely Welsh, Sean Connery Scottish and Michael Caine cockney.

Arthur Bach, one of Dudley Moore's most original creations, is the irresponsible 35-year-old heir to $900 million. His father's hopes are pinned on his marrying the wealthy Susan Johnson (Jill Eikenberry) so that the two family fortunes can be merged. However true love triumphs when Arthur falls for Linda Marolla (Liza Minnelli), an out-of-work actress who lives in Queens and helps support her unemployed blue-collar father by shoplifting. The cupid in this affair is Arthur's faithful butler Hobson (John Gielgud), whose death from cancer strengthens Arthur's resolve to go against his family and marry Linda.

Arthur was founded on the notion that a poor little rich man who is continuously inebriated and infantile (he wears a top hat in the bath and plays with a model railway in his bedroom) could gain audiences' concern and affection. It is to Dudley Moore's credit that against all odds he managed to give the potentially irritating character some credence and win over more people than he alienated, if the $100 million box-office takings are anything to go by. He makes Arthur into a memorable comic drunk whose guffawing at his own jokes (rather good ones, in fact) diffuses any creeping bar-room boredom. Unfortunately, by the end, saccharine dilutes much of the whiskey sour. More seriously, *Arthur* was a misconceived 1980s attempt to recapture the spirit of the screwball comedies of the 1930s. Coming out of the Depression and into The New Deal, a favourite theme then was the social contrasts of class, the idle rich learning how to be happy from the poor – films epitomised by Gregory La Cava's *My Man Godfrey* and George Cukor's *Holiday*, dominated by a huge Park Avenue mansion owned by a wealthy but bored family, with butlers and maids scurrying around a central staircase. The values of the upper crust were found wanting and their lives offered the questionable palliative to the lower classes that it is better to live in happy poverty (a contradiction in terms) than in unhappy wealth. The films were escapist and sentimental props of the status quo, never presenting egalitarianism or even a whiff of socialism as a goal.

This philosophy rang hollow then and it rings hollow in the 1980s, expecially as *Arthur* compounds it by a retrogressive portrait of the loyal and dedicated servant who actually keeps the family together, the admirable Hobson, played with a contrasting mixture of *hauteur* and foul-mouthed dry humour by an understretched Gielgud (Arthur: 'I think I'll take a bath.' Hobson: 'I'll alert the media.'). Emlyn Williams, who had replaced Sir John in Bennett's *Forty Years On*, commented,

'Never, *never* could the mellifluous Irving tones, the voice of the non-permissive last century, later startle posterity by emanating from the aristocratic valet perched on the edge of a bath and looking superciliously down his nose at his naked employer: "I suppose I am now expected to wash your dick." ' For this role, however, after nearly half a century in films, the 77-year-old Gielgud won his first Oscar – Best Supporting Actor. It is ironic that in a book published in 1984 called *The Movie Stars Story*, in which stars are classified by decades, Gielgud is placed in the 1980s chapter along with the likes of David Bowie and Dolly Parton. It was Moore who had suggested Gielgud to Steve Gordon, who also directed. When Gordon told Gielgud that he had never been to London, Sir John replied, 'Oh, what a pity! You've missed it!'

On 15 April 1982, Dudley escorted Susan Anton to the Dorothy Chandler Pavilion for the Oscar ceremony, in which he had been nominated for Best Actor. Although he came second (along with Warren Beatty, Burt Lancaster and Paul Newman) to the dying Henry Fonda in *On Golden Pond*, he found it extremely gratifying to be considered for the world's most renowned motion-picture award. It meant that he was being taken seriously by the denizens of Tinsel Town.

XVI

Dudley Moore's new status as box-office attraction enabled his agent, Lou Pitt, to negotiate four features in a row for him, to be shot within months of one another. This was not unusual in the heyday of the Hollywood studios when stars had to fulfil their annual quota of movies. As Clark Gable commented (to Arthur Miller) about his days at MGM: 'We'd finish a picture most often on a Friday, and there'd be some parties over the weekend, and I'd come back to start a new picture on Monday . . . They'd have my costume ready, and I'd get into it and go out on to the set and say hi to the director and meet whoever was playing the girl in the picture and try to figure out where the locale was supposed to be . . . By the end of the week you'd have a pretty good idea of what the character was, and then you'd have two more weeks till it was finished, and by the time you really understood anything it was over . . . '

In a sense it was easier for stars like Gable because he always had the same expert backup crew, and the portrayals only differed slightly from film to film. From 1980 to 1985, Dudley made nine films, almost two a year. He also gave several classical and jazz concerts and cut a record, *Smilin' Through*, with Cleo Laine. (In the same period, Jonathan Miller directed eight operas, one stage and six television plays and hosted a fifteen-part television discussion series, while Alan Bennett wrote seven television plays, one stage play and one screenplay. Just to be contrary, Peter Cook confined his activities to a couple of films and a smattering of television appearances.)

This whirlwind activity began with Moore's first and only dramatic role (to date) in *Six Weeks*, another entry in the disease-as-entertainment stakes. If you have tears, prepare to shed them now. The title refers to the length of time an eleven-year-old ballerina has been given to live before she dies of leukaemia. Nicole (Katherine Healy) is the precocious daughter of chilly cosmetics millionairess Charlotte Dreyfus (Mary Tyler Moore), who has become romantically involved with a married would-be Congressman Patrick Dalton (Dudley Stuart John Moore). Mother and daughter decide to spend the girl's last Christmas (the sentimental season *par excellence* in the movies) in New York. When Patrick learns that Nicole's ambition is to dance at the Lincoln Center in *The Nutcracker*, he arranges for her to do so. ('The Dying Swan' might have been more apt.) She dances magnificently and dies soon afterwards on the Lexington Avenue subway. Patrick returns to his wife and son, and Charlotte leaves for Europe.

The syrupy script, by David Seltzer, had been doing the rounds since 1975 and Moore's part had been offered to the likes of Burt Reynolds, Paul Newman, George Segal and even to Sylvester Stallone. The choice of Dudley as the radical chic Californian politician necessitated the justification that he had come to the USA at twenty and become a citizen. The director of this sugar plum picture was producer-actor Tony Bill (he had been in *Soldier In The Rain* with Tuesday Weld in 1963) and Moore himself composed the music.

Like many films about the terminally ill, *Six Weeks* is set in the never-never land of the rich, illustrating George Bernard Shaw's maxim that 'Money doesn't bring you happiness, but it allows you to be miserable in comfort.' Although suffering is certainly not exclusive to the poor, the style and imagery of the movie and its artificial notions of wealth militate against any semblance of reality. The luxurious locales, seen as the natural habitat of the characters in soap opera and glossily photographed through tear-stained lenses, exist merely to feed the material aspirations of the less well-off audiences rather than for any dramatic impulse that informs masterpieces of the performing arts. Not that *Six Weeks* had any such pretensions. It came off the dream factory conveyer belt labelled 'weepie', a genre with many noble predecessors. However this one was a reject, and lasted at the box office about as long as its dying juvenile lead.

If one wanted to find a thematic chord running through Dudley's films, it is of a man torn between two women. The millionaire Californian-based Moore plays predominantly very wealthy professionals in his films – senators, orchestra conductors, doctors, scientists, psychiatrists. (The sole worker he's played has been one of Santa Claus's elves.) In *Romantic Comedy*, one of three of Dudley's films released in the USA in 1983, Moore is the male half of a successful playwriting duo in New York, the distaff side being played by Mary Steenburgen. The two of them hover on the edge of an affair, though each is married to another. Finally, they learn to live as workmates instead of playmates. Adapted by Bernard Slade from his Broadway hit, *Romantic Comedy* was neither romantic nor comic nor a hit. Mary Steenburgen was ill-used in the role of his co-writer and Dudley, in the part taken by Anthony Perkins on Broadway, smoothly manages another of his middle-aged, wish-fulfilment-fantasising small guys. Directed by Arthur Hiller in his usual slickly superficial manner, the film had one thing to its advantage – it was set in New York. As a rule, films by run-of-the-mill directors, with whom Moore has mostly worked, are lent a little more wit and intelligence when they are shot in the Big Apple. Manhattan Movies have it over Malibu Movies every time.

New York was also the setting of Dudley Moore's next two films of 1983 before the clammy hand of California reclaimed him. Although they did not do much to put him back on the pedestal from which he had slipped since *Arthur*, they left him with his reputation still intact. Each was connected with subjects he knew something about, psychiatry and music respectively. In *Lovesick* (originally titled *Valium*) he plays Dr Saul Benjamin, a New York psychiatrist, and in *Unfaithfully Yours*, he is orchestral conductor Claude Eastman.

'Ever heard of a Freudian slip?' asks Dr Benjamin of the shade of Sigmund Freud (Alec Guinness) in the back of a taxi cab. 'No, what's that?' says the bemused father of psychology. According to director-screenwriter Marshall Brickman, there is a lot in the film about the 'psychology industry' that old Freud would not recognise, although many of his terms are still used. Moore (again married to a 'career woman' over occupied with her work) has a 'counter transference' affair with one of his patients (Elizabeth McGovern) with whom he argues, in one of the best scenes in the film, about the 'castration complex' and 'penis envy' – 'If we envy you your penis so much,' she says, 'why is it that you spend so much time trying to get what we've got?' *Lovesick* is an amiable enough satire on psychotherapy – there is an amusing collection of patients and doctors – and displays a modicum of intelligence and wit, something one would expect from the co-writer of *Annie Hall* and *Manhattan*. In fact, the extremely corporeal ghost of Freud plays a similar advisory role to Humphrey Bogart's in Allen's *Play It Again, Sam*. Dudley gives one of his most restrained and attractive performances in the part and seems far more at ease with the material than he did in his two previous films.

The ghosts of Preston Sturges and Rex Harrison hung over *Unfaithfully Yours*. Although the original 1948 movie had been one of Sturges's least funny and characteristic, coming after his best period, it was still far more inventive and stylish than the 1980s version directed by Howard Zieff. The Sturges screenplay had had Harrison, spitting out epigrams on his lounge-lizard tongue, as a temperamental British conductor who imagines, while conducting three different works, three different ways of killing his lovely wife (Linda Darnell) whom he suspects of infidelity. The character of his dastardly imaginings is dictated by the character of the music – Rossini, Wagner and Tchaikovsky – an audio-visual experiment along the lines of Raymond Queneau's *Exercises de Style*. This three-toned dimension is reduced to monotone in the remake by using only one work, a concerto at that (the Tchaikovsky violin played by Pinchas Zukerman, future husband of Tuesday Weld), thus diminishing the conductor's musical role even further. Yet Moore's film did have an advantage: where 'Sexy Rexy' had been more convincing as an international conductor, 'Cuddly Dudley' handled the slapstick comedy better. Despite the movie being as flimsy as the evidence of adultery on which this pocket Othello builds his murderous intentions, it is mildly diverting.

Then came Dudley's return to California, the scene of his first triumph in the movies, and to the man who had made it possible, Blake Edwards. *Micki And Maude* (1984) brought the constant Dudley Moore dilemma of being a shuttlecock between two women to its logical conclusion by making him a bigamist. The painfully contrived plot has Dudley as Rob Salinger, a well-known TV frontman of a current affairs programme. His wife, Micki (Ann Reinking) is an ambitious lawyer about to be appointed a judge and who doesn't want to have a baby. (A woman's career is again seen as a threat to a marriage.) Moore wants to be a father and begs her to have 'just one child, a small one'. While his wife dares to neglect him for her job, he meets Maude (Amy Irving), a young cellist, with whom he has an affair. 'I feel guilty about not feeling guilty,' Moore says. A short time later, just before a symphony concert is about to begin at the Hollywood Bowl, Maude tells him she is pregnant. They naturally continue to talk through the first movement of Beethoven's Fifth and nobody tells them to shut up. He is determined to get a divorce and marry Maude, but a few days later Micki tells him she too is going to have a baby. Under pressure from Maude's wrestler father, Rob marries her at a big wedding ceremony in LA. Despite his fame, this piece of news apparently doesn't reach Micki or her parents and leads to the final farcical twenty minutes or so, the *raison d'être* of the film, during which Dudley Moore has to shuffle frantically between his two wives in the same maternity ward, while the two women have their babies at the same time. Unfortunately, despite some funny moments, the farce cannot support a sentimental theme of paternity *and* role reversal, with characters that exist merely as pawns in the plot. In the end, the two women pursue their careers while Dudley is left literally holding the babies.

Although the crass screenplay and direction were at the root of the problem, it was Dudley Moore, the star, who ended up taking the rap. As for *Best Defense*, made the same year, there can be no defence other than a financial one. He didn't even get to go to Israel (standing in for Kuwait), where much of the film was shot. These Middle East episodes featured 'Strategic Guest Star' Eddie Murphy as an American army commander of an out-of-control tank that knocks down an Arab village. 'How do you say, "Get the fuck out of the way" in Arabic?' he shrieks. Clumsily and confusingly parallel to these ham-fisted episodes (inanely using America's intervention on the side of Kuwait in a possible war with Iraq as a peg on which to hang several slapstick episodes) is a silly tale which takes place in California two years previously. Moore, as an engineer for a defence manufacturer, unwittingly (and unwittily) had become involved in an espionage plot to get hold of a design of a gyroscope that is part of a missile guidance system. These 'satiric' goings-on, that once served in the 'sixties in comic James Bond spin-offs, are laced with infantile sexual innuendos, i.e.

a machine discussed in term of anatomy – a nine inch insertion, thermal penetration (nudge, nudge) – and take place between Moore (whose wife is seen rejecting his advances early in the morning when he wakes up, thus offering an excuse for his philandering) and his blonde boss.

Best Defense was the nadir (to date) of Dudley Moore's career. Of the six films he has made since *Arthur*, only *Lovesick* and, to a lesser degree, *Unfaithfully Yours*, had any quantifiable quality. No wonder there were people who agreed with Freud's remark to Moore in *Lovesick*; 'I see that you are flushing a brilliant career down the toilet.'

XVII

Moore continued to be in demand as a 'personality' on TV and as a treasured guest at Hollywood parties, as well as being the recipient of many a film offer. One of the most curious was the suggestion that he play the outrageous drag queen Albin to Frank Sinatra's Renato in a screen version of the musical *La Cage Aux Folles*. Another mercifully aborted project was a proposed remake of Billy Wilder's *Love In The Afternoon* (itself a remake), with Dudley playing opposite the teenage Brooke Shields. He made his Carnegie Hall debut in 1983, playing Beethoven's Triple Concerto with Robert Mann (violin) and Nathaniel Rosen (cello) and the St Paul Chamber Orchestra under Pinchas Zukerman. A couple of years later Moore became a partner in a restaurant called '74 Market Street' in Venice, California, where he would sometimes play the piano for the entertainment of delighted and often pleasantly surprised clients. The restaurant is not far from his 'early beach Colonial' home in Marina Del Rey, built on sand. He had to move out and stay for long periods at the Beverly Hills Hotel while the builders and decorators were making structural changes and redecorating the house. It was therefore an opportune moment for him to return to England to appear in his first British-made film since the dire *Hound Of The Baskervilles* eight years earlier.

During the making of *Santa Claus: The Movie* at Pinewood, Moore stayed at the St James's Club. When there was a fortnight's break in the shooting, he decided to fly back to California by Concorde in order to play at the opening of his restaurant. As his house was still uninhabitable, he stayed at the Beverly Hills Hotel for two weeks, while continuing to pay £150 a night at the St James's in order to keep his room. This extra expense made an imperceptible dent in the salary he was earning for the £30 million picture.

'Money. I don't know much about that,' says Dudley as Patch the Elf in *Santa Claus*.Perhaps one motive for making the movie was that since kids are taken to the cinema most often at Christmas, the film could become a hardy, money-making perennial. Yet the post-Fordian message underlying the film's invented explanation for the origin of the Americanised legend, is to show how it has become over-commercialised in the twenteth century. 'People don't want to wait a whole year for Christmas', says B Z (John Lithgow), the deliciously ruthless toy-manufacturing tycoon, contemplating a way of increasing the market. 'We'll call it Christmas II.' Difficult not to be reminded that the producers, Alexander and Ilya Salkind, had made *Superman I, II, III* and *IV*.

It was probably inevitable that Dudley Moore should one day play an elf in a green pixie cap, brown knee-breeches and rouged cheeks. And he does it with 'a real feeling of elf-confidence'. The screenplay's running joke is elf-consciously and elf-indulgently to use as many elf words as possible. The sparse humour is still better than the songs, mostly by Henry Mancini and Leslie Bricusse, which are elf-destructive. True, there are enough high-tech special effects to quieten down kids brought up on video games rather than on good children's literature, but eventually Santa cloys. At the end, as the final credits roll, we see the words 'AND Dudley Moore'. One wag suggested unfairly that it should read 'BUT Dudley Moore'.

XVIII

Moore's five-year liaison with Susan Anton was drawing to an end and a new one with former model and actress Brogan Lane started to blossom, flowering into marriage in February 1987, three years after they had first begun to live together. Dudley had first met Brogan, a striking green-eyed Jane Fonda-ish brunette 24 years his junior, on the set of *Six Weeks*, in which she had a walk-on. A divorcee, she had a son two years older than Dudley's. 'It was love at first sight . . . I was mesmerised. She's very much younger than me but my mother always said "I like being around young people, it keeps me young," ' Moore explained. This Peter Pan persona was indulged to its utmost degree in his next picture, *Like Father, Like Son*, which he made after a two-year break from films.

'I guess I turned off acting a bit. I needed to take a pause,' he told *Films and Filming* on the set of his 'comeback' movie. 'It certainly had something to do with being fifty. I think I felt when I turned fifty that I'd got to stop something. I couldn't stop growing older so I decided to stop working. It was an amazingly effective remonstration! Of course, it was totally ineffective. It just meant that I didn't work for two years! I thought I'd do some extraordinary reassessment of my life or marinate in some wonderfully creative juices and do something marvellous, but nothing really happened. So in the end I thought I'd better just get back to work. Because there seems no alternative to doing something that keeps you active.'

During the 'inactive' period Dudley rigorously practised the piano at home, played a concert with the LA Philharmonic at the Hollywood Bowl and was (for the second time) the astonished recipient of the *This Is Your Life* red book, handed to him by Eamonn Andrews while at the piano in his LA restaurant.

Like Father, Like Son was another in a sudden spate of 'body swap' and 'time warp' movies where the generations older than the teen audiences, for whom the films were made, can satisfy their desire to be young again. Of course, the theme was not new. In 1947 Peter Ustinov had made *Vice Versa*, based on F Anstey's novel, in which sixteen-year-old Anthony Newley was transmogrified into the body of Roger Livesey, as his stern Victorian father, and *vice versa*. The 1987 version concerned a doctor who accidentally drinks a mysterious elixir that has the effect of exchanging his brain power with that of his teenage son. As a result the boy in the doctor's body has to go to work at the hospital and the father in his son's body goes to school.

The main problem with *Like Father, Like Son* was the casting of Dudley Moore. Surely any comic potential inherent in a role reversal plot should be a complete 'turnabout' (the title of a 1940 comedy where a man exchanges bodies with his wife), with the character in a new situation. As Moore always comes on as a middle-aged man playing a sixteen-year-old, the contrast is not as marked as it would have been with someone more conspicuously 'grown-up'. Not for a moment do we believe that Cuddly Dudley would turn away a dying patient through lack of insurance cover. However, he does have some good moments, especially in the scenes when the squeamish school-boy, in the doctor's body, does his rounds at the hospital; later, at a hospital meeting, he has a nice piece of business with a cigarette and chewing gum. Unfortunately there is also a Blake Edwards-type (i.e.

unfunny) slapstick scene which ends up with a sofa on fire in a swimming pool. Rod Daniel, whose only previous movie was *Teen Wolf*, does direct with the necessary slickness and speed but for any relatively mature persons to enjoy it, they too would have to have a brain swap with a relatively immature teenager. As the critic of *The Scotsman* put it, 'The message is, you can't understand anyone unless you become them. The second message is, thank God for the National Health Service. The third message is, American teenage culture sucks. The fourth message is, come home, Dud.'

XIX

Obviously, after a number of 'bummers', Dudley started hankering for the days when he was 'odour friendly' in Hollywood, covered with the sweet smell of success which emanated from *Arthur*, and when the possibility of a sequel to *Arthur* came up, he was delighted. Sadly, Steve Gordon had died prematurely of a heart attack in 1982 but 32-year-old Andy Breckman had come up with a script that Dudley felt so 'completely captured the irreverent wit, spirit and joy of the original that I said yes immediately'. The director chosen was Bud Yorkin, whose filmography consisted mainly of rather minor, mindless comedies, among which was *Inspector Clouseau* (1968), as maladroit as the title character in its attempt to put Alan Arkin into Peter Sellers's boots.

Arthur 2, ominously subtitled *On The Rocks*, had all but one of the ingredients to make it as great a hit as the first. Never considering the possibility of a follow-up movie, Steve Gordon had killed off John Gielgud's Hobson, thus posing a dilemma for the producers of the sequel. This was sneakily circumvented by contravening the Trade Descriptions Act and giving Gielgud third-billing to appear for a few welcome minutes as Hobson's ghost (in the manner of previous visitations by Bogart and Freud) to offer Arthur some hope. It's Christmas, naturally, and the drunken millionaire playboy has lost $750 million, his wife has left him, and he's become a wino. In the best scene in the film Arthur regales other deadbeats with his history. 'You were rich?' one asks. 'Yes, $750 million. And this was back when $750 million was considered a lot of money . . . I used to buy a new couch every week to match the TV Guide. (Laughter). I was rolling in it, rolling in it. I used to buy a new couch every week to match the TV Guide. (No laughter). You've heard that one before?' Moore's comic timing is as good as ever and Liza Minnelli is wonderfully natural as his wife who tells him she can't have children. 'Well, at least we don't have to have sex any more!' he jokes. But good one-liners do not a picture make. The plot involves financial chicanery, a completely unbelievable rival for Arthur's love (the jilted rich girl of the first film), the couple's attempts to adopt a child and Arthur's to get a job. The 'happy' (but unhappily realised) ending has Arthur getting his money back, the couple adopting a child and the wife finding herself pregnant.

Dudley puts the film's failure in America (it didn't do too badly in Britain) down to the anti-alcohol lobby, especially MADD (Mothers Against Drunken Drivers) and the police, who claimed that both *Arthur* movies glamorised drinking. The fact that Arthur is always chauffeur-driven and that the film has an anti-drinking message worthy of a Victorian temperance tract did not seem to appease MADD. 'What's odd is that people found Arthur funny in the first one when he was drunk, they found him funny in the second one when he was drunk, but then objected that he became boring when he was sober, but they were relieved when he became sober,' Dudley commented in bemusement.

There was no doubt he was desperately disappointed that the character he loved playing, and which brought him megabucks, was now thrown into the cold. There is only one pointer in the film to imply that the makers thought it might not achieve the success of the first: in the end Arthur takes the pledge, thus precluding any further sequel.

XX

Like a battered bantamweight boxer after nine losing rounds, Dudley Moore is still on his feet. There is, however, a certan amount of bitterness. 'I was going through this old box of clippings the other day,' he told *The Illustrated London News* in December 1988. 'It was all "Dudley Moore's English and he was in *Beyond The Fringe*" and there was this whole air of respectability. Isn't-it-wonderful sort of thing. Now it's fuck Dudley time. Get back where you came from. Then you can come out of obscurity and we'll discover you again.'

In 1977 Moore had appeared on Jonathan Miller's TV series *The Body In Question* to demonstrate how the hand and the brain coordinate in piano playing. In March 1987, half of the *Beyond The Fringe* quartet came together again. When Miller's non-Japanese *Mikado* opened at the LA Music Center, Dudley made his acclaimed light operatic debut as Ko-Ko, the Lord High Executioner. It was another proof that if the film career dried up he was still versatile enough to make a good living on the stage and on the concert platform. When asked to estimate, setting modesty aside, how good a musician he was, Dudley replied: 'I think as a musician I am very good, although I do have a great deal of problems in certain areas. I have an innate melodic sense and a delight in contrapuntal activity, but I may well be, as my tutors kindly put it, a miniaturist. I do not seem to have the attention span or the desire to erect more dramatic or theatrical canvases in my music. I am a good sightreader, which partly came from having an insatiable desire to read music when I was young.'

He may not rank among the top jazz pianists yet there is no doubt that he would have no shortage of gigs were he to give up acting. He does not possess the instant recognisability of an Oscar Peterson, Dave Brubeck, Art Tatum or Errol Garner, but according to George Melly 'It falls to very few to be truly original in jazz and even fewer English people and even fewer who come from Dagenham.' He might also have made a decent living as a soloist at classical concerts or recitals, although many necessary years of dedication to his vocation have been lost to him.

As a comedian, Moore was initially overshadowed by his three companions in *Beyond The Fringe* and then by his partner, who was considered to be funnier and more original. It is thought in some circles that anyone who lives in a pink house at Venice Beach, California cannot be taken seriously. The London and New York intellectual finds it difficult to imagine Arnold Schoenberg playing tennis in Beverly Hills, Bertolt Brecht walking down Sunset Boulevard or Thomas Mann in Schwabs. Surely it's brain death in Venice, Cal. However, these views are often tinged with a certain amount of envy. How many actors sitting in draughty rehearsal rooms in England would not have taken the chance to be well-paid and famous in Hollywood, especially if they share Dudley's humble and unpromising beginnings. He's conscious of it: 'I'm not one who walks on to the street and needs to see the Pantheon!' But he hasn't been sucked into Hollywood vacuity. He works hard at his music, practising, experimenting and recording, and is catching up on reading the classics he had ignored for many years.

'Once during the *Beyond The Fringe* days I observed that Dudley went from being a subservient little creep, a genial serf, to become an obstinate bastard who asserted himself,' said Peter Cook, true to form. 'There was a vague truth behind that because at the time, although he wasn't treated with disdain, Jonathan, Alan and myself did not recognise him as a writer although he was always a terrific actor.' When he made a film on his own or appeared in a play, general reactions were not favourable. In artistic terms, his roles don't amount to a hill of beans in this world'. If judged in terms of box-office returns, ten out of the twelve Hollywood films he starred in were just average earners. Still, despite his flops, there are only a handful of stars today who can boast two of the biggest box-office hits in movie history. And what other Hollywood comedian could claim to have sung in *The Mikado*, cut jazz albums and played the Brahms Triple Concerto with Itzhak Perlman and Yo Yo Ma?

Dudley is a wonderful natural clown, a wizard with words and a physical performer of grace. He has splendid comic timing, which comes from his musical training, and can improvise comedy as he does jazz. His muddly, bubbly comic persona, his dark good looks and his warm personality have overcome many weaknesses in scripts and direction. He retains his popularity both in America and in England, where he is still affectionately seen as 'Our Dud'. His presence is always sought for award ceremonies, where he brings a welcome irreverence and 'naughty' humour to gooey self-congratulatory events.

Jonathan Miller, who has described Dudley as a 'grubby cherub', says: 'I once went to lunch with him at a rather smart restaurant in California and I had the rather dubious pleasure of walking behind him, enjoying the wave of sexual excitement which he created as he made his way through the restaurant.' Everyone knew Alan Ladd was 'deficient in the tall department' but the film-makers went to any lengths to disguise his lack of length. On the other hand, Moore has played up his proximity to the ground, proving that small is sexy as well as beautiful. He has, more than any other screen star, given stature to shortshanks and brought a new meaning to the phase 'brevity is the soul of wit.'

11

THE PRIVATE EAR AND THE PUBLIC EYE

The irresistible rise and rise of Peter Cook can be traced from Radley, through Cambridge to West End revues. *Pieces Of Eight, One Over The Eight, Beyond The Fringe* and *Behind The Fridge*; The Establishment; *Private Eye* magazine; and *Not Only . . . But Also* on TV have made him one of the most important influences on post-Suez British comedy. The resistible fall and fall of Peter Cook can only be seen in relation to how much the bitch-goddess Success needs to satisfy her constant desires.

The laughter he engendered at public school and especially university lingered on long after he had gone into the wider world. 'Cook's influence was so thick in the air for two or three years you could cut it with a knife,' said John Cleese, who went up to Cambridge in 1960. 'The way Cook uses words is really quite original – the way he can make a perfectly blunt and banal statement sound terribly funny, just by a choice of certain words. I remember Trevor Nunn . . . used to sit around and convulse us merely by recounting sketches Peter had done.' The title of the 1961 Footlights revue, *I Thought I Saw It Move*, was a homage to one of Cook's catch-phrases. It was David Frost who attempted to carry on the comic style of his master. In Ned Sherrin's vivid phrase, 'Frost had an artistic crush on Cook at Cambridge'.

Some years before *Beyond The Fringe* was a twinkle in John Bassett's eye, Cook, while still at Cambridge, was formulating his idea of opening a satirical nightclub in London which would provide political cabaret and jazz. The determination came during an all-night drinking session with Nicholas Luard, a would-be writer and painter who had spent a year in Paris before coming up and reinforced a dream the lad with the satirical bent had had while in France and Germany in the year between school and university. Political cabaret has had a long tradition on the Continent, the most famous manifestations being in Berlin during the Weimar Republic, and it still flourishes vigorously in countries where most other channels of dissidence are closed. The very notion of an English hotbed of subversion as pictured by George Grosz and Otto Dix, with its Marxist teeth biting the necks of the bourgeoisie, was anathema to entrenched Toryism, to the stultifying British class system and the ancient sexual and social taboos that hung like a brown fog over the nation. Of course, much of the force of European cabaret or of, say, Brecht's 'serious comedies', was the desire for change to come about through laughter and derision. The English were much more inclined to see laughter as an end in itself, being conservatively suspicious of change. It was more in this latter spirit that Cook envisaged his club. After all, as he ironically says, 'The nightclubs in Berlin stopped Hitler coming to power, didn't they'?

As soon as Cook came down he began looking for a suitable site for the club and in the summer of 1961, during the first flush of *Beyond The Fringe*, heard about a strip club in Soho being closed down after a police raid. He immediately contacted Luard, who was researching a thesis on Hemingway in New Orleans: 'I got together with the treasurer of the Footlights, a guy called Nick Luard: not a performer – as he was treasurer, I imagined he was a financial wizard,' recalls Cook. 'He also had a bit of money. I was panicking that somebody would do it first; we eventually found premises in Greek Street and Sean Kenny agreed to design it; we negotiated a lease – it was all quite chaotic. Because of adverse publicity, about seven thousand people joined before it had even opened; they joined on the idea, at two guineas a time, which roughly financed the building of it.' The annual subscription and membership of the club (restricted to the over-eighteens) was three guineas. Ironically dubbed 'The Establishment', Britain's first satirical nightclub opened in October 1961.

A long article by Jonathan Miller, headed 'Can English Satire Draw Blood?', appeared in *The Observer* on the Sunday before the club's opening. In it he explained how The Establishment would have the chance to bring back the style of savage political satire that had dwindled to a 'a whimsical form of self-congratulation' since the eigthteenth century: 'Cook had already written many of the numbers for the highly successful *Pieces Of Eight* but the bony outlines of his contributions were softened and blurred by their gay commercial setting. Tinselly dance routines, a-fidget with glow-paint and fishnet, would follow one of his dour screwy little numbers and promptly erase it from the mind of the audience.' Miller went on to state that Cook now had the chance to escape the Lord Chamberlain's 'bloodshot gaze', being free from his control and managerial restraint and able to put on shows of 'scurrilous vigour, daring and adventure'. He concluded: 'The ranks are drawn up and the air resounds with the armourer's hammer. When battle is joined one can only hope that blood will be drawn.'

Blood was drawn alright but not in the sense Miller had intended, Cook was hit on the head with a handbag early on in the proceedings, the owner of which was a supporter of Pat Arrowsmith, who went into action after a sketch taking the mickey out of the doughty anti-nuclear campaigner, thus demonstrating that the left was not immune to barbs. 'That's not what you're here for!' shouted the pacifist assailant.

'I was very, very lucky in the cast I got,' Cook says. 'I also persuaded Dudley Moore to play with his trio in the basement, at slave labour rates, but he just enjoyed himself a lot and had a fantastic opportunity to meet young women.'

The first revue at the new club featured David Walsh, John Bird, John Fortune, Jeremy Geidt and Hazel Wright, later replaced by Eleanor Bron. One sketch was of the Crucifixion (nearly twenty years before *The Life Of Brian*) with Geidt and Bird as the thieves complaining that Christ (Fortune) was higher up than they were and getting all the attention. John Bird first mimicked Jomo Kenyatta in a scene where the Kenyan leader is being interviewed about football but persists on talking about his taking over the office of Queen of England. These sketches were typical of the club's tone of humour, more in the harmless English nonsense tradition than the satirical, but seemingly more biting because Sacred Cows were involved rather than Runcible Cats.

Cook himself used frequently to come in from the Fortune Theatre to perform either solo or in sketches, always trying to reach new depths of excess. He had one particular piece, a perceptive monologue about how men like to stand over a lavatory bowl and try to pee off the bits of brown that had been left there. The rest of the cast felt vaguely uneasy about it but Peter insisted that this was pushing back the barriers of comedy. One night they couldn't understand why he didn't include it in his routine. All became clear when Cook's parents were ushered into his dressing-room after the show.

Yet, although the shows did not draw as much blood as Jonathan Miller had foreseen in his *Observer* piece, it could be argued that the irreverent stance of The Establishment *vis-à-vis* the establishment, backed up by *Beyond The Fringe* plus the beginnings of *Private Eye* and the coming *TW3* which took up the London-based trend and disseminated it round the nation, were the vehicles that carried the message of dissatisfaction to the electorate and back again more forcefully than did the more conventional means of communication – the national press, TV or radio news and comment.

The Establishment also, less surprisingly, became the launching pad for new talents, spotted and enouraged by Cook. Among them was Barry Humphries in an early incarnation of Australian suburban housewife 'Edna Everage', as modest and dowdy as her name and profession suggest, a long way from the extravagantly bespectacled and begowned Superstar Dame who emerged in the 1970s. Another 'discovery' was Frankie Howerd, an extremely popular comedian in the 1950s who had fallen into neglect and hard times. Although only 40, he was considered a has-been by the younger generation until his revelatory appearances at The Establishment. Among his past triumphs had been variety shows, *Charley's Aunt*, Bottom at the Old Vic and the lead in the 1954 film comedy, *The Runaway Bus*. Part of his perfectly rehearsed impromptu routine, punctuated by comic hesitations and exhortations to audiences not to laugh, was his puzzlement at finding himself part of the satire movement in front of such trendy people.

But The Establishment's biggest coup was the appearance of outrageous American nightclub comedian Lenny Bruce, 'the most original, free-speaking, wild-thinking gymnast of language this inhibited island has ever engaged to amuse its citizens', according to Kenneth Tynan. Cook had seen and met Bruce in the USA and it was his dream to get him to London. For Cook, Bruce 'was a revelation. I watched him every night for four weeks and I've never got over it ... What Bruce did was daring and revealing, but it was his funniness that most impressed me rather than his crusading spirit. He was a very gentle person'. During Bruce's month-long season at The Establishment, Cook had to keep his star supplied with cream buns, for which he had a passion.

Provocation was an essential element of Bruce's act and more often than not he would succeed in his aims. One night during his performance the actress Siobhan McKenna stormed out rather noisily. She accosted Cook, who accused her of scratching his face. 'These hands are clean,' she yelled. 'These are Irish hands and they are clean.' 'Well, this is a British face,' replied Cook, 'and it's bleeding.' In April 1963, just before Bruce was due for a second appearance at the club, the then Home Secretary, Henry Brooke, clamped a ban on the comedian entering the country, or the ***try, as *Private Eye* would have it.

Cook, for whom the past is a happy country, says, 'For two years it was a great place, which I still look back on with tremendous fondness. Those were tremendous times'. The club certainly had its share of excitement. One evening Cook was visited by a thick-eared type who seemed to suggest that the place could get smashed up some time by a mob of thugs, and that protection might be needed. This was followed by a visit from a Detective-Sergeant Challenor who told Cook to report any sign of trouble to the police. Challenor, whom Cook thought 'a man possessed', later went to prison for planting a brick on a student during a protest march. However, all such fun and games had to be left behind when Cook went to Broadway with *Beyond The Fringe*. George Melly recalls that 'Peter wrote me a very flattering letter asking me to take over The Establishment when he went to America. I thought that was beyond my capabilities.' Instead, his beloved brainchild was left in the hands of Nick Luard.

II

Do the English and Americans have everything in common except their humour? There has been a fair amount of incomprehension on both sides of the Atlantic over the years with certain theatrical exchanges that never came off. On the other hand, there has always been a sophisticated, cosmopolitan coterie in the larger cities to support humorous imports. In 1959, Flanders and Swann's undiluted Englishness successfully transferred to Broadway, paving the way for the more abrasive *Beyond The Fringe*. The Establishment revue also reconnoitred in the USA a short while before the New York opening of *The Fringe* in October 1962. At the very same time, *The Premise*, an improvisational satirical show from Chicago's Second City Company premiered at the Comedy Theatre in London and ran for 186 performances. It looked as though 'have satire will travel' was a viable proposition.

The Establishment show, which included a number of sketches by Peter Cook, played to enthusiastic audiences in Chicago and Washington before the company took a lease on the derelict El Morocco club in New York. By that time, *Beyond The Fringe* had made English satire *the* thing, especially after the quartet had been invited to have dinner with Jackie Kennedy. As a publicity stunt, Cook decided to take a leaf out of the book of famous impresario, David Merrick. The year before, a Merrick-produced musical called *Subways Are For Sleeping* had received terrible reviews from the powerful New York critics. Merrick combed the telephone directory for people with identical names to the critics, offered them free tickets to the musical and quoted their rave reviews. Although *The New York Times* withdrew his ad after one edition, the ploy brought the show enough publicity to help it limp on for a little longer. It was just the kind of practical joke that tickled Cook's sense of humour.

'When I opened The Establishment, I found a David Merrick, who was a black postman from Philadelphia. He came to see the show and he liked it – and so he wrote all these rave reviews, saying The Establishment was better than *Oliver, Stop the World* . . . and whatever David Merrick shows were on, rolled into one.' The Merrick was not amused and threatened to sue Cook for pulling the same confidence trick as he had, but it came to nothing.

In fact Cook had no need for such a ruse – the show was liked by public and critics alike – but the joke was enjoyed for its own sake. It was this show's success that led to the offer from Ed Sullivan in May 1963 to do the short-lived *What's Going On Here?* in which Cook appeared and which Jonathan Miller directed. The title echoed what the conservative and sponsor-minded Sullivan said every time something strayed from the bland, thus emasculating the whole enterprise.

At this time Cook set up The Establishment Theatre Company, with Ivor David Balding and Joseph E. Levine, to present a number of plays off-Broadway. The first was Ann Jellicoe's *The Knack*, directed by Mike Nichols, which ran for 685 performances from May 1964 at the New Theater, 154 East 54th Street. Subsequent plays included J P Donleavy's *The Ginger Man* and John Arden's *Sergeant Musgrave's Dance*, which used Dudley Moore's music from the original Royal Court production. (Dustin Hoffman was fired from the Arden play by Stuart Burge, the director, after a few weeks' rehearsal.)

In between his many activities in New York, Cook found time to marry attractive Wendy Snowden, whom he had met at Cambridge where she was an art student. She later became known for having worn false eyelashes throughout the delivery of their first child.

While the prime mover behind The Establishment was appearing nightly on Broadway, and while John Bird, Eleanor Bron and John

Fortune, the best of the show's performers, were entertaining New Yorkers at the old El Morocco, the London Establishment began to languish. Deprived of Cook and Co. (Dudley Moore's jazz piano was also sorely missed in the basement) and faced with *TW3*, a rival satirical revue on Saturday night TV which few citizens in the pre-video age would have dared miss, it began to look inevitable that the club would go under. Another good reason was The Establishment's financial difficulties. Luard had invested a vast amount of the money of Cook-Luard Productions Ltd in an ambitious arts magazine called *Scene*, which folded after a few loss-making months. As a result The Establishment was sold to two shady characters called Raymond Nash and Anthony Coutt-Sykes (the 'Coutt' was added to give the name more class), owners of several gambling and strip clubs. Cook was offered a half-interest but on his return from the USA 'I took one look at the club and said No. The whole atmosphere had gone – the place was filled with rather large men, and I didn't think it was salvageable; and I think the entire cast – who had returned from the States – felt exactly the same way. And so I got out – that was the end of The Establishment for me.' It was soon turned into a night club more typical of the Soho area, and is now the site of a porno cinema.

III

In October 1961, the same month as The Establishment opened, there appeared the first issue of a satirical magazine entitled *Private Eye*. The 300 copies, sold at sixpence apiece, were printed on an offset litho press on yellow paper and stapled together. The journal had been the creation of Peter Usborne, Christopher Booker, Andrew Osmond and William Rushton, with contributions from John Wells and Richard Ingrams: a group of public school and university friends, all of whom had had some experience in Oxbridge magazines. Osmond, the 'proprietor and driver', thought up the name after *The Yellow Press*, *The British Letter*, *Flesh's Weekly*, *The Finger* and *The Bladder* had all been rejected. (The last had been suggested by Ingrams but overruled by Rushton, whose grandmother was dying of a bladder disease.)

The first 'dummy' issue bore on its cover the little crusader knight with his bent lance, a take-off of Beaverbrook's *Express* logo. It contained an interview by Harold Throbson (Hobson) of Sir John

Feelgood (Gielgud) written by John Wells, and also 'Bore of the Week', Mr Punch, a dig at the long-established and arthritic *Punch*.

Peter Cook's first tentative association with the magazine was with the Christmas issue, Vol. 1 no. 3, for which he suggested to Booker, a friend from Cambridge, that they use a comic-book word balloon on the cover. Most of the successful innovations over the years were Cook-inspired, and this was one of the most durable. There were many people who wouldn't dream of buying the magazine but who could quote the often witty cover balloons. The initial example showed an attractive young woman in Santa Claus garb saying, in Gothic lettering, 'Ad Majorem Dei Glorium' over a list of figures whom the magazine had decided were worth attacking. These included Chris Chataway, Ken Tynan, Penelope Gilliatt, Stansgate (Anthony Wedgwood-Benn), Jeremy Thorpe, Jocelyn Stevens, Snowdon, Kenneth Allsopp and 'all Ad-men, Brubeck fans, PRO's, Bow Groupers, striped shirts and pseuds everywhere.'

In March 1962 the magazine started a series of comic strips called 'Aesop Revisited', the first being 'The Satirist' featuring Jonathan Crake, who had more than a passing resemblance to Cook. It begins with a drawing of the boy as a witch in *Macbeth* putting the 'skool cat' into a cauldron. The caption reads: 'Young Jonathan Crake shows an early talent for raising laughs in School Play,' and continues: 'At Cambridge his gay, witty, little pieces in all the mags have the chaps in fits' under a picture of three straightfaced students reading *Gland* magazine and commenting, 'God, that's funny!' The third picture is captioned 'Sparkling revue *Short Back and Sides* mentions Prime Minister. Crake acclaimed as biting satirist of our time.' Crake is then seen in a TV studio above the words 'Instantly besieged by press, TV men seeking views on Monarchy, Mr Gaitskell, Common Market, Schedule A, the Bomb . . . ' We move on to a drawing of what looks like The Establishment. Crake is on stage saying 'Funny thing happened to me on my way to the theatre tonight' to an appreciative audience, one of whom is boasting 'Of course I know all the "Fringe" boys.' The next picture shows a boozy Crake, with a glass in his hand, asking 'Where's the Gents?' of a group of laughing people. 'Ho ho. Very Satirical,' says one. The caption reads: 'Cannot open his mouth without everyone collapsing at brilliant satirical comment.' He then reacts to them by shouting, 'Go away, you ugly bone-headed bastards!' but they laugh even more. Crake is finally revealed copying jokes from *Punch* of 1890 and the Moral above him reads: 'Humour Is A Serious Business.'

Very satirically, it was Jonathan Crake, *alias* Peter Cook, the butt of the cartoon's jibes, who would soon take over *Private Eye*, lock, laughing stock and barrel.

Private Eye grew in circulation with each issue and the small staff settled into an office at 41 Neal Street in Covent Garden, temporarily offered to them rent-free by Welsh millionaire publisher Gareth Powell before their move to Greek Street. However by April 1962 Andrew Osmond felt that the workload and financial pressures weighed too heavily upon him and decided to pursue his original intention of going into the Foreign Office. He began to look around for a buyer. Who better than fellow members of the satirical fraternity – Cook-Luard Productions Ltd? Despite mutual distrust between the Oxford hacks and the Cambridge hams, Osmond sold 75 of his 99 shares in the company to Cook and Luard for £1,500. Luard, Cook, Ingrams and Booker made up the four-man editorial board. Booker was subsequently fired, Luard sold his shares to Cook, and William Rushton and Ingrams became joint editors.

Peter Cook, star of *Beyond The Fringe*, now found himself co-owner of a nightclub (and an off-Broadway theatre) and proprietor of a magazine, though he bore little relation to the loathsome Lord Gnome, its mythical owner. His influence on the *Eye*, as it is affectionately known, soon became noticeable. One of his earliest contributions was a sequence of four photos of a weary baggy-eyed 'Rab' Butler, one of which carried the legend 'I'm just a flabby-faced old coward.' Followed by 'P.S. And what's more, he's such a flabby-faced old coward he won't even sue us. P.P.S. And even if he does sue he's STILL a flabby-faced old coward.'

Cook continued to contribute items while he was in America from October 1962 to April 1964, one of them based on a rumour he had heard that President Kennedy had been previously married and divorced. This piece of news was presented above a note which read: 'We have attempted to check the validity of this grotesque story. . . Unfortunately we have failed, so, as usual, we have printed it without verifying our facts.'

Curiously, for outspoken Jonathan Miller, Cook's magazine became the evil *Eye*. The animosity between the doctor and the satiric organ began after Miller, while in America, sent them a humorous piece entitled 'The Hounding Of The Pooves' which purported to be a learned investigation into homosexuals. It was illustrated by a series

---

of nineteenth-century engravings, some of them demonstrating life-saving techniques with men astride men and the caption 'Pooves or queers at their filthy practices.' Unfortunately, the editors ran the piece as by Dr J. Miller, under a picture of Jonathan.

'I was angry at them for misusing my name by calling me *Doctor* Miller. At the time I was thinking of going back into medicine. *Private Eye* was in the hands of Christopher Booker, that awful, slimy little Christian wanker.' (Miller occasionally says 'Christian' with the same emphasis of distaste that an antisemite would use to say 'Jew'.) Accordingly he sent them a letter which began, 'You stupid bloody irresponsible cunts.' The now yellowing and tattered note is still pinned to the magazine's notice board.

Thereafter, the *Eye* took every opportunity to portray Miller as a pseud of pseuds. As George Melly says, '*Private Eye* was a bully boy's magazine, and for the bully the reaction from the bullied is as important as the bullying. The fact that they knew Jonathan was infuriated and maddened by it meant they continued with even greater vigour.' Although they never felt they had much in common, the event distanced Miller from Cook even further. 'There is some sort of awkwardness between Peter Cook and myself,' Miller says, 'because he's the proprietor of *Private Eye*, a magazine of which I disapprove and which clearly disapproves of me.'

During the Profumo affair in 1963 the circulation of *Private Eye* reached 85,000, riding the crest of the satire wave. A year later the sales had nearly halved and 'satire' had become a dirty word on TV, before Tynan replaced it with another. It looked as if the paper, like Samson, had 'heroically . . . finish'd a life heroic' and that Britain would soon be *Eyeless*. However, according to William Rushton, 'We were saved by the return of Peter Cook from New York, who kept us going while Ingrams slowly discovered about the business of editing and getting the right people in.' Cook was able to contribute far more to the style and content of the magazine. He used to come in to the office at 22 Greek Street and tell his jokes to a delighted audience. One of his most effective covers, on his return, was the depiction of Gericault's *Raft of Medusa* with a bubble coming out of one of the dying saying 'This is the last time I go on a John Bloom Holiday.'

'There was such an unstoppable flow of ideas,' says John Wells. 'He seems to have initiated all sorts of things I've ever had a go at. He initiated "Mrs Wilson's Diary" [almost immediately after the Labour victory in 1964] which Richard Ingrams and I then took over. He came in on the opening writing session of that. Similarly, he was in on the first two sessions of the "Dear Bill" letters. He was tremendously inventive all through those first few years of *Private Eye*. He just never stopped those wonderful ideas. He used to go slightly glazed like a medium and then produce these wonderful, complicated Lewis Carroll-like ideas.'

It was Cook who brought in Barry Humphries, latterly of The Establishment and *TW3*, to write the Barry McKenzie cartoon strip drawn by Nicholas Garland. It detailed the scatological adventures of a vulgarly innocent Aussie at large in London, whose language was peppered with vivid expressions like a 'Technicolor yawn' to describe 'chundering' or vomiting. The strip got filthier and filthier, and more and more culty over its ten years' existence. The Antipodean idiot even became the hero of two movies, *The Adventures of Barry Macken-zie* and *Barry Mackenzie Holds His Own*, Technicolor yawns in their own right.

Peter Cook and veteran radical journalist Claud Cockburn edited one or two issues of the *Eye* in mid-1964. One of the most sensational pieces was an article by Cook which named the Kray twins as leaders of an East End gang that had been terrorising parts of London. Just to be safe from any reprisals, Cook lived up to his philosophy of 'publish and be absent' by taking himself off to Tenerife until the gangsters were under lock and key.

He had been absent in the USA in February 1963 when Randolph Churchill served a writ for libel on the magazine after an 'Aesop Revisited' strip entitled 'The Greatest Dying Englishman' showed Winston's boozy son, named Rudolph Rednose, bowdlerising a version of his father's biography. On that occasion the editors escaped with a full-page withdrawal in *The Evening Standard*. However, two years later Cook was in the firing line of a libel action brought by Lord Russell of Liverpool. 'Lord Liver of Cesspool' had become a regular member of *Private Eye's* rogues' gallery ever since Cook had seen Lord Russell's bestseller, *The Scourge of the Swastika* in a 'dirty book' shop lying between *Rubber News* and *Miss Whiplash*. The *Eye* implied that Russell was a pornographic writer. Unwisely, Ingrams decided to fight in court with the result that the plaintiff was awarded £5,000 damages plus £3,000 costs. As the magazine's total weekly income was around £650, it looked as if it would be doomed. For the first time a readers' appeal came to the rescue along with a benefit concert at the Prince of Wales Theatre for which Larry Adler, Bernard Braden, John Bird,

David Frost, Manfred Mann, George Melly, Spike Milligan, Bob Monkhouse, John Neville, Peter Sellers and Peter Cook and Dudley Moore (it was just after the first run of *Not Only . . . But Also*), 'with a host of lovely ladies', gave their services free.

IV

'I, with utter arrogance, said that *Beyond The Fringe* should stop after we'd all left because it would be a pity for it to dribble away,' commented Peter Cook. 'I felt that once we'd all left, nobody would come and see it. Of course, it was still running when I got back from the States and was looking for a job. I came back expecting to be enormously well known, and of course nobody knew me from Adam.'

Although the 27-year-old 'father of the satire boom', who had seen his baby grow into something that resembled David Frost, was working his whimsical wonders in the offices of *Private Eye*, Cook still saw himself principally as a performer. It was not long before he was back in the public eye. Bernard Braden, the London-residing Canadian broadcaster, invited Cook to re-create his E W Wisty routine on his snappy, investigative weekly late-night ITV show, *On The Braden Beat*. These monologues, delivered unsmilingly straight to camera, were highlights of the programmes for twenty weeks. Cook would improvise them on a tape-recorder the night before the show, after which they were transcribed on to a teleprompter. Typical of the park-bench philosopher's wide-ranging discourse was the following view on royalty: 'Even if it's the most boring thing in the world, people still say, isn't it interesting that a royal person is doing something so boring.'

Semiologists and linguistic philosophers would find much to chew on in Cook's use of language. Although Wisty is a comic creation of great originality, he is a more lunatic relation to some of the vagrants in Samuel Beckett's work and to Davies in Harold Pinter's *The Caretaker*: 'If there's one thing I can't bear, it's when hundreds of old men come creeping in through the window in the middle of the night and throw all manner of garbage all over me. I can't bear that. I think that's unbearable. Ghastly old men, with great pails of garbage, throwing it all over me. I don't think it should be allowed, I think there should be a place for those people to go. And I don't think it should be my room. I'd vote for any party that would say "I won't allow people to throw garbage all over me." But none of the parties seems to be particularly interested. That's why I formed the World Domination League . . .'

Soon after *On The Braden Beat* Cook was asked to guest on a Dudley Moore Special on BBC2, and a new comedy team was born. Like most of Cook's work, *Not Only . . . But Also* was improvised into a tape-recorder. 'We were always late on deadlines,' he says. 'We always had enough material for the show, but practically inevitably we'd change it – we'd become dissatisfied with the stuff we'd written, and do something at the last minute.' The show's centrepieces were the moronic dialogues on lofty subjects between Pete, the stone-faced informed idiot, and Dud, the twitching uninformed idiot, which had a real improvisational feel to them. During the Art Gallery sketch, Dudley, ever prone to giggle, almost collapsed with laughter when crumbs from the sandwich he was eating were splattered into Peter's face.

Dud: Have a sandwich. My feet are killing me.
Pete: What's that got to do with the sandwich?
Dud: Nothing. I just said it afterwards, that's all.
Pete: Well, you mustn't say things like that together. It could confuse a stupid person.

In the same scene Pete informs Dud, with great authority, that the sign of a good painting is 'If the eyes follow you around the room, it's a good painting. If they don't it isn't.' Their intellectual pretensions are satisfied when Dud comes across Pete listening to Debussy.

Pete: You can almost see the scene, can't you?
Dud: Yer.
Pete: *La Mer.*
Dud: Yer.
Pete: There she is – Debussy's mother – comes into the room, a silver tray covered with a silver teapot, silver cups . . .
Dud: Silver hair . . .
Pete: Silver hair on the mother. She comes in – Debussy sitting there on the sofa in his little blue smock – she pours the tea. D'you hear the tea being poured?

Women are a continual subject, the two losers' conversations couched in the language of romantic fiction, i.e. in clichés.

> Dud: Did I tell you about that girl Joan Harold, who I used to know? She used to travel on the 148 bus route a lot.
>
> Pete: Wasn't she the tempestuous gypsy beauty with raven hair down to her waist?
>
> Dud: Yes, delicately boned hands.
>
> Pete: Alabaster body, perfectly formed . . .
>
> Dud: Thrusting through her dress.
>
> Pete: Yes, Joan Harold, thrusting through her dress, yes . . .
>
> Dud: Well, anyway, as you know, or as you don't know, she used to travel on the 148 bus.
>
> Pete: 'Course she did, Dud.

Apart from the regular Dud 'n' Pete set piece were other sketches still lodged in people's memories, an achievement of some note in the ephemeral and congested world of television. One extreme example of Cook's flights of fancy, derived from and enlarged upon clichés of English upper-class speech, was the sketch in which Moore interviews Cook as Sir Arthur Streebe Greebling, a man who in an earlier sketch had tried to teach ravens to fly underwater and was now the owner of an out-of-the-way restaurant called The Frog and Peach.

'I thought to myself, where on earth in this country can you get a decent frog's leg with a decent boiled peach?' The menu consists of spawn cocktail, frog *à la pêche* – a frog done in Cointreau with a peach stuffed in its mouth – and *pêche à la* frog. 'The waiter comes to your table, it's got this huge peach on it which is covered in boiling liqueur, you see, and then he slices it open to reveal about two thousand little black tadpoles squiggling about . . .' When asked if his wife does all the cooking, Cook replies, 'Yes, my wife does all the cooking and, thank goodness, she does all the eating as well. An amazing creature – of course she's not a well woman. Not a well woman at all, so she very much resents having to go down the well every morning to sprinkle Swoop on the toads . . . an amazing creature, my wife . . . I met her during the war, actually . . . She blew in through the drawing-room window with a bit of shrapnel, and became embedded in the sofa, and one thing led to her mother and we were married within the hour.'

Cook was seen in drag as Garbo in the famous last shot of *Queen Christina*, when she stands like a mast-head at the bow of the ship. The expressionless Cook was perfect casting in the scene, for which the director had told Garbo, 'I want your face to be a blank sheet of paper. I want the writing to be done by every member of the audience. I'd like it if you could avoid blinking your eyes, so that you're nothing but a beautiful mask.' That is almost an exact description of the way Cook appeared in most of his fims.

'As Garbo, I thought I looked incredibly beautiful – I fancied myself rotten! I thought I looked rather better than she did!' he confessed.

V

The success of that first comedy series, which ended in April 1965, brought the Cook-Moore team into the movies. Making their screen debuts as physically and morally contrasting brothers, they were as amusing as they were allowed to be in Bryan Forbes's starry but unscintillating package, *The Wrong Box*, Robert Louis Stevenson with Carnaby Street treatment. Still in the nineteenth century, Cook was then aptly cast as the Mad Hatter in Jonathan Miller's TV film version of *Alice in Wonderland* before getting the chance to write his first screenplay. Cook's previous attempt at screen-writing had been an adaptation with John Bird in 1965 of Evelyn Waugh's *Scoop* which, due to the absence of backing, never saw the dark of a cinema. Cook recalls some trouble over a line in which a character calls a taxi driver 'a black bastard', 'What did they want the man to say?' he asks. 'Something like "You wicked Ethiopian" I suppose.'

In the episodic screenplay of *Bedazzled*, Cook was guilty of self-plagiarism (who isn't?), plundering the sketch of the leaping nuns from *Not Only . . . But Also*. He was a bit worried about this but Stanley Donen, the film's director, explained that the TV show hadn't been seen outside Britain and that the sight of Cook, Moore, Eleanor Bron and others in nuns' habits leaping on a trampoline belonged to the world. 'I'm extremely grateful to Stanley Donen for making the movie; but I think we were too over-awed,' remarked Cook. 'I don't think we relaxed enough in performing and we did takes we weren't satisfied with which were too tight. I think we were acutely aware the film was costing money'.

Kathleen Tynan thought Peter looked 'considerably prettier than usual, masquerading as a melancholy though winsome Beelzebub' and Donen considered he could be another Cary Grant, 'so witty and good-looking. It's about time he was discovered in the States,' In fact, there was an opening for a Cary Grant replacement as the 62-year-old Bristol-born star had just made his final film before retiring from the screen. Although the possibility of Hollywood fame as a handsome, romantic, light-comedy lead seemed an attractive possibility, something in Cook's mentality and personality could never fully accept this option. Yet there was no doubt then that of the comedy duo it was Cook who had the better chance of making it in Hollywood.

In the late 'sixties he had three offers of 'straight' film roles that seemed potential stepping stones to international stardom, only one of which he took. First, he refused the role of a trendy photographer opposite Brigitte Bardot (a 'Pete' dream come true) in a French-British co-production called *Two Weeks in September*. Mike Sarne (where is he now?) played the part and the film, directed by Serge Bourguignon, ran about two weeks in 1967. 'I'm one of the few men stupid enough to have turned down a chance to make a film opposite Brigitte Bardot,' Cook recalls ruefully. 'I said I didn't like the script. Must have been mad!'

The second role was offered to him by none other than Federico Fellini. *Bedazzled* had been a big hit in Italy (probably something to do with the Order of Leaping Nuns) and it showed in the period when long-haired young English actors were very fashionable with European directors, especialy Italian ones. Antonioni had used David Hemmings in *Blow Up* (1966) and Terence Stamp appeared in films by both Fellini and Pasolini in 1968. Obviously Fellini saw Cook in this way when he interviewed him for one of the leads in *Satyricon* – an ancient Roman student vying with his friend for the love of a pretty boy and then having various picaresque adventures including a drunken orgy, an involvement with an albino hermaphrodite, a threesome with an Ethiopian slave (female) and a fight with the Minotaur. But audiences were deprived of the pleasure of seeing him in the role because, according to Cook, Fellini rejected him on finding out that he was born under the sign of Scorpio, which wouldn't have done at all. The great Italian director chose the younger, unknown blond Englishman Martin Potter (where is he now?) and Cook remained unFellinified.

However, he did end up in a spy thriller called *A Dandy In Aspic*. The plot, which needed a windscreen-wiper, became more and more blurred as it progressed. What made things worse was that the director, Anthony Mann, died before he could complete the film and the dour star, Laurence Harvey, had to take over. Neither the picture nor Cook made much impression. 'I don't think I was *that* embarrassing, but I was slightly embarrassed by it,' he commented on his role as a bowler-hatted FO type.

Hollywood producers failing to line up pen in hand, Cook was soon back with his half-pint other half down the batting list in *Monte Carlo Or Bust* and *The Bed Sitting Room* (both 1969). In the latter, a surreal post-nuclear-war movie directed by Richard Lester, Cook remembers having to go up in a balloon with Moore, and a balloon expert crouched at the bottom of the basket. 'When we got up there, he said, "I wouldn't go up on a day like this." I said, "You are up on a day like this, what do you mean?" He said, "Well, it's just for Mr Lester, but I wouldn't normally go up – we're at the mercy of the winds." Whereupon we fell violently to the ground and I had to have my cartilage out. I was planning a four-week holiday – I spent it in hospital.'

VI

'Peter gives the finest parties I've ever been to,' said former world middleweight boxing champion Terry Downes, beginning to make a career as a film heavy in the late sixties. 'It might be Michael Caine or John Lennon or one of these top people you see on TV, but everybody's mixing. It boils up to a great evening. Peter never makes himself too busy, never makes himself Jack the Lad. He looks after everybody, especially the women, gives them that little bit of extra attention. My bird's knocked out by Peter. He's a real hundred per cent diamond person.'

This opinion was shared by the many guests who poured into the Cook home in the heady days at the end of his first decade of fame. According to Kathleen Tynan, 'His instantaneous invention comes out most purely in conversation, as he is one of the few people who can keep a whole room laughing without causing hysteria.' In the biography of her husband, Kenneth, she describes an evening early in 1968 when they had invited the Cooks, the Snowdons and the Pinters (Harold and Vivien Merchant) to see avant-garde films as an after-dinner entertainment. One of them was Jean Genet's *Chant d'Amour*. 'Genet's film is about convicts in love with one another and themselves, and it contains many quite unmistakable shots of cocks – cocks limp and stiff, cocks being waved, brandished, massaged or just waggled – intercut with lyrical fantasy sequences as the convicts imagine themselves frolicking in vernal undergrowth. Silence became gelid in the room. Suddenly the inspired Peter Cook came to the rescue. *Chant d'Amour* is a silent film and he supplied a commentary, treating the movie as if it were a long commercial for Cadbury's Milk Flake Chocolate and brilliantly seizing on the similarity between Genet's woodland fantasies and the sylvan capering that inevitably accompanies, on TV, the sale of anything from cigarettes to Rolls-Royces. Within five minutes we were all helplessly rocking with laughter.'

Ian Hislop tells of Cook's performance at a dinner party in Brighton to celebrate Hislop's accession to the post of editor of *Private Eye* in 1987, replacing Richard Ingrams. 'Richard and I prepared short speeches. Cookie prepared nothing. He gave a speech on the sauté potatoes we'd just eaten. He spoke for about fifteen minutes. Willie Rushton sat in the front row crying with laughter, saying "that is the funniest man there is."' Making unexpected connections is an essential component in Cook's ability to be funny about inanimate objects – comical *chose*-ism. Meeting Nicholas Henderson, British ambassador to Washington, after a period of around fifteen years, the first thing Cook uttered was, 'What I can't understand is why you have such awful fucking food in the Embassy!'

The Cook humour often moved from the *salon* to the streets. John Bassett recalls an occasion in the early days when the two of them were getting ready to take the tube at Marble Arch during rush hour, 'Peter, suddenly putting on a woman's voice, fought to get on to the train shouting, "I've lost my baby! Where's my baby? Let me back in. My baby's in there! Ohhh!" People immediately made way'.

It was now some years since Cook had referred to David Frost as the 'Bubonic Plagiarist' and vetoed him as his substitute in *Beyond The Fringe*. A few months before the finalising of arrangements for the 'Fringe' quartet to go the USA, Ned Sherrin organised a pilot for what was to be *TW3*, with a great space open for Cook. Frost and Brian Redhead were the co-link men, and Bernard Levin confronted and tore apart 40 Tory ladies (the sort with flower-covered hats always caricatured by the cartoonist 'Vicky') who had come straight from the Conservative Party Conference. Cook didn't turn up, according to John Bassett 'perhaps because David was linking it.' However, they continued to have a guarded relationship. (Cook is still seen at Frost's parties.) After *TW3* had made Frost a household name, he was staying as a guest at the house the Cooks had rented in Connecticut during their American sojourn. 'He had gone into the swimming pool,' Cook recalls. 'I suddenly saw him struggling in the water and I thought, ho, ho, David is making a satirical attack on drowning. Then he went under. When he went under for a third time, I decided he was serious and pulled him out. David said he had "failed to make the swimming motions".'

In 1969, Frost started his own film production company and for his first venture tackled a script by Graham Chapman and John Cleese that had been gathering dust on his shelf for a couple of years until Cook saw it and thought it had possibilities. *The Rise and Rise of Michael Rimmer* was rewritten by Chapman, Cleese, Cook and Kevin Billington, the film's director. Rimmer is an amoral bastard who claws his way up from being a business efficiency expert to becoming a dictatorial President of England. 'Frost got quite paranoid in that he thought we were exactly mirroring his career – which to an extent we were, some of the character was based on David,' Cook said with his usual grain-of-truth absurdity. 'The ultimate irony was that the set designer, who had never seen David's living room, and which we'd never talked about to her, produced an almost exact replica of David's room.'

Playing another authority figure, Cook, using the fashionable classless accent, was as stiff in the title role as the surrounding range of British character actors were animated: they included Arthur Lowe, John Cleese, Dennis Price, Denholm Elliott, Ronald Fraser, Roland Culver, Ronnie Corbett and Harold Pinter as a TV interviewer. Several years later Cook recognised his shortcomings as a film actor. 'Whenever I made movies I used to suffer Cook's disease, which involved a terrible glassy-eyed look . . . I belong to the school of acting which consists of doing nothing in particular. The variety of my expressions between shock, joy and terror are very hard to define.'

The script and the direction aimed at so many targets (unscrupulous politicians of all parties, manipulation by the media, the gullibility of the public, swinging churchmen, referenda, Black Power, etc,) that it was bound to hit a few bull's eyes, but while the blunderbuss technique provoked some laughter it diminished the satirical intent. *Michael Rimmer* remains an interesting sociological document on 1970 modes.

With the ending of *Not Only . . . But Also* after three seasons, a film career that had fizzled like a wet firework and the sundering of his marriage to Wendy, with whom he had two daughters, Lucy and Daisy (born 1964 and 1965 respectively), 1971 did not begin propitiously for Peter Cook. When BBC2 offered him the chance to be the host of a chat show, he jumped at it: it would allow him to move into David Frost's territory. Ned Sherrin, who was one of the guests on the last of the 'disastrous' shows, comments, 'My instinct is that as Frost had attained celebrity simply as a chat show host, somewhere at the back of Peter's mind, although he's infinitely more humorously clever than David, he thought that obviously I must be a chat show host. It's easy. If Frost can do it, I can do it better.'

Unfortunately Cook found out on the first programme that 'I was no good at talking to people on TV. The first minute of the first show, I realised that I was not going to be interested in anything the guests said.' Entitled *Where Do I Sit?*, the show was supposed to run for twelve weeks but was axed after three. One of the more serious problems was that Cook had insisted on doing the shows 'live'. 'There's so little live TV,' he confidently told the BBC, 'People will enjoy disasters if they happen.' But he found the experience a nerve-racking one and displayed a complete and baffling inability to frame intelligent questions that would elicit intelligent answers. He looked so glazed by it all that there were suggestions that he was either on drugs or drink.

'He appeared perfectly sane but frightened the night I was on with him,' remembers Sherrin. 'It was chaos. He isn't very interesting when talking to other people, he's much more interesting when other people talk to him. Being a chat show host is pretty negligible compared with being a comic genius, but it does require certain skills.' The programme proved beyond doubt that the chat show format did not suit Cook's free-wheeling, free-associative humour. The secret of this form of superficial, predictable and cheap television is that the interviewer must be less interesting than the interviewee. Peter Cook asking Terry Wogan questions – disaster. Cook being questioned by Wogan *et al* – success.

Visits to the Greek Street offices of *Private Eye* provided some solace for Cook, striding up and down, improvising and inventing a string of characters such as Sir Herbert Gussett (the habitual letter writer to newspapers), Sir Basil Nardly-Stoads (chief Rammer of the Seductive Brethren) and Rhandhi P'Hurr, while Richard Ingrams did more mundane things like editing the magazine. The 'Special Judges' issue of 13 August 1971, however, was edited by Cook himself and attacked Judge Michael Argyle for his role in the obscene libel case brought against the *Eye's* rival magazine, *Oz*, which saw its editor, Richard Neville, imprisoned for 'conspiracy to produce a magazine with intent to debauch and corrupt the morals of children and young persons within the Realm'. On the cover was a drawing by Ralph Steadman of the judge in the nude apart from his wig, with his face blacked out. A note explains that 'To avoid prosecution under the Obscene Publications Act, the obscene parts have been blacked out.'

VIII

Behind The Fridge celebrated the reunion of the Cook-Moore comic duo but it was what was in the fridge that caused a few problems on their tour of Australia and New Zealand. According to Dudley Moore, 'Peter suddenly turned into an alcoholic. He had always drunk rather a lot but suddenly he turned the corner. He came out drunk on stage one night and I had to ignore it. If I had acknowledged it that would have turned all our sketches into something else – me and my drunken friend, me and the drunken clergyman. After that it seemed like he was drunk every night. So one night I got drunk, which I had never done before a performance. He complained that it was the worst performance I'd ever given. He saw it from my side and stopped.'

It was not the end of Cook's running battle with the bottle, which continued over the next few years. In mid-1977, however, after warnings from his doctor about the state of his liver and worries about his beginning to resemble the *Private Eye* creation, journalist Lunchtime O'Booze, Cook went on the wagon, gallons of coffee and Coca-Cola intermittently breaking the chain of cigarettes.

During the long and successful Cambridge Theatre run of *Behind The Fridge*, Peter had married former Deb of the Year, 27-year-old Judy Huxtable, whom he liked to call Lady Judy Sexburga Cook; her surname was also adapted into an obscene adjective by some ribald wags at the *Eye*. Judy had recently been divorced from the brilliant stage designer, Sean Kenny, he of The Establishment Club, who died at the age of 41 in the same year as the Cooks' marriage. Their first years together were spent in the USA, where the show, renamed *Good Evening*, ran from October 1973 to August 1975. Thereafter Peter and Judy returned to Hampstead, and Dudley and Tuesday settled in Los Angeles. The friends did not meet again until Dudley came over to England to record the three smutty Derek and Clive records – 'For the sheer pleasure of being an evil yobbo', says Cook – and to make *The Hound Of The Baskervilles.*

Of the lascivious Derek and Clive, Cook felt 'They are, basically, the epitome of all that is best about mankind and the eternal search for the numero uno wank. The Primal Wank is what they're after. And they'll strive to attain it. They don't give up easily.' Sexual inhibitions long since conquered by Cook and Moore, not much was needed to liberate their libidos, although drink should have helped to lubricate their masturbatory fantasies. At one stage in *Derek and Clive Come Again*, Clive-Peter says slurringly to Derek-Dudley: 'You're so fucking drunk you can't fucking speak . . . You're a fucking alcoholic.' Unfortunately, the only way to appreciate the records is to be as inebriated or as stoned as they are or to believe that taboo-breaking in itself is amusing. Despite the motivation behind the records, Derek and Clive's messy ejaculations against the walls of puritanism were never exposed to a wide enough public to serve any revolutionary purpose. All unwittingly these stink bombs reached the enemy camp when several hundred copies of the first album were sold bearing the label 'Readings from *Black Beauty*', provoking an irate father of a seven-year-old girl to take the distributor to court. *Derek and Clive – The Movie* was edited by Cook down to 93 minutes from twelve hours' footage in the hope of a cinema release. By this time Moore, who had become a hot Hollywood 'property', resisted a cinema showing. 'It was so naughty, I knew Dudley might not like it,' said Cook. 'He has this wholesome image, you know.' Nevertheless, the film began to be passed around as a video tape at the beginning of the 'eighties. The late decadent era of the Cook-Moore partnership ended with the whimpering *Hound Of The Baskervilles*, seventeen years after *Beyond The Fringe*. In order to give birth to the silly little mouse of a script, Cook and Moore laboured eight hours a day holed up in Cook's Beverly Hills Hotel suite. When asked by the press about it, Cook explained: 'It's about the fiftieth remake of *Hound Of The Baskervilles*. I shall be playing Sherlock Holmes and Dudley will be the hound.' As the film sank slowly in the west, it was time for Cook and Moore to say 'Goodbye-ee' to one another.

IX

Dud and Pete remained friendly rivals after they went their separate ways; like Beatrice and Benedick, they indulged in 'a kind of merry war . . . and skirmish of wit between them'. Cook complained of Moore's 'megalomania tendencies' and his 'constant desire to please'. Moore spoke of Cook's 'relentless and perverse cynicism'.

Cook: Dudley is selfish, greedy and vain – and therefore a fully rounded human being.

Moore: Peter has a desire to shock like a flasher on Hampstead Heath. He wants to see the lady indignant but without any interest in molesting her.

Cook: Like many smallish men, Napoleon and Hitler to name but two, Dudley has a superficial charm and warmth that deceives many. Underneath lurks a demented sadist, capable in private of many unspeakable deeds. It is my personal belief that his secret ambition is to initiate World War III. I can only hope that my unfailing modesty and tact may prevent this disaster for a few years to come.

This kind of banter has been maintained for many years in the time-honoured manner established by Bing Crosby and Bob Hope, on-and off-screen, with most of the tongue-lashings coming from the more acerbic Cook, a fact which in some quarters has been ascribed to jealousy on his part, even by those who know them both personally. Perhaps it is true that Moore benefited most obviously from the break-up of their partnership, but as Cook has said: 'I've always shagged off Dudley and there is no reason for me to stop doing so now that he's a Hollywood star. He complained to me that in Hollywood he's surrounded by fools and sycophants who laugh at everything he says. I reminded him that when he was living here he was surrounded by intelligent people who kept telling him what a toad he was!'

In the August 1988 edition of *Vanity Fair*, however, Cook did appear to cross the bounds of good-natured repartee. In an interview with English writer Glenys Roberts he laid into his friend's 'vacuous' LA lifestyle, and criticised Brogan, Moore's wife of eighteen months: 'She has had a special boot made for his foot. She marches him up and down the side of the Grand Canyon before breakfast.' Cook claims to have made these remarks off the record, after the interviewer had switched off her tape, and was shocked to find them printed. 'She behaved shittily to me,' he said. 'I, being my normal bitchy self, spilled the beans about Dudley. I was just trying to make her laugh.' Moore was not amused although Cook 'had the grace to apologise for the picture he painted of Brogan with a whip out to me'.

For short period in 1977 Peter Cook was able to indulge his 'normal bitchy self' in a weekly full-page humorous column in the right-wing *Daily Mail* called 'Peter Cook's Monday Morning Feeling'. But 'I had to give it up,' he explained. 'I felt bogus about having opinions.' Plenty of his opinions were aired before reaction set in, over a wide range of subjects from 'How I unwittingly bugged Harold Wilson' to robots in the underground being used to catch fare dodgers like himself. Jimmy Carter was referred to as The Martian President and the Prime Minister of India was Goosey Goosey Gandhi. Seizing upon the news item that 'Women Against Rape' had occupied the Athenaeum, he explained that 'a small but lively counter group, "Women For Rape", were trying to storm my house. Unlike the Athenaeum, this is no pushover. Lady Judy Sexburga Cook and I have erected a system of alarms, barriers and watchdogs unparalleled in the free world.'

One Monday morning he managed a poke at his old sparring partner, David Frost: 'For some reason the black-and-white repeat of the 1963 *That Was The Week That Was* showed up pink on my set. Presumably the performers were retrospectively blushing . . . I did admire David Frost for his guts in doing such an appalling imitation of one of my least favourite people, "our Gracie Fields" . . . *TW3* was a very important programme.' Cook's column was also peppered with digs at the *Daily Mail*'s rival rag, *The Daily Express*, together with its new owner, Victor Matthews, and editor Derek Jameson: 'When I saw the new editor, Derek Jameson on *The Editors* I experienced something only paralleled by my first exposure to Elvis and Marlon Brando. Some would call it "love", others infatuation, but this man has all the allure of JFK, combined with the mystique of Garbo.'

After this stint as a Monday morning anti-depressant he continued to express opinions from time to time in silly-serious letters to the newspapers: 'Sir, You state that without the support of the record and film companies The Sex Pistols and Sid Vicious would have remained problems for their parents rather than for almost every parent in Britain,' he wrote in October 1978 to *The Sunday Times*. 'I myself turned to crime on learning that my idol, Robert Mitchum, had been convicted on a drug charge.'

The letter was in reply to criticism levelled at an ATV late Saturday night pop music programme called *Revolver*, with which he was inexplicably involved. Philip Purser of *The Sunday Telegraph* thought it a 'deplorable entertainment' in which 'Peter Cook, eyes wavering on some indeterminate point ahead of him, as if reading from a dodgy teleprompter, is supposed to be the manager of a dance hall reluctantly turned over to a pop and rock music clientele.' From his control box, he introduced the bands with distaste, reminiscing about the better music of his day and receiving catcalls from the young people on the floor. Stanley Reynolds in *The Times* felt that 'removed from the action in this way, the full impact of his personality was weakened. Perhaps the physical presence of the tall and debonair Peter Cook, one of the few really witty performers in Britain, would have dwarfed the performing punks.'

There were two outstanding occasions in the late 'seventies when Cook unmistakably demonstrated his comic genius among peers and without Dudley Moore: in the 1976 Amnesty International charity show, released on a record as *A Poke In The Eye With A Sharp Stick* and filmed by Roger Graef as *Pleasure At Her Majesty's*; and in *The Secret Policeman's Ball*, the 1979 Amnesty Gala, also filmed by Graef.

For those too young to have seen 'So That's The Way You Like It', the Shakespeare sketch from *Beyond The Fringe*, the 1976 show had Miller, Cook and Bennett from the original cast plus Terry Jones of Monty Python standing in for Moore, who was stranded by work permit regulations in America. On the day Roger Graef came to record the rehearsals for the sketch at Miller's house, Cook didn't turn up till rather late. He was there on time on the night and also offered the audience the chance to see E W Wisty explaining why he'd rather be a judge than a miner. The 'Bee in the Box' duologue, which Cook had written in 1959 for Kenneth Williams in *Pieces Of Eight* while still at Cambridge, was performed by the author and John Fortune. When Fortune corpsed, Cook quickly responded, 'There's nothing to smile about here.' He later joined the Monty Python team in a courtroom sketch as a man in the dock, 'Michael Norman Smith *alias* Michael Norman Smith.'

At *The Secret Policeman's Ball*, 'slightly directed by John Cleese', the interesting facts sketch, written before *Beyond The Fringe*, came up as fresh and as funny as ever, with Cleese playing straight man to a trivia-stuffed Cook expostulating on, *inter alia*, the length of one's intestines, in a manner that puts *The Body In Question* to shame. But the outstanding number of the whole evening – notwithstanding Billy Connolly's monologue on Scots in Rome or Rowan Atkinson's school roll call or the perennial Python Parrot sketch, all seen previously – was Cook's topical, trenchant and pointed parody of the judge's summing-up at the Jeremy Thorpe trial. Using a supercilious, plummy, upper-class voice, he openly instructs the jury to find the defendant not guilty by maligning the prosecution witnesses; one of them is described as 'a piece of ordure – a piece of excrement – unable to carry out a simple murder plot without cocking the whole thing up'. He finished by saying, 'You are now to retire as indeed should I.' Among the silliness, surrealism and slapstick of the evening, Cook's voice emerged as the only true satiric one, demonstrating with ease that it was possible to make a serious point and be hilarious at the same time.

Cook was one of the first satirists off the mark after Thatcher's victory in 1979, participating in a radio programme on the night of the election called *Why Vote, It Only Encourages Them*. Not long afterwards his domestic life hit the tabloid headlines. Apparently, he could become rather violent during arguments with his wife, Judy, who took out an injunction to restrain him from molesting her. There followed a short period of reconciliation.

X

After Peter Sellers's death in 1980, Blake Edwards, not surprisingly, looked around for a possible substitute. Dudley Moore and '10' had just brought him back to Hollywood in triumph, and Dudley's former partner was considered for the role of Inspector Clouseau. Cook threw cold water on the suggestion: 'In fact, what I am tipped to take over is Jacques Cousteau's underwater TV programmes if ever he perishes, which he should do, being under water. I'm definitely a snorkel and flippers man.' Needless to say Cook neither took over from Clouseau nor from Cousteau. (However he did replace Sellers in a Barclay's Bank commercial in which he played Harry Hodges, a spiv whose prey is an innocent student, for which exercise he received the fee of £20,000.) He later made another commercial as a suave estate agent for Diet Coke.

As the activities of his former 'Fringe' colleagues went into over-drive at the beginning of the 1980s, so Cook's began to slow down. Between rare appearances on TV – he had an LWT special called *Peter And Co.* in April 1980 – and fortnightly visits to *Private Eye*, he was being 'good at doing nothing in particular. I can be happily indolent.' Golf and football occupied much of his time.

Michael Parkinson relates a golfing story about Cook's greatest ambition, to play a round with Lee Trevino. When he finally did get an invitation, Cook hoped to learn something from the master. 'Aim straight for the flag,' advised Trevino on the first tee. 'Lee, I'm glad you told me that because you see I had a better idea,' Cook responded. 'I was going to take a 3-wood and knock the ball straight down the clubhouse chimney where it would bounce through the secretary's office, across the bar and through the dining-room window on to the green.'

Cook has been a keen supporter of Tottenham Hotspurs for over 25 years and has a season ticket at White Hart Lane, where he attends most of the home matches. 'I've never been in awe of anyone except footballers,' he asserts. 'I played a charity match at White Hart Lane, but I turned nasty. I was kicking the players not only after the ball had gone, but long after the game had finished.' It is perfectly possible that his love of football is one of the principal reasons he never pursued a career in America.

'Hollywood is not a good town to be in without any real or specific ambitions. Dudley has them to be successful. I do not,' Cook commented. 'It's far too hectic there. People are only interested in what you are doing, and they are always lying about what they are doing. Saying they're busy. The people who work on films go to bed early so they'll look good for early call in the morning. And those out of work don't go out in case anybody accuses them of not working.'

While on holiday in Los Angeles in 1981, he was asked by CBS to do a pilot for a sit-com based on the British TV series *Two's Company*, in which Donald Sinden was butler to Elaine Stritch, his American employer. The pilot went well and *The Two Of Us* hit the US screens for 30 minutes over 20 weeks. Then, in the mercenary manner of American TV, the show was axed as soon as it failed to make the top ratings. No great loss to Western culture. Someone once said that 'No sit-com with a sofa in it can be any good,' a criticism which covers the genre pretty extensively. Naturally, there was a sofa in *The Two Of Us*, but Cook cleverly avoided bumping into it. He played Robert

Brentwood (the kind of English name Americans dream up; there isn't one Brentwood in the London directory), a snobbish, supercilious butler to a disorganised talkshow hostess (Mimi Kennedy) with an outspoken teenage daughter (Dana Hill). The series coincided with Dudley Moore's blockbusting *Arthur*, in which John Gielgud played another exponent of the Arthur Treacher Method of butlering, rarely practised outside the confines of American comedy.

'This is not acting. I'm just being English. I don't have to dredge deep within my resources to be sardonic,' Cook commented at the time. 'In a way I find many things in America ridiculous and say so. So it is nice to be playing somebody who is a slightly more ridiculous version of myself.' The role didn't stretch him, it shrank him. The 'most original comic genius of his generation' was deadened in the insipid, neatly tailored straitjacket of American sit-com, but Cook allowed the circumstance no poignancy – 'Tormented Carnivorous Comic Genius Reduced To Eating Pap' – because he is so self-aware and his acting ambitions are so modest. Miller, Bennett and Moore are the clowns who wanted to direct, write and play *Hamlet* respectively. Cook is the clown who wanted to play the clown. 'I don't want an Oscar. I'd have to play an alcoholic, or a drug addict, for that,' he said. 'Scream a lot, and you'll get an Oscar. I stick to the show-off theory about actors. That's why they do it. To show off.'

Dudley Moore does assume that Cook wanted the sort of Hollywood fame he himself had achieved, but blew his chances: 'The trouble was, Peter was apologising all the time for being here and it showed in his work. If he'd made it big here, he would have been at home with it and relaxed and enjoyed it. But because it didn't work, and God knows we've all had our failures, there's this strange residual contempt.' And yet could it be that the Hampstead-Spurs-*Private Eye*-British TV-loving Peter Cook did not join the 'face-lifted androids on the beach in California' because he had no real desire to? Reluctance to accept this notion is based on the assumption that Hollywood is the nirvana to which all entertainers aspire and against which all careers are judged.

'There's an elitism and a snobbery in LA which is pretty insufferable,' Cook told Clive Hirschhorn in *The Sunday Express*. 'I'm a bit of a snob myself, but an amateur compared to some of those Hollywood types. Six months was about the most I could take of it. In fact, when filming came to an end and it was time for me to return home to England, I deliberately left my golf-clubs and tennis racket at the

Chateau Marmont where I was staying. I thought to myself, if I leave them behind, fate will make quite sure the series and my contract will not be renewed and that I'd forfeit some very expensive sports equipment. Which, of course, is what I was hoping would happen. And I'm happy to say it did. The series wasn't the success the network had hoped for and the show was dropped. It cost me a set of clubs and a racket, but at least I've retained my sanity.'

In 1981, back in Britain, *Private Eye* celebrated its twentieth birthday. For the occasion they put out a record album consisting of all eleven of the magazine's give-away flimsy discs plus some which had originally been thought too offensive to distribute. The rudest and funniest was one of Cook as a homosexual discussing his 'liaisons' with famous politicians over the past 25 years. That same year Cook stirred up a storm in a teacup by crossing teaspoons with minor actor (and later biographer of theatrical impresario 'Binkie' Beaumont), Richard Huggett. The portly thespian had already provoked the wrath of Auberon Waugh, writer on the *Eye* since 1970, for daring to portray his father in a one-man show at the Arts called *A Talent To Abuse*. The magazine now made the terrible mistake of accusing Huggett of once being Lady 'Bubbles' Rothermere's butler, an error deriving from the fact that when Cook had gone to interview her at her home, he mistook Huggett for the butler when he served tea. Huggett insisted that he was Lady Rothermere's 'social secretary' while 'resting'. Scarcely an example of the kind of hard-hitting investigative journalism with which the *Eye* had made its name.

XI

'It all started when Keith Moon, Sam Peckinpah, Graham Chapman and myself were dining at Trader Vic's . . . Keith suggested doing a movie about pirates and we were all discussing it and being enthusiastic, when I saw Sam, who was too tired actually to go to the lavatory, relieving himself in the artificial palm tree by the table. It was then that I thought the idea was unlikely to get off the ground.' Peter Cook's pessimism was unfounded and *Yellowbeard*, his first feature film for six years, was released in 1983 following two paltry screen versions of *The Pirates Of Penzance*, and preceding Roman Polanski's pathetic *Pirates*. Filmed in England, the USA and Mexico, and with a cast whose very names were enough to provoke a smile of expectant pleasure, it promised to be a sort of Monty Pirate romp and the resultant dull parade was all the more disappointing. Cook, Chapman and Bernard McKenna, who wrote it, would have been well advised to watch *The Crimson Pirate* a few times before putting quill to paper; parody needs more invention and style than this puerile patchwork of buccaneer buffoonery offered, with its mistaken assumption that 'shit' and 'tits' are funny words when coming from the mouth of an angelic nine-year-old girl. Opportunities were created, then thrown overboard. There were half-hearted stabs at *Treasure Island* and *Mutiny On The Bounty*, with James Mason as a Captain Bligh figure; in the plot, Mason smuggles a girl on board who poses as an officer called Mr Prostitute. Michael Hordern (thrice Jonathan Miller's *King Lear*), Eric Idle, Beryl Reid, Spike Milligan, Susannah York, David Bowie, Marty Feldman (in his last role) and Cook, as Lord Lambourne, waste their talents on this drivel. Only John Cleese as Blind Pew ('I have acute hearing'; 'I'm not interested in your jewellery') and Graham Chapman, hiding behind the beard of the title, are mildly amusing.

Yellowbeard did not give the expected boost to Cook's film career, either as performer or scriptwriter and he retreated behind the walls of his Hampstead home until tempted out by an offer to make a lot of money for doing very little. Alexander Salkind and nephew Ilya, who had made a fortune from three *Superman* movies, had the notion that they would repeat the process with a 'feminist' version, an idea immediately undermined by the title, *Supergirl*, not Super<u>woman</u>, although Helen Slater was in the same age range as Christopher Reeve when he first took to the skies. Cook played Nigel, a warlock maths teacher at a girls' school who assists the evil witch Selena (Faye Dunaway) in her plans to take over the world by means of a Krypton power source.

'I sat around on the set for sixteen weeks. I did that very well,' was Cook's honest assessment of his contribution to the proceedings.

Since the ending of *Not Only . . . But Also* in 1970, Peter Cook's involvement with television has been as an avid and addicted viewer rather than as a performer. In fact, as a viewer he has been more successful. In 1986 two events caused sympathetic headshaking among his friends. One was his neutral appearance on the *Joan Rivers Show* for BBC2, the other was being prosecuted for drunken driving (he had long since fallen off the wagon). The former gained him more disapprobation. Some bright spark at the BBC had the idea of getting the raunchy, aggressive, anorexic-looking American comedienne to do a six-week chat show in London, with Cook as her co-host. 'I was there to help her out if she got into trouble,' Cook explained, 'but she never thought she was in trouble so I never helped her out. I was meant to spring to her aid if we ever got into very intricate areas, such as the English language or things she didn't comprehend. I told them that if they did another series I'd do it for the same fee but I'd just like to come on at the very end and kiss everybody.'

The fact that the six programmes were shot in a rushed six days could not have helped the rather indolent Cook, who looked as if he were an uninvited guest trying not to be conspicuous on the end of a sofa. While Rivers was in full flow, he sank lower and lower from view. It would be kind to think that the whole thing was a sublime satire on the idiocies of the genre, yet the brash hostess's obsession with sexual matters did, at least, diverge from the usual bland chat show beaten track. It might have been a better idea to have 'Derek and Clive' on the programme to dish some real dirt. It was generally agreed that the show was more of an accident than what befell Cook on the night of his 49th birthday on 17 November 1986 when he was found, after his Honda saloon rammed a police car on a zebra crossing near his Hampstead home, to have had twice the legal limit of alcohol. In mitigation he claimed that 'It's my birthday. I had three drinks earlier this evening.' The court fined him £200 and banned him from driving for a year.

He and Judy had decided to separate. Since she was a lover of country life and disliked London, she spent most of her time 150 miles away at their eight-acre home near Porlock; when in London she occupied her own half of the house. If Peter wasn't on the golf course or tennis court he would spend a lot of the week 'reading the newspapers or watching Brazilian soap operas on Channel 4'. His enjoyment of the schlocky end of the television spectrum has led him to guest on the chat shows of Clive James and Jonathan Ross to comment on the medium; he could well have made a living as an entertaining TV critic if only he had had the application – or the Latin.

XII

In the year of the Joan Rivers debacle, Cook was sent the script of *Whoops Apocalypse*. 'It seemed very funny to me, and it is one of the most convincing parts I have ever played. Most stuff goes straight to my agent, who sifts out quite a lot of crap. If he can't bear reading it, I certainly can't.' The role, as the crazed British Prime Minister Sir Mortimer Chris, was his first lead part in a film since *The Rise And Rise Of Michael Rimmer* sixteen years before. Written by Andrew Marshall and David Renwick (who scripted the TV series of the same name and the Fleet Street send-up *Hot Metal*) had imagined Cook in the part which was in fact a throwback to his Macmillan imitation from *Beyond The Fringe*. In a grey wig and sporting an Eden moustache on his stiff upper lip, Cook played a potty PM who believes that unemployment is caused by pixies. In order to create jobs, he arranges for 10,000 volunteers to leap to their deaths off Beachy Head, cheering him as they go. He also proclaims that 'We in this Conservative government have always felt that it is utterly immoral to spend millions of pounds on nuclear weapons which are never used.'

Commenting on his performance Cook announced that 'I let my moustache do the work, actually. The only thing I felt absolutely certain about was that I had to have a moustache. I don't think Anthony Eden would have invaded Suez if he hadn't had a moustache. Look at Margaret Thatcher – a triumph of the depilator's art. Moustaches give you the confidence to invade people.' The plot is a parody of the Falklands crisis: the USA, headed by President Loretta Swit, invades the British protectorate of Maguadora, the Russians are drawn into the conflict, and nuclear war threatens. Overextended, as are most screenplays deriving from short comic blocks laid end to end, it can be gauged as a laughter-provoking rather than a thought-provoking satire. In the cast were members of the third generation of comedians to follow from the 'Fringers', Rik Mayall and Alexei Sayle, who look upon Cook as their comic mentor. His only other notable contact with the new breed was his appearance as Richard III in Rowan Atkinson's *Blackadder* comical-historical series, in 1983.

XIII

Despite describing his politics as being on the right, Cook was once a self-proclaimed 'Attlee groupie' and voted Labour in the 1988 General Election.

'I was once asked to stand as a Liberal. I said why? I never thought of myself as a Liberal or anything. And they said we heard you on *Any Questions* and you seemed to fit in with our values.' As a satirist, he has a longing for the old-style Tories. 'We had scandals like the Profumo affair. There used to be a rule that any big scandal involving Labour would concern corruption and with the Tories it would be sex, but there's a cross-pollination these days . . . It's all got a bit drab since. What have you got? Leon Brittan not having an affair with an Alsatian. Cecil Parkinson having an affair with his secretary. That's too dull and he's too dull.'

'It has got to the point where the entire population has to be seen live on television every night to prove that they are still alive or haven't got AIDS,' Cook exclaimed, when reports of his death between television engagements became exaggerated. The staff at *Private Eye* knew that he was alive almost every other week when he trundled into the Soho offices to contribute some of the better jokes anonymously. The *Eye* was important to Cook, not just as means of keeping him in the comfortable lifestyle to which he has long been accustomed, as well as somewhere to go on rainy afternoons, but as the last remaining doric column of the ruined temple of satire that he had built.

George Melly called it 'that bible of forty-year-old adolescent fifth-formers armed with satirical wet towels'. Former contributor Peter McKay, who left when Ingrams promoted Ian Hislop to editor, complained that the magazine had 'become very poor. I certainly don't get as many laughs out of it. It used to be that *Private Eye* was mentioned in the papers every other week.' The gentleman proprietor, like the gentleman farmer, remained loyal. 'I think it's a good laugh every two weeks; and good writing. It's as funny recently as it ever was.'

If Cook had ever wished to sell his 75 per cent of the magazine, he would not have made a profit. By a special provision inserted in the articles of association, he had to offer them first to other shareholders (among them Anthony Blond, Andrew Osmond, Barry Fantoni, Dirk Bogarde, Bernard Braden and Jane Asher) at cost – that is £1,500. When Sir James Goldsmith won huge damages against the *Eye* in 1977, Cook was approached by prospective buyers. At a meeting 'Two people turned up, both called Simon Fraser,' narrates Cook. 'One of them owned half Scotland, and the other did not. They said they wanted to buy *Private Eye*. I was quite suspicious of them because I thought they might be put up to it by Goldsmith, but anyway they rambled on for a couple of hours about their plans for the paper. Then Oscar Beuselinck, my lawyer, got a bit bored and suddenly said, "What about the fucking ackers then?" It turned out they were thinking of between £25,000 and £50,000 . . . Finally I told them I would sell it to them for £5 million. So we heard no more about it.'

The £30,000 which Goldsmith settled for, plus costs, was raised from the public's response to a 'Goldenballs' appeal. Though the *Eye* could ill afford libel payments over its 28 years' existence, it was part of the nature of a satirical magazine to take risks. In 1981, however, the magazine published a story claiming falsely that Sonia Sutcliffe, wife of Peter Sutcliffe, the 'Yorkshire Ripper' had 'caroused' with reporters after clinching a £250,000 deal with *The Daily Mail*. It took eight years for this time-bomb to explode. A jury awarded the plaintiff the monumental sum of £600,000 plus costs, an amount far beyond the magazine's resources. The largest shareholder put on a brave face as the comfortable carpet was pulled from under him: 'I suppose henceforth we'll have to run controversial stories about kind vicars spending nice days at the seaside, but without naming the vicars or committing ourselves to the weather for fear of comebacks. I can't see the point of running a magazine like this if you're going to allow it to become bland.'

XIV

'Whatever happened to Peter Cook?' is the question most people ask. If Miller is criticised for doing too much, Cook is taken to task for doing too little. He may have been one of the main instigators of the satire movement but for anyone under 40, it is ancient history. 'Peter Cook has had a funny career, starting in an incandescent blaze . . . After that his career has seemed to fizzle and fart, to break down into individual, often brilliant, but sporadic outcroppings,' commented Alexei Sayle. His contribution to *Private Eye* is minimal and his occasional TV appearances provide only glimpses of the artist Peter Ustinov once called 'the funniest man in the world'.

A colleague at the *Eye* thought that although Cook can still be very brilliant, 'He's quite badly wounded by life. He's rather hesitant and not as confident as he used to be.' His recent screen roles have certainly necessitated the 'Don't blink' warning to those who wish to see him. Perhaps it would be best to shut one's eyes to his brief role of the 'Impressive Clergyman' in *The Princess Bride*, in which he put on a silly high voice 'somewhere between the Archbishop of Canterbury and a female sheep', as Cook himself describes it, although he was amusing as the smarmy owner of a fashionable hairdressing salon in *Getting It Right* (1989). He also cropped up way down the cast list, as the editor of *The Strand Magazine* in *Without A Clue* (1989), an unfunny Sherlock Holmes spoof which had Ben Kingsley's Watson the brains behind Michael Caine's Holmes. Twelve years previously Cook himself had starred as Sherlock Holmes to Moore's Watson. But . . . There is a delicious moment in *Bedazzled* when a man with a severe stammer, speaking with some difficulty, makes a rather contentious statement to which Peter Cook replies, 'Easy for you to say, Colonel!' Perhaps that answer would serve when he is criticised for not being as prolific as his three former partners. 'If there's one thing I can't stand,' he says, 'it's people telling me what to do.'

'There's always a sense of excitement when he comes out again,' says Ned Sherrin. 'You feel it's the Grand Old Man coming out to prove he can still do it amongst the kids. He has a more oblique and original approach than most of them.' One of the 'kids', Jonathan Ross, interviewing Cook on *The Last Resort* in December 1988, said 'I'm a big fan of yours, but I'm always intrigued as to how you survive as you don't seem to work on a regular basis. I wonder what you actually do with yourself.'

'I'm not from a working class family, ' replied Cook, lighting the first in a chain of cigarettes. 'Independent wealth and blackmail.'

Alexei Sayle, in a *Time Out* piece called 'Cook's Apocalypse', wrote: 'From what you read, from what I remember and from what you can still see, Peter Cook was the best; unbelievably quick-witted, moving lizard-like to the best line and then onward to complex, mad improvisations of daredevil skill. But there seems to be some immutable rule about comedy: the truly talented stumble and founder while the ruthless self-promoters and self-advertisers – the Dudleys and the Frosties – go forever onward and upward.' Sayle's 'immutable rule' does not bear scrutiny; There are as many of the truly talented who ascend without stumbling as those who fall. Neither did Cook fall. He just sat down.

It was plain from the start that Cook's 'genius', a word that frequently comes to people's lips when describing him, would not be confined just to performing. In John Wells's view 'Peter is the great originator of ideas, the most original of our generation.' Although multifarious factors brought about the 'satire boom', if one were to point the finger at one man in the identify parade of comic suspects responsible for its advent, Peter Cook would be singled out more than anyone else. Nick Luard, one of Cook's oldest friends, explains: 'I think Peter has never really found the vehicle for his astonishing gifts, even though he's incomparably more talented than any of the other three in *Beyond The Fringe* – much more so than Miller, and, in my view, Bennett – which is a pretty high standard.'

It is clear that people wish to picture Cook as a tortured comic genius wandering the wilderness (or Hampstead Heath), having been expelled from his own lunatic kingdom. But Cook, so often conjugated into the past tense, believes the very best work he ever did was *Beyond The Fringe*: 'I don't know if I agree with the notion of progress. Why does everybody have to progress – why can't you stay in the same place?'

George Bernard Shaw (cribbing from Goethe) said that 'There are two tragedies in life. One is not to get your heart's desire. The other is to get it.' Cook had most of his wishes granted by the time he was 30. He had starred in the West End and Broadway in a hit revue predominently written by himself; he ran a satirical nightclub, owned a magazine; ran a theatre in New York, and had starred in films. He was happily married with two daughters, and had a comfortable house and bank balance. Some of these assets remain, and he makes occasional sorties into the limelight to prove that he himself is still there. His relative inactivity has become just as much part of his public persona in the 1980s as was his Wisty character in the past. 'Ambition can lead people to take pretty desperate measures at times. I'm not that desperate.'

PART FOUR

. . . and Beyond

The intellect of man is forced to choose
Perfection of the life, or of the work,
And if it take the second must refuse
A heavenly mansion, raging in the dark.
When all that story's finished, what's the news?
In luck or out of toil had left its mark:
That old perplexity an empty purse,
Or the day's vanity, the night's remorse.

W B Yeats *The Choice*

. . . AND BEYOND

'Biography is all about cutting people down to size,' claims Alan Bennett. 'Getting an unruly quart into a pint pot.' My task in this book was to get four quarts into a pint pot; as an author in search of four characters, I began with four caricatures.

Jonathan Miller has been described as looking like a 'camel after it's been through the eye of a needle', tying himself into physical knots as well as semantic ones. He is pictured either as an intellectual Gulliver in a corduroy jacket with leather elbows, fending off the pinpricking swords of the Lilliputian critical fraternity, or as a dilettantish Dr Know-All, spinning uncertainly and confusingly between medicine and the arts. A case of 'Miller, Miller on the wall, Who is the cleverest of us all?'

Alan Bennett is viewed as shy, schoolmasterly, spinsterish and schoolboyish, an owl in a tweed jacket, NHS specs and a woollen jumper, who writes upmarket *Coronation Street* TV plays and otherwise spends his time eavesdropping on old ladies on buses or peeping out of the closet in his home in NW1, where he lives a melancholy and solitary existence.

Dudley Moore is invariably depicted as an ingratiating Munchkin who has squandered his talent by selling out for a Hollywood lifestyle, appearing with beautiful starlets at Oscar ceremonies, and acting in execrable movies in between visits to the shrink.

Received opinion of Peter Cook is that this once slim, dark, good-looking, aquiline dandy, now wasted by alcohol, his T-shirt hanging over his beer belly, spends his days morosely watching TV alone in his Hampstead home, seething with jealousy over Moore's Hollywood fame, occasionally paying a visit to *Private Eye* to contribute a few lazy jokes belittling someone, or making a jaded appearance on some chat show or in a film.

At the time of *Beyond The Fringe* they were just four clever, funny young men who seemed to set the 'sixties swinging. It took some time for them to gain acceptance in their new roles, and still one wonders if they have really strayed that far from each other or from their concerted beginnings in show business.

Beyond The Fringe enabled Peter Cook to buy a mansion in Perrin's Walk, Hampstead that once belonged to H G Wells; Miller and Bennett bought houses in Gloucester Crescent, Camden Town (where they continue to live) and Moore a Maserati and later a seven-bedroomed Georgian house on The Mount in Hampstead. The show gave them not only fortune but fame and they are linked forever with it and with each other, in spite of their Promethean attempts to break the chains.

'I've often amused myself by thinking of what it would be like if the four of us rather geriatric figures were to get together again and do the show more or less as it was written,' mused Jonathan Miller. 'It would probably still be as funny as it was then.'

The combination of irreverent, anarchic, often childish, very English humour, tinged with melancholy, is what they still have in common. Englishness is the theme that comes out more strongly than any other in Bennett's plays, but without too obvious symbolism, rhetorical gestures, chauvinism, 'state of the nation' pronouncements or 'message'. It is what makes his reputation, in his own words, 'scarcely extend beyond the Isle of Wight'.

Despite Miller's cosmopolitanism and claims that 'I can imagine myself being at home in Italy . . . and I make eight times more money in the USA than I do here', he too is as much part of the English scene as the BBC, the Proms and Wimbledon. 'Every part of my memory is saturated with English imagery,' he says and his language is certainly saturated with English humour; even when talking about Alzheimer's disease (of which his mother died) on television, he will suddenly crack a joke to make a point.

Looking back; Miller has very equivocal views on *Beyond The Fringe.*

'It's something about which I'm enormously proud and I had an enormously enjoyable time doing it. But it really did divert me from something I intended to do, that I was enthusiastic about – scientific neurology. I feel remorse for the teachers who invested so much in me and felt there was a future for me, and I feel remorse for myself because I think I could have made a contribution. I feel like Marlon Brando in *On The Waterfront.* "I coulda been a contender." On the other hand it's given me all sorts of things I would never have had.

I've had a much jollier life. I've been all over the world. I've met and become friends with a much wider range of people than if I'd continued medicine. There is something rather grey about institutional medicine these days.'

Peter Cook, who apotheosised the Great English Bore and Underachiever, was patently not at home in LA where they don't know a bore when they see one, and where underachievers are definitely not a subject for humour. His bailiwick stretches from Hampstead to Soho, despite the far-off fantasising of 'Pete'; 'Bloody Greta Garbo. Diaphanously clad in a shortie nightie, holding on to the window sill her knuckles all white, screamin' at me. I had to poke her off with a broomstick . . . and bloody Betty Grable. Transatlantic call. She said come over immediately, get on a plane, come dance with me, be mine tonight.'

For Cook, the *Fringe* days were the happiest days of his life, even happier than his public schooldays when he did much the same thing on a smaller scale. 'I never had it so good,' he recalled in a postscript to *The Complete Beyond The Fringe* in 1987. 'I look back on the show with nothing but pleasure . . . There is only one depressing side effect of re-reading the text – I may have done some other things as good but I am sure none better. I haven't matured, progressed, grown, become deeper, wiser, or funnier. But then, I never thought I would.'

In 1963, with two West End revues to his name, *Beyond The Fringe*, *The Establishment* show running in London and New York, and *Private Eye* picking up sales, Cook was only 26, the same age as Orson Welles when he directed *Citizen Kane*. But, as Welles said of himself, 'I started at the top and worked my way downwards.'

His old partner Dudley Moore feels a stranger in Britain after fourteen years away, but his personality and habits have made sure there's some corner of California that is for ever England. Speaking of the *Fringe* days, the Hollywood star and jazz musician, 'never had a better experience. I felt an urgency about it. It was the easiest physical job I have ever done – wandering on and off stage – just terrific to do . . . It was everything I ever wanted . . . to be on stage in a revue.'

'He's a child, to be sure, but he pleases me,' sings Julie Andrews of Dudley in '*10*'. In his beach house filled with toys, china ornaments, rag dolls, teddy bears, dogs and a cat, and a bathroom with fish-shaped tap handles, Moore is undeniably enjoying 'the blissful childhood I never had'. Miller considers *his* job as 'being allowed to pursue the life of a child well into adulthood', a phrase that echoes what he said a decade previously: 'Being allowed to produce an opera is really like being licensed to go on playing with one's toys until one's an old man.' He continually uses the language of children in reference to his profession. 'If someone rings at the door and says "Come out to play", I'll come out and play.' Even his book, *The Human Body*, is based on children's pop-up books.

Private Eye gave Cook the opportunity to prolong his adolescence by thinking up gags for that truant-playing school magazine. Bennett, an inveterate giggler, is likewise unrepentant about his weakness for 'terrible' puns and smutty schoolboy jokes. According to John Wells 'Infantilism is possibly the hallmark of our generation.' But Bennett appears to be the only one of the four who takes a dispassionate view of the *Fringe* years.

'I can't look back on *Beyond The Fringe* with any nostalgia . . . Looking back on it now I think of it as the work of another person. Some years later I was invited to a dinner by Harold Wilson at 10 Downing Street. The Wilsons met the guests as they arrived. The Prime Minister asked me what I did. I said I was a playwright but that I'd started off in *Beyond The Fringe*. "Well, I don't remember you. You weren't one of the original four, surely?" I felt like Trotsky when he was cut out of the history of the revolution.'

Despite their initial entry into the public arena as four matadors flashing provocative capes at sacred cows, all four 'Fringers' are rooted in the soil of tradition. None of them can remotely be called *avant-garde*. They cling on to the wreckage of what George Steiner calls 'the inventory of that great polyglot, liberal, humanistic culture; in many ways a world of ash, a dead world'.

Yet, paradoxically, they are dissidents; not in the meaning that the word implies in less fortunate countries but in that they are four people who have never swum in the cultural mainstream. Twenty-five years since *Beyond The Fringe* has not really mellowed them. In four differing styles, their tongues continue to lash abuses of authority and idiocies around them. They are still, despite the trappings of bourgeois comfort, four of life's natural anarchists. If they began by finding the 'Never had it so good' society ripe for disdain and humour, neither has the 'May the market forces be with you' society of the 1980s been spared their derision.

Jonathan Miller makes no bones about his views on 'the leaderene': 'She is loathsome and repulsive in almost every way, with her odious suburban gentility and sentimental saccharin patriotism.' Not the sort of language one expects from a CBE awarded under Mrs Thatcher's government. Alan Bennett has his own viewpoint. 'You wish you had an instrument that would give her an electric shock in the bum.' As surely as he is willing to excuse Guy Burgess of any 'crime' because of his sense of humour, Bennett condemns Mrs Thatcher for what he considers her lack of it.

'The response of a human being would be to throw something at her,' says Peter Cook. 'The trouble is that it's like being at school and there's the awful boring one who knows everything and no matter how much you rush about tittering and sniggering about how ghastly they are, they're always the ones who end up Prime Ministers . . . I think there's terrific merit in having no sense of humour, no sense of irony, practically no sense of anything at all. If you're born with these so-called defects you have a very good chance of getting to the top. That's what's enabled her to turn Britain into a cross between Singapore and Telford.'

Tucked away in California, the non-political Dudley Moore expresses his attitude to his birthplace: 'I don't know what is happening to this country but I do know it is being demoralised and I don't like that at all . . . What the bloody hell is monetarism? Does anyone understand it? And how much worse must things get before they start getting better?'

But overriding their various involvements with opera, Shakespeare, Kafka, betrayal, psychiatry, medicine, alcohol, divorces, soul-searching etc., they will be remembered as four very funny men. They have added to the gaiety of the nation, as the saying goes.

'If I laugh at any mortal thing, 'Tis that I may not weep.' So wrote Lord Byron and that seems to go for our Childe Harolds too.

'Happiness is such a nebulous, evanescent sort of thing,' reflected Moore. 'Happiness for me is doing the things I want to do – to become a concert artist, to be scholarly in certain directions.' Alexander Goehr believes with Schopenhauer that the face reflects character, and sees Miller's as a sensitive but not a contented one. A colleague says of him, 'He becomes increasingly tormented when he is in one of his fits of melancholia.' Cook, who 'can only compare today with a visit to the dentist combined with a coronary', thinks 'Happiness is one of the great delusions of living. You think back on the times when you think you were happy – but you probably didn't notice it then. You remember the unhappiness, though.'

'The only time you're really happy is when you're looking back,'

Bennett muses. 'I wouldn't describe myself as unhappy. It's like that phrase in *The Old Country*, "I'm not happy but I'm not unhappy about it."' There were four days in his life when Bennett knew at the time he was happy, but he refuses to reveal the source of the emotion. The only clue comes in an entry in the diary he kept during rehearsals of *Forty Years On* in October 1968: 'A group of boys have written a pop song on themes arising out of the play and in gaps of rehearsal they orchestrate it with the help of Carl Davis. This afternoon they sing it over to me, George Fenton and Anthony Andrews singing in high altos above the guitar and organ accompaniment . . . I sit in the Tea Centre in Manchester's Oxford Road, working on the lyrics with George Fenton and Keith McNally, and I see suddenly how I shall look back on this time as very happy.'

None of them finds consolation in religion. Christian John Wells thinks Miller is 'the most God-haunted atheist I've ever come across', and 'would not be surprised if he didn't have some kind of late religious experience'. Atheist George Melly refers to Miller as 'firmly agnostic yet, as a Jew, he holds a continuous dialogue with God', Jonathan himself says he will never 'lapse into conviction unless attacked by oncoming dementia'.

Bennett has renounced the strong faith he held in his adolescence as a 'censorious Christian Tory' but still knows the Book of Common Prayer by heart, and can weep at hymns. The non-believer Cook was brought up Church of England and 'I'm still trying to work it out.' Moore has become 'not irreligious, but anti-religious in my declining years . . . I doubt if I could tell you the difference between one religion and another. Being Anglo-Catholic, in my view, merely meant going to the church where they didn't use incense and Latin.' Dud 'n' Pete inevitably had views on the subject:

Dud: Do you think God's been listening while we've been talking?

Pete: Well, if He exists, He's been listening because He's omnipresent. He's heard every word we've said.

Dud: Oh, we'd better look religious, then.

Pete: It's no good just looking religious Dud. He can see through that. You have to *be* religious. What do you *really* believe in?

Dud: I believe in having a good time. Food and kip and Joan Whittaker and that.

Pete: That's not religion, Dud. That Hedonism. You're an Heddist.

Dud: No, I'm a Duddist. That's what I call it.

Henry James believed that the 'artist was what he did – he was nothing else'. As the inner processes of a creative artist or performer can only be guessed at by outsiders, I have allowed my four subjects mostly to speak for themselves. I leave judgements on their personalities and unfinished lives to the reader; my opinions are reserved for their work, which they have offered to the world at large for its reactions. All four *provocateurs* seem disarmingly vulnerable and unresilient to criticism, the idle chatter of the *agora*.

The only good subject for a biography is a dead one. Then the narrative can at least be satisfactorily rounded, even if posthumous information comes to light or reinterpretation is offered from the standpoint of different eras. Besides the need to tread much more softly to avoid stepping on too many toes, biography of the living must of necessity remain open-ended, in this case with four loose ends sticking out; a freeze frame taken at a particular moment in four lives. As soon as the book is finished, the image begins to move once more into action.

ENVOI

Cambridge, April 1989. Nothing had changed very much over the years, or as a valedictory song from a Footlights Revue has it:

So let's take a last look round
If it's going down well, it always will,
It was Cambridge then and it's Cambridge still
It will always be the same.

Cambridge continues to be primarily an institution for the 'well born' and students still spend, as Simon Raven put it, 'four years of misty autumns and green springs, of gaiety and neurosis . . . of vacuity and intensity, of love and hate'. Of course, education is no longer an end in itself; it has now entered the market place, with more and more students crowding into the careers advice offices. And the President of the Student's Union is a punk-haired Lesbian Tory. 'It's years since one of *them* has become President!' exclaimed an undergraduate. 'Imagine! A Tory!'

The Footlights Club is in rehearsal. During breaks, its members have been listening to the record and reading the text of *Beyond The Fringe*. Roland Kenyon, the President of the Footlights, a postgraduate in linguistic philosophy, was born in the year *Beyond The Fringe* opened in London. The rest of the year's Footlighters are some years younger. (Will any of them have their biographies written in the year 2017?) Sitting in Kenyon's rooms in Fitzwilliam Street, the Footlighters of 1989 were astonished to find how much of the 29-year-old show was still funny enough to be put on unchanged now, and how much it had influenced later British comedy.

Transplanted to these times when ailing Liberty is on a hospital waiting list, the show was described by these 'Thatcher's Children' as mildly irreverent rather than bitingly satiric. The present-day Cambridgians in their twenties do not remember Prime Ministers in the urbane Eden-Macmillan mould, so Cook's TVPM seemed too gentle. However, the parodies of the preacher and Shakespeare, the sort of things regularly performed in student revues, 'have never been better done'.

There were sensitive areas, like the camp actors and the black politician, that they wouldn't dare touch in their revues today, and the trendy TV vicar had been overtaken by different religious preoccupations such as the question of the ordination of women priests. As they were even further away than audiences of the 1960s from World War II, which had ended over twenty years before most of them were born, there was incomprehension as to why anyone would have found the 'Aftermyth of War' sketch offensive in any way. This was put into perspective when it was pointed out that perhaps they would not yet risk a sketch mocking similar attitudes that had been dusted off for the Falklands War.

But the youthful laughter greeting the efforts of the young Bennett, Cook, Miller and Moore across the years reveals that *Beyond The Fringe* continues to live up to its legendary reputation.

CREDITS

The following is a list of stage productions, theatre and TV plays, books, films, stage and TV appearances of my four subjects. I have tried to be as comprehensive as possible, although I haven't itemised every single sighting.

BEYOND THE FRINGE

1960, Edinburgh Festival
1961, Fortune Theatre, London
1962, John Golden Theater, New York
1964, John Golden Theater (Paxton Whitehead replacing Jonathan Miller)

BEYOND THE FRINGE recordings

1961, recorded at the Fortune Theatre
1962, recorded in New York
1964, recorded in New York

JONATHAN MILLER

Theatre productions

1962   UNDER PLAIN COVER by John Osborne. Royal Court Theatre, London
1964   THE OLD GLORY, two plays by Robert Lowell adapted from Herman Melville (*Benito Cereno*) and Nathaniel Hawthorne (*My Kinsman Major Molineux*). American Place Theater, New York
1966   COME LIVE WITH ME by Lee Minoff and Stanley Price. New Haven, Connecticut

1967   BENITO CERENO by Robert Lowell adapted from Herman Melville. Yale Drama School

1967   PROMETHEUS BOUND by Robert Lowell adapted from Aeschylus. Yale Drama School

1968   BENITO CERENO. Mermaid Theatre, London

1968   SCHOOL FOR SCANDAL by Richard Brinsley Sheridan. Nottingham Playhouse

1969   THE SEAGULL by Anton Chekhov. Nottingham Playhouse

1969   KING LEAR by William Shakespeare. Nottingham Playhouse

1970   HAMLET by William Shakespeare. Arts Theatre, Cambridge

1970   THE TEMPEST by William Shakespeare. Mermaid Theatre

1970   KING LEAR. National Theatre, Old Vic, London

1970   THE MERCHANT OF VENICE by William Shakespeare. National Theatre

1971   PROMETHEUS BOUND. Mermaid Theatre

1971   DANTON'S DEATH by Georg Büchner. National Theatre

1971   JULIUS CAESAR by William Shakespeare. Arts Theatre, Cambridge

1972   SCHOOL FOR SCANDAL. National Theatre

1972   THE TAMING OF THE SHREW by William Shakespeare. Chichester Festival Theatre

1973   THE MALCONTENT by John Marston. Nottingham Playhouse

1973   THE SEAGULL. Chichester Festival Theatre

1974   MEASURE FOR MEASURE by William Shakespeare. National Theatre

1974   THE MARRIAGE OF FIGARO by Pierre Augustin Caron de Beaumarchais. National Theatre

1974   THE FREEWAY by Peter Nichols. National Theatre

1974   GHOSTS by Henrik Ibsen. Greenwich Theatre

1974   THE SEAGULL. Greenwich Theatre

1974   HAMLET. Greenwich Theatre

1975   THE IMPORTANCE OF BEING EARNEST by Oscar Wilde. Greenwich Theatre

1975   ALL'S WELL THAT ENDS WELL by William Shakespeare. Greenwich Theatre

1976   A POKE IN THE EYE WITH A SHARP STICK a.k.a. PLEASURE AT HER MAJESTY'S. Her Majesty's, London

1976   THE THREE SISTERS by Anton Chekhov. Cambridge Theatre, London

1979   SHE WOULD IF SHE COULD by George Etherege. Greenwich Theatre

1982   HAMLET. Donmar Warehouse, London

1986   A LONG DAY'S JOURNEY INTO NIGHT by Eugene O'Neill. Haymarket Theatre, London; Broadhurst Theater, New York

1987   THE EMPEROR by Michael Hastings adapted from Ryszard Katuscinski. Royal Court Theatre

1987   THE TAMING OF THE SHREW. Royal Shakespeare Company, Stratford-upon-Avon; Barbican Centre, London

1988   ANDROMACHE by Jean Racine. Old Vic, London

1988   ONE WAY PENDULUM by N F Simpson. Old Vic

1988   BUSSY D'AMBOIS by George Chapman. Old Vic

1988   THE TEMPEST. Old Vic

1988   CANDIDE by Leonard Bernstein, co-directed with John Wells. Old Vic

1989   KING LEAR. Old Vic

1989   THE LIAR by Pierre Corneille. Old Vic

Opera productions

1974   ARDEN MUST DIE by Alexander Goehr. Sadler's Wells Theatre, London

1975   COSI FAN TUTTE by Wolfgang Amadeus Mozart. Kent Opera

1975   RIGOLETTO by Giuseppe Verdi. Kent Opera

1975   THE CUNNING LITTLE VIXEN by Leos Janacek. Glyndebourne

1976   LA FAVOLA D'ORFEO by Claudio Monteverdi. Kent Opera

1977   EUGENE ONEGIN by Peter Ilyich Tchaikovsky. Kent Opera

1978   THE MARRIAGE OF FIGARO by Wolfgang Amadeus Mozart. English National Opera, Coliseum, London

1979   LA TRAVIATA by Giuseppe Verdi. Kent Opera

1979   THE FLYING DUTCHMAN by Richard Wagner. Frankfurt

1979   THE TURN OF THE SCREW by Benjamin Britten. English National Opera

1980   ARABELLA by Richard Strauss. English National Opera

1980   FALSTAFF by Giuseppe Verdi. Kent Opera

1981   OTELLO by Giuseppe Verdi. English National Opera

1982   RIGOLETTO. English National Opera; Metropolitan Opera, New York

1982   COSI FAN TUTTE. St Louis Opera, Missouri

1982   FIDELIO by Ludwig Von Beethoven. Kent Opera
1983   THE MAGIC FLUTE by Wolfgang Amadeus Mozart.
        Scottish Opera
1985   DON GIOVANNI by Wolfgang Amadeus Mozart. English
        National Opera
1986   TOSCA by Giacomo Puccini. Maggio Musicale, Florence; English
        National Opera
1986   THE MIKADO by Arthur Sullivan. English National Opera
1987   THE BARBER OF SEVILLE by Gioacchino Rossini. English
        National Opera
1987   THE MIKADO. Los Angeles Music Center Opera
1987   TRISTAN AND ISOLDE by Richard Wagner. Los Angeles Music
        Center Opera

Television (director)

1962   WHAT'S GOING ON HERE? NBC New York
1965   THE DRINKING PARTY after Plato's Symposium (also producer).
        BBC TV
1966   ALICE IN WONDERLAND (also producer). BBC TV
1968   OH WHISTLE AND I'LL COME TO YOU after M R James (also
        producer). BBC TV
1973   CLAY after James Joyce. BBC TV
1975   KING LEAR. BBC TV
1980   THE TAMING OF THE SHREW (also producer). BBC TV
1980   ANTONY AND CLEOPATRA (also producer). BBC TV
1981   TIMON OF ATHENS (also producer). BBC TV
1981   OTHELLO (also producer). BBC TV
1981   TROILUS AND CRESSIDA (also producer). BBC TV
1982   KING LEAR (also producer). BBC TV
1984   THE BEGGAR'S OPERA by John Gay (also producer). BBC TV
1985   COSI FAN TUTTE. BBC TV
1986   LONG DAY'S JOURNEY INTO NIGHT. BBC TV
1989   DIALOGUE IN THE DARK by Michael Ignatieff. BBC TV

Television (presenter)

1964   MONITOR. BBC TV
1977   THE BODY IN QUESTION, 13-part series (also writer).
        BBC TV
1982   STATES OF MIND, 15-part series. BBC TV

1984   IVAN. BBC TV
1989   WHO CARES?, 6-part series. BBC TV
1989   EQUINOX Channel 4

Film

1964   (Actor.) Kirby Groomkirby in ONE WAY PENDULUM
       (Woodfall Films), Director Peter Yates
1967   (Director.) SCOTCH (documentary short for John Walker and
       Sons)
1970   (Director.) TAKE A GIRL LIKE YOU (Columbia Pictures)

Publications

1971   McLUHAN, Fontana Modern Masters
1972   (Editor.) FREUD: THE MAN, HIS WORLD, HIS INFLUENCE,
       Weidenfeld and Nicolson
1972   CENSORSHIP AND THE LIMITS OF PERMISSION, British
       Academy
1978   THE BODY IN QUESTION, Jonathan Cape
1982   (With Boris Van Loon.) DARWIN FOR BEGINNERS, Unwin
       and Writers and Readers Publishing Co-op
1983   STATES OF MIND, BBC Publications
1983   (With David Pelham.) THE HUMAN BODY, Jonathan Cape
1984   (With David Pelham.) THE FACTS OF LIFE, Jonathan Cape
1986   SUBSEQUENT PERFORMANCES, Faber and Faber

ALAN BENNETT

Plays (theatre)

1968   FORTY YEARS ON. Apollo Theatre, London
1971   GETTING ON. Queen's Theatre, London
1973   HABEAS CORPUS. Lyric Theatre, London
1975   HABEAS CORPUS. Martin Beck Theater, New York
1977   THE OLD COUNTRY. Queen's Theatre
1980   ENJOY. Vaudeville Theatre, London
1986   KAFKA'S DICK. Royal Court Theatre, London
1988   SINGLE SPIES—*An Englishman Abroad* (also director) *and*

A Question of Attribution (also actor). National Theatre, London; Queen's Theatre

Plays (television)

1972 A DAY OUT, Director Stephen Frears. BBC TV
1975 SUNSET ACROSS THE BAY, Director Stephen Frears. BBC TV
1977 A LITTLE OUTING, Director Brian Tufano. BBC TV
1978 A VISIT FROM MISS PROTHERO, Director Stephen Frears. BBC TV
1978 ME, I'M AFRAID OF VIRGINIA WOOLF, Director Stephen Frears. LWT
1978 DORIS AND DOREEN, Director Stephen Frears. LWT
1978 THE OLD CROWD, Director Lindsay Anderson. LWT
1979 AFTERNOON OFF, Director Stephen Frears. LWT
1979 ALL DAY ON THE SANDS, Director Giles Foster. LWT
1979 ONE FINE DAY, Director Stephen Frears. LWT
1982 INTENSIVE CARE, Director Gavin Millar. BBC TV
1982 A WOMAN OF NO IMPORTANCE, Director Giles Foster. BBC TV
1982 OUR WINNIE, Director Malcolm Mowbray. BBC TV
1982 ROLLING HOME, Director Piers Haggard. BBC TV
1982 MARKS, Director Piers Haggard. BBC TV
1982 SAY SOMETHING HAPPENED, Director Giles Foster. BBC TV
1983 AN ENGLISHMAN ABROAD, Director John Schlesinger. BBC TV
1986 THE INSURANCE MAN, Director Richard Eyre. BBC TV
1988 TALKING HEADS, Six monologues; A CHIP IN THE SUGAR, Director Stuart Burge; A BED AMONG THE LENTILS, Director Alan Bennett; A LADY OF LETTERS, Director Giles Foster; HER BIG CHANCE, Director Giles Foster; SOLDIERING ON, Director Giles Foster; A CREAM CRACKER UNDER THE SETTEE, Director Stuart Burge. BBC TV

Screenplays

1984 A PRIVATE FUNCTION, Director Malcolm Mowbray
1987 PRICK UP YOUR EARS, Director Stephen Frears

Performances (theatre)

1962   Archbishop of Canterbury in BLOOD OF THE BAMBERGS
by John Osborne. Royal Court Theatre

1964   Reverend Sloley-Jones in A CUCKOO IN THE NEST by Ben
Travers. Royal Court Theatre

1968   Tempest in FORTY YEARS ON. Apollo Theatre

1974   Mrs Swabb in HABEAS CORPUS. Queen's Theatre

1976   A POKE IN THE EYE WITH A SHARP STICK a.k.a.
PLEASURE AT HER MAJESTY'S. Her Majesty's Theatre,
London

1988   Tailor in AN ENGLISHMAN ABROAD and Blunt in A
QUESTION OF ATTRIBUTION in double bill SINGLE SPIES.
National Theatre and Queen's Theatre

Performances (film)

1987   The Bishop in LITTLE DORRIT, Director Christine Edzard

Performances (television)

1965   Various roles in MY FATHER KNEW LLOYD GEORGE,
Director Jack Gold. BBC TV

1966   ON THE MARGIN (comedy series), also writer. BBC TV

1966   The Mouse in ALICE IN WONDERLAND, Director Jonathan
Miller. BBC TV

1979   Stanley in AFTERNOON OFF. LWT

1982   Midgley in INTENSIVE CARE. BBC TV

1986   Mr Posner in BREAKING UP by Nigel Williams, Director
Stuart Burge. BBC TV

1987   Lord Pinkrose in THE FORTUNES OF WAR by Alan Plater,
Director Sir James Cellan Jones. BBC TV

1988   Graham in A CHIP IN THE SUGAR (one of the TALKING
HEADS). BBC TV

1988   DINNER AT NOON (documentary). BBC TV

Recordings

ALICE IN WONDERLAND and ALICE THROUGH THE LOOKING
GLASS
THE WIND IN THE WILLOWS
WINNIE THE POOH and THE HOUSE AT POOH CORNER

DUDLEY MOORE

Performances (theatre)

1969   Alan Felix in PLAY IT AGAIN, SAM by Woody Allen. Globe
       Theatre, London
1972   BEHIND THE FRIDGE – Revue by Peter Cook and Dudley
       Moore. Cambridge Theatre, London
1973   GOOD EVENING a.k.a. BEHIND THE FRIDGE. Plymouth
       Theatre, New York
1987   Ko-Ko in THE MIKADO by Arthur Sullivan. Los Angeles
       Music Center
1989   THE SECRET POLICEMAN'S BIGGEST BALL. Cambridge
       Theatre

Performances (film)

1966   John in THE WRONG BOX, Director Bryan Forbes. Columbia
1967   (Also music and co-screenplay.) Rupert Street in 30 IS A
       DANGEROUS AGE, CYNTHIA, Director Joseph McGrath.
       Columbia
1967   (Also music.) Stanley Moon in BEDAZZLED, Director Stanley
       Donen, Twentieth Century-Fox
1969   Lt Barrington in MONTE CARLO OR BUST, Director Ken
       Annakin. Dino De Laurentiis
1969   Sergeant in THE BED-SITTING ROOM, Director Richard
       Lester. United Artists
1972   Dormouse in ALICE'S ADVENTURES IN WONDERLAND,
       Director William Sterling. Fox-Rank
1977   (Also music and co-screenplay.) Dr. Watson and Mrs Ada
       Holmes in THE HOUND OF THE BASKERVILLES, Director
       Paul Morrissey. Hemdale
1978   Stanley Tibbets in FOUL PLAY, Director Colin Higgins.
       Paramount
1979   George Webber in '10', Director Blake Edwards. Columbia-
       EMI-Warner
1980   Harvey Orkin and Herschel in WHOLLY MOSES!, Director
       Gary Weis. Columbia
1981   Arthur Bach in ARTHUR, Director Steve Gordon, Columbia-
       EMI-Warner

1982 (Also music.) Patrick Dalton in SIX WEEKS, Director Tony
Bill. Rank

1983 Claude Eastman in UNFAITHFULLY YOURS, Director
Howard Zieff. Twentieth Century-Fox

1983 Saul Benjamin in LOVESICK, Director Marshall Brickman.
Columbia-EMI-Warner

1983 Jason Carmichael in ROMANTIC COMEDY, Director Arthur
Hiller. UIP

1984 Wylie Cooper in BEST DEFENCE, Director Willard Huyck.
Paramount

1984 Rob Salinger in MICKI AND MAUDE, Director Blake
Edwards. Columbia-EMI-Warner

1985 Patch in SANTA CLAUS, Director Jeannot Szwarc. Rank

1987 Dr Jack Hammond in LIKE FATHER LIKE SON, Director Ron
Daniel. Columbia

1988 Arthur Bach in ARTHUR 2: ON THE ROCKS, Director Bud
Yorkin. Warner

1989 CRAZY PEOPLE, Director Tony Bill. Paramount

Performances (television)

1964 OFFBEAT. BBC TV

1965 NOT ONLY . . . BUT ALSO (first series). BBC TV

1966 NOT ONLY . . . BUT ALSO (second series). BBC TV

1969 GOODBYE AGAIN. ATV

1970 NOT ONLY . . . BUT ALSO (third series). BBC TV

Music (film)

1968 INADMISSIBLE EVIDENCE, Director Anthony Page.
Paramount-Woodfall

1969 STAIRCASE, Director Stanley Donen. Twentieth
Century-Fox

Music (theatre)

1959 SERGEANT MUSGRAVE'S DANCE by John Arden. Royal
Court Theatre

1959 ONE WAY PENDULUM. Royal Court Theatre

1961 THE OWL AND THE PUSSYCAT – Ballet. Prince of Wales
Theatre, London

1962 ENGLAND OUR ENGLAND – Revue by Keith Waterhouse and Willis Hall. Princes Theatre, London
1962 THE CAUCASIAN CHALK CIRCLE by Bertolt Brecht. Royal Shakespeare Company, Aldwych Theatre, London
1963 COLLAGES – Ballet. Edinburgh Festival
1964 THE EMPEROR JONES by Eugene O'Neill. Boston Arts Festival

Recordings

1962 Theme from 'BEYOND THE FRINGE AND ALL THAT JAZZ'
1965 (With Peter Cook.) GOODBYE-EE
1965 NOT ONLY PETER COOK . . . BUT ALSO DUDLEY MOORE
1965 THE OTHER SIDE OF THE DUDLEY MOORE TRIO
1966 GENUINE DUD
1967 (With Peter Cook.) L S BUMBLEBEE
1967 30 IS A DANGEROUS AGE, CYNTHIA
1968 BEDAZZLED
1969 THE DUDLEY MOORE TRIO
1972 TODAY
1973 (With Peter Cook.) GOOD EVENING
1976 DUDLEY MOORE AT THE WAVENDON FESTIVAL
1976 (With Peter Cook.) DEREK AND CLIVE LIVE
1977 (With Peter Cook.) DEREK AND CLIVE COME AGAIN
1978 (With Peter Cook.) DEREK AND CLIVE AD NAUSEAM
1978 THE DUDLEY MOORE TRIO
1982 (With Cleo Laine.) SMILIN' THROUGH

PETER COOK

Writing (theatre)

1959 PIECES OF EIGHT. Apollo Theatre, London
1961 ONE OVER THE EIGHT. Duke of York's Theatre, London

Performances (theatre)

1972 BEHIND THE FRIDGE. Cambridge Theatre, London

1976 A POKE IN THE EYE WITH A SHARP STICK a.k.a.
PLEASURE AT HER MAJESTY'S. Her Majesty's Theatre,
London

1979 THE SECRET POLICEMAN'S BALL. Her Majesty's Theatre

1989 THE SECRET POLICEMAN'S BIGGEST BALL. Cambridge
Theatre

Performances (film)

1966 Morris in THE WRONG BOX, Director Bryan Forbes.
Columbia

1967 (Also screenplay.) George Spiggott in BEDAZZLED, Director
Stanley Donen. Twentieth Century-Fox

1968 Prentiss in A DANDY IN ASPIC, Director Anthony Mann,
(completed by Laurence Harvey). Columbia

1969 Major Dawlish in MONTE CARLO OR BUST, Director Ken
Annakin. Dino De Laurentiis

1969 Inspector in THE BED-SITTING ROOM, Director Richard
Lester. United Artists

1970 (Also co-screenplay.) Michael Rimmer in THE RISE AND
RISE OF MICHAEL RIMMER, Director Kevin Billington.
Warner

1972 Dominic in THE ADVENTURES OF BARRY McKENZIE,
Director Bruce Beresford. Austral

1977 (Also co-screenplay.) Sherlock Holmes in THE HOUND OF
THE BASKERVILLES, Director Paul Morrissey. Hemdale

1983 (Also co-screenplay.) Lord Lambourn in YELLOWBEARD,
Director Mel Damski. Orion

1984 Nigel in SUPERGIRL, Director Jeannot Szwarc.
Cantharus/Ilya Salkind

1986 Sir Mortimer Chris in WHOOPS APOCALYPSE, Director
Tom Bussmann. ITC

1987 Impressive Clergyman in THE PRINCESS BRIDE, Director
Rob Reiner. Vestron

1988 Greenhough in WITHOUT A CLUE, Director Thom
Eberhardt. Rank

1989 Mr Adrian in GETTING IT RIGHT, Director Randall Kleiser.
MCEG

1990   First English Reporter in GREAT BALLS OF FIRE, Director
        Jim McBride. Orion

Performances (television)

1963   WHAT'S GOING ON HERE? NBC TV New York
1964   ON THE BRADEN BEAT. ITV
1965   NOT ONLY . . . BUT ALSO. (First series)
1966   NOT ONLY . . . BUT ALSO. (Second series)
1966   The Mad Hatter in ALICE IN WONDERLAND. BBC TV
1969   GOODBYE AGAIN. ATV
1970   NOT ONLY . . . BUT ALSO. (Third series)
1971   WHERE DO I SIT? BBC TV
1978   REVOLVER. ATV
1980   PETER AND CO. LWT
1982   THE TWO OF US. CBS, USA
1986   THE JOAN RIVERS SHOW. BBC TV

Recordings (all with Dudley Moore)

1965   GOODBYE-EE
1965   NOT ONLY PETER COOK . . . BUT ALSO DUDLEY MOORE
1967   L S BUMBLEBEE
1973   GOOD EVENING
1976   DEREK AND CLIVE LIVE
1977   DEREK AND CLIVE COME AGAIN
1978   DEREK AND CLIVE AD NAUSEAM

INDEX

Index

Bennett, Walter (father) 74, 75, 76, 78,
    164, 176
Bergson, Henri 57
Beyond The Fringe 3, 4
    first meeting (1960) 7–8,
        rehearsals for Edinburgh
        Festival 8–11, opening 11,
        reviews 11–12
    at Cambridge 17, 50, and Brighton
        17, reviewed by FTG 18–19
    at Fortune Theatre, London (1961)
        21, 72, reviewed 21–2, 26, 40
    on Broadway (1962–3) 45–6,
        47–8, 60, (1964) 49, reviews 51
    in West End, with second cast 43–
        4
    issues: black politician 29–30, 289,
        homosexuality 28–9, 289,
        politics 30
    impact of its satire 22–5, 245
    sketches: 9, 10, 36–7, 72
        'The Aftermyth of War'
            10–11, 37–8, 288
        'And The Same To You' 27
        'The Ballad of Gangster Joe' 49
        'Boring Old Man' 31, 46
        Civil Defence sketch 31
        'The End Of The World' 40, 45
        'The English Way of Death' 50
        Great Train Robbery 50
        'The Heat–Death Of The
            Universe' 9, 39–40
        Jim's Inn parody 12
        'Little Miss Britten' 28
        'Man Bites God' 36
        'One Leg Too Few' 50–1, 204,
            212, 218
        'Porn Shop' 40
        'Real Class' 8
        'The Royal Box' 34, 41
        'Sitting On The Bench' (E L
            Wisty) 9, 34–5 (*see also*
            Cook, Peter)
        'So That's The Way You Like It'
            (Shakespeare parody) 10,
            38–9, 109, 266, 289
        'Star Spangled Banner' 49

'Steppes In The Right Direction'
    26
'Under Canvas' 17
Billington, Michael 81, 87, 106, 141,
    161
Bird, John 29, 47, 68, 70, 73, 100, 103,
    142, 149, 150, 163, 206, 244, 247, 252,
    256
Birdsall, Timothy 64, 70
Blakemore, Michael 114, 118
Blunt, Anthony 4, 124, 181, 185, as
    'character' 184
Booker, Christopher 22, 32, 45, 248,
    249, 250, 251
Boston Arts Festival 197
Boyd, Hugo 12, 88, 195
Braden, Bernard 252, 253, 274
Brady, Terence 44
Bricusse, Leslie 59, 236
Bridge, Peter 16, 20
Brighton, Theatre Royal 17–19
Britten, Benjamin 27–8, 126
Bron, Eleanor 68, 69, 73, 150, 204, 244,
    247, 256
Browne, Coral 182, 183–4, 186
Bruce, Lenny 245–6
Burgess, Guy 181, 182, 285, as
    'character' 185, 186
Burge, Stuart 105, 128–9, 187, 188, 247
Burrough, Tony 187

Callow, Simon 183, 184
Cambridge: Arts Theatre 17, 106;
    School of Slavonic Studies 77;
    University 77, 106, 242, 249
Cambridge Footlights 3, 5, 6, 17, 23, 44,
    55–6, 58, 59, 64, 69, 71, 88, 134,
    287–8
        revues: *Out Of The Blue* (1954) 59,
        68–9; *Between The Lines* (1955)
        60, 61, 68–9; *Springs To Mind*
        (1958) 64; *The Last Laugh* (1959)
        14, 68–70, 71; *I Thought I Saw It
        Move* (1961) 43, 242
Chapman, Graham 7, 260, 271
Chelton, Nick 122, 124
Chester, Hal 102, 103

303

Index

Index